Ancient Prophecies
of the Mahdi?

*The Book of Revelation
as prototype for
the Islamic end-time Hadiths*

Matthias Key

Ancient Prophecies
of the Mahdi?

*The Book of Revelation
as prototype for
the Islamic end-time Hadiths*

by Matthias Key

New American Standard Bible
(NASB) edition

PROCLAIM PUBLISHERS

ORLANDO, FLORIDA

Ancient Prophecies of the Mahdi?
The book of Revelation as prototype
for the end-time Islamic Hadiths

New American Standard Bible 2020 (NASB) Edition

Copyright © 2026 by Matthias Key

ISBN-13 paperback NASB edition: 978-1-954858-79-4
ISBN-13 hardback NASB edition: 978-1-954858-80-0
ISBN-13 e-book NASB edition: 978-1-954858-78-7

Cover artwork:
• M'Siouri, Amine, *Sculptures at the Foot of the Burj Khalifa Skyscraper in Dubai*, https://www.pexels.com/photo/burj-khalifa-28291078/, free to use for commercial purposes.
• Konopatzki, Christian, *Statues and Burj Khalifa behind*, https://www.pexels.com/photo/statues-and-burj-khalifa-behind-11118288/, free to use for commercial purposes.
• Musely royalty-free AI image generator, *Glowing futuristic key hovering vertically over processor*, https://musely.ai/tools/ai-non-copyright-image-generator, free to use for commercial purposes.

Printed through Proclaim Publishers, Orlando, Florida
Manufactured in the United States of America

John 16:33 These things I have spoken to you so that in Me
you may have peace. In the world you have tribulation, but
take courage; I have overcome the world.

Revelation chronology key

Verse(s)	Section(s)
1:1-6	K00
1:7	K38
1:8-20	K00
2:1-7	K06
2:8-11	K07
2:12-17	K08
2:18-24	K09
2:25	K09, K13
2:26	K46
2:27	K42
2:28	K46
2:29	K09, K13
3:1-6	K10
3:7-9	K11
3:10-11	K11, K13
3:12	K47
3:13	K11
3:14-22	K12
4:1-11	K14
5:1-7	K00
5:8	K00, K14
5:9-10	K14
5:11-14	K00
6:1-2	K16
6:3-4	K21
6:5-8	K25
6:9-11	K26
6:12-17	K27
7:1-8	K18
7:9-17	K26
8:1-6	K28
8:7-9	K29
8:10-11	K30
8:12-13	K31
9:1	K15, K32
9:2-11	K32
9:12-21	K33
10:1-11	K00
11:1-2	K18
11:3	K19, K34
11:4-6	K19
11:7-10	K34
11:11-13	K35
11:14-19	K36
12:1	K03
12:2	K04
12:3-4	K01, K04, K15
12:5	K05, K42
12:6	K18
12:7-10	K15
12:11	K26
12:12	K15
12:13-17	K18
13:1-2	K21
13:3-10	K23
13:11-18	K24
14:1-3	K43
14:4	K18
14:5	K43
14:6	K41
14:7	K41, K42
14:8	K21
14:9-11	K42
14:12-13	K24
14:14-18	K36
14:19	K38
14:20	K40
15:1	K36
15:2-4	K43
15:5-8	K36
16:1-11	K37
16:12-16	K38
16:17-21	K39
17:1	K02, K17, K20
17:2	K20
17:3-5	K17
17:6	K20
17:7-11	K02
17:12-13	K21
17:14	K38
17:15	K17
17:16-17	K21
17:18	K17
18:1-5	K21
18:6-7	K20
18:8	K20, K21, K25
18:9-10	K22
18:11	K21
18:12-13	K20
18:14-16	K21
18:17-20	K22
18:21-24	K20
19:1-4	K22
19:5-10	K48
19:11-14	K38
19:15	K38, K42
19:16-19	K38
19:20	K40
19:21	K38
20:1-2	K42
20:3	K42, K45
20:4	K24, K43
20:5	K43, K46
20:6	K44, K46
20:7-10	K45
20:11-15	K46
21:1-3	K47
21:4-7	K49
21:8	K46
21:9-21	K47
21:22-27	K49
22:1-5	K49
22:6-21	K50

Contents

Foreword

Every reader, and especially Muslims, will find this reference study by Matthias Key to be an excellent book. It is a systematic comparison between the eschatological prophecies of the Book of Revelation, framed as an open "Letter to the Tribulation," versus Islamic Hadiths which tell of the Mahdi.

The analysis reconstructs the end-time chronological timeline from Revelation's seals, trumpets, and bowls. It then integrates the fragmented hadith narratives to identify parallels as well as divergences.

Matthias points out that such a timeline analysis between the two prophecies can only be done by conducting a thoroughly literal interpretation of Revelation, as given in the model of pretribulational premillennialism. He reminds us the biblical teaching that a saving faith in the Jesus Christ of the Bible does not depend on one's understanding of the book of Revelation, or the timeline of the end times.

But Matthias, who personally holds to the literal view, goes on to show Revelation as a cohesive prophetic blueprint, whereas Hadiths constitute a reactive, less-structured counter-narrative that is influenced by biblical motifs. Key figures – such as the antichrist beast versus the Mahdi, and the false prophet versus ʿIsa ibn Maryam – are examined through thematic alignment, with a timeline of tribulation, resurrection, and judgment. This approach highlights how Islamic eschatology echoes and inverts Revelation. This affirms my own research on the Qur'an, which echoes numerous biblical themes, meanings, and whole verses taken verbatim, as I show in my book *The Good News to Muslims*.

In Matthias Key's unmatched work, central parallels emerge in the end-time motifs.

Revelation's seven-year tribulation aligns with the Mahdi's rule. The antichrist's coming on a white horse to conquer (Revelation 6:2) mirrors the Mahdi's conquest at the head of black banners from

Khorasan. The woman of Babylon (Revelation chapter 17) parallels the "Romans" as a decadent western entity in the Hadiths. In both accounts they are overthrown: by the beast (17:16), and by the Mahdi (hadith on *al-Malhamah al-Kubra* or Great War). The tribulation plagues of the seals, trumpets, and bowls (chapters 6, 8-9, 15–16) echo hadith signs such as famine and smoke. The two witnesses (chapter 11) invert as the Dajjal, a deceptive messiah who opposes the Mahdi. The resurrection of the two witnesses (Rev. 11:11) contrast against the failure of the Dajjal's miracles to tempt Muslims to reject their faith.

Armageddon (16:16) parallels the Islamic conquest of Jerusalem and the Dajjal's defeat outside Mecca. Cosmic judgments such as earthquakes (6:12, 16:18, etc) and hail (8:7) match landslides and celestial signs, like the sun rising from the west. All these further underscore inversion.

Divergences include Revelation's rapture (the pretribulation escape), which is absent from the Hadiths, and Christ's millennial reign (chapter 20), which contrasts with the Mahdi's fleeting "silver age" before the coming of the Yajuj and Majuj.

Those motifs won't be complete until you read *End Times: Eschatology in Judaism, Christianity, and Islam, Will the Real Messiah Please Stand Up!*, by Dr. Ed Hoskins. There you will get the Jewish perspective in a complete 360 view.

Matthias Key's comparative exegesis will reveal Revelation's internal coherence as a prophetic canon to you, in contrast to the disjointed, derivative structure of the Hadiths. This suggests that Islamic eschatology is a post-biblical reconfiguration that supplants biblical authority. Ultimately, this unique analysis affirms biblical inerrancy, positioning Revelation as sovereign prophecy, whereas the Hadiths reflect a human, and ultimately infernal adaptation. In the end, there is underscored an unwavering eschatological faith in Christ's sure return.

Dr. Ahmed Joktan
December 25, 2025

Ancient prophecies of the Mahdi?

Hello. My name is Matthias Key. I am writing to you from the year 2024. I am writing especially to you of the Islamic faith. It has been one hundred years since the caliphate was abolished. Will you have to wait another hundred years? Many of you would like to see the end time come soon, so that your struggle could come to a rewarding end. You are drawing on the prophecies which tell of the coming of the Mahdi, the awaited savior of Islam. He will usher in a final glorious age, that will involve a series of great wars to bring peace.

I am also writing to you Christians, who are mostly unaware of Islamic prophecies and the theology behind them.

Perhaps you are reading this book in your future time of unending wars worldwide, and unprecedented trials on a global scale. Could you be living in the prophesied end-time tribulation? The Almighty can bring you safely through this most terrible time. I hope my book will help.

I am named after Matthias, the last of the twelve apostles of ʿIsa al-Maseeh, also known as Jesus the Messiah. Matthias was one of the disciples who followed Jesus during all three years of his intensive ministry in Israel two thousand years ago. He took the place of Judas Iscariot as apostle. Matthias grew to know that Jesus was sent by God. Along with the other apostles he confessed him to be Jesus the Christ.

Islam recognizes ʿIsa among the great prophets. Matthias and almost all the other apostles were put to death for following him. They died at different times, and in different places.

The Jewish, Christian and Muslim traditions all talk about an extreme seven-year period of many deaths at the end of our era. In the Jewish Old Testament it is prophesied in the book of Daniel. The Christian New Testament expands on Daniel in great detail, in the book of Revelation. In the Muslim traditions, the end-time prophecies are scattered across the holy written Qur'an, and also in the sayings of Muhammad recorded in the *Hadiths*. All three religious traditions agree that the seven years are not just a time of political upheaval, but that they also have a profoundly spiritual dimension.

My book will make the case that the coming of the Mahdi was prophesied not only by Muhammad.... There were much more ancient prophecies of the Mahdi, hidden five hundred years earlier in the book of Revelation!

The Christian version of the seven-year period is commonly called the *tribulation*, which is prophesied in many different books of the Bible. The second half of this time will be particularly fearful. It is known as the *great tribulation*. The primary source that looks ahead to the seven years is the final book of the Bible, titled Revelation. It recounts a long vision that came to John, another of the twelve apostles. He was deep in worship when Jesus showed him the things of the future.

Prophetic visions and dreams were regarded with great significance by both Jews and the early Christians. Records of them are scattered throughout the Bible. Individual Muslims have an even higher opinion of dreams. From them they try to find divine guidance for their everyday lives.

The vision of Revelation is possibly the most fantastic one ever recounted. Muslims ought to study it, especially because it closes out the New Testament, which they know as the *Injil*. The Injil is regarded as one of the holy writings of Islam.

A prophecy is a *foretelling* of future events. It can also be a *forthtelling*, that rebukes people and guides them through trials. Revelation is even more than both. It is *apocalyptic* prophecy. It comes to us as a vision and warning of the future, portrayed in fantastic imagery. The events of Revelation will have eternal consequences for each and every person on earth, those long dead, alive today, and still to be born.

Even though Revelation comes from the Christian scripture, many Muslims do not realize that its prophecies are foundational to your own end-time traditions.

John foresaw the future events in the order that they were shown to him. But we shall see that they are not given in the actual sequence that they will be fulfilled. It's as if John was being twirled back and forth through space and time during the vision. To extract the timeline, it is necessary to freeze-frame it into pieces, then correlate them out of the swirl to make a coherent flow of events.

The spine of the timeline is driven by the seven seals, followed by the seven trumpets, followed by the seven bowls. Many of the other events of the vision are disjointed in time. But we can find their best placement in the timeline by asking where they logically fit into the three series of sevens.

In my first book, *Letter to the Tribulation*, I used this technique to extract the timeline of Revelation. I pointed out the cross-linking between specific prophesied events. You will see references to the chronological order when I refer you to the designations K00 through K50. In this current book I will cover each section. But for additional detail, please refer to my earlier book.

By employing this chronological method, we can see that Revelation touches on all of human history, going back to when God created Adam and Eve. Indeed, Revelation spans past, present, and future, a period of thousands of years, with special attention to the seven-year period of the tribulation.

Unlike Revelation, the Hadiths were not all given in one source document. They are the oral sayings and actions of Muhammad, narrated by many of his companions. After Muhammad died, they transmitted them to more followers, who eventually recorded them in writing in the several centuries that followed. But these sayings were never combined into one authoritative book like the Qur'an. Instead, over time they were gathered into various collections of Hadiths.

The sayings of the Hadiths were uttered over five hundred years after Revelation. Thus, Muhammad's words about the end times are actually the second, after Revelation, to claim divine inspiration.

I will use my earlier book as a basis to recount Muhammad's prophecies, again in the chronological order that they are meant to be fulfilled. Along the way, I will gather the end-time Hadiths, along with relevant surahs from the Qur'an, and piece together the letter that Muhammad could have penned about the end of the world. I will quote almost a hundred Hadiths in detail, according to their sequence in the timeline. The timeline sections will be chronologically designated as H00 through H49.

This will be a type of presentation that I don't believe has ever been attempted, in English translation from the original Arabic.

The result will be a second letter about the end-time tribulation, as dictated by the prophet Muhammad. He meant for his prophecies to supersede Revelation. That was the first letter to the tribulation, given by God to the apostle John five hundred years earlier, to close out the Christian Bible.

Muhammad's predictions revolve around three main characters: the Mahdi, 'Isa ibn Maryam, and their enemy the Dajjal. We shall see that 'Isa ibn Maryam is much different from the 'Isa al-Maseeh of the Bible.

What was happening during those five hundred years after the writing of Revelation that resulted in the Hadiths? How is it that the end-time Hadiths are comparable to John's vision? I will discuss that, and will argue the case that Revelation is the prototype of the Hadiths' predictions of the Mahdi. Also that Revelation is an inverted prototype. The Hadiths are an echo. They have inverted mirror images of the prophecies we read in Revelation.

I will be referring to Hadiths in the Sunni tradition, but a similar effort could be made using the Shi'ite sources. Most of the Hadiths quoted are regarded as authentic (*sahih*) by Islamic scholars. Others are graded as reliable (*hasan*). Those considered weak will be marked as *da'if*, but some will be presented because of their affirmation by many Muslims. Hadiths that are fabricated (*mawdoo*) will certainly be avoided.

As I recount the Hadiths regarding the end time and the Mahdi, I will show how those prophecies line up with those of Revelation. The timeline of the Hadiths can be explained in large part by Revelation's own chronology. The Islamic prophecies, in their own hidden way reflect the actions of the main characters of Revelation: the beast, the false prophet, the woman of Babylon, the two witnesses, and Jesus Christ.

The analysis will show that Muhammad was influenced by the events of Revelation to construct an alternative universe in time. By drawing on Revelation, you can be informed in even greater detail of the happenings that will occur in the last days. In fact, God's word in Revelation, by its greater detail and consistency, will commend itself as superior to anyone who is open to examining it.

I will also show how Jesus Christ enters the end-time narrative of Revelation. He will bring ultimate peace to the people whom he ushers into eternity, in very surprising ways that bring gladness and blessing of the heart.

I will warn you that my findings are controversial. In years to come, I have no doubt that my book will be officially banned by different governments. It is amazing that you have found it, because a surveillance state is in action around you. My prayers go with you that almighty God in heaven will protect you until you have fully read this, shared it with others, and take it to heart.

The sacred texts

The Bible is the holy book of Christianity and Judaism. The Jewish Bible consists of the 39 books of the Old Testament. The Christian Bible adds to it the 27 books of the New Testament.

The authors of the different New Testament books were apostles who knew Jesus Christ first-hand, like Matthew, John, Paul, and Christ's brothers James and Jude. Others were written by direct associates of the apostles, like Mark, Luke, and the unknown author of the book of Hebrews.

The authors of the Old Testament books were prophets such as Moses, Isaiah, Jeremiah, Ezekiel, Daniel, and others. There are also books compiled by unknown chroniclers that record the succession of judges and kings in Israel; collections of songs or psalms, mostly by King David; and the proverbs and wisdom of King Solomon. Each book of the Bible records words spoken audibly by the Almighty God of Heaven, and holy words inspired by him.

The Old Testament was written over the period from approximately 1440 to 440 BCE. The New Testament books date between 40 and 90 CE.

The common thread of the Old Testament is the expectation that God will send a messiah to save his people from their sins, and to restore them to fellowship with him. The New Testament, is about the coming of this messiah in the person of Jesus Christ. It testifies how he died on the cross, rose from the dead three days later, and after forty more days ascended into heaven. On the fiftieth day, the day of Pentecost, God poured his Holy Spirit upon Christ's disciples. They became the Church of God. The New Testament also includes many promises from Jesus, that one day he will return to earth.

The Old Testament is considered authoritative by believing Jews, Christians and Muslims. The New Testament is regarded as so by Christians and Muslims.

The *Qur'an* is the primary holy book of Islam. It means "recitation" in Arabic, written by Muhammad, the prophet of Allah. It consists of 114 chapters called *surahs*. They claim to record the literal words of *Allah*, the Arabic name for God.

The Qur'an dates to approximately 650 CE. At that time all alternative manuscripts were destroyed, and only the version officially sanctioned by the third caliph, Uthman ibn Affan, was allowed. Thus, we do not have multiple manuscripts that would permit an assessment of the level of consistency of the Qur'an. It is taken as an article of faith that the destroyed manuscripts do not contradict what became accepted as the Qur'an.

Many Muslims are taught that the text of the Bible is corrupted. But simultaneously they read in the Qur'an that the *Taurat* (Torah portion of the Old Testament), *Zabur* (Old Testament Psalms and Prophets) and *Injil* (New Treatment) are earlier writings from Allah (Surah 4:136). It therefore seems inconsistent that Islam teaches these earlier sacred texts to be corrupt. For the Qur'an declares "there is none that can alter the words and decrees of Allah" (Surah 6:34), "none can change his words" (6:115), "no change can there be in the words of Allah" (10:64). And nowhere in the Qur'an are the Christians accused of distorting or corrupting the New Testament. Instead, in a few passages the Christians are referred to as honest people, the group closest to the Muslims (5:82).

The Bible testifies to its own inerrancy by the majesty of its words, and its internal consistency that has survived criticism by thousands of unbelieving scholars over many centuries. Unlike the Qur'an, we can assess the accuracy of the different books of the Bible as they were handed down in the decades after authorship, because there are hundreds of early manuscripts in the Greek, Hebrew and Aramaic languages. They have been shown to be consistent with one another to a level of 98.33%. Most of the differences involve merely mechanical errors that occurred when manuscripts were copied – in spelling, change of word order, or use of paraphrase. Thus, the degree of substantial purity is actually 99.75%. The differences between manuscripts do not impact the spiritual teachings of the Bible.[1]

Of equal importance to the Qur'an for Muslims is the *Sunnah*. This word means "a clear or well-trodden path." It is the record of Muhammad's sayings, teachings, and doings. Muslims are taught that the Muhammad of the Sunnah is the example they should strive to follow, because Islam considers him to be the perfect man. Without the Sunnah, the Qur'an cannot be properly understood. Many practices and beliefs of Islam are found only in the Sunnah.

There are two types of literature that make up the Sunnah. The first are the *sirats*, the ancient biographies of Muhammad. An example is Ibn Ishaq's *Sirat Rasul (The Life of Muhammad)*. The second are the *Hadiths*, which are records of the sayings and deeds of Muhammad.

Beyond the Sunnah, in high regard also are the *tafsirs*, which are commentaries on the Qur'an and ancient histories of early Islam. Next are the oral sayings of the companions and immediate followers of Muhammad, eventually recorded in the *athars*.[2] The sirats, Hadiths, tafsirs, and athars, all written in Arabic, make up the Islamic traditions.

The Hadiths have their origin during the lifetime of Muhammad, when his companions began to orally hand down their memories of the prophet. Each hadith has two parts – an *isnad* and a *matn*. An isnad is found at the beginning of each hadith. It gives the names of people involved in the oral chain of transmission before the hadith was written down. The matn is the actual text of the hadith that records the saying or action of Muhammad.

In the Sunni branch of Islam, the canonical hadith collections are the *Kutub al-Sittah*, "the six books," compiled by six Sunni Muslim scholars in the ninth century CE, approximately two centuries after the death of Muhammad. They were grouped and defined by Ibn al-Qaisarani in the

---

[1] Mark Tabata, *Hundreds Of Thousands Of Errors In The Bible Manuscripts?*, https://marktabata.com/2016/08/06/hundreds-of-thousands-of-errors-inthe-bible-manuscripts/, accessed November 13, 2022.

[2] According to Imam Jalalud-Din As-Suyuti (15th century Egyptian hadith master), cited in Seifeddine-M, *The Meaning of the Words 'Hadeeth', 'Khabar' and 'Athar'*, October 29, 2014, https://muftisays.com/blog/Seifeddine-M/3767_29-10-2014/the-meaning-of-the-words-hadeeth-khabar-and-athar.html.

11th century. Of those six books, *Sahih al-Bukhari* and *Sahih Muslim* have the highest status. The other four are *Sunan Abu Dawood, Jami' al-Tirmidhi, Al-Sunan al-Sughra* and *Sunan ibn Majah*.

In the Twelver Shi'a branch of Islam, the canonical hadith collections are the *Kutub al-ʾArbaʿa*, "the four books": *Kitab al-Kafi, Man la yahduruhu al-Faqih, Tahdhib al-Ahkam*, and *Al-Istibsar*.

The *musnads* are collections of Hadiths arranged by the narrator's name. For example, the Musnad of Aḥmad ibn Hanbal (died 855) consists of 27,000 Hadiths. Ibn Hanbal is said to have scrutinized nearly 750,000 reports, sifting out forgeries and keeping only those which he deemed to be reliable.

Islamic scholars have an ongoing debate about the interpretation of Hadiths, even those that are considered sound. There is also significant disagreement about which Hadiths are sound or weak in their transmission.[3]

Out of the tens of thousands of Hadiths, several hundred are on the topic of the end times. I will rely on English translations of such Hadiths given at https://sunnah.com. Wherever possible, in the footnotes I will provide the hadith English web reference volume, book, and hadith number, as catalogued by the USC-MSA Muslim Students Association at the University of Southern California. I will also rely on the interpretation of the various Hadiths given by Islamic scholars on different web sites, and in these books:

- *Al Mahdi and the End of Time*, by Muhammad Ibn ʿIzzat and Muhammad ʿArif, Dar al Taqwa press, London, second edition 2007.
- *Al-Mahdi, The Promised Caliph*, by Abu Rahma, self-published, Middletown Delaware USA, 2018.

---

[3] *Hadith*, https://www.britannica.com/topic/Hadith, accessed October 29, 2022.

Main actors of the end-time Hadiths

The Parallel Reference portion of this book will quote many Hadiths that reference the end times. It will not be an exhaustive collection. However, you will find representative Hadiths that include the meaning of most other Hadiths that are similar.

Let me introduce you to the main actors that we shall encounter.

According to Islam, before the Major Signs of the end times, the Mahdi will appear. In Arabic, *al-Mahdi* means the rightly guided one. The vast majority of Muslims believe in his coming, including most serious Sunnis and all religious Shi'ites.

The Mahdi is considered to be the awaited savior of Islam. He is an end-time eschatological figure who will emerge after a period of great turmoil and suffering. He will be a devout Muslim, the leader of Muslims worldwide. He will invade opposing lands, win many wars, and will establish a new world order. Under his rule there will be a great social transformation. All things will come under divine guidance. He will establish purity of the faith, bring true and uncorrupted guidance to all, and will create a just social order. The world will be free from anti-Muslim oppression. This will come as a consequence of the Mahdi compelling the entire world to become Muslim, either by persuasion, by war, or by conquest.

The words of Muhammad in the Hadiths prophesy that the Mahdi will make a seven-year treaty with "the Romans" through a Jew of priestly lineage. Later he will conquer Israel for Islam, and will lead the faithful Muslims in a final slaughter of the Jews and Christians.

The Mahdi will be loved by all the people of the earth. At the end of the seven years, he dies.

After the Mahdi appears, a great enemy will come to oppose all that he stands for. He will be known as the Dajjal. His full title is *Al-Maseeh Ad-Dajjal*, or the Messiah Liar and Deceiver. He will have miraculous powers. He will be blind in one eye, with the word "unbeliever" written between his eyes. He will claim to be Jesus Christ and be divine. He will be Jewish and his followers will be the Jews.

Interestingly, the Mahdi and the Dajjal do not appear in the Qur'an, but only in the Hadiths. This is even though they are the most important end-time figures in Islam.

The third main character in the end-time Hadiths is Jesus. But Christians should understand that this Muslim Jesus is drastically different from the Jesus they know from the Bible. Muslims believe that the New Testament books were corrupted in their transmission, and that the versions of them validated by the Church are fatally flawed. They are taught this despite the degree of substantial purity of the New Testament manuscripts discussed in the previous section, when we presented the sacred texts of Judaism, Christianity and Islam. This is their rationale for putting forth a different Jesus.

Jesus, according to Muslims, is one of the great prophets that Allah sent. He bears the honorific title of Messiah, as he does for Christians. But he is not in any way a savior for the sins of mankind, as Christians expect from the word Messiah.

The Qur'an denies that Jesus was ever crucified or that he ever experienced death. Instead, Allah miraculously delivered him from death. He later ascended into heaven alive. Since then, he has remained with Allah, awaiting to return to earth to finish his ministry and complete his life.

The Hadiths that refer to him do not call him by the name Jesus, but rather 'Isa (or Eisa). Muslims occasionally will refer to Jesus by his English name for westerners' sake, but the names that the Qur'an gives him and which most Muslims use is *'Isa al-Maseeh* (Jesus the Messiah), *Hadrat 'Isa* (Honorable Jesus), or *Nabi 'Isa* (Prophet Jesus). Most Christians call him Jesus Christ (Jesus the Messiah translated to Greek). Jewish believers in Jesus call him *Yeshua HaMashiakh* (Jesus the Messiah in Hebrew). To avoid confusion with Messiah Jesus of the Bible, whenever I speak of the Muslim Jesus, I will refer to him by another title they use, *'Isa ibn Maryam* (Jesus son of Mary). This title emphasizes their belief that Jesus is just another man, and is definitely not the divine son of God.

When ʿIsa ibn Maryam returns, it will not be to restore the nation of Israel to the Jewish people. His mission will not be to save and deliver faithful Christian followers from persecution. Instead, ʿIsa will return as a Muslim.

ʿIsa ibn Maryam will descend from heaven to join the army of the Mahdi. He will subordinate himself to the Mahdi, and will lead them in prayer to Allah. He will be the greatest Muslim evangelist ever, and will oversee the institution and enforcement of Islamic *Sharia* law all over the world. He will kill the Dajjal, kill the Jews, and abolish Christianity. Then he will eventually die some decades later.

There are also two supernatural actors in end-time Hadiths. The main one is Allah, the god of Islam. Allah was revealed to the world by his messenger Muhammad.

Before Muhammad was born, his Arabian tribe the Quraysh profited from travelers who came in pilgrimage to their local shrine, the Kaaba in the city of Mecca. It was a pagan shrine with idols of local gods of all the area tribes. Allah was the name of one of those gods, probably the tribal god of the Quraysh.

Muhammad was born in Mecca to that tribe in 570. As a young man, his habit was to spend many continuous days in private worship to the god Allah. At the age of forty he experienced a visitation by an angel, whom he came to believe was the angel *Jibreel* (the Arabic version of Gabriel). The angel conveyed to him the words of Allah, and commanded him to commit them to writing. The angel made many such appearances over the next twenty-three years. These written revelations became the Qur'an.

Muhammad became regarded as the foremost prophet of Allah. In his lifetime he founded Islam as a monotheistic religion, and violently spread the creed that Allah is to be worshipped to the exclusion of all other gods. He began the conquest of neighboring tribes and countries for Islam. The exciting new religion expanded to an even greater degree after his death. The black stone of the Kaaba became the holiest site of Islam. It is the most desired place of pilgrimage for all Muslims around the world. A pilgrimage to the Kaaba, known as the *hajj*, during a Muslim's lifetime earns him or her merit before Allah.

In the end-time Hadiths, Allah takes direct action frequently. Allah sends and withholds rain. He sends a cold wind that causes death. He takes away Sharia law from the earth, then sends the Mahdi and ʿIsa ibn Maryam to enforce Sharia everywhere through a final Islamic caliphate. He expresses his anger over sexual acts of adultery. Allah specially empowers the armies of the Mahdi to achieve their victories. He prolongs the times for battles, and restores the power of Islam by crushing its enemies.

Allah causes landslides to swallow his opponents, and to punish the grossly immoral. He promises to take care of every Muslim. He commands them to behead their foes. He grants forgiveness of sins for Muslim soldiers in return for their participation in certain military campaigns that he expressly authorizes. He is directly involved in the defeat of the Jews. Finally, he is the one who revealed these future end-time events by way of the angel Jibreel to his messenger, Muhammad. He arranged for these prophecies of the end time to be transmitted as additional revelation by way of the Hadiths of Muhammad.

The second supernatural character is *Shaytan*, Arabic for Satan.

In my book, I will be making a distinction between the Islamic Shaytan and the Satan of the Bible. We shall see that the two are different characters.

In Surah 38:71-85, the Qur'an has the story of al-Shaytan, or Iblis, the first of the shaytans (devils).[4,5] He was a glorious creature made of fire. When Iblis saw that the newly created Adam was a mere man made of clay, he refused to bow to him. Therefore, Allah banished him and the other devils from heaven to earth. Iblis swore revenge on Adam and his descendants: "by your glory [Allah]! I will certainly mislead them all, except your chosen servants among them" (Surah 38:82-83 Clear Qur'an translation).

Allah then promised him to "surely fill up hell with you and whoever follows you from among them, all together." (Surah 38:85, Clear Qur'an

---

[4] https://islamqa.info/en/answers/6297/will-iblees-enter-hell-and-why, source: Sheikh Muhammed Salih Al-Munajjid, accessed February 18, 2024.
[5] Brian Duignan. *Iblis*, February 2, 2024, https://www.britannica.com/topic/Iblis, accessed February 18, 2024.

translation). Elsewhere, the Qur'an speaks of the fulfillment of this promise (see Surah 26:91-95 in H46).

However, in the Hadiths that prophesy the time of the Mahdi, Iblis or Shaytan is mentioned sparingly. In the one notable reference, he appears to be the Dajjal's sponsor (see H21).

The main showdown in the end-time Hadiths will occur between the Dajjal and 'Isa ibn Maryam. They are leaders of fundamentally conflicting belief systems. In Muslim eyes, the Dajjal is the antichrist, because he opposes the Mahdi who is their messiah. In this sense it can be said that the Dajjal is the Islamic antichrist.

The overall timeline of Islamic end-time events

There is consensus among Islamic teachers regarding main events of the end-times, as prophesied by Muhammad in the Hadiths.[6] But there is not agreement on the sequence of subsidiary events.

There will come a period of civil war among Muslims. At that time an army carrying black banners will arrive from the eastern region of Khorasan. The Mahdi will be revealed, and will be compelled to become caliph. People will gather around him and pledge their allegiance. He will end the civil war, begin the institution of a global caliphate government, and take power.

His main competitor for military and political power will be a future incarnation of Romans, who wish to reestablish a reflection of the Roman empire of old.

The Romans will make a truce with the Muslims. They will then fight together against a common enemy, whose identity is not revealed. Perhaps those are remnants of nations who do not accept the global government, or Christians and Jews that are concentrated in certain places. The Mahdi and the Romans will invade these areas. They will fight and defeat this common foe.

Afterward, the Muslims and the Romans will break the truce, and will fight each other in a great battle. In the Hadiths this is called the greatest massacre. The Mahdi will defeat the Romans, and his armies will capture Constantinople and then Rome.

At this time, the Dajjal will appear, as defender of Jews and Christians who have not yet submitted to the Mahdi. He will perform various miraculous acts, and will be successful at deceiving many. He will assemble a great army of his own.

---

[6] Abu Rahma, *Al-Mahdi, The Promised Caliph*, self-published, Middletown Deleware USA, 2018, p.102.

'Isa ibn Maryam then returns to earth, by descending from heaven to Damascus. He becomes the Mahdi's deputy and religious leader of the caliphate.

The Muslims will be fighting on multiple fronts, and will march to India to defeat the infidels there. But the main army of the Mahdi will battle that of the Dajjal. Toward the close of the campaign, 'Isa ibn Maryam will kill the Dajjal near Jerusalem, as he attempts escape through the Ludd Gate.

Every Christian and Jew will now embrace Islam. Those who don't will be killed. The Mahdi and 'Isa ibn Maryam will jointly rule over a Muslim planet. They will dispense great blessings to all. After seven years, the Mahdi dies, and 'Isa ibn Maryam passes away after that.

After more years comes the true end of history, and Allah's final judgment of all humanity.

This is the general chronology of the end-time Hadiths. There are also many Hadiths that describe the person of the Mahdi, and his opponent the Dajjal. Others tell of conditions of life among the Mahdi's followers, his armies, and among people who reject Sharia law.

There are additional events in the end-time Hadiths that are difficult to fit into the overall chronology of the Mahdi's wars. We shall see that the timeline of Revelation will suggest when they will occur.

Main actors of Revelation

The book of Revelation from the Injil or New Testament is a record of the vision that the apostle John received from ʿIsa al-Maseeh, Jesus Christ. The book has 21 chapters.

Jesus is the main character in the first four chapters. In them he dictates seven letters of prophecy to the churches of Asia, which was a province of the Roman empire in the western part of today's Turkey. The prophecies in the seven letters span the time from the writing of Revelation to my own day, which is before the tribulation.

In chapter 5 the scene shifts to heaven, where Jesus appears as "the Lamb that was slaughtered" (5:12 K00). This is a re7ference to God sending him to Israel two thousand years ago, his death on the cross, his resurrection with a glorified, deathless body, followed by his ascension into heaven. Those events were seen by many eye witnesses, as testified elsewhere in the New Testament. Because he is the Lamb, Jesus alone is worthy to open the heavenly book of prophecy, bound with seven seals. He then sends his angels to convey the contents of the sealed book to John through a series of visions.

Jesus then waits until late in the vision to reappear as the main character, in Revelation chapter 19 to 22.

More than half of Revelation, chapters 6 to 18, concerns the seven-year tribulation period. During that time, many people will trust their eternal destiny to Jesus. But the main actors of the seven years are the beast, the false prophet, the woman of Babylon, and the two witnesses.

The title of antichrist is not mentioned in Revelation. But obvious implications from the rest of the Bible are that the beast of Revelation is also the antichrist. He is *anti* because he is against Christ (1 John 2:22 K16), and portrays himself as an imitation Jesus, a superior messiah. He is *the* antichrist because he is not merely another in a long line of antichrists that have arisen since the first coming of Jesus. He is the final one.

The antichrist is the man of lawlessness (2 Thessalonians 2:8 K16) who hates God's standards of righteousness. He is the "prince who is to come," prophesied in the Old Testament (Daniel 9:26 K16) – his goal is to rule over a worldwide empire that opposes God. The beast's intention is to take the place of the true God, and become God in his own right (2 Thessalonians 2:3-4 K24).

At the beginning of the tribulation this beast will ascend out of the abyss (Revelation 17:8 K02) to make his appearance on earth. This origination point of the beast identifies him as a tool of Satan, because Satan is the angel of the abyss (9:11 K32). Indeed, Satan is instrumental in raising up and molding the character of the beast.

The beast's deputy is the false prophet. He is a separate character who is described as "another beast" (13:11 K24). Whereas the first beast is a charismatic military-political chief, this one is a religious leader. We know this from his title of prophet. But he is a false one, because he does not speak the word of almighty God in heaven. Instead, his words are motivated by the power of Satan. His credential as a religious leader is also based on having "two horns like a lamb" (13:11 K24). In the Old Testament the lamb was the preferred sacrificial animal that Jews brought to the temple in Jerusalem to atone for their sins before God. But the false prophet, unlike Jesus, certainly does *not* offer himself up for the sins of the people.

The false prophet is completely loyal to the beast. He is second to him in authority. He makes fire come down from heaven to earth, and works many other miracles in his name (13:12-13 K24).

The woman of Babylon is a prostitute who appears at the beginning of the tribulation. It is not clear whether this is an actual person, or whether she symbolizes a group of rulers whose aim is a global anti-God system rooted in materialism, immorality, opportunism, and power. The woman represents a culture promoting temptation, that enforces itself through a politically controlling system. It is a system that works visibly and invisibly to oppose the commandments of God. It cannot rest until it establishes dominance over others that will allow no opposition or criticism. Such an orientation to the snares of this world has powered many great empires throughout history.

We shall see that the woman of Babylon makes an alliance with the beast at the beginning of the tribulation. But later she is overthrown by him.

The other major characters of Revelation are the two witnesses. They are prophets sent by God to Jerusalem. They are present there during much of the great tribulation. As fitting with their description as witnesses, they shine light on the true things of God. They are two in number, for "On the testimony of two or three witnesses every matter shall be confirmed" (2 Corinthians 13:1b K19). God gives them miraculous power to oppose the plans of the woman and the beast. They are clothed in sackcloth (Revelation 11:3 K19), which indicates their concern for the rebelliousness of the world against the true God. In view of the approaching judgment, their mission is to call people to repentance, and direct them back to God. Some heed their warnings and accept Jesus Christ as their Lord and Savior. We shall see that many will be killed for doing so.

We must not forget the other important actor of Revelation – God the Father. He is the God of the Bible, the God *Yahweh* (or *Jehovah*) who revealed himself to Jews, Christians, and the whole world. He is omnipresent from the beginning, in the six days of creation, and to the end, in the new heaven and the new earth. He sent his son Jesus, without sin, to Israel two thousand years ago, to suffer and die on the cross for our sins. He orchestrates all of time, and the end times, and will send his son to earth again.

In Revelation, God the Father is ever-active from his throne in heaven. He jealously defends his commandments and his righteousness. He directs his angels to announce his judgments and avenge his wrath upon evildoers. He protects his people, and commissions them as evangelists of good news. He proclaims his word, and continually offers forgiveness through the everlasting gospel of salvation. He turns the hearts of many men and women to repent, and trust their lives to his son Jesus Christ. The Father then sends his Holy Spirit to live in the hearts of all those who accept his son Jesus as Lord.

We will see that before the tribulation, God will cast Satan out of heaven. This will allow the martyrs of the tribulation to rest in their souls after death without accusation, while they wait on God to resurrect their physical bodies. He takes them to himself in heaven, and wipes away their tears. He is always good, always God.

The overall timeline of end-time events in Revelation

Ever since Revelation was written, there has been disagreement about what it means. Many say that the apocalyptic tribulation scenes are not meant to be interpreted literally, but are symbolic pointers that encourage present-day followers of Jesus who are going through persecution. They allow that some of the foreseen events will indeed literally come to pass. They include: the second coming of Christ; God's judgment of all humanity, both those dead and those still alive; the unveiling of the new heaven, the new earth, and the new Jerusalem; and finally, the ushering of the faithful followers of Jesus into the eternal state.

But there is a large group of Christians who believe that all of Revelation is meant to be taken literally wherever possible, unless obvious symbolic language is being used. In this view the book is a comprehensive set of prophecies from the God of Heaven, all of which will be fulfilled in the future.

To take Revelation literally, it is important to recognize that an apocalypse is not necessarily given in a time-ordered sequence. Individual pieces of the vision have flashbacks to previous events. The vision can then suddenly jump far into the future. In this way Revelation consists of cross-linking spirals. The different motifs of the book are repetitive and intertwined.

In my earlier book I laid out the timeline of Revelation by looking for these cross-links. From that analysis, I presented the verses of the book, not in the order they were written, but in the most consistent chronological order possible.

The main waypoints of Revelation, which introduce new events of the vision, are the seven seals, seven trumpets, and seven bowls. To help with the chronological ordering, I took the view that these series of sevens are not rehashes of one another, as symbolic interpreters would say. Instead, the seventh seal is followed event-wise by the seven trumpets, and the seventh trumpet is then followed by the seven bowls. I also took the majority approach among literal interpreters, which holds that there will be a brief coming of Christ to earth called the rapture, shortly before the seven-year tribulation period.

In the book of Revelation, the church is not referred to at any time during the tribulation, and is not mentioned until after the new heaven and the new earth are revealed. It makes sense that the church is missing, because other passages of the New Testament (1 Thessalonians 4:15-17, 5:2, 5:9; 1 Corinthians 15:51-53; John 5:28-29, 14:2-3), describe a "last trumpet" event, which will be sudden and unexpected. This is the rapture (K13). Jesus will descend from the clouds. All the church believers, who have put their complete trust in him, will suddenly be caught up with Christ in the air. The dead, even those whose dust has been scattered throughout the earth or the seas, will be resurrected first. Then the living will also ascend. Jesus, in his love for the church, brings them all home to heaven, so that none of those alive would experience the extreme trials of the tribulation. Instead, they are welcomed with joy into God the Father's house (K14).

This interpretive model is called pretribulational premillennialism, because it holds that Christ raptures the church prior to the tribulation. Then, after the tribulation, his second coming comes prior to a thousand-year millennial kingdom. After the thousand years comes the last and final judgment.

The rapture event is coupled with the withdrawal of the Holy Spirit of God from active intervention in the world (K13), and Satan being cast down to earth (K15). He and the fallen angels are permanently barred from heaven. God withdraws his common grace, and leaves the world to its own devices. For the time that follows, sin and rebellion against God will predominate.

The seven-year period will then be inaugurated by a rider on a white horse. He carries a bow and wears a crown (K16). He is called the beast, and comes to conquer the world. He is acting in line with Satan's plan to afflict humanity. His description fits the man of lawlessness, the antichrist (2 Thessalonians 2:3, 6-8).

In another image we see the woman of Babylon riding the beast, also at the beginning of the tribulation (K17). They rule the world together for three and a half years. The woman is known for promiscuity, fornication, and adultery. She rules from "Babylon," which in the day of the apostle John was a code word for Rome, the capital of the Roman empire. Her future capital may be Rome, Constantinople (today's Istanbul), Brussels, or a yet-to-be capital of Europe. She has the ways of a prostitute, and lives off the masses by enslaving them to an ideology of materialism, pleasure, and promises of security. Her aim is to reestablish a godless worldwide system in the end time through her alliance with the beast, and to maintain power by making her lifestyle desirable and mandatory.

Besides his alliance with the woman of Babylon, the beast makes a seven-year treaty with Israel. It supposedly establishes permanent peace in the Middle East for the first time in history, and allows the Jews to continue worshipping at the temple in Jerusalem. The temple had likely been built just prior to the beast and the woman establishing worldwide power. Despite this treaty, the Jews are targeted by the beast and the woman.

The rulers also make it a top priority to persecute Christ-followers and other non-conformists. Those people are not parties to any treaty, so they lack even the false promises of a paper document. Many are put to death for their beliefs.

God acts in response, and brings a remnant of Jews into safety. Many of them put their faith in Christ. God specially seals 144,000 out of them (K18), guaranteeing their lives for the rest of the tribulation. They become evangelists to the world. Despite immense pressure, they lead many Jews and non-Jews to turn away from following the beast and the woman, and instead to repent of their sins against God. The evangelists bring them good news – that when Jesus died on the cross, he paid for their sins and reconciles them to God. In this way, God grants believers life after death, and fellowship with him in heaven.

Before the midpoint of the seven years, two witnesses appear in Jerusalem (K19). They are fearless in pronouncing woe against the evils propagated by the government of the beast and the woman. By God's power they perform miraculous acts of judgment, such as sending fire against their enemies, stopping rain from heaven, and turning waters to blood.

The sins of Babylon result in a promise from Almighty God that the woman and her city will be judged (K20). God then surprisingly uses the beast as his instrument of judgment, coming again as the rider on the red horse. In a related scene, the beast reappears out of the sea with ten horns. The horns represent ten nations that are completely loyal to him (K21). At the mid-point of the tribulation, they overthrow the woman and set fire to her city. A great smoke arises from the burning (K22).

The beast then becomes the supreme ruler during the next three and a half years, with claim to the entire world (K23). This is the terrible period known as the great tribulation. It is a time of continuous war. The beast breaks the treaty with Israel, enforces a uniform religion, makes it necessary that all people worship him, and blasphemes the God of Heaven. He targets for death all those who have turned to Christ.

Immediately after the overthrow of the woman, the false prophet comes to assist the beast (K24). He takes over the Jerusalem temple from the Jews. He compels his subjects to erect an image of the beast inside the temple, the *abomination that causes desolation*, and to worship it. He forces all people to be branded with the *mark of the beast* to show their allegiance to him, and seeks to kill those who refuse it. Revelation also speaks of the *number of the beast*, 666, but leaves it to our imagination on how the beast and the false prophet use it.

A rider on a black horse then signals famine and death upon a fourth of mankind. This is the logical outcome of the beast's hegemony (K25).

The Christ-followers who die as a result have their souls transported to heaven. They cry out to God for retribution against the beast (K26). He responds with heavenly omens and an earthquake (K27). There is a long silence in heaven (K28) before the wrath of God continues with hail, fire, and blood sent upon the earth (K29); with wormwood upon the waters (K30); and with darkening of the heavens (K31). God also allows Satan to let loose his fellow demons whom God had imprisoned, so that they could torment the beast's worshippers for five months (K32). Four evil angels gather armies that slay another third of men (K33).

The beast and the false prophet have been unable to stop the testimony of the two witnesses in Jerusalem. Therefore, they enlist the aid of Satan. God allows Satan to kill them (K34). Then after three and a half days, God demonstrates his power over death to the whole world by raising the two witnesses from the dead (K35).

God is not finished with the beast and with Satan. He sends boils on the flesh of people, blood on the sea and waters, heat and darkness to the world (K37). This is a last prelude to the final showdown.

Jesus becomes the main character once again in the closing chapters of Revelation, 19 to 22.

At this point the seven-year mark of the tribulation has been reached. The beast has gathered an army of 200 million men, the largest army ever known, in a final invasion of Israel. Now occurs the second coming of Christ. Lightning flashes across the world. He unexpectedly descends from heaven to earth. All will see him. His first action is to defeat the armies of the antichrist/beast at the battle of Armageddon (K38). The city of Babylon, burnt earlier, is destroyed (K39), and so are the beast's armies. The beast and the false prophet are cast into the eternal lake of fire (K40).

After these expressions of God's wrath against those who hate him so, he sends an angel to offer the saving message of the everlasting gospel one last time. Our loving God is gracious even to the last minute to undeserving people (K41).

Another angel of God then captures Satan, binds and chains him for a thousand years (K42).

Jesus invites those who came to believe in him during the tribulation into his new earthly kingdom (K43). It is known as the millennial kingdom, for it lasts for a thousand years. His deputies are the tribulation martyrs who died for believing in him – they are now also resurrected and have glorified bodies (K44). The Old Testament gives indications that the glorified deputies will include those who put their trust in the future messiah during that ancient time, even before Christ was born of the virgin Mary.

At the end of the thousand years, God allows Satan to be unchained. He comes back to earth in one last attempt to overthrow God. Many who were born during the millennium join Satan in the rebellion, despite the unmatched goodness and glory of Christ's kingdom that they grew up in. God sends fire from heaven to defeat them. And Satan finally meets his end by being cast into the lake of fire (K45).

In a literal interpretation of Revelation, all these things occur before the very end of time.

We have now reached the events that almost all interpreters of Revelation agree on.

A great resurrection of the dead takes place. They appear in heaven before God, in the great white throne judgment. The wicked are condemned to join Satan in hell (K46). But the believers who confessed faith in Christ are taken to see the new Jerusalem descend from the new heaven to the new earth (K47). All the faithful then rejoice at the marriage supper between Christ and his church (K48). The vision of Revelation ends with scenes of the eternal state (K49).

The close similarities between Revelation and the end-time Hadiths

In the introduction, I described how in my earlier book I reorganized all the content of the biblical book of Revelation into chronological order. I used the timeline designations K00 through K50.

This second book has a Parallel Reference area that repeats the "K" sections. Every verse of Revelation will be found in one of those time sections. Section K00 is the introduction, and K50 the concluding revelations and exhortations.

In the parallel left column, you will find the verses from Revelation, using the New American Standard Bible 2020 (NASB) translation. The NASB is widely embraced and trusted as a literal English translation, using formal equivalence to translate word-for-word and sentence-by-sentence from the original biblical languages. Thus it maintains faithful accuracy to the original texts, yet provides a clear understanding using modern English. The NASB relies on the most reliable and scholarly accepted manuscripts available, and in doing so, it excludes some verses that are found only in later manuscripts or more dubious historical sources.

Revelation is the last book that was added to the Bible. As such, it refers to many prophecies of the Old and New Testament. Some of those prophecies had a double fulfillment – with a partial fulfillment during Jesus' first coming two thousand years ago, and a future fulfillment in the end-times period.

Similarly, there are some verses of Revelation that you will find in more than one K section. I will indicate them by a double dagger mark ‡ that points to the other section(s), for example 12:3‡[K04,K15]. This happens when there are two or three parts to the verse and only one part is applicable to the section, or when it is a verse that has double or triple fulfillment. There will also be verses with only a portion that is relevant to the section under consideration. The other portion will be in italics. For example, in this verse from K04, the dragon ready to devour the child is the portion that is relevant:

> 12:4‡[K01,K15] *And his tail swept away a third of the stars of heaven and hurled them to the earth.* And the dragon stood before the woman who was about to give birth, so that when she gave birth he might devour her Child.

My earlier book, *Letter to the Tribulation*, goes into detail on each section. Here in the second book, I will attempt to summarize my earlier commentary, and leave room for comparison with the timeline of the Hadiths.

In the parallel right column, you will also see Hadiths for 28 of the sections. They are marked with "H" designations, with numbers matching the corresponding Revelation sections, H00 through H49. There you will also find quotations from the Qur'an, using the Abdullah Yusuf Ali translation, as updated in 1991 by the King Fahd Holy Qur'an Printing Complex.[7] The updated Ali translation will be used, unless otherwise indicated.[8]

If we compare the overall timelines of the two prophecies, we will see striking similarities, and also glaring differences. Let's consider them.

Revelation/the Hadiths have the following in common:

- There will be a seven-year period of extreme trial at the end of our era.
- A supreme ruler over the entire world will arise for the seven years – the beast/the Mahdi.
- He will inaugurate his rule by making a dramatic and unexpected treaty, and will gain a great following by doing so.
- He will concentrate his activities on Jerusalem and the surrounding areas.
- He will temporarily align himself with a co-ruler based in the capital of Europe – the woman of Babylon/the Romans. Together they will go after a common foe.

---

[7] https://archive.org/details/the-holy-quran-english-translation-of-the-meanings-and-commentary-king-fahd-prin; see Huda, https://www.learnreligions.com/top-english-translations-of-the-quran-2004604, June 25, 2019.
[8] For various English translations of the Qur'an, see https://www.islamawakened.com/index.php/qur-an, accessed June 11, 2024.

- After their joint action together, the supreme ruler and his closest allies will surprisingly overthrow the co-ruler.
- The capital city of the co-ruler/a massive area, will be burnt with fire. The great smoke that results is of special significance.
- After the overthrow of the co-ruler, a charismatic duo/figure comes forth as the chief antagonist(s) to the supreme ruler and his government – the two witnesses/the Dajjal. They proclaim the biblical faith. Many believe in their preaching. (In the case of the two witnesses, they started their activity a few months before the co-ruler's demise. By comparison, the Hadiths do not mention the Dajjal's preparatory activity prior to the co-ruler's overthrow. They merely emphasize that afterward, the Dajjal became the Mahdi's main opponent.)
- A deputy arises to assist the supreme leader – the false prophet/ʿIsa ibn Maryam.
- The supreme ruler unilaterally breaks the treaty.
- His deputy compels all people to worship the supreme ruler and his religion.
- The leader and his deputy raise armies that hunt down and kill Christians, Jews, and others who refuse to submit to them.
- The world leaders manage to kill their charismatic opponent(s).

At this point the following divergences take place, and only in the Revelation prophecy:

- The God of Heaven takes control of events, by resurrecting the two witnesses whose bodies had been left lying in the streets of Jerusalem. They ascend into heaven, for all the world to see.
- God sends plagues upon those who worship the supreme ruler and are thereby complicit. He sends boils, blood on the sea and waters, heat, and darkness.
- God sends his own son Jesus Christ from heaven to earth. Jesus assumes the place of the two witnesses as champion of those persecuted for their faith in him.

After this, the book of Revelation and the Hadiths once again converge in their general subjects and time flow:

- A battle of epic proportions is fought. In Revelation the supreme ruler is vanquished in the battle of Armageddon/In the Hadiths the supreme ruler is victorious and emerges as unopposed after the defeat and killing of the Dajjal.
- All those on the losing side are put to death.
- All those remaining now put their complete faith and trust in the victor – Jesus Christ/the Mahdi.
- After the continual wars that resulted in countless deaths, the victor rules over a completely peaceful world and dispenses great blessings to all – for a millennium of a thousand years/the remainder of the seven years.
- In the Hadiths, after seven years are over, the Mahdi dies, and ʿIsa ibn Maryam passes away sometime later/In Revelation, Jesus Christ does not die, because God already resurrected him after his death on the cross two thousand years ago. By death he defeated death. Jesus brings life after the grave to all who repent of their sins and believe on him.
- Finally, both prophecies come to the true end of history. At that time occurs the final judgment of all humanity by the supreme being who lords over all creation.

This list of similarities is absolutely amazing. Though the name "Mahdi" does not appear in Revelation, and Islam as a religion was still centuries into the future, it could well be said that Revelation contains many ancient prophecies of the Mahdi. We shall explore that in exhaustive detail in the rest of this book.

How the timeline of Revelation guides interpretation of the end-time Hadiths

The way that the prophecies of the Hadiths overlay those of Revelation is very intriguing, though each has a different cast of actors. Whether your background is Muslim, Christian, or another worldview, the knowledge of the parallel prophecies can have an amazing impact on your own relationship with God.

In the Parallel Reference area that follows, you should consider five alternatives at interpreting the prophecies.

The Mahdi will rule for seven years: "He will be the glorious one sent by Allah to establish Sharia across the world. The Muslim end-time prophecy is the true one. Allah is supreme, and it is blasphemy to say that he has a Jewish son who is a god. Islam is the true religion, and the falsehoods of Christianity and the Jews will be smashed once and for all."

An Islamic antichrist will rule for seven years: "The Christian end-time prophecy is the true one, in all its literal detail, with the Mahdi and an impostor Jesus, ʿIsa ibn Maryam, taking on the roles of the beast and the false prophet. They will act in the name of Allah. But they will be the ones defeated by Jesus Christ the son of God at the battle of Armageddon. God the three in one – Father, Son, and Holy Spirit – is the true God over all."

A non-Islamic antichrist will rule for seven years: "The Christian end-time prophecy is the true one, again in all its literal detail, including an evacuation (rapture) of church believers to heaven before the tribulation period, and a thousand-year kingdom of Christ that follows it. But the beast and the false prophet of the tribulation will not be Muslims."

The world will eventually be ensnared in an antichrist spirit: "The Christian end-times prophecies foresee a spirit of antichrist and lawlessness descending upon the world, perhaps spearheaded by a charismatic leader; to be followed by the second coming of Jesus; a final judgment; and concluding with the eternal state. But the other images of Revelation do not correspond to an intricate series of additional future events."

Skepticism: "Neither the Muslim nor the Christian so-called prophecies are prognostications of the future. Both are merely expressions of ingrown belief patterns among hardened segments of humanity."

In my own searching for truth, I started as a skeptic. When I came to repent of my sins and put my trust in Christ, I accepted that the world will eventually be ensnared in an antichrist spirit.

But when God turned me to the depths of Revelation, he persuaded me to believe that its prophecies will come true in literal detail. As I stated in my earlier book, I came to this position because I was forced to deal with this important question: what is God's purpose in providing all the inner detail of the numerous specific events in Revelation? What more would God have to write in his Word to make it clear it should be taken literally?

However, let us leave open the question of the identity of the future antichrist. Yes, the fact that the Islamic prophecies of the Mahdi are so similar to Revelation is striking. As we go through both sets of prophecies, we will consider whether the Hadiths are proof that the Mahdi will be the antichrist.

The book of Revelation is indeed worthy to be used as an authoritative guide to understanding the end-time Hadiths and their fulfillment. That is because of its richness, structure and coherence, its total theological agreement with the rest of the Bible, and the fact that it is evidently the inspired word of the Lamb of God Jesus Christ. Though the Hadiths are more numerous in number, Revelation in its succinctness has more detail in its end-time account. Revelation also has precedence over the Hadiths, as it was written 500 years before Muhammad's day.

Each section of the Parallel Reference will have three parts: the prophecy of the time period in question according to Revelation; the prophecy (if present) according to the Hadiths and the Qur'an, and a comparison of the two. The Revelation commentaries will be a rehash of my earlier book, *Letter to the Tribulation*. If you have already read it, you can save time by skipping to the Hadiths and comparison commentaries within each section.

Muhammad definitely had some exposure to the Bible, Christianity and Judaism. His sayings as recorded in the Hadiths regarding the end times are an echo of what Revelation and the rest of the Bible have to say on that topic. We shall see that the Hadiths often unknowingly have Revelation in mind, but that they anticipate the end-time events through a totally different lens.

Parallel Reference: Revelation vs the end-time Hadiths

Koo :

John is called to receive this apocalyptic prophecy

: Hoo

The greatest future trial will be the coming of the Dajjal the false Messiah

1:1 The Revelation of Jesus Christ, which God gave Him to show to His bond-servants, the things which must soon take place; and He sent and communicated it by His angel to His bond-servant John,
1:2 who testified to the word of God and to the testimony of Jesus Christ, everything that he saw.
1:3 Blessed is the one who reads, and those who hear the words of the prophecy and keep the things which are written in it; for the time is near.
1:4 John to the seven churches that are in Asia: Grace to you and peace from Him who is, and who was, and who is to come, and from the seven spirits who are before His throne,
1:5 and from Jesus Christ, the faithful witness, the firstborn of the dead, and the ruler of the kings of the earth. To Him who loves us and released us from our sins by His blood—
1:6 and He made us into a kingdom, priests to His God and Father—to Him be the glory and

It (the Last Hour) will not come until you see ten signs … the smoke, Dajjal, the beast, the rising of the sun from the west, the descent of 'Isa ibn Maryam, the Yajuj and Majuj (Gog and Magog), and land-slides in three places, one in the east, one in the west and one in Arabia at the end of which fire would burn forth from the Yemen, and would drive people to the place of their assembly.[9]

There will not be any tribulation on earth, since the time Allah created the offspring of Adam, that will be greater than the tribulation of Dajjal. Allah has not sent any Prophet but he warned his nation about Dajjal…. He will undoubtedly appear among you…. He will start by saying "I am a Prophet," and there is no Prophet after me. Then a second time he will say: "I am your Lord." But you will not see your Lord until you die. He is one-eyed, and your Lord is not one-eyed, and written between his eyes is *Kafir* [Unbeliever]. Every

---

[9] Narrated by Hudhaifa b. Usaid al-Ghifari, *Sahih Muslim 2901a,* Book 41, Hadith 6931, https://sunnah.com/muslim:2901a, accessed July 6, 2024 ; also referenced in Rahma p.144.

the dominion forever and ever. Amen.

believer will read it, whether he is literate or illiterate.[10] *(da'if)*

1:8 "I am the Alpha and the Omega," says the Lord God, "who is and who was and who is to come, the Almighty."

1:9 I, John, your brother and fellow participant in the tribulation and kingdom and perseverance in Jesus, was on the island called Patmos because of the word of God and the testimony of Jesus.

1:10 I was in the Spirit on the Lord's day, and I heard behind me a loud voice like the sound of a trumpet,

1:11 saying, "Write on a scroll what you see, and send it to the seven churches: to Ephesus, Smyrna, Pergamum, Thyatira, Sardis, Philadelphia, and Laodicea."

1:12 Then I turned to see the voice that was speaking with me. And after turning I saw seven golden lampstands;

1:13 and in the middle of the lampstands I saw one like a son of man, clothed in a robe reaching to the feet, and wrapped around the chest with a golden sash.

1:14 His head and His hair were white like white wool, like snow; and His eyes were like a flame of fire.

1:15 His feet were like burnished bronze when it has been heated to a glow in a furnace, and His voice was like the sound of many waters.

1:16 In His right hand He held seven stars, and out of His mouth came a sharp two-edged sword; and His face was like the sun shining in its strength.

1:17 When I saw Him, I fell at His feet like a dead man. And He placed His right hand on me, saying, "Do not be afraid; I am the first and the last,

1:18 and the living One; and I was dead, and behold, I am alive forevermore, and I have the keys of death and of Hades.

1:19 Therefore write the things which you have seen, and the things which are, and the things which will take place after these things.

1:20 As for the mystery of the seven stars which you saw in My right hand, and the seven golden lampstands: the seven stars are the angels of the seven churches, and the seven lampstands are the seven churches."

5:1 I saw in the right hand of Him who sat on the throne a scroll written inside and on the back, sealed up with seven seals.

5:2 And I saw a strong angel proclaiming with a loud voice, "Who is worthy to open the scroll and to break its seals?"

5:3 And no one in heaven or on the earth or under the earth was able to open the scroll or to look into it.

5:4 Then I began to weep greatly because no one was found worthy to open the scroll or to look into it.

---

[10] Narrated by Abu Umamah Al-Bahili, *Sunan Ibn Majah 4077*, Vol. 5, Book 36, Hadith 4077, https://sunnah.com/ibnmajah:4077, accessed May 13, 2024.

5:5 And one of the elders said to me, "Stop weeping; behold, the Lion that is from the tribe of Judah, the Root of David, has overcome so as to be able to open the scroll and its seven seals."
5:6 And I saw between the throne (with the four living creatures) and the elders a Lamb standing, as if slaughtered, having seven horns and seven eyes, which are the seven spirits of God sent out into all the earth.
5:7 And He came and took the scroll out of the right hand of Him who sat on the throne.
5:8‡[K14] When He had taken the scroll, the four living creatures and the twenty-four elders fell down before the Lamb, each one holding a harp and golden bowls full of incense, which are the prayers of the saints.
5:11 Then I looked, and I heard the voices of many angels around the throne and the living creatures and the elders; and the number of them was myriads of myriads, and thousands of thousands,
5:12 saying with a loud voice, "Worthy is the Lamb that was slaughtered to receive power, wealth, wisdom, might, honor, glory, and blessing."
5:13 And I heard every created thing which is in heaven, or on the earth, or under the earth, or on the sea, and all the things in them, saying, "To Him who sits on the throne and to the Lamb be the blessing, the honor, the glory, and the dominion forever and ever."
5:14 And the four living creatures were saying, "Amen." And the elders fell down and worshiped.
10:1 I saw another strong angel coming down from heaven, clothed with a cloud; and the rainbow was on his head, and his face was like the sun, and his feet like pillars of fire;
10:2 and he had in his hand a little scroll, which was open. He placed his right foot on the sea and his left on the land;
10:3 and he had in his hand a little scroll, which was open. He placed his right foot on the sea and his left on the land;
10:4 When the seven peals of thunder had spoken, I was about to write; and I heard a voice from heaven, saying, "Seal up the things which the seven peals of thunder have spoken, and do not write them."
10:5 Then the angel whom I saw standing on the sea and on the land raised his right hand to heaven,
10:6 and swore by Him who lives forever and ever, who created heaven and the things in it, and the earth and the things in it, and the sea and the things in it, that there will no longer be a delay,
10:7 but in the days of the voice of the seventh angel, when he is about to sound, then the mystery of God is finished, as He announced to His servants the prophets.
10:8 Then the voice which I heard from heaven, I heard again speaking with me, and saying, "Go, take the scroll which is open in the hand of the angel who stands on the sea and on the land."

10:9 And I went to the angel, telling him to give me the little scroll.
And he said to me, "Take it and eat it; it will make your stomach
bitter, but in your mouth it will be sweet as honey."
10:10 took the little scroll from the angel's hand and ate it, and in
my mouth it was sweet as honey; and when I had eaten it, my
stomach was made bitter.
10:11 And they said to me, "You must prophesy again concerning
many peoples, nations, languages, and kings."

Revelation. The author is John, the last survivor of the twelve original apostles of Christ. He wrote it around the year 95 CE. He was living in exile on the Greek island of Patmos in the Aegean Sea, where he had been sent by the authorities of the Roman Empire as punishment for following Jesus. He wrote it as a long letter meant to be circulated to seven churches in the Roman province of Asia, a region in western-central Asia Minor (today's Turkey). John knew that persecution was about to come upon the churches.

John begins the book (1:1) by saying that this Revelation is not his own, but is from Jesus, God's specially anointed one. Jesus' honorific title for anointed one is *Messiah* in Hebrew, *Christ* in Greek.

John is writing to the seven churches of Asia (1:4). He sees seven spirits before God's throne, who are seven angels. John recognizes that many different angels are sent by Jesus to help convey the vision.

John praises Jesus as the one who loved us and washed us from our sins in his own blood. By giving his life on the cross of Calvary, Christ substituted his perfect sinless life in our place. John hears Jesus announce that he is the Alpha and Omega (1:8), the beginning and end of all things.

Then John uses the word *tribulation* for the first time (1:9). By this he means the trials that are coming upon the seven churches because of their faith.

John sees the son of man (1:13). This was Jesus' favorite title for himself in the New Testament gospels of Matthew, Mark, Luke, and John. Jesus is holding seven stars (1:16), which are the seven angels of the seven churches (1:20).

We jump to chapter 5, where the vision flashes back to the subject of John's commissioning to write the book. That is why we are including this passage from a different chapter here in section K00. A mighty angel calls out (5:2): "who is worthy to open the scroll and break its [seven] seals?" The book in question is this book of Revelation being given to John. The mighty angel takes the scroll (5:8). Then many angels and elders fall down before the Lamb of God, another biblical title for Christ.

Much further, in chapter 10, the vision again visits John's commissioning. A mighty angel comes down from heaven with a little scroll open in his hand. This is the book of prophecy about to be transmitted to John. John is instructed (10:10) to eat the little scroll. It is sweet in his mouth because it is God's word of grace, but bitter in his stomach because divine punishment will be poured out.

This completes the introduction of Revelation, K00.

Hadiths. The sayings of Muhammad regarding the end-times are sprinkled among the thousands of Hadiths. There is no introduction to them. But I have selected two Hadiths to serve as a preface. They include the hadith about the ten signs of the Last Hour, and the hadith that warns of the future trial that will be brought by the Dajjal.

Every Muslim is expected to believe in the Last Day. It is one of the six articles of *iman* (faith). Five are given in Surah 2:177:

1.   Belief in Allah.
2.   Belief in the Last Day.
3.   Belief in angels.
4.   Belief in the scripture.
5.   Belief in the prophets.

The sixth and last article comes from Surah 9:51, and from other passages of the Qur'an:

6.   Belief in the divine decree.

To compare, every true follower of Christ expects him to come again and bring the judgment of heaven or hell. But they are certainly not required to understand the events surrounding his return in all their complexity.

However, Muslims are additionally required to believe in certain events associated with the Last Day called the Major Signs. Of lesser importance to the faith are the Minor Signs.

In future sections I will be touching on the Major Signs. There is no set number of them that Islamic theologians agree upon, but ten are given in the hadith at the top of this section:

- o   the smoke (see H22)
- o   the Dajjal (H19)
- o   the beast, or Dabbat al-ard (H45)
- o   the rising of the sun from the west (H45)
- o   the descent of ʿIsa ibn Maryam (H24)
- o   the Yajuj and Majuj (Gog and Magog) (H45)
- o   landslides, three in number: in the east, in the west, and in Arabia (H39)
- o   a fire will burn forth from the Yemen (H46)

All the Major Signs involve great trials that come upon humanity. But the second hadith in our current section tells us that the greatest of the trials will be brought by the Dajjal. He will claim to be a prophet even greater than Muhammad, the prophet of Islam. That is blasphemous, because Muhammad is regarded by Muslims as the greatest man who will ever live. The Dajjal has the word "unbeliever" tattooed between his eyes, and is blind in one of them. He will come as the defender of the Jews. He will demand to be recognized as a god, Lord over all. The greatest trial will be that the Dajjal will deceive many people into leaving Islam.

This Dajjal hadith is a suitable preface to all the end-time Hadiths. It is a grave warning to all Muslims during the seven-year period not to be tempted to forsake their faith because of the Dajjal and his miracles. It is also an implicit warning that Muslims should always be on guard against the Jews, out of whom the Dajjal will come, and their deceptions. There are other Hadiths that hint that the Dajjal will be Jewish. Some even say that in the lifetime of Muhammad a child was born as a premonition among the Jews of Medina, who fit the description of the Dajjal.[11]

Comparison. Here at the beginning of the parallel timeline, both Revelation and the Hadiths single out a character. In the Hadiths it is surprisingly not the Mahdi, but the Dajjal. They warn how he will tempt people to leave Islam. In Revelation, it is Jesus Christ. The apostle John is filled with praise for Christ, the beginning and end of all things. But his praise is coupled with bitterness (10:10) when he senses that the vision he is about to see will be the greatest divine punishment ever upon living men and women.

The Dajjal and Jesus Christ have some things in common according to Islamic doctrine. Islam opposes the idea that Jesus shares all the divine attributes of God the Father. The Bible attests to this in many passages. For example, Colossians 1:19, written by the apostle Paul, says that "it was [God] the Father's good pleasure for all the fullness to dwell in Him [Christ]." Islam also is opposed to the Dajjal, the anticipated end-time adversary, for the similar reason that he is predicted to claim divinity. In this way, the Hadiths attempt to map the well-known Jesus Christ of the Bible into the caricature of the Dajjal.

At his first coming, Jesus certainly was not a great deceiver, or blind in one eye. But the Jesus whom the Bible says will come at the end of the seven-year tribulation, will in many ways match the Muslim expectations of the Dajjal. Christ will come against the beast and the false prophet as defender of Jews and of Israel's spiritual children, the Christians. This compares with the Dajjal coming on the scene when the rulers of the world are the Mahdi, called by Allah to establish the Muslim world order, and his deputy who holds the name of Jesus, 'Isa ibn Maryam.

In Revelation, before Jesus comes, many Jews and non-Jews will turn away from following the world rulers, and will trust their destiny to

---

[11] Tabrīzī, III, p. 1521, quoted in *Dajjal*, Encyclopaedia Iranica, https://www.iranicaonline.org/articles/dajjal-the-great-deceiver-in-islamic-tradition-the-maleficent-figure-gifted-with-supernatural-powers-whose-advent-and-bri, accessed December 14, 2022.

Christ. This again matches the expectation of the Hadiths for the Dajjal's success at turning many Jews and non-Jews toward him.

The Hadiths expect a Muslim messiah, a Muslim Jesus and an anti-Muslim Jesus – in the persons of the Mahdi, ʿIsa ibn Maryam and the Dajjal. We shall see that Revelation is a mirror image of the Islamic eschatology. It prophesies the coming of one false messiah, one false prophet, and one true messiah – they will be the antichrist known as the beast, his assistant the false prophet, and Jesus Christ the son of God.

K01 :
Satan and the devils rebel against God
and are cast out of heaven

12:3‡[K04,K15] Then another sign appeared in heaven: and
behold, a great red dragon *having seven heads and ten horns,
and on his heads were seven crowns.*
12:4‡[K04,K15] And his tail swept away a third of the stars of
heaven and hurled them to the earth. *And the dragon stood
before the woman who was about to give birth, so that when
she gave birth he might devour her Child.*

Revelation. The earliest event in the chronology of Revelation goes
back to the time after God created Adam and Eve. It tells of the wonder
of the great red dragon, whose tail sweeps the third part of the stars
from heaven down to earth. The image symbolizes the rebellion of
Satan and a third of the angels against God. It describes the fall of
Satan, and the origin of the devils.

We will consider the italicized parts of 12:3 and 12:4 in sections K04
and K15. They refer to later points in the timeline of history.

The back story of the red dragon involves Adam and Eve.

A study of the Bible tells us that Satan and the devils, along with the
rest of the angels, are spirit beings created by God. This happened
during the six days of creation, of Genesis chapter 1. Initially, all the
angels had free access to heaven. But Satan was not satisfied. He said "I
will make myself like the Most High" (Isaiah 14:14). God responded to
this challenge by casting him out of heaven. This was the fall of Satan
and the evil spirits. Afterward, they made it their mission to torment
men and women on earth.

Satan then appeared to Eve as the talking serpent in the garden of
Eden. In this guise, he deceived her into eating of the tree of Good and
Evil, which was the only thing that God expressly forbid Adam and Eve
not to do. The temptation that Satan held out to her was the same that
brought about his own fall – that she and Adam would "become like
God" (Genesis 3:5). Adam willingly followed into the same sin, instead

of correcting his wife. But the two of them did not become like God. Instead, they learned evil. This act of original sin is shared by all the descendants of Adam and Eve, including you and me. Each of us secretly or openly wants what we want, instead of desiring to follow God with all our heart.

The fall of the human race into sin happened more than four thousand years before Muhammad. In their shame, Adam and Eve recounted exactly what happened to their descendants. The record was carefully relayed through the line of Noah, then through the line of Abraham and Israel, until Moses wrote it down at God's direction two thousand years before Islam.

God created the human race to be immortal. But our first parents rejected this perfection in favor of Satan's lie. The result was that God sentenced them to eventually die. And so, all of us will die a physical death, because we share in the sin and rebellion of our original ancestors.

God gave additional revelation about the fall of Satan to his Jewish prophet Ezekiel, more than one thousand years before Muhammad.

Ezekiel sees Satan in the form of the prince of Tyre (the premier seaport of the eastern Mediterranean at the time). He was the signet of perfection, an anointed cherub in the garden of Eden, until God dealt with his rebellion:

> Ezekiel 28:11 Again the word of the Lord came to me, saying,
> 28:12 "Son of man, take up a song of mourning over the king of Tyre and say to him, 'This is what the Lord God says: "You had the seal of perfection, Full of wisdom and perfect in beauty.
> 28:13 "You were in Eden, the garden of God; Every precious stone was your covering: The ruby, the topaz and the diamond; The beryl, the onyx and the jasper; The lapis lazuli, the turquoise and the emerald; And the gold, the workmanship of your settings and sockets, Was in you. On the day that you were created They were prepared.
> 28:14 "You were the anointed cherub who covers, And I placed you there. You were on the holy mountain of God; You walked in the midst of the stones of fire.
> 28:15 "You were blameless in your ways From the day you were created Until unrighteousness was found in you.

> 28:16 "By the abundance of your trade You were internally
> filled with violence, And you sinned; Therefore I have cast
> you as profane From the mountain of God. And I have
> destroyed you, you covering cherub, From the midst of the
> stones of fire.
> 28:17 "Your heart was haughty because of your beauty; You
> corrupted your wisdom by reason of your splendor. I threw
> you to the ground; I put you before kings, That they may see
> you.
> 28:18 "By the multitude of your wrongdoings, In the
> unrighteousness of your trade You profaned your
> sanctuaries. Therefore I have brought fire from the midst of
> you; It has consumed you, And I have turned you to ashes on
> the earth In the eyes of all who see you.
> 28:19 "All who know you among the peoples Are appalled at
> you; You have become terrified. And you will cease to be
> forever." ' "

After he was cast out of heaven, Satan could only return there when
summoned, for example when he appeared before God to discuss the
righteousness of Job (Job 1:6, see K15).

Why is Satan not satisfied until he is like God? Many say he was filled
with the sin of pride, and wants company in his rebellion by getting as
many men and women as possible to build up his own kingdom. My
answer is that it was not pride, but jealousy of Christ, and of all human
beings created in his image. Satan's goal is to destroy both Jesus and all
mankind.

By many evidences and testimonies, the Bible shows Jesus Christ to be
the eternal and divine son of God, the second person of the Trinity. In
Letter to the Tribulation Appendix A, *Why Satan hates Christ*, I discuss the
biblical evidence that even before God created the universe in six days,
Jesus was already the perfect God-man, with an eternal spirit and
glorified body. He was the template for Adam and Eve and all their
descendants. This is supported in the New Testament by Hebrews 13:8:
"Jesus Christ is the same yesterday and today, and forever." The word
"yesterday" looks back from when Hebrews was written, all the way to
before the creation.

When God created the angels, he brought his eternal son Jesus before
them. Most of the angels willingly worshipped him out of profound
gratitude:

> Hebrews 1:6 And when He again brings the firstborn into the world, He says, "And let all the angels of God worship Him."

But Satan and his associate angels did not worship. When he understood that Jesus was the eternal God-man, and that Adam, Eve, and their descendants to come were created in his image, an unrelenting hatred arose in Satan's heart toward Jesus and toward God the Father. Satan saw Jesus Christ as the supreme obstacle in his goal to become equal to God. He determined to undermine the position of Jesus by attacking those created in his image. To this day, he attacks people. He does so physically, by promoting disease, abortion, and war. He also attacks them spiritually, by promoting religions and ideologies that challenge God's word. We shall see that one of these religions violently enforces the ideas that God must be singular, that the three-in-one God of the Bible is anathema, and that there cannot be a divine Son of God.

Hadiths. The fall of Satan in the Bible inspired the character of Shaytan in the Qur'an. I already mentioned its story of Iblis, the first of the shaytans (devils), in the section on the Main actors of the end-time Hadiths. In the Qur'an he was a glorious creature made of fire, who refused to bow to Adam. That is the reason given why Allah banished all the devils from heaven to earth. Shaytan then swore revenge on Adam and his descendants.

In the Hadiths of section H15, we shall see an echo of the red dragon's tail drawing a third of the stars down to earth. A star with a tail will signal the coming of the Mahdi.

Comparison. Compared with the Qur'an, the Bible gives much more insight into Satan's fall, and his aim of turning all humanity to destruction.

K02 :

The spirit of Babel in the empires of the Old Testament period and the coming tribulation

: H02

After the prophet, Allah sends a caliphate, a kingdom, then a caliphate based on prophethood

17:1‡[K17,K20] Then one of the seven angels who had the seven' bowls came and spoke with me, saying, "Come here, I will show you *the judgment of* the great prostitute who sits on many waters."
17:7 And the angel said to me, "Why do you wonder? I will tell you the mystery of the woman and of the beast that carries her, which has the seven heads and the ten horns.
17:9 Here is the mind which has wisdom. The seven heads are seven mountains upon which the woman sits,
17:10 and they are seven kings; five have fallen, one is, the other has not yet come; and when he comes, he must remain a little while.

Prophethood will remain amongst you for as long as Allah wishes. Then Allah will remove it whenever He wishes to remove it, and there will be a caliphate upon the prophetic methodology. It will last for as long as Allah wishes it to last, then Allah will remove it whenever He wishes to remove it. Then there will be an abiding dynasty, and it will remain for as long as Allah wishes it to remain. Then Allah will remove it whenever He wishes to remove it. Then there will be an enforced monarchy, and it will remain for as long as Allah wishes it to remain. Then He will remove it whenever He wishes to remove it, and then there will be a caliphate upon the prophetic methodology.[12] *(hasan)*

17:11 The beast which was, and is not, is himself also an eighth and is one of the seven, and he goes to destruction.
17:8 The beast that you saw was, and is not, and is about to come up out of the abyss and go to destruction. And those who live on the earth, whose names have not been written in the book of life from the foundation of the world, will wonder when they see the beast, that he was, and is not, and will come."

---

[12] Narrated by Ibn Ḥanbal, *Musnad Aḥmad, 30:355, no. 18406,* https://yaqeeninstitute.org/read/paper/the-prophecies-of-prophet-muhammad, accessed May 13, 2024; also referenced in `Ibn Izzat, *Al Mahdi and the End of Time,* Dar Al Taqwa Ltd., London, 1997, p.39-40.

Revelation. In this section, John is given to see the overmlarching vastness of human history, from the time after Noah's flood, to the casting of Satan into hell at the end of days.

This macro view occurs late in the vision, in chapter 17, after the seven seals, seven trumpets and seven bowls have been completed.

We are introduced to the prostitute. We know from verses 17:4-5 K17 that this is the woman of Babylon, one of the main characters of the letter. She sits on many waters (17:1), and also on seven mountains (17:9).

We also see seven kings (17:10). Five of them are in the past, one is ruling much of the world in the time of John, and one is coming in the future.

We see an unreal beast, who is carrying the woman (17:7), ascending from the abyss (17:8). The pit ties him to Satan, who by the names Apollyon or Abaddon is the angel of the abyss (9:11 K32). The beast "is one of the seven" kings (17:11). He is therefore associated with them, or perhaps he is one of them in some manner. It is promised that the beast will reappear as an eighth king. His eternal destiny will be destruction (17:8), which will be in hell.

Some of the kings of 17:10 are an echo of Daniel 2, written after 600 BCE. There the Jewish prophet Daniel interpreted to King Nebuchadnezzar of Babylon his dream of another beast, one with a head of gold, chest and arms of silver, middle and thighs of bronze, and legs partly of iron and partly of clay. By God's leading, Daniel explained the dream in terms of empires in the centuries to follow, that expanded and contracted over much of the world: Babylonia, Medo-Persia, Greece and Rome. Two additional empires of great power existed before Daniel's time: Assyria and Egypt. All these kingdoms at some point had sovereignty over Jerusalem. The first five came before John's day, they are the kings that are *fallen*. The Roman empire is the nemesis of John's day. It is the sixth king, the one who *is*.

All six empires were crucial in the history of Israel, God's chosen people. Egypt enslaved the Israelites, Assyria dispersed the ten northern Israelite tribes, and Babylon brought the Jewish tribes of Judah and Benjamin into captivity for seventy years. Medo-Persia was the only empire favorable to God's people. It allowed the Jews to return to Jerusalem and rebuild God's temple. Greece desecrated the temple with unholy sacrifice, which Daniel prophesied as the abomination that causes desolation (Daniel 9:27). It is the precedent for an even greater abomination that will happen during the tribulation (13:15 K24). Finally, Rome demolished the temple completely.

The prostitute or woman of Babylon ultimately links back to Babel, the precursor to all these empires. Nimrod, the king of Babel, rejected the judgment of the worldwide flood that occurred less than 200 years before his time. He and his followers rebelled against God yet again, by building their tower of Babel as high to heaven as they could reach. God foiled their plan by confusing their speech. This was the origin of languages. The people of Babel then turned against each other. Most of them started a migration to the distant lands of the earth: Europe, Africa, India, China, the Pacific, and the Americas. They brought with them syncretistic religions that Babel had given birth to.

The woman and the beast will use each other until halfway through the tribulation period. But Revelation leaves us uncertain as to the identity of the woman and the beast. We shall see that the Hadiths have something to say about that.

Here in Revelation we are given three points about the beast:

- There will be a seventh kingdom coming after Rome the sixth kingdom (17:10).
- The beast "is one of the seven" kings, and will also be an eighth. So, he will be an eighth king who was somehow operative in all seven kingdoms, or possibly he will be king of both the seventh and eighth kingdoms (17:11).
- In between the seventh and eighth kingdom the beast will be eclipsed (17:8).

The vision then plunges ahead to the time after the tribulation, when the beast will be cast into hell (17:8, which will be fulfilled in 19:20 K40).

Hadiths. Muslims believe that Muhammad was the last and greatest prophet. His words recorded in the hadith of this section can be compared with our Revelation passage, since they give a view of Islam far into the future.

Muslims see themselves as members of one *ummah*, or community of believers. Ideally, this community is structured around the caliphate. The Hadiths foretell the reestablishment of the caliphate, and the future triumph of Islam over the whole world.

Muhammad's prophecy of *caliphate upon prophetic methodology* (or *prophetic prophethood*) came to fulfillment as the political-theocratic structure that he constructed. It resulted in a long succession of caliphs, over many centuries. Each was regarded as the worldwide leader of Islam of his day. Their political influence extended to wherever their boundaries reached. But their spiritual influence extended further, to all Muslims throughout the world.

After Muhammad's death, three caliphates succeeded each other, each with a hereditary line of caliphs. The Rashidun Caliphate (632–661) ruled from Medina in Arabia, then Kufa in Iraq. The Umayyad Caliphate (661–750) ruled from Damascus, then Harran in Turkey. The Abbasid Caliphate ruled much of its time from Baghdad (750–1258), then shifted to Cairo (1258-1517).

During the period of Ottoman expansion, after Sultan Selim I conquered Cairo and Mamluk Egypt in 1517, he claimed the caliphal authority. By this conquest the Ottoman sultan took on the title of Defender of the Holy Cities of Mecca and Medina. That strengthened the Ottoman claim to caliphate in the Muslim world. Only a few decades earlier, in 1453, the Ottoman Turks finally subjugated Constantinople, which had been capital of the eastern Roman empire (also known as the Byzantine empire) for a thousand years. And so the power of Islam was shifted to Constantinople, renamed Istanbul. The Ottoman Caliphate (1517-1924) became the last caliphate recognized by all Sunnis.

The hadith continues with the prophecy that *Allah ... will remove it whenever he wishes*. This happened in 1924 with the abolition of the Ottoman caliphate by the government of Ataturk and his recently formed nation of Turkey.

What is the caliphate, or *khilafah*? An idealist Islamic answer is:

The Caliph must be just and rule the people by Islamic Sharia law. Sharia is a comprehensive system that legislates on ruling, social, economic and judicial matters. Economic progress and enhancing the living standards of the people is one of its major objectives. The Caliphate's army must follow strict rules of engagement when fighting war (jihad). The soldiers do not fight the enemy out of anger or hatred, but to please their creator – Allah. The restoration of the Caliphate will usher in a new era of peace, stability and prosperity for the Muslim world and beyond, ending years of oppression by some of the worst tyrants this world has ever seen such as Islam Karimov of Uzbekistan and Hosni Mubarak of Egypt and finally solving the long running problems of Palestine, Iraq, Kashmir and Chechnya to name but a few.[13]

Those who do not believe in Allah are outside the ummah. They are the *kuffar* (plural of *kafir*), the heathen or infidels, who refuse to convert to Islam. Under the caliphate they are treated as *dhimmi*, the people of contract. These are subjugated persons, having lesser rights granted by contract, compared with the much fuller rights of Muslims. Treated worse are the *murtad*, those who once adhered to Islam, then left it.

Many Muslims regard the politicians who are running their countries as traitors to the vision of this ideal caliphate. They see the modern Muslim political states as non-Islamic constructs forced upon them by infidel Western powers, who took advantage of a weakened caliphate, terminated it, and oppose its reestablishment.

The hadith concludes *then there will be caliphate based on prophetic methodology*. This refers to the coming of the Mahdi. Since Muhammad is regarded as the final prophet, the Mahdi will not be a prophet himself. However, he is predicted to come from the bloodline of Muhammad. He will be the final and rightly guided caliph.[14] He will create a global Islamic state.

Throughout the centuries there have been many self-styled Mahdis who wished to bring about the end time by their own means. Prominent examples were Ibn Tumart and the Almohads in the Maghreb (North

---

[13] *What is the Caliphate?*, https://islamciv.com/what-is-the-caliphate/, accessed December 23, 2022.
[14] *Who Is Imam Al-Mahdi?*, http://www.islamicweb.com/history/mahdi.htm, accessed December 21, 2022.

Africa, 1120's), nine different Sufi leaders who led Mahdist revolts against Ottoman authority (1240-1665), Shah Ismail and the Safavids (Iran, 1501), the Ottoman Sultan Suleiman who besieged Vienna twice (16th century), and Muhammad Ahmad against the British (Sudan, 1885).[15]

The fall of the Ottoman caliphate set the stage for Wahhabi jihadist influence over all of Sunni Islam, and the 1979 Iranian Shi'ite Sharia revolution. Sunnis and Shi'ites each look with hope for the Mahdi to soon emerge. Some have already proclaimed themselves to be him. Juhayman al-Utaybi announced he was the Mahdi Muhammad al-Qahtani (Saudi Arabia, 1979). In 2012, the Muslim Brotherhood candidate for presidency of Egypt styled himself as the Mahdi.[16]

But neither these, nor the self-pronounced Mahdis of centuries past, were anything close to what the end-time Mahdi is prophesied to be. At best, Muslims consider some of them to be *mujaddid*, or "renewers" of Islam that the following hadith predicts will come every hundred years:

> At the beginning of every century God will send one who will renew its religion for this people.[17]

Major events and dates in the Islamic calendar bring on elevated expectations that instead of more renewers, the long-awaited end-time Mahdi will come, who will bring about a final and valid caliphate.

My year of writing, 2024, is the 100-year anniversary of the demise of the caliphate. In another hundred years 2124 will come. It will be another date of Mahdist fever. Eschatological expectations also spike at the turn of each Muslim century. The year 2076 CE will be 1500 AH in the Muslim calendar. Will the glorious Mahdi appear at one of those times?[18]

Comparison. The Islamic view of salvation is communal. Muslims cannot expect a personal relationship with Allah, because he is

---

[15] Timothy Furnish, *Ten Years Captivation with the Mahdi's Camps*, no publisher, 2015, pp.1-2, 101.
[16] Furnish, pp.1-2.
[17] Narrated by Abu Dawud, *Mishkat al-Masabih 247*, https://sunnah.com/mishkat:247, accessed July 7, 2024.
[18] Furnish, p.83.

unapproachable. But they believe they can gain his favor by maintaining solidarity with the ummah, establishing the caliphate, serving it, and fighting jihad to expand Islam.

By contrast, followers of Jesus Christ come into a personal relationship with him, the son of God. He knows each one of them individually, by name. Everyone who believes in Christ knows a special bond with him, because God created us in his image.

The yearning for caliphate has a great parallel in the expected seventh and eighth kingdoms of this Revelation passage.

Many Christian commentators believe that the seventh kingdom will be a reconstituted Roman empire, with Rome as capital. They say it will be established during the first three and a half years of the tribulation, and will rule over the whole world. The beast will be one of its powerful leaders. The eighth empire will succeed it in the second half of the tribulation. In that final kingdom, the beast will not be merely part of a leadership coalition. He will be supreme.

In answer to this interpretation, note that historically, as one biblical empire fell, a new one was rising: first Egypt, then Assyria, Babylon, Medo-Persia, Greece, and then the sixth kingdom of Rome. This unbroken continuity was true even after Babel – when it fell, Noah's son Ham and grandson Mizraim immediately went to Egypt to start the kingdom there. But in 17:10, John sees that when the seventh king comes, "he must remain a little while." This could be interpreted to mean that that the seventh will be cut short. The result would be a discontinuity in the series of empires. Afterward there will be a time gap until the next empire.

The question becomes, what would then be the seventh kingdom that immediately succeeded the sixth one of Rome, and was later cut short?

The Hadiths suggest an answer. They point to a totally different understanding of how the sixth could be immediately followed by a seventh, and still have the seventh rehashed as an eighth.

The Hadiths say that the caliphate will be reestablished in the end times by the Mahdi. If that does take place, it will give clarity to the three time periods indicated by the words "the beast ... *was, and is not*, and *is about to come up out of the abyss*" (17:8). It will also resolve the three points about the beast posed above:

- The coming of the Mahdi will indicate that the seventh kingdom of Revelation happened long after John wrote the book, but before my time. It was the Ottoman empire. It succeeded the sixth kingdom, the Roman empire, with no time gap. That occurred when Constantinople fell to the siege of the Ottoman armies in 1453. Not long after, the Ottomans assumed the caliphate in 1517. This is the beast *that was* (17:11).
- If the Mahdi becomes worldwide ruler, we can be sure that Islam is the beast king of both the seventh and eighth kingdoms (17:11).
- When the Istanbul caliphate was abolished in 1924, the beast was eclipsed. This is the pause in empire history, the beast that *is not* (17:11). The Ottoman empire and the caliphate in Constantinople were cut short. Then the first gap between empires started. It will last until the eighth kingdom of the tribulation comes, in the person of the Mahdi, the king of the tribulation period. He will be the beast that *is about to rise* (17:8).

Not all the sayings of Muhammad regarding the long-term future of the caliphate are truly prophetic. His prediction that the caliphate would succeed him was a self-fulfilling one. It came true at the hands of the military complex that he forged. If the caliphate had not followed, Muhammad would be a minor historical footnote. It is also self-fulfilling that the caliphate would eventually come to an end, for that has been the fate of every earthly kingdom in history. Because of these self-fulfillments, we can dispense with the idea that Islam, or Satan, can out-do the prophecies of the Bible.

Yes, it is striking that what is left of the six empires of Revelation are largely Muslim today, and that the end-time Hadiths seem to be a logical fulfillment of the seventh and eighth kingdoms of Revelation. Yet they do not prove that the Mahdi will be the beast of the tribulation.

Only God can ordain what will happen down the corridors of time. No human being, angel, or evil spirit can do so.

The true God of the Bible may indeed intend, for his own sovereign purposes, that the Mahdi will appear as the head of the opposing Islamic religion. I believe that we should be prepared for that possibility, and be aware of the intentions of the end-time Hadiths. We must remember that God sent the godless Assyrian and Babylonian armies in judgment upon Israel, with the ultimate purpose that people would come to repentance, and turn to him for salvation. He may have already planned a similar movement to repentance by millions during the end-times, when they experience the Mahdi's rule.

K03 :
God founds the nation of Israel

12:1 A great sign appeared in heaven: a woman clothed with the sun, and the moon under her feet, and on her head a crown of twelve stars.

Revelation. The God of history has always known there will be a succession of empires who lead their people in opposition to him. His response occurred early in the history of Egypt, the first empire. He raised up a tiny nation that would outlast all the empires. From this nation would be born a baby, who would grow up to save God's people from their guilt and sin.

This verse (12:1) pictures a great wonder in heaven, a woman with a crown of twelve stars. The number twelve refers us to the book of Genesis, where Jacob, also known as Israel, had twelve sons who became the tribes of Israel. In an incredible story of slavery and redemption, God guided one of the sons, Joseph, to become prime minister of Egypt and to deliver his family and millions of Egyptians from a seven-year famine.

In his youth Joseph had a prophetic dream (Genesis 37:9). In it he saw that "the sun and the moon, and eleven stars were bowing down to me." The dream stayed with him, but he had little idea what would happen. Many years later, during the famine, his father Jacob, his mother Rachel, and his eleven brothers did indeed bow down to him, and recognized that God had transformed him from a household slave into the deputy ruler of Egypt. The twelve sons of Jacob went on to become the nation of Israel.

Here in Revelation, God brings similar imagery before John. He sees a woman clothed with the sun, the moon under her feet, and a crown of twelve stars. This woman is Israel, God's chosen people. The wonder in God's timeline is that he established this small and special nation for his great and special purposes.

God uses his people to present truth to the world against its spirit of rebellion. That spiritual rebellion translates to a spiritual famine. After

Jesus was born in a manger in Bethlehem, and died on a cross in Jerusalem, he brought that truth to all the nations. Many people in their midst recognized that Jesus was the true king of their hearts. They became Christians. Many more will do so until the end of days.

The coming of Jesus into the world will be the subject of the next section.

Qur'an. The Bible depicts the Jews as the people that God chose to reveal himself to, and a people whom he loves despite their faults. The Qur'an on the other hand, sees the Jews as a totally despicable people.

Hatred of Jews originates in the actions of Muhammad. In 622 he and his small group of early followers were forced out of Mecca. They headed north to the city of Medina, in a migration that became known as the *hijrah*. There, Muhammad built up his following. Together they returned eight years later to Mecca to defeat his enemies, and make it the permanent center of the new religion.

While Muhammad was in Medina, there were several Jewish tribes living there who refused to accept Muhammad's prophethood. The leaders of the Jewish Banu Qurayzah tribe were supposedly plotting to have him killed. Muhammad pronounced that the Qurayzah were "brothers of monkeys," and found one of their own numbers to hand down a judgment upon them: "the men should be killed, the property divided, and the women and children taken as captives." Muhammad's men then besieged the Jewish forces, captured the men, and beheaded more than 600 of them.[19]

This pattern set by the prophet of Allah against the Jews has inspired centuries of his militant jihadist followers.

Comparison. Israel and the Jews play extremely important roles in the Bible and Revelation, and also in the Qur'an and the Hadiths. Jesus Christ was born Jewish. He remains so to this day, since he is immortal God. But the Hadiths go to great lengths to explain that their Jesus, 'Isa ibn Maryam, will forsake his Jewishness. He will return as the greatest

---

[19] `Abd al-Malik Ibn Hisham, *Life of Muhammad. A Translation of Ishaq's Sirat Rasul Allah*, pp. 459-466, quoted in Furnish, pp.14-15.

Islamic religious figure. He will not rest in his mission to do away with Jews, Christians, and all others who do not accept the Mahdi.

The importance of the Jews in both end-time narratives is another clue that the Hadiths are meant to be a replacement for Revelation in the hearts and minds of Muslims. I believe you should compare both carefully to see where the truth lies.

K04 :

Satan attempts to kill the baby Jesus through King Herod

> 12:2 and she was pregnant and she cried out, being in labor
> and in pain to give birth.
> 12:3‡[K01,K15] Then another sign appeared in heaven: and
> behold, a great red dragon *having seven heads and ten horns,
> and on his heads were seven crowns.*
> 12:4‡[K01,K15] *And his tail swept away a third of the stars of
> heaven and hurled them to the earth.* And the dragon stood
> before the woman who was about to give birth, so that when
> she gave birth he might devour her Child.

Revelation. In the next verses we are told that the woman Israel, with her crown of twelve stars, will give birth to a child.

The Old Testament has many prophecies of the anointed one, titled the *Messiah* in Hebrew, in Greek the *Christ*. He would deliver God's people from their earthly oppressors, and from Satan. But more importantly, he would atone for their sins against God, so that they could enter God's eternal presence.

One of the prophecies was from Isaiah:

> Isaiah 9:6 For a Child will be born to us, a Son will be given
> to us; And the government will rest on His shoulders; And
> His name will be called Wonderful Counselor, Mighty God,
> Eternal Father, Prince of Peace.

That prophecy came true in the birth of Jesus, as recorded in the New Testament book of Matthew:

> Matthew 1:20 But when he had thought this over, behold, an
> angel of the Lord appeared to him in a dream, saying,
> "Joseph, son of David, do not be afraid to take Mary as your
> wife; for the Child who has been conceived in her is of the
> Holy Spirit.
> 1:21 She will give birth to a Son; and you shall name Him
> Jesus, for He will save His people from their sins."
> 1:22 Now all this took place so that what was spoken by the
> Lord through the prophet would be fulfilled:

> 1:23 "Behold, the virgin will conceive and give birth to a Son,
> and they shall name Him Immanuel," which translated
> means, "God with us." [Isaiah 7:14]
> 1:24 And Joseph awoke from his sleep and did as the angel of
> the Lord commanded him, and took Mary as his wife,
> 1:25 but kept her a virgin until she gave birth to a Son; and
> he named Him Jesus.

The baby of Revelation 12:2 is this Jesus – born miraculously of the virgin Mary, a daughter of Israel. She was of the bloodline of David, the greatest king of Israel, the man after God's own heart who wrote most of the Psalms and defeated all of Israel's enemies. Jesus the eternal king of kings was conceived in Mary's womb not by Joseph, her betrothed, but by the Holy Spirit of God (Matthew 1:20).

The other character of this section is the great red dragon. In section K01 we already identified this creature as Satan.

Satan knows the Bible. Israel and the promised messiah are a mortal threat to his plan for universal domination. In the italicized part of 12:4 he was cast out of heaven along with all the fallen angels (K01). Here, in the second part of 12:4, he stands before the woman, ready to devour her child when she gives birth.

This image refers to the massacre of the innocents, which happened soon after the birth of Jesus. At that time, wise men from afar called the *magi*, were led by a special star to Jerusalem. They asked Herod the king where to find the newly born king of the Jews. Herod's advisors told him that the birth of the messiah was prophesied in Micah 5:2, and that he would be born in Bethlehem, the city of David. Herod then sent soldiers to kill all baby boys age two and under who were in Bethlehem. He thought that in this way he could kill this future rival to his throne.

Satan was the one working behind the scenes.

However, God, who arranges all things, sent an angel to warn Joseph to flee temporarily to Egypt with Mary and the baby. Satan will have to try again to kill Jesus.

Qur'an. The virgin birth of ʿIsa ibn Maryam is also described in the Qur'an:

> And mention in the Book, O Prophet, the story of Maryam when she withdrew from her family to a place in the east, screening herself off from them. Then We sent to her Our angel, Jibreel, appearing before her as a man, perfectly formed. She appealed, "I truly seek refuge in the Most Compassionate from you! So leave me alone if you are God-fearing." He responded, "I am only a messenger from your Lord, sent to bless you with a pure son." She wondered, "How can I have a son when no man has ever touched me, nor am I unchaste?" He replied, "So will it be! Your Lord says, 'It is easy for Me. And so will We make him a sign for humanity and a mercy from Us.' It is a matter already decreed." So she conceived him and withdrew with him to a remote place. Then the pains of labour drove her to the trunk of a palm tree. She cried, "Alas! I wish I had died before this, and was a thing long forgotten!" So a voice reassured her from below her, "Do not grieve! Your Lord has provided a stream at your feet. And shake the trunk of this palm tree towards you, it will drop fresh, ripe dates upon you. So eat and drink, and put your heart at ease." (Surah 19:16–26a, Clear Qur'an)

Comparison. The Qur'an surprisingly joins the Bible in praising Jesus, not just as a prophet, but as the Messiah. He is even honored as the word of Allah (Surah 3:45). This is similar to his title of divine *logos*, or word of God in the New Testament book of John (1:1, 14).

In the Qur'an, ʿIsa is born not in Bethlehem, but in some "distant place." Maryam is all alone to give birth, and there is no Joseph or anyone else to help her. ʿIsa is born under a palm tree, next to a miraculous stream. And just as Isaiah prophesied, he was miraculously born of a virgin, as described in the above passage.

Despite recounting the virgin birth of ʿIsa ibn Maryam, Muhammad rejected the logical conclusion that ʿIsa was therefore a son of God. He certainly could not be God the son. He could be nothing more than another messenger of God.[20]

---

[20] Mustafa Akyol, *Jesus' Birth Between Islam and Christianity, How the Quran's account of the Nativity echoes both the Bible and non-canonical Eastern Christian texts*, https://newlinesmag.com/essays/the-palm-and-the-spring/, December 23, 2022.

In its story, the Qur'an makes no mention of Shaytan or the massacre of the innocents.

<table>
<tr><td>

K05 :
The incarnation and
ascension of Jesus

</td><td>

: H05
The Mahdi will be born in
the line of Muhammad

</td></tr>
</table>

12:5‡[K42] And she gave birth to a Son, a male, *who is going to rule all the nations with a rod of iron;* and her Child was caught up to God and to His throne.

The Prophet said: The Mahdi will be of my family, of the descendants of Fatimah.[21] *(sahih)*

The world will not end until a man from my family rules over it (the world); his name would the same as my name.[22]

Revelation. The next verse (12:5) tells us that despite Satan's schemes, the virgin Mary "gave birth to a Son, a male." The God who created us loved us so much that he descended to our level. He adopted the fallen flesh of sinful man, and was born a babe. Jesus "became flesh, and dwelt among us" (John 1:14). This is celebrated by the word *incarnation*, which applies to only one man who ever lived, the Christ.

Jesus grew up, and ministered throughout the land of Israel for three years. He proclaimed the word of God, and miraculously healed people. Many demons chose this time to oppose him, to possess people's hearts and minds, and make their claim on souls. But on frequent occasions, Jesus drove them out, and showed that he had the power of God over Satan.

At the end of his ministry, Satan once again schemed, this time by way of the Jewish religious establishment, to have Jesus put to death on the cross (Matthew 27:45-54, Mark 15:33-39, Luke 23:44-48, John 19:17-30). There were many who saw him breathe his last. One of the Roman soldiers who crucified him pierced his side with a spear, and blood and water poured out (John 19:34). Three days later, Jesus rose from the

---

[21] Narrated by Umm Salamah, Ummul Mu'minin, *Sunan Abi Dawud 4284*, Book 37, Hadith 4271, https://sunnah.com/abudawud:4284, accessed May 13, 2024.

[22] *Mustadrak al-Hakim 8455, Musnad al-Bazzar 1619, 1620, and 1643, Musnad lil-Shaami 583, Mu'jam al-Sagheer of Tabarani 1179, Mu'jam al-Aswat of Tabarani 7009,* quoted in Rahma p.11.

dead (Matthew 28:1-7, Mark 16:1-11, Luke 24:1-12, John 20:1-18), never to die again.

Forty days later, Jesus was "caught up to God" (12:5). This is his ascension into heaven, which is described in eye-witness detail in Acts 1:

> Acts 1:6 So, when they had come together, they began asking Him, saying, "Lord, is it at this time that You are restoring the kingdom to Israel?"
> 1:7 So, when they had come together, they began asking Him, saying, "Lord, is it at this time that You are restoring the kingdom to Israel?"
> 1:8 but you will receive power when the Holy Spirit has come upon you; and you shall be My witnesses both in Jerusalem and in all Judea, and Samaria, and as far as the remotest part of the earth."
> 1:9 And after He had said these things, He was lifted up while they were watching, and a cloud took Him up, out of their sight.
> 1:10 And as they were gazing intently into the sky while He was going, then behold, two men in white clothing stood beside them,
> 1:11 and they said, "Men of Galilee, why do you stand looking into the sky? This Jesus, who has been taken up from you into heaven, will come in the same way as you have watched Him go into heaven."

The onlookers heard the two angels in white say that someday Jesus will return from heaven to earth in like manner, in a cloud. That will be the second coming of Christ (1:7 K38).

Verse 12:5 also emphasizes the divinity of Christ. After his ascension he was "caught up to God and to his throne." Then he sat down at the right hand of God the Father, as explained in Mark's account:

> Mark 16:19 So then, when the Lord Jesus had spoken to them, He was received up into heaven and sat down at the right hand of God.

We know' from the psalms that the right hand of God is the place of divine standing:

> Psalm 110:1 The Lord says to my Lord: "Sit at My right hand Until I make Your enemies a footstool for Your feet."

Hadiths. These are just two of the Hadiths where Muhammad predicts that the Mahdi will be his descendant. He will also be called Muhammad. He will come as *the* Islamic messianic figure to save the world. He will be the universal leader for all Muslims, and will rule the world.

Even though the Mahdi is not mentioned in the Qur'an, he is the future hope of hundreds of millions of Muslims. In 2012, the Pew Forum on Religion and Public Life released a survey of 28,000 Muslims across 23 countries, titled "The World's Muslims: Unity and Diversity." Of those questioned, 42% believe that the Mahdi would come before the year 2050. Belief was highest in Afghanistan, 83%; Iraq, 72%; Turkey, 68%; Tunisia, 67%; Malaysia, 62%; Pakistan, 60%; Lebanon, 56%; Morocco, 51%; Palestinian territories, 46%; and Egypt, 40%. It proves that Mahdism is not some medieval holdover in Islam, believed only by the uneducated. It is very strong throughout all strata of the Islamic world.[23]

In section H02 we saw examples of men who prematurely claimed to be the Mahdi over the past thousand years. There have also been many movements in Islam that have sought to prepare the way for the Mahdi. They desire to hasten his coming by constructing a Sharia framework on his behalf, and launching violence and war on Jews, Christians and other infidels. In this way sentinels of the Mahdi believe they can "hotwire" the long-awaited apocalypse.

Examples include the Mahdist Isma'ili Shi'a dynasty that ruled Egypt in the 10th through 12th centuries. Nigeria had the *Yan Tatsine* movement from World War II to the late 1970's. In my day the Islamic Republic of Iran has espoused Mahdism since it overthrew the Shah in 1979. The major jihadist group in Syria, *Jabhat al-Nusra*, reveres the 9/11 (2001) destruction of the World Trade Center as the commencement of the "age of great wars" which will lead to the Mahdi. Iraq in the years after the 2004 defeat of Saddam Hussein saw Muqtada al-Sadr's *Jaysh al-Mahdi* (Army of the Mahdi). In Morocco there is *Ansar al-Mahdi* (Helpers of the Mahdi). In Kyrgyzstan there is another *Jaysh al-Mahdi*. Beheadings of Christians by ISIS (Islamic State in Iraq and Syria), and

---

[23] Furnish, p.6, 76.

their mass murders of Shi'a and Yezidis, are intended to bring on the Mahdi.[24] Iran's *Hojjatieh* Society is aimed to speed the Mahdi by the creation of a period of chaos on earth.[25]

Comparison. The Old Testament has many prophecies of the coming Messiah, which came true in the first coming of Jesus Christ. In several places the New Testament indicates that Christ will briefly return before the tribulation, in the rapture. And throughout the Bible, there are many prophecies of his second coming at the end of the tribulation. Many of these prophecies strongly support the divinity of the son of God, of the same substance as the Father and the Holy Spirit.

The Hadiths are similar, in that they also tell of the coming of the messiah. But their's is the Islamic one, the Mahdi. Over the centuries, many of Muhammad's followers have been impatient waiting for him. Instead, they have taken preemptive actions against Christians, and the rest of the *kuffar*.

Why do many Muslims aggressively take on the role of persecutor, and Christians largely submit?

Jesus told his followers to wait for his return. In the meantime, Christians ought not to attack their enemies, but to pray for them:

> Matthew 5:43 "You have heard that it was said, 'You shall love your neighbor and hate your enemy.'
> 5:44 But I say to you, love your enemies and pray for those who persecute you,
> 5:45 so that you may prove yourselves to be sons of your Father who is in heaven; for He causes His sun to rise on the evil and the good, and sends rain on the righteous and the unrighteous."

But the Qur'an supports aggression against Christians, because one of its core teachings is that it is the worst blasphemy to say that Jesus is God's son.[26] Encircling the inside of the Dome of the Rock Mosque in Jerusalem are the words "Far be it from God that he should have a son!" The attitude is that there can only be one God. He has no equals, and

---

24 Furnish, p.47,70,77-78.
25 Walid Shoebat, *God's War on Terror: Islam, Prophecy and the Bible*, self-published, United States, 2008, p.446.
26 Joel Richardson, *The Islamic AntiChrist*, WND Books, Los Angeles, 2009, p.103-110.

has no need of a son to do his work. Ironically, these words are stamped in the location of the destroyed Old Testament temple, where Jews worshipped in expectation of their coming messiah. In the millennial kingdom after the tribulation, Jesus Christ will return to this same spot. Islam has built a monument there that defies that promise.

The Qur'an pronounces Allah's curse on people who trust in Christ as God's son:

> In blasphemy indeed are those that say that Allah is Maseeh the son of Maryam. (Surah 5:17a)

> They say: "(Allah) Most Gracious has begotten a son!" Indeed ye have put forth a thing most monstrous. At it the skies are ready to burst, the earth to split asunder, and the mountains to fall down in utter ruin. That they should invoke a son for (Allah) Most Gracious. For it is not consonant with the majesty of (Allah) Most Gracious that He should beget a son. (Surah 19:88-92)

> They say: "Allah hath begotten a son!" - Glory be to Him! He is self-sufficient! His are all things in the heavens and on earth! No warrant have ye for this! say ye about Allah what ye know not? (Surah 10:68)

> The Christians call Christ the son of Allah. That is a saying from their mouth; (in this) they but imitate what the unbelievers of old used to say. Allah's curse be on them: how they are deluded away from the Truth. (Surah 9:30b)

This curse is used as justification for jihadists to attack the blasphemers.

Second, Islam declares as blasphemy the Trinity, the belief that God is three-in-one: Father, Son, and Holy Spirit:

> They do blaspheme who say: Allah is one of three in a Trinity: for there is no god except One Allah. If they desist not from their word (of blasphemy), verily a grievous penalty will befall the blasphemers among them. (Surah 5:73)

Third, Islam denies that it was Jesus who died on the cross:

> That they said (in boast), "We killed 'Isa al-Maseeh, the son of Maryam, the Messenger of Allah";- but they killed him not, nor crucified him, but so it was made to appear to them, and those who differ therein are full of doubts, with no (certain)

> knowledge, but only conjecture to follow, for of a surety they
> killed him not: Nay, Allah raised him up unto Himself; and Allah
> is Exalted in Power, Wise. (Surah 4:157-8).

This is despite the corroborating written accounts in the four Injil gospels of Jesus speaking and praying, as he died on the cross. It also flies in the face of the Qur'an's own warning (Surah 6:34b) that "there is none that can alter the words and decrees of Allah," whom they believe inspired the Injil.

The Islamic declaration of faith, the *Shahadatan*, stakes out the red lines that are crossed by Jesus as son and Jesus as savior. It states: "There is no God but Allah, and Muhammad is his messenger." This makes it clear that Allah is a unitary god, and not the Yahweh three-in-one God of the Bible. It also places Muhammad, and his future descendant the Mahdi, in the position that only Jesus the Messiah can fill.

Muslims believe they can gain Allah's favor and gain entrance to paradise if their good deeds counterbalance their bad. For them, the greatest deeds are those that further the religion of Allah and defeat his enemies. Engaging in jihad against infidels and blasphemers is such a deed.

Unfortunately, a Muslim cannot have a saving relationship with Allah, because he is utterly remote. No one can be sure what acts of jihad will appease him. Therefore, there will always be some who go to the absolute extreme of suicidal attack on the blasphemers, as the ultimate good deed. Surely that will give them a guarantee of eternity in Allah's heaven.

The Bible teaches that no one can gain favor in God's eyes by works that you do, even if you believe they are on his behalf. We are not saved because of our good works – we are saved by putting our faith in Christ:

> John 6:28 Therefore they said to Him, "What are we to do, so
> that we may accomplish the works of God?"
> 6:29 Jesus answered and said to them, "This is the work of
> God, that you believe in Him whom He has sent."

> Ephesians 2:8 For by grace you have been saved through
> faith; and this is not of yourselves, it is the gift of God;
> 2:9 not a result of works, so that no one may boast.

Then you can do the good works that God planned since the beginning of time, according to his love and standards of righteousness:

> Ephesians 2:10 For we are His workmanship, created in Christ Jesus for good works, which God prepared beforehand so that we would walk in them.

If you are in Christ, you can be sure that he has saved you. You need not be anxious. You can serve God in thankfulness for what he has already done for you.

God will forgive every sin through the blood of Christ, even murder of Christians and Jews, or abortion of babies, if we come to him in repentance. But there is one sin that is unforgivable, the sin against the Holy Spirit. In the words of Jesus:

> Matthew 12:31 "Therefore I say to you, every sin and blasphemy shall be forgiven people, but blasphemy against the Spirit shall not be forgiven.
> 12:32 And whoever speaks a word against the Son of Man, it shall be forgiven him; but whoever speaks against the Holy Spirit, it shall not be forgiven him, either in this age or in the age to come.

What is this sin against the Holy Spirit?

The work of the Spirit is to convict us of sin and bring us to Jesus Christ:

> 1 Corinthians 12:3 Therefore I make known to you that no one speaking by the Spirit of God says, "Jesus is accursed"; and no one can say, "Jesus is Lord," except by the Holy Spirit.

To forsake the Holy Spirit is therefore to deny Christ the son, insult God the Father, and altogether resist his work in you. But even if you have done so in your life, you can still repent of this to your dying breath, and God will forgive you.

The end-time prophecies of the New Testament anticipate the rejection of the son of God coming into the world in human flesh, and of his payment for our sins on the cross. Such opposition is done in the spirit of the antichrist:

> 1 John 4:3 and every spirit that does not confess Jesus is not
> from God; this is the spirit of the antichrist, which you have
> heard is coming, and now it is already in the world.
> 2:22 Who is the liar except the one who denies that Jesus is
> the Christ? This is the antichrist, the one who denies the
> Father and the Son.
> 2 John 7 For many deceivers have gone out into the world,
> those who do not acknowledge Jesus Christ as coming in the
> flesh. This is the deceiver and the antichrist.

In Revelation, the antichrist spirit will receive personification in the beast, who will come riding on a white horse (K16). His counterpart in the Hadiths is the Mahdi, who is also expected to come on a white horse (H16). The Mahdi by his character would qualify to be the antichrist. Both are predicted to be a supreme world military and spiritual ruler, who will attack Israel, make and break a seven-year treaty with the Jews, change all laws and worship, and oppress those who profess Christ.

K06 :

The church of the apostles
30 to 98 CE (death of the apostle John)

2:1 "To the angel of the church in Ephesus write: The One
who holds the seven stars in His right hand, the One who
walks among the seven golden lampstands, says this:
2:2 'I know your deeds and your labor and perseverance, and
that you cannot tolerate evil people, and you have put those
who call themselves apostles to the test, and they are not,
and you found them to be false;
2:3 and you have perseverance and have endured on account
of My name, and have not become weary.
2:4 But I have this against you, that you have left your first
love.
2:5 Therefore, remember from where you have fallen, and
repent, and do the deeds you did at first; or else I am coming
to you and I will remove your lampstand from its place—
unless you repent.
2:6 But you have this, that you hate the deeds of the
Nicolaitans, which I also hate.
2:7 The one who has an ear, let him hear what the Spirit
says to the churches. To the one who overcomes, I will grant
to eat from the tree of life, which is in the Paradise of God.'"

Revelation. We are done with images in the vision that refer to events
in John's past. Now I will pick up where most commentators begin,
with the letters to the seven churches of Asia.

While John was in exile on the Aegean island of Patmos, he was in
correspondence with Christians who gave news of the seven churches.
He laid them out before the Lord Jesus in prayer. In the vision of
Revelation, Jesus gave him the words to write to each church – words of
encouragement, advice, warning, and prayer.

The first letter is to the church at the ancient city of Ephesus, near the
present-day city of Selçuk, Turkey. Some preachers who came to the
church were proclaiming false doctrines. The Nicolaitans, a false sect
that espoused tolerance for adultery, were also active in the area. Their
teaching took advantage of God's grace and forgiveness, and allowed

license for sin. The Ephesians were careful in distinguishing falsehood from truth in these various teachings, and Jesus praised them for this.

However, the Ephesians were forgetting their first love. They were replacing their passion for Christ with religious routine. Jesus encourages them to overcome this, and to come back to a living relationship with him. If they do, he will grant them to eat of the tree of life in the eternal paradise to come.

It is not so obvious that the seven letters also represent seven future time periods of the worldwide Church, viewed prophetically. A thousand years ago, expositors could not even think of this. But we now have the advantage of two thousand years of church history. In hindsight, some have noted parallels between the situations of the seven churches and periods of time during church history. I will follow that trail of interpretation.

The time period that corresponds to the Ephesian church is the apostolic age, beginning with the resurrection of Christ in 30 CE, and ending with the death of John, the last living apostle, in 98 CE. The churches which spread across the Roman empire and surrounding regions in this first century responded with overflowing joy to the good news of Jesus.

But in the next couple of generations, many felt the continuing temptation of the sexual lifestyle around them, and justified a blend of Christianity with immorality. Some understood this was happening, and attempted to counter it by condemning it.

One of Satan's schemes in the early decades of the Christian church was to subvert the faith by setting aside the need for repentance, and tolerating sexual sin. Satan thought by doing this he could reduce Christianity to just another of the empire's gnostic sects, some of which involved sexual initiation into the mysteries of the universe.

In our own day, the gnostic religions of Rome are forgotten. But dealing with our surrounding culture, that extends its tentacles of immorality inside the church, is a constant trial for God's people to the present day.

In the teaching of Jesus, forgiveness for sin is coupled with repentance. To repent is to turn away from sinful activity that violates God's law.

The temptation to sin will remain, however. Reasoning or rules are not enough to counter this. A replacement that totally eclipses the desire for temptation is needed. That replacement is a desire to know Christ, and to grow in the knowledge of him.

Hadiths. The Qur'an and the Hadiths are over five hundred years into the future with respect to this apostolic age.

K07 :
The persecuted church
98 to 313 (Constantine's edict of Milan)

> 2:8 "And to the angel of the church in Smyrna write: The first and the last, who was dead, and has come to life, says this:
> 2:9 'I know your tribulation and your poverty (but you are rich), and the slander by those who say they are Jews, and are not, but are a synagogue of Satan.
> 2:10 Do not fear what you are about to suffer. Behold, the devil is about to throw some of you into prison, so that you will be tested, and you will have tribulation for ten days. Be faithful until death, and I will give you the crown of life.
> 2:11 The one who has an ear, let him hear what the Spirit says to the churches. The one who overcomes will not be hurt by the second death.'"

Revelation. The second letter is to the church at Smyrna. The city is known today as İzmir in Turkey. John foretold that ten days of concentrated trouble would be coming to the church. He was writing during the rule of the Roman ruler Domitian, 90 to 96 CE, who mandated that all his subjects across the empire offer incense to the genius of the emperor. The Roman authorities were beginning the persecution of Jews and Christians who refused to do so. Some Jews were tempted to submit, and inform on Christians who did not conform. They may be the ones that John calls "a synagogue of Satan."

Smyrna was the church in suffering. In the letter Jesus does not rebuke them. Their steadfastness in Christ safeguarded them from compromise with evil. He encourages the church to endure the trials that are coming and stay faithful unto death. In doing so they will receive the crown of life.

This message is also to the wider church in the age of persecution that came after John's death.

The precedents for the persecution were already set by the emperor Nero, who in 64 CE set fire to his own capital city of Rome. He then accused Christians of the arson, and crucified many of them on the streets of the city. Both the apostles Peter and Paul met their deaths at that time.

Throughout the second and third centuries, persecution became a recurring theme in different parts of the Roman empire.[27] Emperors Trajan (98-117) and Hadrian (117-138) had Christians executed for disloyalty. Bishop Polycarp, the most famous son of Smyrna, was martyred under Antoninus Pius (155). Marcus Aurelius (161-180) blamed Christians for natural disasters. Septimus Severus (202-211) forbid conversion to Christianity, and executed many new believers. Maximus (235-236) executed many Christian pastors.

The worst was empire-wide persecution under Decius (249-251). He ordered an annual offering to the gods and the genius of the emperor. Many Christians, fearing for their lives, renounced their faith. After Decius' death the church had to face the difficult issue of whether these lapsed believers could be allowed holy communion once again. This controversy was known as Donatism. Valerian (257-260) confiscated houses of Christians, and made worship assembly illegal. Diocletian (303-305) destroyed churches, burned Bible manuscripts, suspended the civil rights of Christians, and made sacrifices to the gods mandatory.

During this age, Satan realized that the church was a lasting phenomenon that could not be easily turned into an obscure mystery religion. He therefore added persecution as his main attack vector on the church.

Despite all this, Christians continued to proclaim the good news of Jesus Christ. There were many among the elites who heard it, and some pledged themselves to Christ. One of them was Constantine, who converted to Christianity and became emperor. He allowed freedom of Christian worship in the edict of Milan (313). They were now free to preach and evangelize across the empire. The centuries of troubles finally ended.

---

[27] Steven Flick, *Persecution of the Early Christian Church,* https://christianheritagefellowship.com/persecution-of-the-early-christian-church/, July 15, 2021.

In 330, Constantine transferred his capital from Rome to the city of Byzantium on the Bosphorus strait. It took on the emperor's name as Constantinople. It was also known as the New Rome, or the Second Rome. It became the seat of the ecumenical patriarch of the Eastern Orthodox Church. We know this city as Istanbul.

Hadiths. The Qur'an and the Hadiths are still more than three hundred years into the future. We will see that Constantinople will be an important location for Islam.

K08 :

Church and state
313 to 610 (Muhammad's revelation)

2:12 "And to the angel of the church in Pergamum write: The One who has the sharp two-edged sword says this:
2:13 'I know where you dwell, where Satan's throne is; and you hold firmly to My name, and did not deny My faith even in the days of Antipas, My witness, My faithful one, who was killed among you, where Satan dwells.
2:14 But I have a few things against you, because you have some there who hold the teaching of Balaam, who kept teaching Balak to put a stumbling block before the sons of Israel, to eat things sacrificed to idols and to commit sexual immorality.
2:15 So you too, have some who in the same way hold to the teaching of the Nicolaitans.
2:16 Therefore repent; or else I am coming to you quickly, and I will wage war against them with the sword of My mouth.
2:17 The one who has an ear, let him hear what the Spirit says to the churches. To the one who overcomes, I will give some of the hidden manna, and I will give him a white stone, and a new name written on the stone which no one knows except the one who receives it.'"

Revelation. The first century city of Pergamos was known for the worship of Aesculapius the serpent god. It is no wonder that John writes to the Pergamite Christians that they were living "where Satan's throne is." One of their numbers, Antipas, had already been killed for his faith (2:13).

Plus, the believers were being seduced into sexual compromise and impure religious practices by the Nicolaitans (2:15, previously mentioned in 2:6 K06). Jesus warns the church to repent of these teachings, and hold fast to the faith. If they do, God will reward each one in heaven with a glorious white stone emblazoned with a new and distinctive name (2:17). It will be their treasured possession through all eternity.

Pergamos was the church in compromise.

Pergamos represents the church age that followed Constantine giving the Christians their freedom, after centuries of persecution. He went further than that. He took the first steps to coalesce the church with the state. Future emperors furthered this practice. Many people professed Christ, not because their hearts were transformed by him, but to advance their worldly standing. The church would have its conscience blurred, like the Old Testament prophet Balaam when he sold his prophetic gift for money.

In the decades after Constantine, the church did take steps to strengthen its faith in view of the new challenges. It came to agreement on exactly which letters and gospels were originally put to ink by the apostles and their helpers, under the inspiration of God, and which were not. The contents of the New Testament were determined by these criteria.

The church leaders also had the freedom and the time to compare these holy scriptures with each other and with the Old Testament. Intensive Bible study brought about a comprehension of God as Trinity – Father, Son, and Holy Spirit – and also the divine-human nature of Christ.

Unfortunately, there were some who only chose favorite passages from the apostolic writings, and mingled them with ideas from Greek philosophy that were current in their day. This led them to imagine a different Father God, and a Christ that was less than him. They roiled the church with their controversies, and confused many who were less knowledgeable of the Bible. They held onto their ideas with such stubbornness, that in many cases the church had to declare their theologies as heresies, in the hope that it would clarify matters for the faithful. The most troublesome were the Arians, who held that the Son was not co-eternal with the Father, but was created by him.

Church representatives from all corners of the Roman empire and beyond came together to carefully interpret the scripture, in gatherings called councils. They formulated biblically oriented statements of doctrine in answer to the questions that had arisen. The best known was the Council of Nicea (325), which issued the Nicene Creed. It gained wide acceptance across many Christian denominations down the centuries:

> I believe in one God, the Father Almighty, maker of heaven and earth, and of all things visible and invisible;
>
> And in one Lord Jesus Christ, the only begotten Son of God, begotten of his Father before all worlds, God of God, Light of Light, very God of very God, begotten, not made, being of one substance with the Father; by whom all things were made; who for us men and for our salvation came down from heaven, and was incarnate by the Holy Ghost of the Virgin Mary, and was made man; and was crucified also for us under Pontius Pilate; he suffered and was buried; and the third day he rose again according to the Scriptures, and ascended into heaven, and sitteth on the right hand of the Father; and he shall come again, with glory, to judge both the quick and the dead; whose kingdom shall have no end.
>
> And I believe in the Holy Ghost the Lord, and Giver of Life, who proceedeth from the Father [and the Son]; who with the Father and the Son together is worshipped and glorified; who spake by the Prophets.
>
> And I believe in one holy Catholic [Universal] and Apostolic Church; I acknowledge one baptism for the remission of sins; and I look for the resurrection of the dead, and the life of the world to come.
>
> Amen.

This confession of the Christian faith is not the philosophical thinking of men, but is based on many passages from the Bible, such as these:

> Isaiah 9:6 For a Child will be born to us, a Son will be given to us; And the government will rest on His shoulders; And His name will be called Wonderful Counselor, Mighty God, Eternal Father, Prince of Peace.
>
> Micah 5:2 "But as for you, Bethlehem Ephrathah, Too little to be among the clans of Judah, From you One will come forth for Me to be ruler in Israel. His times of coming forth are from long ago, From the days of eternity."
>
> Matthew 3:16 After He was baptized, Jesus came up immediately from the water; and behold, the heavens were opened, and he saw the Spirit of God descending as a dove and settling on Him,
> 3:17 and behold, a voice from the heavens said, "This is My beloved Son, with whom I am well pleased."
>
> Luke 1:30 And the angel said to her, "Do not be afraid, Mary, for you have found favor with God.

1:31 And behold, you will conceive in your womb and give birth to a son, and you shall name Him Jesus.
1:32 He will be great and will be called the Son of the Most High; and the Lord God will give Him the throne of His father David;
1:33 and He will reign over the house of Jacob forever, and His kingdom will have no end."

Luke 9:33 And as these two men were leaving Him, Peter said to Jesus, "Master, it is good that we are here; and let's make three tabernacles: one for You, one for Moses, and one for Elijah"—not realizing what he was saying.
9:34 But while he was saying this, a cloud formed and began to overshadow them; and they were afraid as they entered the cloud.
9:35 And then a voice came from the cloud, saying, "This is My Son, My Chosen One; listen to Him!"

John 1:1 In the beginning was [always, *imperfect tense*] the Word, and the Word was with God, and the Word was God.
1:14 And the Word became flesh, and dwelt among us; and we saw His glory, glory as of the only Son from the Father, full of grace and truth.

John 3:16 "For God so loved the world, that He gave His only Son, so that everyone who believes in Him will not perish, but have eternal life."

John 8:58 Jesus said to them, "Truly, truly I say to you, before Abraham was born, I am."

John 10:28 "and I give them eternal life, and they will never perish; and no one will snatch them out of My hand.
10:29 My Father, who has given them to Me, is greater than all; and no one is able to snatch them out of the Father's hand.
10:30 'I and the Father are one."

John 17:1 Jesus spoke these things; and raising His eyes to heaven, He said, "Father, the hour has come; glorify Your Son, so that the Son may glorify You,
17:5 And now You, Father, glorify Me together with Yourself, with the glory which I had with You before the world existed.

Colossians 1:19 For it was the Father's good pleasure for all the fullness to dwell in Him [Christ].

The Nicene creed, with its biblical description of each person of the trinity, is an awesome complement to the gospel message of salvation. God never withdraws the offer of salvation, from anyone, while they are still alive. We shall see that even at the very end of the seven-year tribulation, God will send an angel to the army defeated at the battle of Armageddon, and offer the everlasting gospel, or "good news," one last time. We shall discuss the gospel at length in that section, K41.

But the controversies of the post-Constantine age brought trouble. There were even wars fought between Arian and orthodox Christian nations. Too many expended their energies arguing about the nature of God. They forgot to embrace and proclaim the gospel. They claimed they were followers of Christ, but did not humble themselves to be discipled by him.

Worse was to come in the church age that followed.

Satan's evolving plan. During the first century's apostolic age, Satan tempted churches to set aside the need for repentance, and instead to tolerate sexual sin. His goal was to reduce them to just another insignificant religious sect.

In the age of the second and third centuries, when the church was rapidly growing, Satan shifted to encouraging raw persecution.

In the age of integration of church and state, Satan worked to weaken the church from within by stirring up controversy regarding the divine person of Christ and the three-in-one nature of God. During that time, Revelation was finally accepted by the entire church as the last book of the New Testament. There were many Christians who regarded it as God's word already in the second century. After many decades of discussion of its difficult nature, Revelation was officially adopted into the canon by the Council of Carthage in 397.[28]

Despite the church's defense of biblical truth, many were prone to confusion caused by departures from the Bible, and compromise with worldly lifestyle. How could Satan take advantage of this?

---

[28] Glenn Davis, *The Canon approved by the third Synod of Carthage (397 CE)*, 2010, http://www.ntcanon.org/Carthage.canon.shtml, accessed July 12, 2024.

Satan is a great student and twister of the Bible. He quoted scripture to tempt Jesus after he spent forty days fasting in the wilderness. Satan analyzes and re-analyzes the end-time prophecies. For him, Revelation is the greatest of all prophecy reference books. He came to understand the literal principles of prophetic interpretation, more than a thousand years before Christians fleshed out their own fuller understanding in pretribulational premillennialism. He knows that Revelation forecasts that he will be bound with a chain for a thousand years, and will ultimately be cast into the lake of fire.

If Satan knows the ending, why doesn't he submit to the Almighty God of heaven, king of the universe, and plead for mercy?

A first reason is that Satan feels he has no choice. His initial rebellion with the rest of the evil angels was so extreme, on such a cosmic level, that he sees no possibility for reconciliation with God. God has already spoken that his coming judgment on Satan will be irrevocable. We saw this already in Ezekiel 28:19 (K01): "you have become terrified And you will cease to be forever."

Satan thus feels compelled to continue his war with God, with the devils as his allies. He refuses with every fiber of his being to go through with the destiny spelled out for him.

A second reason is that Satan and his followers do not believe in God's absolute sovereignty over the universe. As proof, he puts forward his own rebellion against God, and the sin and depravity of human beings. If God was almighty, why doesn't he simply put a stop to this? In Satan's thinking, God lost control of events long ago, shortly after the beginning of creation. Revelation is just wishful thinking on God's part. Perhaps Satan can work out boundaries so that God's rule can be strictly limited within a certain sphere. Then Satan would be supreme forever on earth and other key places. He could then resume his efforts to multiply his following, and better yet, to arrange for his demon followers to increase in number (see the discussion of the Nephilim in Appendix A of *Letter to the Tribulation*, titled *Why Satan Hates Christ*).

Satan is the great opportunist. He is always looking for an off-ramp where he can take control of the end-time plan. In the fourth century, with the book of Revelation accepted as normative, Satan sees it as a way to avoid submission to God. His antidote is to find something in its prophecies to leverage and exploit, with the goal of taking over God's supreme place in the universe. He would replace Revelation with his own revelation that would deviate in a direction of his choosing. In line with this he has been scheming surprises based on different contingencies. He wants to catch people completely off guard, and spring on them something unheard of in any of the thousands of Revelation commentaries ever written (including this one). This would be a fresh attack on the children of God, and a way to sharply decrease the number of people turning in repentance to Christ.

But God won't be surprised. Satan is bound by time. He operates within it, the way you and I do. He does not know the future. Only God operates outside of time. He created it. He has already arranged all the details of the future that all his creation will live through, including human beings and the angelic spirit creatures.

Satan counters God by inspiring people to invent their own religions and ideologies. There were many founded before the first coming of Christ, going back to Noah's day. At that time, God judged all of mankind in the flood. Many among the generations afterward unwittingly followed Satan's cue, and embraced the sins of their antediluvian ancestors. They founded new religions that were meant to replace God's promise of a messiah, salvation from sin, and a future hope of eternal life. They included Animism, Hinduism, Confucianism, and Buddhism. Satan and the evil spirits took great advantage of these to lead people away from a relationship with their creator God.

The next religion that fits this scheme appears on our timeline at the end of this age of church and state. It is Islam.

Islam has its ancient roots in the conflict between the two sons of Abraham: Ishmael, his first son by his wife's Egyptian maidservant Hagar, versus Isaac, the son whom God promised and miraculously conceived in the womb of Abraham's ninety-year-old wife Sarah. Among the descendants of Isaac were the Jews and Jesus Christ. Among the descendants of Ishmael were the Arabs.

Islam would be a simpler, unitarian religion, that would stir the emotions of millions. It would come as the answer to the theological confusion of the church and state age, proclaimed by a new self-styled prophet in Arabia named Muhammad. He would announce that Allah alone was the true God, he was one and one only, he had no son, and that Muhammad was his messenger.

Islam seems to be purpose-built as the counterfeit of Christianity.

Certain signatures point to Satan's direct influence in the founding of Islam.

The first is the very word *Islam*. It translates to "submission." Ironically, Satan assists in the founding of Islam, so that he can avoid submitting to the God of the Bible.

The second signature – Islam teaches that the core Christian beliefs are evil, and must be opposed with utmost vigilance. As explained in H05, they are:

- the trinity
- the divine incarnation
- the atoning sacrifice and crucifixion of Jesus

Large numbers of Muslims are also taught that they must therefore fight holy jihad against Christians. They deserve death for believing these abominations in the here and now.

While many ideologies do not agree with all Christian doctrines, only Islam fills the role of a religion that exists to deny core Christian beliefs.[29] This Muslims willingly do in the spirit of the antichrist (H05).

The third of Satan's signatures – Islam would have its own story of the end time. But not in its holiest scripture, the Qur'an, which has little information about it. This is Satan's influence. He could not fake an official written narrative equal in richness and detail to Revelation. Therefore, best not to place it in the Qur'an. He would rely on the inherent difficulties and many possible alternate interpretations of Revelation. He would call into question that God inspired that book, and for that matter all of the Bible.

---

[29] Richardson, p.108.

Then he would stake out an alternate end-time narrative via an oral tradition, transmitted by many different sources. Hence the Hadiths, the many collections of Muhammad's sayings. Despite their sheer volume and lack of organization, the Hadiths only touch on a portion of the end-time events of Revelation. Coupled with the Qur'an, the military example of Muhammad, and the discipline of the Islamic religion and culture, the Hadiths are a very potent competitor to Revelation for the hearts and minds of Muslims.

The fourth signature – unlike in Revelation, where Satan is an obvious key actor, in the new account the Shaytan character would take on a minor role. This subterfuge suits him fine, for it would deceive many more than otherwise.

It is striking that Islam and Satanism are the two religions that have the strongest contempt and mockery toward the Gospel.[30] They both advocate violence in opposition to the concept of the sonship of Christ. But in Islam, Shaytan is not an obvious actor. In that way Muslims cannot be accused of being Satanists. Far greater numbers of people can be deceived into doing his bidding without realizing it.

The fifth signature – the crescent moon and star became an accepted symbol of Islam. It is found on Islamic coins within a hundred years of Muhammad's death.[31]

The word for crescent moon in Arabic is *hilal*. The related Hebrew word *heylel* means "light-bearer." It appears in Isaiah 14:12, in its description of the rebellion of Satan:

> Isaiah 14:12 "How you have fallen from heaven, You star of the morning [Hebrew *heylel* meaning "light-bearer"], son of the dawn! You have been cut down to the earth, You who defeated the nations!
> 14:13 "But you said in your heart, 'I will ascend to heaven; I will raise my throne above the stars of God, And I will sit on the mount of assembly In the recesses of the north.
> 14:14 'I will ascend above the heights of the clouds; I will make myself like the Most High.'
> 14:15 "Nevertheless you will be brought down to Sheol, To the recesses of the pit."

---

[30] Richardson, p.108.
[31] https://wikiislam.net/wiki/Crescent_Moon, accessed January 7, 2023.

The above is in the modern New American Standard Bible translation. The 17th century King James translators chose to substitute the word *Lucifer* for *heylel*. They followed the example of St. Jerome's pioneer Latin translation, the Vulgate, finished in 405. Lucifer is a Latin word formed from the Latin root lux- meaning "light", and suffix -fer, meaning "bearing" or "bearer." Thus, Lucifer means "light-bearer" or "light-bearing." This is the only place the name Lucifer appears in the Bible.

In the crescent moon symbol of Islam, Satan is embracing the title of Lucifer, the light bearer.

In the additional star symbol, Satan doubles down. Though he originally came to earth as the fallen star whom God expelled from the highest heaven (Isaiah 14:12), he became the hidden star that inspired Islam. Muslims unwittingly pay homage to the chief of the evil angels when they make pilgrimage to the Kaaba and its stone fallen from heaven, the *Hajr e Aswad* or black stone, and when they use the star alongside the crescent moon in their symbology.

With these signatures planned out, Satan chose an initial target of deception carefully. He would be a descendant of Ishmael, the eldest son of Abraham, man of God. The people of the new religion could therefore claim Abraham as forebear. This would allow them to take over the promises that God gave to him.

Qur'an. Muhammad was born to the Quraysh, a tribe of Arabs based in the city of Mecca.

In pagan Arabia there were frequent blood feuds between tribes. Women were chattel. Child marriage and female infanticide were normal. Islam would take on these characteristics. Jewish and Christian tribes also lived nearby.

The Quraysh did a lucrative trade from those doing pilgrimages to the Kaaba, the local shrine. It housed many pagan idols, representing the gods of local tribes, special trees and stones. One of these gods was Allah, which may have been the god preferred by the Quraysh. Another was Hilal, the crescent moon, whom we have seen has a tie-in to the light-bearer Lucifer of the Bible.

According to the Qur'an, the Kaaba was originally built in Mecca by Abraham and Ishmael, at the direction of Allah. They constructed a simple unroofed structure with a rectangular shape. To finish the Kaaba, the angel *Jibreel* brought the sacred black stone, the *Hajr e Aswad*, which Abraham placed in the eastern corner. The Kaaba then became the first house of worship for mankind. Allah urged Ishmael's descendants to perform the annual pilgrimage of hajj to the Kaaba.[32] According to this hadith:

> The Black Stone descended from the Paradise, and it was more white than milk, then it was blackened by the sins of the children of Adam.[33] *(hasan)*

In keeping with this health, touching this black stone expiates previous sins.[34]

The keepers of the Kaaba have never allowed a scientific study to be done on the stone. Various theories are that it is a basalt, agate, or obsidian rock. Many Muslims believe the stone is a meteorite with supernatural powers, originating from beyond the earth.[35] This is a conspicuous parallel to the expulsion of Satan from heaven, and his casting down to earth, which we will discuss in K15.

Muhammad, born in Mecca, declared himself a prophet of Allah when he was about forty years old, around 610. Even as a boy, after learning of the different deities in the Kaaba, he devoted himself to Allah as the only god. As a young man, he spent long periods of prayer to Allah. One night during the month of Ramadan he had a vision, with a visitation from a spirit being. He recorded the words of the spirit, which became the first revelation of the Qur'an:

---

[32] Omar Ayoub, *History Of Kaaba: From Origin To Its Last Renovation In 1626*, https://zamzam.com/blog/history-of-kaaba/, May 31, 2021, accessed January 8, 2023.
[33] Narrated by Ibn Abbas, *Jami` at-Tirmidhi 877*, Vol. 2, Book 4, Hadith 877, https://sunnah.com/tirmidhi:877, accessed July 12, 2024.
[34] *History of Hajr-e-Aswad- The Black Stone of Kaaba*, https://www.hajjumrahpackages.us/blog/history-hajr-e-aswad-black-stone-kaaba/, August 25, 2017.
[35] Bryan Hill, *The Kaaba Black Stone: A Holy Stone from Outer Space?*, https://www.ancient-origins.net/artifacts-other-artifacts/kaaba-black-stone-holy-stone-outer-space-003661, April 3, 2020.

> Proclaim! (or read!) in the name of thy Lord and Cherisher, Who created man, out of a (mere) clot of congealed blood. Proclaim! And thy Lord is Most Bountiful, He Who taught (the use of) the pen, Taught man that which he knew not. (Surah 96:1-5)

Muhammad described his interaction with the spirit in a hadith:

> The angel caught me (forcefully) and pressed me so hard that I could not bear it anymore. He then released me and again asked me to read, and I replied, "I do not know how to read," whereupon he caught me again and pressed me a second time till I could not bear it anymore. He then released me and asked me again to read, but again I replied, "I do not know how to read (or, what shall I read?)." Thereupon he caught me for the third time and pressed me and then released me and said, "Read: In the Name of your Lord, Who has created (all that exists). Has created man from a clot [of blood]. Read and Your Lord is Most Generous [the One who taught by the pen, taught man] that which he knew not.[36]

We read that Muhammad obeyed only after the third time that the spirit nearly strangled him.

After this first violent and terrifying encounter, Muhammad believed that the demons possessed him, in the same way that Arabs of his day thought that poetry was created under the inspiration of devils. This is according to the ancient biography (*sirat*) of Muhammad by Ibn Ishaq:

> So I read it, and he departed from me. And I awoke from my sleep, and it was as though these words were written on my heart…. Now none of Allah's creatures was more hateful to me than a poet or a man possessed: I could not even look at them. I thought, "Woe is me poet or possessed – never shall Quraysh say this of me! I will go to the top of the mountain and throw myself down that I may kill myself and gain rest." So I went forth to do so and then, when I was midway on the mountain, I heard a voice from heaven saying, "O Muhammad! Thou are the apostle of Allah and I am Jibreel."[37]

---

[36] Narrated by `Aisha, *Sahih al-Bukhari 6982,* Vol. 9, Book 87, Hadith 111, https://sunnah.com/bukhari:6982, accessed May 19, 2024; also referenced in Robert Spencer, *The Truth about Muhammad*, Regnery Publishing, Washington, 2006, p. 41.
[37] Ishaq, Ibn, Sirat Rasul Allah -The Life of Muhammad, A. Guillaume, translator, Oxford University Press, 1955, p. 106.

Many of his tribe also believed that Muhammad's visions were demonic and that he was demon possessed:

> Yet they turn away from him and say: "Tutored (by others), a man possessed!" (Surah 44:14)

> And say: "What! shall we give up our gods for the sake of a Poet possessed?" (Surah 37:36)

Allah himself had to respond within the Qur'an to Muhammad's critics:

> And (O people!) your companion [Muhammad] is not one possessed. And without doubt he saw him [Jibreel] in the clear horizon. Neither doth he withhold grudgingly a knowledge of the Unseen. Nor is it the word of an evil spirit accursed. (Surah 81:22-25)

> It [the Qur'an] is not the word of a poet: little it is ye believe. Nor is it the word of a soothsayer: little admonition it is ye receive. (This is) a Message sent down from the Lord of the Worlds. (Surah 69:41-43)

Richard Spencer, a modern biographer of Muhammad, explains that over time, the people of the Quraysh tribe became weary of Muhammad's revelations and his insistence that they stop worshipping their variety of gods. They came to him with a compromise proposal:

> "Muhammad, come and let us worship that which you worship and you worship that which we worship, and we shall make you a partner in all of our undertakings."[38]

He then pondered upon the three favorite goddesses of the Quraysh:

> Have ye seen Lat. and 'Uzza? And another, the third (goddess), Manat? (Surah 53:19-20)

An angel answered:

> "These are the exalted gharāniq, whose intercession is hoped for."[39]

---

[38] Ibn Ishaq, pp. 165, quoted in Spencer, p. 79.
[39] Ibn Ishaq, pp. 165.

The *gharāniq* are cranes that fly at great height. Muhammad understood the implication, that they were near to Allah's throne.[40] Muhammad returned with the answer that Muslims were allowed to pray to these goddesses as intercessors before Allah.

The Quraysh were delighted. But the angel Jibreel came to Muhammad and said:

> "What have you done, Muhammad? You have read to these people something I did not bring you from Allah and you have said what he did not say to you."[41]

Muhammad realized the gravity of his error:

> "I have fabricated things against Allah and have imputed to him words which he has not spoken."[42]

Allah gave Muhammad a stern warning:

> So Allah sent down (a revelation), for he was merciful to him, comforting him and making light of the affair and telling him that every prophet and apostle before him desired as he desired and wanted what he wanted and Shaytan interjected something into his desires as he had on his tongue. So Allah annulled what Shaytan had suggested and Allah established his verses i.e., you are just like the prophets and apostles.[43]

From then on Muhammad regarded the verse about the gharāniq as being from Shaytan, and did not include it in the Qur'an. This event became known as the "Satanic verses" incident. It has caused Muslims great embarrassment ever since, and casts a shadow over Muhammad's claim to be a prophet. Many deny that it really happened. But it is hard to understand how trusted Muslim ancients such as Ibn Ishaq, Tabari (who attributed his version to Ibn Ishaq), and Ibn Sa'd[44] could have fabricated the story, given their absolute devotion to Muhammad.

---

[40] Spencer, p. 204.

[41] Abu Ja'far Muhammad ibn Jarir al-Tabari, *The History of al-Tabari, Volume VI: Muhammad at Mecca*, W. Montgomery Watt and M.V.McDonald, translators, New York, SUNY Press, 1988, p. 111, quoted in Spencer, p. 80.

[42] Ibid.

[43] Ibn Ishaq, p. 166.

[44] Ibn Sa'd , *Kitab Al-Tabaqat Al-Kabir*, Vol. I, S. Moinul Haq and H.K.Ghazanfar, translators, Kitab Bhavan, 1967, p. 236-9.

Muslims believe that over the next 23-year span, the angel Jibreel then continued to appear to Muhammad to dictate the Qur'an word by word.

After the five signatures discussed earlier in this section, the sixth signature of Satan's influence in the founding of Islam is this Satanic verse incident. It is a trademark of his character that he leaves such a memorable trace, but with plausible deniability. Is it possible that he spoke words on other occasions which Muhammad did not doubt, but that did get into the Qur'an?

Many careful scholars have concluded that Muhammad was epileptic, or demon possessed, or both.[45] The evidence is that Muhammad's earliest critics were right. Satan had a direct inspiration on Muhammad, the prophet of Allah.

Our continuing comparison of the book of Revelation with the Hadiths spoken by Muhammad will bear this out. We shall show how Satan aspires to the title ascribed to Allah in the Qur'an: The Lord of the Universe.

Muhammad died in 632. He had fifteen wives (eleven at one time), four concubines, and eleven broken marriage contracts.[46]

Comparison. Muhammad's experience with his spirit visitations was far different from appearances recorded in the Bible of angels, or the Lord God himself. They almost always began with the comforting phrase, "Do not be afraid" (Genesis 15:1, 26:24, 46:3; Daniel 10:12, 18-19; Matthew 28:5, 10; Luke 1:13, 30, 2:10; Revelation 1:17 K00).

---

[45] Richardson, pp. 97-102.
[46] https://wikiislam.net/wiki/Muhammad%27s_Marriages, accessed August 24, 2024. "According to Anas ibn Malik, the Prophet Muhammad used to visit all eleven of his wives in one night; but he could manage this, as he had the sexual prowess of thirty men."

K09 :
False teaching corrupts the church
610 to 1054 (the Eastern and Roman church split)

2:18 "And to the angel of the church in Thyatira write: The Son of God, who has eyes like a flame of fire, and feet like burnished bronze, says this:
2:19 'I know your deeds, and your love and faith, and service and perseverance, and that your deeds of late are greater than at first.
2:20 But I have this against you, that you tolerate the woman Jezebel, who calls herself a prophetess, and she teaches and leads My bond-servants astray so that they commit sexual immorality and eat things sacrificed to idols.
2:21 I gave her time to repent, and she does not want to repent of her sexual immorality.
2:22 Behold, I will throw her on a bed of sickness, and those who commit adultery with her into great tribulation, unless they repent of her deeds.
2:23 And I will kill her children with plague, and all the churches will know that I am He who searches the minds and hearts; and I will give to each one of you according to your deeds.
2:24 But I say to you, the rest who are in Thyatira, who do not hold this teaching, who have not known the deep things of Satan, as they call them—I place no other burden on you.
2:25‡[K13] Nevertheless what you have, hold firmly until I come.
2:29‡[K13] The one who has an ear, let him hear what the Spirit says to the churches.'"

Revelation. The fourth letter of the series is to the church at Thyatira, now the modern Turkish city of Akhisar. The believers there have some good qualities: their love, their service, their faith, and their patience.

But the church was guilty of catering to evil in their midst. They permitted a woman calling herself a prophetess to carry on activities among them. The letter gives her the name of Jezebel, which might be comparing her to the evil queen of that name in the Old Testament. This new Jezebel was tempting the church-goers to eat food sacrificed to idols, and enjoy themselves at the pagan festivals of their city, where sexual immorality regularly took place.

The letter transmits a warning of judgment from Jesus to the Thyatirans (2:22-23). They will suffer the consequences of their adulteries. He urges them, and all the churches, to instead hold fast to their faith. If they do, he promises to return for them (2:25). We will see that come to pass when the rapture takes in K13.

Thyatira was the church tolerating apostasy.

The church age represented by Thyatira was the first half of the Middle Ages. At that time most in the church lessened the role of Jesus in their Christian life. Instead, they offered their prayers to Mary the mother of Jesus. She was exalted almost to the level of a female deity. People also prayed to dead saints. They felt that they could not pray directly to God the Father or to Jesus, because their divine nature would not allow sinners into their presence.

There was also organizational discord. The Eastern Orthodox church based in Constantinople, and the western, Roman Catholic church based in Rome, slowly drew apart. The two officially separated in the year 1054 over a little understood doctrine known as the *Filioque* clause, regarding the relationship within the trinity (in theological terms the "procession") of the Spirit of God from the Father and the Son. The filioque added the words "from the father *and from the Son*" in describing the procession of the Holy Spirit. The Roman Catholic church made this addition, which the Eastern Orthodox vehemently rejected. This was considered suitable grounds for separation. But the two parent churches were already functioning separately, because of their geographical distance and disagreement about the pope in Rome being the highest earthly spiritual authority.

Unfortunately, this misplaced emphasis on theological controversies, human authority, and unbiblical teaching took hold of most of the church, its leadership, and the broader culture of countries where people called themselves Christians. Over time, the evangelistic gospel message, the good news, was slowly forgotten. The church drifted away from joy in Christ. The biblical teaching of Christ's all-sufficient death on the cross, and justification by faith and not by works, was largely lost. The church persisted in a religious pose. In reality it was falling into apostasy.

Islam. The new religion proclaimed by Muhammad, the prophet of Allah, burst upon the world at this time. Millions were attracted to its simple message of a unitary God who was unapproachable and separate from humanity. Muhammad finished the Qur'an under dictation from the angel Jibreel, after many visitations. He died in 632. Over the succeeding centuries, all his oral sayings were collected and catalogued into the Hadiths. His was not a message of good news. It was a message of power.

Muhammad had laid sufficient groundwork for the Arab armies to be victorious far abroad, and to establish the Sharia government of the caliphate. Islam experienced great expansion, from Arabia to Spain to Pakistan. It came knocking at the walls of the greatest city west of China, Constantinople. The first Muslim siege of the city was in 674, the second in 717. Both were repelled. Constantinople would remain in Christian hands for seven hundred more years.

K10 :

The dead church
1054 to 1517 (Martin Luther's 99 theses)

3:1 "To the angel of the church in Sardis write: He who has
the seven spirits of God and the seven stars, says this: 'I
know your deeds, that you have a name that you are alive,
and yet you are dead.
3:2 Be constantly alert, and strengthen the things that
remain, which were about to die; for I have not found your
deeds completed in the sight of My God.
3:3 So remember what you have received and heard; and
keep it, and repent. Then if you are not alert, I will come like
a thief, and you will not know at what hour I will come to
you.
3:4 But you have a few people in Sardis who have not soiled
their garments; and they will walk with Me in white, for
they are worthy.
3:5 The one who overcomes will be clothed the same way, in
white garments; and I will not erase his name from the book
of life, and I will confess his name before My Father and
before His angels.
3:6 The one who has an ear, let him hear what the Spirit
says to the churches.'"

Revelation. The little group of Christians in the city of Sardis, near the
modern town of Sart in Turkey, was outnumbered by pagans who were
devoted to the mother goddess Cybele. The temple of the city was built
in her honor. These idolaters held festivals that were known across the
region for their sexual orgies.

Though the Christians had a reputation of displaying their religiosity,
they were compromised by their worldliness. Theirs was a church in
name only (3:1). They were no longer doing works of salt and light to
the unbelievers around them (3:2).

There were only a handful of believers who oriented every area of their
lives to Jesus (3:4). Yet he promises to stand by them, when they
ultimately come in judgment before God (3:5).

But the overall message that Jesus conveys in the letter to Sardis is one of warning (3:3). It does not have a single word of praise for the church. It is the only one of the seven letters like this.

The church of Sardis was the church that was dead.

The message to Sardis is one that should humble the Christians of my time. Churches are full of activity. Pastors speak of saving faith in Christ. But they do not train up disciples to follow Christ in his righteousness. They issue little challenge to the world around them of the need for repentance, and to turn back to God's commandments. To unbelievers, the faith of the Christians seems to be irrelevant.

This letter to Sardis also serves as a prophecy of the church of the Middle Ages. During this time, the Roman Catholic Church arbitrarily added many new innovations with no basis in scripture. These were the centuries before the Bible was rediscovered during the Protestant Reformation.

Priests were no longer allowed to be married. Many of them did not hold to this vow and did not stay celibate. This resulted in much scandal. The inquisition was instituted, which held people in fear of speaking out for biblical truth. The concept of purgatory was developed. This was an imagined place where sinners supposedly went after death to undergo chastening, which would then allow them entry into heaven.

The church added to its substantial money flow by selling indulgences, which promised people relief in purgatory. Five additional holy sacraments were added to the baptism and the Lord's supper, which were the only two that Jesus gave in the New Testament. The bread and the wine of the Lord's supper, which Jesus taught his followers to observe regularly in remembrance of his sacrifice on the cross for their sins, was now said to have miraculous power. The Roman Catholic church decreed this by the doctrine of transubstantiation. It states that in the Eucharist ceremony, the ordinary bread and wine get transformed into the actual blood and flesh of Jesus Christ. He is crucified anew every week inside every Roman Catholic church.

The Bible was only available in the dying language of Latin. Translations into understandable languages were placed on the index of forbidden books.[47]

To the east, the Eastern Roman empire was continuing in existence. It became known as the Byzantine empire, and promoted the Eastern Orthodox church.

Constantinople withstood many attacks from different barbarian armies coming from the north. The Byzantines countered by bringing Eastern Orthodoxy to their enemies. The kingdoms of the Balkans became Christian. The kingdom to the north of the Black Sea adopted Christianity in 988, centered in Ukraine. That kingdom spawned the city of Moscow, founded in 1147. It became the capital of a new state called Russia, which began its own quest for dominance.

But further to the east, south, and west, Islam was claiming more people for its cause than the Eastern Orthodox Church was doing.

Islam. East of Constantinople, a new Muslim sultanate was founded in the year 1299, by the Turkish sultan Osman Ghazi. In 1354, the armies of his successors bypassed Constantinople, penetrated Europe, and started conquering the Balkans. The sultanate was transformed into a transcontinental state, which became the Ottoman empire.

In 1391, 1394, and 1422, the Ottoman armies returned to besiege the walls of the great city.

In the year 1453, after more than a thousand years of existence, the capital Constantinople of the Eastern Roman empire finally fell to an Ottoman army. The greatest church edifice in the world, Hagia Sophia, was transformed into a mosque.

Aftermath. With its fall to the Muslim Ottoman Turks, Constantinople lost much of its influence as the center of the eastern church. Afterward, the rulers of Russia began calling themselves Caesar, or Tsar. They laid claim to the Christian heritage of the cities of Rome and Constantinople, by referring to Moscow as the Third Rome. The Russian empire would take the integration of church and state to its

---

[47] https://www.britannica.com/topic/Index-Librorum-Prohibitorum, accessed July 25, 2024.

greatest extreme. This sets the stage for Russia as a rogue player in the Bible's end-time prophecies.

The lasting Christian heritage of Constantinople was its biblical scholars, who fled to Roman Catholic territories to the west. They brought with them original manuscripts of the New Testament in the Greek language. Since Greek was their native language, these scholars were able to deposit a great seed of knowledge. The lost perspective of the Bible was once again found. The rediscovery of God's word sparked the rebirth of Christian faith. We are now ready for Martin Luther to nail his 99 theses onto the door of the castle church at Wittenberg, Germany. They exposed the corrupt practices of the Roman Catholic Church.

K11 :

Church of the Reformation
1518 to 1682 (founding of modern Philadelphia)

3:7 "And to the angel of the church in Philadelphia write: He
who is holy, who is true, who has the key of David, who
opens and no one will shut, and who shuts and no one opens,
says this:
3:8 'I know your deeds. Behold, I have put before you an
open door which no one can shut, because you have a little
power, and have followed My word, and have not denied My
name.
3:9 Behold, I will make those of the synagogue of Satan, who
say that they are Jews and are not, but lie—I will make them
come and bow down before your feet, and make them know
that I have loved you.
3:10‡^{K13} Because you have kept My word of perseverance, I
also will keep you from the hour of the testing, *that hour
which is about to come upon the whole world, to test those
who live on the earth.*
3:11‡^{K13} *I am coming quickly;* hold firmly to what you have,
so that no one will take your crown.
3:13 The one who has an ear, let him hear what the Spirit
says to the churches.'"

Revelation. The sixth letter is to the church of Philadelphia, the
original city by that name. Today, it is Alaşehir in Turkey. The letter is
almost entirely one of praise. The faithful there knew that their greatest
gift was salvation in Christ. They gladly shared that gift with the lost
around them. They never denied the name of Christ, but made him
their most important message. Jesus, God's son, is the open door (3:7-
8) to having a relationship with God. The believers of Philadelphia took
full advantage.

The church was not without opposition. The letter calls their accusers a
synagogue of Satan (3:9). This apparently refers to the Jews of the
surrounding area. From God's point of view, they were not truly Jews,
but liars. They told the gentile believers of the church that they could
not be saved by faith in Christ, but that they had to self-justify
themselves by sufficient obedience to the law of Moses. The actions of

these Jews showed they actually served Satan. But the Christians at Philadelphia resisted the efforts of the Judaizers.

Jesus promises that some of these opponents will come to faith and bow down with the church at the feet of the Lord. Their conversion and faith will lead to life everlasting. What a wonderful encouragement to the church. Their faith will bear much fruit.

Jesus will also deliver his faithful in Philadelphia from the hour of trial that is coming. He then shifts this promise to the church at large. The italicized sections of verses 3:10-11 are a promise of the rapture, by which Jesus will bring all true believers to heaven before the end-time tribulation begins. We will discuss the rapture in section K13.

From our vantage point almost two thousand years later, we can see that this letter is also describing the period of the Protestant Reformation.

The best known of the early reformers was Martin Luther. In 1517 he formally challenged the unbiblical practices of the Roman Catholic church that were choking the true faith. He was compelled by his study of God's word to declare far and wide that *Sola Scriptura*, "scripture alone," should be the guide for people to come to saving faith in Christ, and for people to live their lives for him. Many other fearless reformers expanded on this truth.

When the established church, led by the pope in Rome, refused to repent of its faulty ways, these reformers started new churches, with various distinctives. These included Lutheran, Reformed, Presbyterian, and Baptist churches. They rejected an earthly vicar, a pope, as the head of the church. Christ was their head. They also rejected state interference with the teachings of the Bible.

They translated the Old and New Testaments from the original Hebrew and Greek, into the common languages of the people. Together with the invention of the printing press, this allowed thousands for the first time to read the Bible for themselves. The evangelistic message of the reformers was one of great hope and excitement. Millions of people flocked to the new churches. The gospel that had been obscured for so long burst forth to change many hearts. The Holy Spirit called forth preachers, teachers, and translators. Many ordinary people became disciples of Christ. Political leaders in several countries re-examined their thinking about how societies could reorient themselves to be pleasing in God's eyes.

Things were not easy, however. Countries whose kings were still committed to the Roman Catholic church made war on the new churches, to keep religious supremacy in Europe. Many of the rediscovered faith died, and others were tempted away from it. It was the time of the greatest revival in history, but also a time of trial. The new believers certainly were not perfect. At times they made decisions based on old customs or prejudices. But often, the power of God's word would lead them to see error in their ways, to humble themselves, and repent.

The time of the Protestant Reformation does not have an obvious ending date. I will choose 1682, the founding of the modern city of Philadelphia. This city was part of a great migration of believers from Europe to America in search of freedom of religion. Some of them had the goal of establishing a biblically-inspired society. Such were the Judeo-Christian roots of a great new nation, the United States. It held to these roots for several centuries before casting them away.

Islam. The Ottoman caliphate continued to expand militarily during the sixteenth and seventeenth centuries. Their shock troops were the Janissaries. These were children of Christian families, forcibly taken by the state, circumcised and converted to Islam, enslaved to be trained up as elite soldiers.

The Ottomans kept pushing deeper into Europe. They were finally stopped in 1683 at the battle of Vienna, by an unlikely coalition of Christian countries, mostly Catholic (Holy Roman empire, Polish-Lithuanian commonwealth), but including some Orthodox (Ukrainian Cossacks) and Protestant (Saxons). It was a turning point in history, after which the Muslim armies began a slow retreat over the centuries to come.

Early recognition of the antichrist spirit in Islam. Martin Luther, the great reformer, grappled with the Roman Catholic machinery that held people in fear. He saw in the established church a spirit of antichrist. To counter, he led people to life in Christ, by opening God's word to them.

It is little known that Luther recognized the spirit of antichrist in Islam also. "The Pope is the spirit of antichrist, and the Turk (Muslim) is the flesh of antichrist. They help each other in their murderous work. The latter slaughters bodily by the sword; and the former spiritually by doctrine."[48]

The other giant preacher of the Reformation was John Calvin. His fledgling Bible congregations were also hounded by the Roman Catholic church. But he also recognized that Islam had set its goal to turn multitudes away from Christ: "The defection has indeed spread more widely! For, since Muhammad was an apostate, he turned his followers, the Turks, from Christ... The sect of Muhammad was like a raging overflow, which in its violence tore away about half of the church. It remained for the Papal antichrist to infect with his poison the part which was left." Calvin also wrote: "It does seem that the fourth iron kingdom [of Daniel 7] was in fact both the pre-Papal and the pre-Islamic undivided Pagan Roman Empire, as well as the later Western-Roman Papal and the contemporaneous Eastern-Roman Islamic Empire into which it then subdivided.... They correspond to the two legs of the later Roman Empire – Islam and the Papacy."[49] And again: "as Mahomet says that his Al-Coran is the sovereign wisdom, so says the Pope of his own decrees. For they be the two horns of Antichrist."[50]

We shall see that Calvin's words regarding the papacy and Muslims are a portent of the strange alliance between the woman of Babylon and the beast during the tribulation.

---

[48] Martin Luther, *Tischreden*, Weimer ed., 1, no. 330, quoted in Shoebat, p. 329.

[49] John Calvin, *Commentaries on the Book of the Prophet Daniel*, 1561, quoted in Francis Nigel Lee, *Calvin on Islam*, Lamp Trimmers 2000, https://dr-fnlee.org/wp-content/uploads/Calvin-on-Islam.docx, p. 7.

[50] John Calvin, *Sermons on Deuteronomy (18:15 & 33:2)*, 1556-57, quoted in Francis Nigel Lee, *Calvin on Islam*, Lamp Trimmers 2000, https://dr-fnlee.org/wp-content/uploads/Calvin-on-Islam.docx, p. 5.

K12 :

The lukewarm church of the modern age
1682 to present

3:14 "To the angel of the church in Laodicea write: The
Amen, the faithful and true Witness, the Origin of the
creation of God, says this:
3:15 'I know your deeds, that you are neither cold nor hot; I
wish that you were cold or hot.
3:16 So because you are lukewarm, and neither hot nor cold,
I will vomit you out of My mouth.
3:17 Because you say, "I am rich, and have become wealthy,
and have no need of anything," and you do not know that
you are wretched, miserable, poor, blind, and naked,
3:18 I advise you to buy from Me gold refined by fire so that
you may become rich, and white garments so that you may
clothe yourself and the shame of your nakedness will not be
revealed; and eye salve to apply to your eyes so that you may
see.
3:19 Those whom I love, I rebuke and discipline; therefore be
zealous and repent.
3:20 Behold, I stand at the door and knock; if anyone hears
My voice and opens the door, I will come in to him and will
dine with him, and he with Me.
3:21 The one who overcomes, I will grant to him to sit with
Me on My throne, as I also overcame and sat with My Father
on His throne.
3:22 The one who has an ear, let him hear what the Spirit
says to the churches.' "

Revelation. The seventh and final letter is to the church at Laodicea.
The believers there were well-off. But their preoccupation with material
things was lulling the church to sleep spiritually. For this reason, Jesus
has no words of praise. Instead, he rebukes them for being lukewarm,
neither cold nor hot (3:15-16). They were devoted more to the things of
this world than to him. This is a position of comfort. It would be better
for them if they were cold. God has put a spark into many cold hearts,
to turn people to repentance, and flame them forth with zeal for him.

The church is not seeking the Spirit with an eager heart.

The Laodiceans, both pastor and people, are blind to God's leading. To remedy this, they should seek spiritual insight by asking God to anoint their eyes, that they may see (3:18).

This letter to a first century church is yet another prophetic cry to the distant future. This time it is to my time. Its criticism strikingly applies to the church of the past three centuries.

Our modern era began with great hope after the Reformation. Science became a pursuit of many Christians. They found that they could explain numerous phenomena in a predictable manner, because the God who created the world is truthful and reliable. This commendable pursuit gave birth to technical advances and the Industrial revolution.

But the modern era's onset was also marked by the Enlightenment. Its premise is that humanism, the study of man, is the center of all things. Over time it displaced theology, the study of God. Society regressed from trying to intentionally please God, to being indifferent to him (agnosticism), to outright rejecting him (atheism).

For brief periods there were spiritual revivals in some countries. These were movements of many people to repentance and faith. The 1730s saw the Great Awakening in Britain and the American colonies. A second Great Awakening happened in the early 1800s. But afterward there were few mass conversions. Areas which preachers had frequented became known as burnt-over districts, like in western New York in the United States, where people became numb to the gospel message.

Some innovators started congregations that had the outward characteristics of churches, but were actually teaching heresy that was not in keeping with the Bible. One group like this was the Mormons, which had their beginnings in western New York. They believed that God created Jesus Christ at some point in time as a spirit child, and later was incarnated as a human being.[51] They migrated to Utah, where they practiced polygamy for several decades until they were forbidden by the United States federal government.

---

[51] Patrick Zukeran, *Mormon Doctrine of Jesus: A Christian Perspective*, May 27, 2005, https://probe.org/mormon-doctrine-of-jesus/, accessed January 21, 2023.

In Europe, new generations of scientists, who were not committed to the Bible, sought to explain things by natural causes alone. They disparaged the possibility that God could be involved, and disallowed dissenting voices by defining any such approach as "non-scientific." In 1859 Charles Darwin followed this line, and launched the theory of evolution with his book *On the Origin of Species*. But careful analysis shows that "survival of the fittest" is based on data interpretation that involves circular reasoning. Evolution should therefore be regarded as a belief system, and not a science. Unfortunately, many Christian churches were dazzled by this pseudo-science, and retreated from the teachings in the Bible of God as creator. They tried to strike compromises between biblical teaching and the godlessness of evolution.

In the area of politics, the modern age has seen many activists who believe that the world and the human race can be manipulated into a managed sort of perfection. They have no use for the idea of the afterlife, saying that people who believe in that are the biggest impediments to achieving optimal conditions on earth. To a critical observer it is interesting that the conditions imagined have different characteristics, depending on the wishes of successive generations.

One chief architect of such a heaven-on-earth was Karl Marx, who wrote *The Communist Manifesto* in 1848. He proposed to overthrow the oppressors, whom in his system were the upper and middle classes. The proletarian working class would then be freed to establish an economically fair society, by force. The products of his political system were communism, and its less violent and more persuasive variant, socialism.

New generations lost interest in the gospel message of redemption from sin, the message that had changed the lives of their parents and grandparents. Many pastors reset to a new "social gospel." Christ was said to be the champion of the poor. Both rich and poor felt that they could earn their way into God's presence by participating in a redistribution of wealth.

Other churches, such as the Eastern Orthodox church in czarist Russia, were held captive by the embrace of the state. The spiritual oppression of Russia's state-church apparatus was one of the causes of the 1917 communist revolution. Communism in its totalitarian Marxist-Leninist form then swept over half of the world in the next seventy years. It remains strong in China in my day.

In the 1930s, the church in Germany turned inward, self-satisfied with repetitive worship and pietistic sermons. It did little to courageously challenge the murderous antisemitism of Hitler and National Socialism, or Nazism. Dietrich Bonhoeffer, a Lutheran pastor, called on the church to resume its role as representing the righteous God in heaven before the world. He modeled this in his preaching and writings, the most well-known being his book *The Cost of Discipleship*. In it he showed how churches were offering an easy spiritual road to all comers, a cheap grace, which requires no life commitment from Christians. He contrasted this with the grace that Christ extends to us, a costly grace, paid for by his blood on the cross. This saving grace calls on disciples of Christ to carry the cross in their lives as well, before the world.

Bonhoeffer was hanged by Nazi executioners.

In recent decades, after the dismantling of communism in the Soviet Union in 1991, an offshoot of Marxism has been critical race theory. The greatest oppressors in this worldview becomes white Christian men.

All these different movements are belief systems in their own right. They can be seen as Judeo-Christian offshoots. However, sin is not seen as against an Almighty God, but against the collective group that controls public opinion. Redemption is not by the work of Christ on behalf of the repentant. Instead, redemption of society is accomplished by joining in the persecution of all those who don't pledge allegiance to the majority view of the moment.

Under this pressure, countries cast aside their Christian heritage and started condoning practices in direct conflict with God's commandments. These sinful behaviors became widespread and even favored: promiscuous sexual activity, abortion, homosexuality, same-sex "marriage," surgical mutilation of under-age boys and girls (transgenderism).

Bonhoeffer's prophetic words were largely forgotten. Most churches in Europe are now relics of the past. Bible believing churches in North

America became ingrown and downplayed evangelistic outreach to people. Professional pastors preached passages from the Bible without reference to current events, leaving to their listeners' imagination how to deal with societal sin and transformation.

The last three hundred years are a record of the church at large becoming lukewarm.

However, some churches during that time took Christ's great commission to heart:

> Matthew 28:19 "Go, therefore, and make disciples of all the
> nations, baptizing them in the name of the Father and the
> Son and the Holy Spirit,
> 28:20 teaching them to follow all that I commanded you; and
> behold, I am with you always, to the end of the age."

These churches raised up cross-cultural missionaries and sent them to dozens of countries that had not yet heard the gospel message. It was embraced by millions, in places that formerly had few Christians, such as China, the former Soviet Union, South Korea, Brazil, Chile, Mexico, Nigeria, Uganda, Iran, Columbia, Algeria. Believers in these areas now outnumber those in Europe and North America.

But more countries than ever, even those where many of their ancestors once welcomed Christ, now oppress Christians with various levels of persecution. In some, believers are not able to gather in church buildings. Instead, they assemble at private homes in what are known as house churches. These faithful know that imprisonment is possible any day. They are an inspiration for everyone else who believes in Christ.

Very few places are left where the good news of Christ has not been proclaimed. This is a sign in my day that the end is near:

> Matthew 24:14 This gospel of the kingdom shall be preached
> in the whole world as a testimony to all the nations, and
> then the end will come.

Unfortunately, the phenomenon of the burnt-over district is repeating itself in the new countries among the children and grandchildren of the new believers.

We will see that after God raptures all true believers home to heaven, he will overcome the burnt-over district phenomenon. Many from those hard-hearted countries will cry out for Christ to save them.

Laodicea was the lukewarm church, comfortably embedded in the surrounding world. It is also a sad picture of the church of my time. Despite this condition, in these words of Revelation Jesus is inviting anyone to hear him knocking on the door of their heart. If you answer, he will come to live with you forever (3:20).

Islam. The weakening of the caliphate, that set in following its military loss at the gates of Vienna in 1683, caused great angst among Muslims. It severely damaged their confidence that the rule of Allah would irrepressibly expand until Sharia law reached the ends of the earth.

Imams and mullahs felt this failure occurred because Allah was displeased with the deficient level of devotion displayed by most Muslims, and because of organizational faults in their movement.

In 1740s Arabia, Muhammad ibn Abd al-Wahhab[52] began preaching that only the first three centuries of Islam were pure before Allah. Every idea added afterward was false and should be eradicated. He denounced superstitious folk religious practices that had blended into Muslim society, and said they were a regression to the polytheistic religion of Arabia before Muhammad.

Wahhab (d. 1792) was the first modern Islamic fundamentalist.

Wahhabi Islam regarded the new ideologies developed in Europe as an even greater anathema than the syncretistic Muslim folk religion. Wahhabists will not compromise with modernity, secularism, and the Enlightenment. They preach a principled opposition to all these foreign ideas, even to the point of violence. They oppose any reform movement that reinterprets Islamic law to bring it closer to standards set by the West, in areas like male-female relations, family law, personal autonomy, and participatory democracy. They consider the only true Muslims to be those who follow the strict teachings of al-Wahhab, because only they still follow the path laid out by Allah. If someone is

---

[52] Austin Cline, *Origins and Doctrines of Wahhabism, Islam's Extremist Sect*, March 24, 2018, https://www.learnreligions.com/wahhabism-and-wahhabi-islam-250235.

not a true Muslim by that criterion, it is permitted to kill them in war or by an act of terrorism.

In addition, Wahhab and his followers are called *muwahiddun*, or "unitarians," because of their emphasis on the absolute oneness of Allah.

The 1744 pact between emir Muhammad ibn Saud and Wahhab was a milestone in the rise of the first Saudi state, the emirate of Diriyah. By offering the Al-Saud a clearly defined religious mission, the alliance provided the ideological impetus to Saudi expansion.

The influence of Islamic fundamentalism expanded widely beyond Arabia with the outcome of World War I, when the Ottoman empire was defeated. The secular nation of Turkey was established in its place. It took steps to abolish the caliphate in 1924, after 1,292 years of existence. This came as a shock to religious Muslims. They were furious that British and French administration was established over Muslim areas formerly part of the Ottoman zone. This rapidly intensified Wahhabi influence over all of Sunni Islam.

Shi'as had their own fundamentalist movement, which by 1979 resulted in the Iranian revolution.

Since the time of its founder, Wahhabism has been dominant in the Arabian peninsula, and has led by example in holy war against Muslims that do not comply, and against non-Muslims. Osama bin Laden, who masterminded the 9/11 (2001) attack on the World Trade Center, was a Saudi Arabian and an advocate of Wahhabism. He is regard as a hero by many Islamists across the world.

The effort to expand Islam until it reigns supreme against the unbelieving world is called *jihad*. This word is derived from the Arabic root word *j-h-d*, which means "strive." There are five types of jihad that are a requirement for all Muslims[53]:

- *Jihad al-nafs:* striving against one's inner self
- *Jihad al-Shaitan:* striving against Shaytan
- *Jihad al-kuffaar:* striving against the disbelievers

---

[53] Richardson, p.139.

- *Jihad al-munafiqeen:* striving against the hypocrites
- *Jihad al-faasiqeen:* striving against corrupt Muslims

Jihad is not about overcoming adversity, or waging defensive war, despite what Muslims apologists say who want to display Islam as a religion of peace. No, Muhammad himself encouraged the spread of Islam by force:

> Allah's Messenger said, "I have been ordered to fight the people till they say: 'None has the right to be worshipped but Allah.'[54]
>
> Fight those who believe not in Allah nor the Last Day, nor hold that forbidden which hath been forbidden by Allah and His Messenger, nor acknowledge the religion of Truth, (even if they are) of the People of the Book, until they pay the Jizya [tax] with willing submission, and feel themselves subdued. (Surah 9:29)
>
> O ye who believe! fight the unbelievers who gird you about, and let them find firmness in you: and know that Allah is with those who fear Him. (Surah 9:123)
>
> Fighting is prescribed for you, and [though] ye dislike it. But it is possible that ye dislike a thing which is good for you, and that ye love a thing which is bad for you. But Allah knoweth, and ye know not. (Surah 2:216)

Muhammad, and the caliphs that came after him, all attacked the surrounding nations to spread Islam. They obeyed the words of the Qur'an. They set the example of how jihad is to be waged, to force its victims to submit, or else to be crushed.

Shoebat describes the strategy of jihad:

"Islamic Jihad is religious conditioning, using illusions of misery and glory days of the past in order to convert masses into becoming rage and pride filled, remorseless killers and seekers of salvation by their own death. The goal is to re-establish a utopian theocratic world order where Allah and Muslims reign supreme and non-Muslims become subservient."[55]

The goal of jihad is to advance the glory of Allah, and to achieve world domination for Islam.

---

[54] Narrated by Abu Huraira, *Sahih al-Bukhari 2946*, Vol. 4, Book 52, Hadith 196, https://sunnah.com/bukhari:2946; also referenced in Richardson, p.140.
[55] Shoebat, p.97.

The crowning achievement of jihad will be to reestablish the caliphate, then extend it to be worldwide. Many Muslim strategists have considered how this can be achieved in a practical manner, starting from the current situation.

Furnish explains that Abu Mus`ab al-Zarqawi, a leader in the *al-Qa`idah* (AQ) terrorist organization who pledged allegiance to Osama bin Laden in 2004, plotted five stages toward re-creating the khilafah (caliphate): 1) *hijrah*, or flight, of Islamists away from corrupt rulers, 2) creating among them the *jama`ah*, or group community, 3) undermining the *taghut*, the tyrannical regimes of illegitimate oppressive rulers, 4) consolidating power, or *tamkin*, 5) establishing the *khilafah*, the caliphate.[56] This five-step program was followed in the rise of ISIS (Islamic State of Iraq and Syria), which declared itself the caliphate in 2014. However, ISIS was a temporary phenomenon.

Other strategists view transnational organizations as a suitable vehicle for ushering in the caliphate. In my day they include the Organization of Islamic Cooperation, with foreign ministers of Muslim countries as members, whose aim is greater unity between Islamic states. The Muslim Brotherhood is a grass-roots movement that aims to re-Islamize society from the ground up. *Hizb ut-Tahrir* (HT), or "Party of Liberation," issues theoretical tracts, and holds conferences on reconstructing the caliphate. It failed in declaring a caliphate in Zanzibar, and has been banned in many countries as a terrorist group. *Tablighi Jama`at* (TJ) is ostensibly non-political, and has 80 million members. It is not opposed to Islamic mysticism and some Sufi and Muslim folk practices, for this reason it is seen as a "conveyor belt" to terrorism. The Sufis are pre-disposed to TJ's charismatic leadership and already have a ready-made organizational structure that could welcome TJ's accommodating version of Mahdism.[57]

---

[56] Furnish, pp.63-64.

[57] One such group is led by the Turkish neo-mystic Fethullah Gulen, exiled from Turkey in 1991, living in Pennsylvania USA, and accused of plotting to overthrow President Erdogan in the failed 2016 military coup. His followers have created an international charter school system with 135 schools and 45,000 students, ostensibly STEM-oriented, but suspected of being future cells for Islamic indoctrination. See Furnish, pp.235-6.

Furnish further speculates on how Islamists might hotwire the coming of the Mahdi:

"A charismatic, mystically oriented Muslim leader with Mahdist aspirations is probably more likely to emerge from TJ's ranks that from any of these other organizations. If such a man were to bridge the gap between TJ and HT, wedding the former's piety, Muhammadan emulation and transnational reach to the latter's political program, zeal and activism – then a non-state caliphate with a Mahdi in charge is possible."[58]

"An alliance of non-state groups like TJ and or HT with AQ Central (and very possibly the South Asian terrorist organizations) naming one man as caliph, who then reveals that he also considers himself the Mahdi, is the most likely path to modern Mahdism…. Should this new Mahdi and his followers gain the support of a Muslim-majority state, … the world would have its hands full – especially were he to do so where he would gain a nuclear arsenal, such as in Pakistan."[59]

Muslim view of modern Christianity. Beginning with the Enlightenment, the church at large gradually accommodated the various atheistic innovations of the world around it, instead of challenging them and helping people to understand how the good news of Jesus Christ is the only possible hope that we have for heaven. Over this time, Muslims intertwined the actions of seemingly Christian countries with the true Christian faith that is described in the Bible. Thus, the various ideologies such as capitalism, Marxism, globalism, nation-building, etc., are regarded by most Muslims as products of Christianity aimed expressly at them. They also see abortion, pornography, the Hollywood sexual culture, LGBTQ, tolerance of all sorts of behavior, and growing lawlessness, as more outgrowths of Christianity.

The only remedy that Islamists see is the imposition of Sharia law and submission to Allah. This is appealing to Muslims, who are tired of their subservient position within the world order that global elites are slowly advancing. It is also appealing to many lonely or angry westerners, who feel adrift amidst the atheistic culture, and find spiritual answers in Islam. They are intrigued that Muslims are supposed to pray five times a day, fast, and give alms as a way of life. Others believe they can avoid the jihadist terror if they submit and become Muslims.

---

[58] Furnish, pp.79-81.
[59] Furnish, p.83.

Muslims are increasing their percentage in the population of western countries, both by immigration, and by not tolerating abortion. After jihadist successes, such as the 9/11 (2001) destruction of the World Trade Center, conversions to Islam are even more prevalent. In the United States this was estimated to be 60,000 people annually in the years after 9/11. Over 80% of American converts were raised in a Christian church. Islam is sweeping through inner cities. Before the end of the twentieth century, greater New York City already had more than 700,000 Muslims.[60] This is a measure of the lukewarmness of the church, where people do not see the power of Christ to change hearts.

This is also a sign of the great apostasy (*apostasia* in Greek) away from the church that the Bible foretells for the last days:

> 1 Timothy 4:1 But the Spirit explicitly says that in later times some will fall away from the faith, paying attention to deceitful spirits and teachings of demons.

> 2 Thessalonians 2:3 No one is to deceive you in any way! For it will not come unless the apostasy comes first, and the man of lawlessness is revealed, the son of destruction.

Unfortunately, Muslims don't realize that many Christians also oppose the ideologies and behaviors of the world. They instead endeavor to follow biblical teaching and values. The true Christian remedy is the person of Jesus Christ. They pray for others to discover the goodness of Christ, and become his disciples. They also pray for their persecutors, and for God's values to be reinstituted in this broken world, as given in the ten commandments.

While Islamists pursue violent jihad to hasten the coming of the Mahdi, the few Christians who stay true support missionaries and evangelists, who go near and far to bring the good news of Jesus to people who are lost. They believe in God's promise that when the full number of people to be saved is reached, Christ shall return.

The world that I live in is sliding toward the end times. God cares for his people, though they are becoming fewer in number. His plan is to save them from experiencing the coming tribulation. That will happen with

---

[60] Bruce McDowell and Anees Zaka, *Muslims and Christians at The Table*, Phillipsburg NJ USA, P&R Publishing, 1999, pp. 6-7, referenced by Shoebat, p.463.

the rapture, which will be the topic of the next section. After that event, in Revelation (or the Hadiths) we shall see the rising of the woman of Babylon (or the Romans) and the beast (or the Mahdi). But despite the unprecedented power of these opponents of God, the prophecies tell of many who will reject them and their systems. Revelation relates that the most courageous ones will ask Jesus to come into their hearts.

Jesus did not call his followers to war. No, he calls on them to come to him and have rest:

> Matthew 11:28 "Come to Me, all who are weary and burdened, and I will give you rest.
> 11:29 Take My yoke upon you and learn from Me, for I am gentle and humble in heart, and you will find rest for your souls.
> 11:30 For My yoke is comfortable, and My burden is light."

K13 :
The rapture and judgment of the church saints

2:25‡[K09] Nevertheless what you have, hold firmly until I come.

3:10‡[K11] Because you have kept My word of perseverance, I also will keep you from the hour of the testing, that hour which is about to come upon the whole world, to test those who live on the earth.

3:11‡[K11] I am coming quickly; hold firmly to what you have, so that no one will take your crown.

2:29‡[K09] The one who has an ear, let him hear what the Spirit says to the churches.

Revelation. We have finally reached the end-time events of Revelation.

When Jesus Christ came to Israel two thousand years ago, some Jews recognized him as the messiah that was promised in the Old Testament. But most Jews did not. God knew this would happen. After Christ's resurrection and ascension into heaven, God sent his Holy Spirit, who descended like tongues of fire upon Christ's disciples, and supernaturally empowered them to speak in other languages instead of Hebrew (Acts 2). This happened on the day of Pentecost. The church was born. It started with Jewish believers. This gift of languages directed them to tell non-Jewish gentiles about Jesus. After only a couple decades, the church exploded in numbers, and gentile believers outnumbered Jewish ones.

God has been at work ever since to soften the hearts of people and bring them into his church. In every generation, there have been Jews who come into the church by making Jesus their messiah. But most new believers have been from gentile nations. This includes atheists, animists, Buddhists, Confucians, Shintoists, and also people brought up in Christian surroundings. It also includes numerous Muslims, many of whom can trace their ethnic ancestry all the way to Abraham. As such, they are among the closest relatives to the Jewish nation. For this reason, Muslims are also near and dear to God's heart.

God has ordained the lives of all the billions of people who ever lived. He knows who among them will trust in his son Jesus for their salvation. When the full number of the elect is reached, the end will come:

> Romans 11:25 For I do not want you, brothers and sisters, to be uninformed of this mystery—so that you will not be wise in your own estimation—that a partial hardening has happened to Israel until the fullness of the Gentiles has come in.

> Matthew 24:14 This gospel of the kingdom shall be preached in the whole world as a testimony to all the nations, and then the end will come.

> Romans 11:26 and so all Israel will be saved; just as it is written: "The Deliverer will come from Zion, He will remove ungodliness from Jacob ."

This tells us the end will come in stages. The first will involve the New Testament church, when the "the fullness of the Gentiles has come in," and the "testimony to all nations" is completed. In another stage the eyes of Jewish people will be opened. That is when "all (the rest of) Israel shall be saved." Revelation supports this. Below in section K18 we shall see that during the tribulation most Jews will turn to Jesus and be saved.

This separation into two stages is corroborated by the fact that the word "church," so prominent in Revelation chapters 2 and 3 (K06 through K12), is nowhere mentioned during the upcoming events of the tribulation and the millennial kingdom. It will reappear only in the last sections of our timeline, in as the bride of Christ in verse 19:7 (K48) and as the churches in 22:16 (K50).

What happens to the church? What's left of the true church disappears in the *rapture*. This event is only hinted at in Revelation. But it is detailed elsewhere in the New Testament:

> 1 Thessalonians 1:10 and to wait for His Son from heaven, whom He raised from the dead, that is, Jesus who rescues us from the wrath to come.
> 5:9 For God has not destined us for wrath, but for obtaining salvation through our Lord Jesus Christ,

4:14 For if we believe that Jesus died and rose from the dead, so also God will bring with Him those who have fallen asleep through Jesus.
5:2 For you yourselves know full well that the day of the Lord is coming just like a thief in the night.
4:15 For we say this to you by the word of the Lord, that we who are alive and remain until the coming of the Lord will not precede those who have fallen asleep.
4:16 For the Lord Himself will descend from heaven with a shout, with the voice of the archangel and with the trumpet of God, and the dead in Christ will rise first.
4:17 Then we who are alive, who remain, will be caught up together with them in the clouds to meet the Lord in the air, and so we will always be with the Lord.

1 Corinthians 15:51 Behold, I am telling you a mystery; we will not all sleep, but we will all be changed,
15:52 in a moment, in the twinkling of an eye, at the last trumpet; for the trumpet will sound, and the dead will be raised imperishable, and we will be changed.
15:53 For this perishable must put on the imperishable, and this mortal must put on immortality.

John 5:28 Do not be amazed at this; for a time is coming when all who are in the tombs will hear His voice,
5:29a and will come out: those who did the good deeds to a resurrection of life,[61]

The earliest promise of the rapture came directly from the Lord Jesus. At the Last Supper, before he was betrayed and brought to trial, Jesus said he would come again, to receive his faithful to himself:

John 14:3b I am coming again and will take you to Myself, so that where I am, *there* you also will be.

On another occasion, prior to the Last Supper, Jesus also talked about returning, but he used very different words:

Matthew 24:27 For false christs and false prophets will arise and will provide great signs and wonders, so as to mislead, if possible, even the elect.

---

[61] John 5:29b continues "those who committed the bad deeds to a resurrection of judgment." This is another case of double fulfillment of prophecy. John 5:29a will be fulfilled at the rapture, 5:29b at the great white throne judgment (see K46).

> 24:30 And then the sign of the Son of Man will appear in the sky, and then all the tribes of the earth will mourn, and they will see the Son of Man coming on the clouds of the sky with power and great glory.

The two dissimilar passages indicate two separate returns, which matches what we find in Revelation. The first return of Christ, a brief one, will be the rapture. It will be unexpected. He will take the church saints to heaven. After a short period of unspecified length, the seven-year tribulation will begin. The second return will happen exactly at the end of the seven years. This return is commonly known as the second coming of Christ. His immediate task will be the defeat of the antichrist (19:15 K38). Then he will remain on earth as king to rule for a thousand years, in the millennial kingdom (20:6 K44).

Revelation speaks in great detail of the second coming. But it also contains some verses that point to the rapture. Verse 2:25 exhorts the church of Thyatira to "hold firmly until I come." These words of Jesus are speaking of his first return in the rapture. In verse 3:10-11 he promises the church of Philadelphia that he will "keep you from the hour of the testing, that hour which is about to come upon the whole world." Again, he will do this with the rapture. Then in the words of 2:29 – "let him hear what the Spirit says to the churches" – he promises the rapture to the church faithful of all upcoming centuries.

The three persons of God will have different roles in the rapture.

God the Father has planned the exact moment it will happen. We know it is coming closer, because in the last couple of centuries the gospel has been proclaimed to almost every people group on earth (see Matthew 24:14 above). But the Bible does not have prophecies of definite supernatural events that will precede the rapture. Even Jesus, the divine son of God, does not know the exact time of the rapture:

> Matthew 24:36 "But about that day and hour no one knows, not even the angels of heaven, nor the Son, but the Father alone.
> 24:37 For the coming of the Son of Man will be just like the days of Noah.
> 24:38 For as in those days before the flood they were eating and drinking, marrying and giving in marriage, until the day that Noah entered the ark,

> 24:39 and they did not understand until the flood came and
> took them all away; so will the coming of the Son of Man
> be."

That makes it impossible to construct a timeline of concrete events that will occur beforehand. Instead, the rapture will happen unexpectedly, like a thief in the night (1 Thessalonians 5:2 above).

When the rapture does come, the Father will create glorified bodies for those believers long dead, and will resurrect them. They will rise first. The Father will then send Jesus to take them (1 Thessalonians 4:14).

Jesus the son will briefly descend from heaven, with a great trumpet sound, heard across the world. He will be seen in the clouds. All the newly resurrected will rise into the sky to meet him (1 Thessalonians 4:16). The living will also be caught up (*rapere*) with Christ in the air (1 Thessalonians 4:17). Their bodies will be changed. They will be *translated*, or morphed, from natural bodies subject to age, into glorified bodies.

The Latin verb *rapere*, meaning to carry off or to catch up, is the root behind the word rapture. It is an appropriate word for this "last trumpet" event.

Jesus then ushers all the raptured ones into eternity. In his love for the church, he brings them to heaven, so that none of them would experience the terrible trials of the tribulation.

The rapture event implies a judgment immediately afterward of all New Testament era believers, known as church saints, at the throne of God. Such a judgment is a requirement for entrance into heaven. These faithful ones do not justify themselves according to their own works. Based on them they would be condemned:

> Romans 3:23 for all have sinned and fall short of the glory of
> God.

Instead, it is by their faith in Jesus Christ that God embraces them. For Jesus gave his life to pay for their sin:

> 1 John 4:10 In this is love, not that we loved God, but that He
> loved us and sent His Son to be the propitiation for our sins.

The Holy Spirit, the third person of the trinity, also plays a key role in the rapture.

We have already spoken how the Bible supports the divinity of the son of God. But we have not explained the third person of the trinity, the Holy Spirit.

The Bible uses the pronoun *he*, not *it*, for the Spirit. This is because the Spirit is a person, not a force. He has always been with God's children. God promised his people the Jews, whom he rescued by the Exodus, that his Spirit would be present among them:

> Haggai 2:5 'As for the promise which I made you when you came out of Egypt, My Spirit remains in your midst; do not fear!'

The Holy Spirit took on a more intimate role with New Testament church believers than in the Old Testament. We saw how God sent the Spirit to inaugurate the church on the day of Pentecost. Afterward, the Spirit lives in the heart of every believer.

God also works through the Spirit to give shared blessings to believers and unbelievers alike, even though unbelievers are unappreciative. This is known as God's Providence. The influence of the Holy Spirit on human society also restrains sin in the world.

This protection will remain as long as the church is present in the world, and seeks the leading of the Holy Spirit. But when that begins to stop, the church will experience widespread and novel forms of apostasy worldwide (1 Timothy 4:1 and 2 Thessalonians 2:3 in K12). We can expect that to happen before the rapture.

When the church believers are removed from the scene, the Holy Spirit will completely withdraw from the world. He will no longer hold back sin. The most terrible things will happen. The man of lawlessness, the antichrist, will be revealed:

> 2 Thessalonians 2:6 And you know what restrains him now, so that he will be revealed in his time.
> 2:7 For the mystery of lawlessness is already at work; only He who now restrains will do so until He is removed.

> 2:8 Then that lawless one will be revealed, whom the Lord
> will eliminate with the breath of His mouth and bring to an
> end by the appearance of His coming.

We shall see the coming of the antichrist, known as the beast in Revelation, in just three more sections (see 6:2 K16).

Comparison. The Hadiths have an event that can be compared with the rapture. But it does not occur at this point in the timeline. It is the evacuation of true Muslims who are still alive to the mountain Tur by ʿIsa ibn Maryam. It will happen after the death of the Mahdi, but prior to the coming of Yajuj and Majuj (the Islamic Gog and Magog) and Allah's final judgment. The Muslims who are dead at the time of the mountain of Tur will have to await the judgment before they are resurrected.

We will cover Mount Tur in H44.

K14 :

Scene in heaven after the rapture

4:1 After these things I looked, and behold, a door standing open in heaven, and the first voice which I had heard, like the sound of a trumpet speaking with me, said, "Come up here, and I will show you what must take place after these things."
4:2 Immediately I was in the Spirit; and behold, a throne was standing in heaven, and someone was sitting on the throne.
4:3 And He who was sitting was like a jasper stone and a sardius in appearance; and there was a rainbow around the throne, like an emerald in appearance.
4:4 Around the throne were twenty-four thrones; and upon the thrones I saw twenty-four elders sitting, clothed in white garments, and golden crowns on their heads.
4:5 Out from the throne came flashes of lightning and sounds and peals of thunder. And there were seven lamps of fire burning before the throne, which are the seven spirits of God;
4:6 and before the throne there was something like a sea of glass, like crystal; and in the center and around the throne, four living creatures full of eyes in front and behind
4:7 The first living creature was like a lion, the second creature like a calf, the third creature had a face like that of a man, and the fourth creature was like a flying eagle.
4:8 And the four living creatures, each one of them having six wings, are full of eyes around and within; and day and night they do not cease to say, "Holy, holy, holy is the Lord God, the Almighty, who was and who is and who is to come."
4:9 And when the living creatures give glory, honor, and thanks to Him who sits on the throne, to Him who lives forever and ever,
4:10 the twenty-four elders will fall down before Him who sits on the throne, and they will worship Him who lives forever and ever, and will cast their crowns before the throne, saying,
4:11 "Worthy are You, our Lord and our God, to receive glory and honor and power; for You created all things, and because of Your will they existed, and were created."
5:8‡[K00] When He had taken the scroll, the four living creatures and the twenty-four elders fell down before the Lamb, each one holding a harp and golden bowls full of incense, which are the prayers of the saints.

> 5:9 And they sang a new song, saying, "Worthy are You to take the scroll and to break its seals; for You were slaughtered, and You purchased people for God with Your blood from every tribe, language, people, and nation.
> 5:10 You have made them into a kingdom and priests to our God, and they will reign upon the earth."

Revelation. We are transported to the scene in heaven, which welcomes the saints who have arrived after the rapture (5:9). It is the most euphoric and joyous occasion. God makes the newcomers all priests of the kingdom (5:10), to prepare them for the new earth that will be coming (K47).

On each side of God's throne are four living creatures (4:6). They represent four different aspects of God's majesty. The lion stands for nobility and omnipotence. The ox is patience and continuous labor. The man is intelligence and rational power. The eagle is sovereignty and supremacy.

All the persons of the trinity are present in this scene.

God the Father is there. Spread around his throne we see twenty-four elders celebrating in worship (4:4). They are the representatives of the newly raptured citizens of heaven. On their heads are the crowns of victors, crowns of gold.

The Holy Spirit is there. We see seven lamps before the throne, burning with fire, identified as the seven spirits of God (4:5). Together they represent the Holy Spirit.

The son of God is there, in the person of the Lamb. We see the twenty-four elders fall down before him (5:8). A most unique scroll comes into the scene, having many seals (5:9). The elders appeal to the Lamb to open the scroll. They know that only he is worthy to open the seals. He is the one who defeated death by death. The Lamb can be none other than Jesus Christ.

The book is the book of the tribulation. The number of its seals will turn out to be seven. As they are opened, the seals of Revelation will unfold.

The opening of the first seal will inaugurate the tribulation on earth. But before that, God's greatest opponent will take his preferred place.

K15 :
Satan cast down to earth begins the seven-year tribulation

: H15
Sharia is gone, only the unjust remain, then a star with a tail will signal the coming of the Mahdi

12:3‡[K01,K04] Then another sign appeared in heaven: and behold, a great red dragon having seven heads and ten horns, and on his heads were seven crowns.
12:7 And there was war in heaven, Michael and his angels waging war with the dragon. The dragon and his angels waged war,
12:8 and they did not prevail, and there was no longer a place found for them in heaven.
9:1‡[K32] *Then the fifth angel sounded,* and I saw a star from heaven which had fallen to the earth; *and the key to the shaft of the abyss was given to him.*
12:4‡[K01,K04] And his tail swept away a third of the stars of heaven and hurled them to the earth. *And the dragon stood before the woman who was about to give birth, so that when she gave birth he might devour her Child.*
12:9 And the great dragon was thrown down, the serpent of old who is called the devil and Satan, who deceives the whole world; he was thrown down to the earth, and his angels were thrown down with him.

Ye have indeed in the Messenger of Allah a beautiful pattern (of conduct) for any one whose hope is in Allah and the Final Day, and who engages much in the Praise of Allah. (Surah 33:21)

The last hour will not come before Allah takes his Shari`a away from the people of the earth, leaving no one in it but heathens who do not recognize right or object to wrong.[62]

Those who do not judge by what Allah has revealed are truly the wrongdoers. (Surah 5:45, Clear Qur'an)

Do you not see those who claim that they have *iman* [belief] in what has been sent down to you and what was sent down before you, still desiring to turn to a satanic source for judgment in spite of being ordered to reject it? Shaytan wants to misguide them far away. (Surah 4:60, Aisha Bewley translation)

12:10 Then I heard a loud voice in heaven, saying, "Now the salvation, and the power, and the kingdom of our God and the

---

[62] Narrated by Abd Allah ibn Amr ibn al-As, quoted in `Ibn Izzat p.52. Abd Allah was author of *Al-Sahifah al-Sadiqah* (The Truthful Script), the first known hadith compilation document.

authority of His Christ have come, for the accuser of our brothers
and sisters has been thrown down, the one who accuses them
before our God day and night.
12:12 For this reason, rejoice, you heavens and you who dwell in
them. Woe to the earth and the sea, because the devil has come
down to you with great wrath, knowing that he has only a short
time."

Revelation. The dragon becomes the main character once again. We
encountered him earlier when we studied verses 12:3,4 in K01. There
we already identified him as Satan, leading the fallen angels in rebellion
against God the Almighty. The creator had originally made them in
perfection. They had free access to heaven. But Satan and the devils
who followed him into revolt were defeated. Afterward, they spent
much time on earth. Their obsession was to torment men and women,
and tempt them to sin against God.

After his fall, Satan was not completely excluded from heaven. On at
least one occasion, God summoned him back, to consider the
faithfulness of Job. The event is described in Job 1.

Satan accused Job's faith of being a sham, merely a natural product of
God's excessive blessings upon him and his family. God answered by
allowing Satan to take the lives of Job's children, and to torment him
with severe bodily affliction. Incredibly, Job's faith survived these great
trials, and proved to be true. Then God blessed him even more
abundantly than before.

At this point in our timeline, we see verses 12:3,4 again, in a case of
double prophecy. At the time of the rapture, by God's design, Satan and
the devils are in heaven. The rapture comes as a surprise to everyone,
including Satan. His answer is to launch war in heaven. Doubtlessly his
anger was extreme, seeing that so many people are resurrected and
brought to heaven by Christ his enemy.

The archangel Michael and the righteous angels fight back the horde of
devils, and are victorious (12:7-8). Satan and his followers are cast out
of heaven again, this time permanently. They are thrown down to earth
(9:1, 12:4). Satan will never again have the opportunity to accuse the
believers in heaven, as he did against Job. They will be permanently

beyond his reach. Heaven is forever purified from contact with the fallen angels.

This is part of God's eternal plan, and is also prophesied in the Old Testament book of Daniel:

> Daniel 12:1 "Now at that time Michael, the great prince who stands guard over the sons of your people, will arise. And there will be a time of distress such as never occurred since there was a nation until that time; and at that time your people, everyone who is found written in the book, will be rescued."

In verse 12:12 a voice from heaven pronounces woe and great distress upon all who remain on earth after the rapture. God is delivering them into the hands of Satan the master accuser. He is now hurled down to earth to operate among them.

Satan knows that all this may happen. He is reading the same Bible we do. He knows that his time is short (12:12). Ever since Revelation was written, it is logical that he has been developing contingencies for various scenarios. Through them he thinks he can ultimately win out against God with his schemes. His most cunning plan of all is for the time after the rapture. He has been preparing to raise up a suitable candidate to take on the role of the beast of Revelation. This man will be the perfect vehicle through which Satan can finally gain dominion over the entire world.

Through the beast, Satan will gladly fulfill Revelation's prophecy of an eighth and final godless empire (17:10,11 K02). The prophecy of 12:3 adds detail by portraying Satan as the dragon having seven heads and ten horns. He will co-opt the beast as his surrogate, who also will have seven heads and ten horns (17:3 K17 and 13:1 K21). We will examine the meaning of the heads and horns in section K21.

After Satan puts his agent into place, he will look for a way to then hijack control of the prophecies, and make his world order of the tribulation permanent.

We shall see that God has other plans. The upcoming time will not be of distress alone, but also of refinement, as metal is purified by fire. Many people will come to their senses and will ask God to save them.

The antichrist will launch the seven-year tribulation in the next section. But the tribulation will not begin immediately after the rapture. There will first be an interim of some years. This is indicated by some supernatural events prophesied in other books of the Bible, such as Ezekiel 38-39, whose timing is best placed between the rapture and the tribulation.

Hadiths. In these Hadiths, Muslims are exhorted to put their hope in Allah and the end times. At the time Islam was founded, he sent Muhammad to be the role model for all Muslims. In the Last Day he will send another in the beautiful pattern of Muhammad – the Mahdi.

Just before the end time comes, only evil people will remain. This is because Allah will withdraw Sharia law from the earth. Left to their own devices, people will no longer recognize what is good and pleasing to Allah. They will not object to evil.

The hadith says that only heathens (infidels) will remain. This should be reinterpreted in view of upcoming Hadiths about the appearance of the Mahdi. At that time there will still be many faithful Muslims who will recognize and welcome him. But they will be hindered by their false Muslim overlords, and by a multitude of non-Muslims.

The meaning of this hadith could therefore be that no Muslim nation remains which seriously enforces Sharia. Many nations will claim to be Islamic. But all of them will persist in deviance and disobedience to the decrees of the Qur'an. These false Muslims judge by man-made laws, and comply with rulers who are only nominally submissive to Allah. The lot of them are being misguided by Shaytan.

Ka'b al-Ahbar was an early transmitter of Judeo-Christian *isra'iliyyat* traditions, those that are considered uncorrupted by Islam (see section H16). He was active in the generation after Muhammad's death. He had heard many of the oral sayings of the prophet, and was aware of this future time when Sharia would be gone from the world. He was also familiar with the Christian book of Revelation. He tied the two together to make his own prophecy. When the world has reached this awful condition:

> **A star with a luminous tail will rise from the East, before the Mahdi emerges.**[63]

Many Muslims regard this prophecy as authoritative.[64] Some believe that the star with the tail will be a comet,[65] which is widely considered a sign of coming catastrophe and disaster.

Unbelievers will be terrified by the star with the tail. Then the Mahdi will appear.

Comparison. Revelation and the Hadiths both tell of a time when people of the world are living according to their own dictates. For Bible believers, this will be the time after the rapture, after Christ takes his followers to heaven. The Holy Spirit has withdrawn from the world and no longer is the restrainer of sin. In the Hadiths, it is the result of Sharia law no longer being in effect anywhere.

In my day, it is certainly becoming true that more people across the world are living without regard for any divine power. They are redefining reality for themselves. By this measure, both the Christian and Muslim prophecies are closer than ever to fulfillment.

Which account is to be believed?

Let us consider the heavenly signs of the two accounts. In Revelation, it is a star falling from heaven (9:1), who we learn is Satan. He must be cast down to earth first, to set the stage for the coming of the antichrist. In the Muslim tradition, it is a star with a luminous tail, that will be seen before the Mahdi emerges.

The Bible tells us that Satan is the originator of evil. God permits evil, so that he can demonstrate what good really is in comparison. In this way he persuades many to follow him with their whole heart. A passage from Romans speaks to this:

---

[63] In Ka'b al-Ahbar, quoted in `Ibn Izzat p.21.
[64] For example in Ayatollah Sadr al-Din al-Sadr (d.1953), *Al-Mahdi*, English trans. Jalil Dorrani, Naba Organization, 1994, https://www.al-islam.org/al-mahdi-sayyid-sadruddin-sadr/chapter-7, accessed October 14, 2024.
[65] https://www.reviewofreligions.org/16172/the-saviour-of-the-latter-days-signs-of-the-messiah/, July 14, 2019.

> Romans 9:22 What if God, although willing to demonstrate
> His wrath and to make His power known, endured with
> great patience objects of wrath prepared for destruction?
> 9:23 And He did so to make known the riches of His glory
> upon objects of mercy, which He prepared beforehand for
> glory.

Ultimately God will establish a new heaven and earth where evil will be no more. He is preparing a home there for all his faithful followers. But the God of the Bible is definitely not the author of evil. He endures it that we might turn away from it, and embrace him instead.

On the other hand, *Al-Falaq*, or "The Daybreak" chapter of the Qur'an, tells us that Allah is the creator of evil:

> Say, O Prophet, "I seek refuge in [Allah] the Lord of the
> daybreak, from the evil of whatever He has created, and from
> the evil of the night when it grows dark, and from the evil of
> those witches casting spells by blowing onto knots, and from
> the evil of an envier when they envy." (Surah 113:1–5, Clear
> Qur'an)

From an Islamic perspective, this passage is difficult to defend. Could it be that Shaytan, the true creator of evil, is working behind the scenes? It could be the seventh signature of his influence on Islam (see K08). The upcoming sections will guide us to more truth.

K16 :

The rider on the white horse, known as the beast and antichrist, at the beginning of the seven-year tribulation

6:1 Then I saw when the Lamb broke one of the seven seals, and I heard one of the four living creatures saying as with a voice of thunder, "Come!"
6:2 I looked, and behold, a white horse, and the one who sat on it had a bow; and a crown was given to him, and he went out conquering and to conquer.

: H16

Allah sends the Mahdi for a seven-year glorious age

Three will fight one another for your treasure, each one of them the son of a caliph, but none of them will gain it. Then the black banners will come from the east, and they will kill you in an unprecedented manner…. When you see them, then pledge your allegiance to them even if you have to crawl over the snow, for that is the caliph of Allah, Mahdi.[66] *(da'if)*

When you see the black flags coming out from the direction of Khorasan, then go to them even if you have to crawl on snow, for verily among them is the *khalifah* of Allah, the Mahdi.[67] *(sahih)*

Allah Almighty will send the Mahdi after despair has reached a point that people will say, "there is no Mahdi." Three hundred and fifteen of the people of Syria … will bring him out of the valley of Makka from a house at as-Safa. They will force him to accept their allegiance.[68]

[Armies carrying] black flags will come from Khorasan. No power will be able to stop them and they will finally reach Bait al-Maqdis [in Jerusalem] where they will erect their flags.[69] *(da'if)*

---

[66] Narrated by Thawban, *Sunan Ibn Majah 4084*, Vol. 5, Book 36, Hadith 4084, https://sunnah.com/ibnmajah:4084, accessed May 15, 2024; also referenced in Rahma p.42.

[67] Narrated by Abu 'Abd Allah Na'im b. Hammad al-Maruzi, *Kitab al-Fitan* (Dar al-Fikr; 1414 H) [annotator: Prof. Dr. Suhayl Zakar], part 4, p. 188, quoted in Toyib Olawuyi, https://www.al-islam.org/imam-al-mahdi-twelfth-khalifah-sahih-sunni-ahadith-toyib-olawuyi/5-black-flags-khurasan, accessed May 15, 2024; see also Thawban, in Al-Hakim, ad-Dani, Nu`aym ibn Hammad, and as-Suyuti, quoted in `Ibn Izzat p.43.

[68] Narrated by Abdullah ibn `Abbas, in Nu`aym ibn Hammad, quoted in `Ibn Izzat p.28. Narrated by Abu Hurairah, *Sunan al-Tirmidhī 2269*, Vol. 4, Book 7, Hadith 2269, as quoted in Mohammed Ali Ibn Zubair Ali, *Signs of Qiyamah,* New Delhi, Abdul Naeen,

> Surely, Black Flags will appear from the Khorasan until a group (of them) will tie their horse leashes to the Olive Trees between Beit-Lahia (in Gaza district, Palestine) and Harasta (near Damascus, Syria).[70]

> The Prophet said: The Mahdi will be of my stock, and will have a broad forehead a prominent nose. He will fill the earth will equity and justice as it was filled with oppression and tyranny, and he will rule for seven years.[71] *(hasan)*

> He will live for seven or eight years.[72]

> He will divide the property, and will govern the people by the Sunnah of their Prophet and establish Islam on Earth. He will remain seven years.[73] *(da'if)*

> The Messenger of Allah said, a nation which has me at its beginning, 'Isa ibn Maryam at its end and the Mahdi in between will never be destroyed.[74] *(da'if)*

Hadiths. The Mahdi arrives on the scene. Now begins the long-awaited glorious age of Islam.

He will come at a time of despotic rule, corruption, and great cruelty. People will be negligent and heedless. Many have despaired and no

---

2004, p.42, cited in Richardson p. 27; see also https://sunnah.com/tirmidhi:2269 accessed May 15, 2024; Abu Amina Elias, *Are hadith of the black flags of al-Mahdi authentic?* October 2, 2014, https://www.abuaminaelias.com/hadith-black-flags-al-mahdi/.

[70] Nuaim Ibn Hammad (9th century collector of hadiths), *Kitab Al-Fitan*, https://www.scribd.com/document/378445646/Kitab-al-Fitan-of-Nuaym-b-Hammad, p.215, cited in https://ghayb.com/2017/06/the-black-banners-will-appear-6-years-before-imam-mahdi/, accessed May 15, 2024; see also https://daiyah.fandom.com/wiki/Hadith_of_black_flags, accessed March 16, 2023.

[71] Narrated by AbuSa'id al-Khudri, *Sunan Abi Dawud 4285*, Book 37, Hadith 4272, https://sunnah.com/abudawud:4285, accessed May 15, 2024.

[72] *Mustadrak Haakim 8673*, quoted in *Justice and Blessings During the Reign of the Mahdi*, December 26, 2022, https://ihyaauddeen.co.za/?p=20267.

[73] Narrated by Umm Salamah, Ummul Mu'minin, *Sunan Abi Dawud 4286*, Book 37, Hadith 4273, https://sunnah.com/abudawud:4286, accessed May 15, 202994.

[74] Narrated by Abdullah ibn `Abbas, in Ahmad ibn Hanbal, Abu Nu`aym, and an-Nasa'l, quoted in `Ibn Izzat p.8; also narrated by Abdullah Ibn 'Abbas, in Ibn Hajar al-Haytami (10th century Egyptian scholar of hadith), *Al-Sawa'iq al-Muhriqah*, quoted in Ayatollah Sadr al-Din al-Sadr (d.1953), *Al-Mahdi*, English trans. Jalil Dorrani, Naba Organization, 1994, https://www.al-islam.org/al-mahdi-sayyid-sadruddin-sadr/chapter-4, accessed May 26, 2024.

longer believe that the promised Mahdi would ever come. They are saying, "there is no Mahdi." Many imams have become timid and stopped preaching about his coming in their sermons. Muslims will display weakness and faithlessness.

The Hadiths predict how the Mahdi will come forth in these conditions. After the death of a Muslim ruler, there will be civil war between three sons of rulers. Neither of them will achieve victory. But, by the mercy of Allah, a band of warriors brandishing black banners will come from the east. They are from the region of Khorasan, located on the plateau stretching from eastern Iran to northern Afghanistan to Tashkent in Uzbekistan and beyond.

The army of Khorasan will notice a special man among them whom they will identify as the Mahdi. Three hundred and fifteen men of Syria will join them. They will be the first to pledge their allegiance to him. These believers who prepare the way for the Mahdi are selected men whom only Allah knows.

The Mahdi will come before the Major Signs[75].

The Mahdi's army of black flags will then attack Jerusalem and reconquer it for Islam. It will be his capital city. From there he will extend his dominion over the whole world. In the next section we shall see that he will start consolidating rule by first making alliance with the Romans, with whom he will reign jointly for a time. Later he will break the alliance and become the lone sovereign.

Muslims will be ecstatic, for the Mahdi will have arrived, to preside over the rightly guided caliphate. They have been yearning for this ever since 1924, when the last caliphate was abolished, a few years after the demise of the Ottoman empire.

The Mahdi will be recognized and welcomed by millions, then billions. Among them will be people formerly professing to be Christians. In section K12, I discussed the great apostasy within Christian circles before the rapture and the tribulation. Many will forsake the church.

---

[75] https://islamqa.info/en/answers/43840/signs-of-the-judgement-day-in-order, October 25, 2023.

Some will convert to the Muslim faith. They will join those who greet the Islamic deliverer.

The Mahdi will be a descendant of Muhammad, and will be named after him (H05). Muhammad, which means "praiseworthy," is the appropriate name for both. It is derived from one of the 99 names of Allah: *Al-Hameed*, "The Praiseworthy."[76]

The Mahdi will rule for seven years. Some Hadiths say seven, eight, or possibly nine (see H44). He will fill the earth with justice, and give out wealth to the people. His influence will not be limited to the Arab people or to historically Muslim areas. The Mahdi will lead a world revolution that will establish an Islamic world order. He will accomplish this through multiple military campaigns, in holy wars of jihad. Some opponents will convert to Islam peaceably. But most other conversions will be the result of conquest and forced submission.

The inhabitants of the earth are then promised lives of great fulfillment for the rest of the Mahdi's seven years.

Among the first generation of Muhammad's disciples, some were already drawing a comparison between the Mahdi and the untainted Judeo-Christian traditions that became known as the *isra'iliyyat*.

In section H14, we met Ka'b al-Ahbar, An early transmitter of *isra'iliyyat*. He was a Yemenite Jew and convert to Islam. Ka'b came to Medina only a few years following Muhammad's death, after `Umar ibn al-Khattab became caliph in 634. `Umar was a senior companion and one of Muhammad's fathers-in-law. Because of Ka'b al-Ahbar's expertise with *isra'iliyyat*, he became `Umar's trusted advisor.

When `Umar marched with an army into Jerusalem, Ka'b advised him to build a Muslim place of worship at the site of the heap of ruins left over from the Old Testament temple, known as the Temple Rock. `Umar ordered the rubbish on the Temple Rock to be removed, and instituted prayers there. Some years later, in 691, the Umayyad caliph Abd al-Malik built the Dome of the Rock over the site. It became the

---

[76] *99 Names of Allah (Al Asma Ul Husna)*, https://99namesofallah.name, accessed February 16, 2023.

third holiest site in Islam, ranked after the Kaaba in Mecca, and the *Al-Masjid an-Nabawi* (Mosque of the Prophet) in Medina.

Ka'b al-Ahbar's knowledge of both the Old and New Testaments allowed him to also boldly connect their prophecies with the end-time appearance of the Mahdi:

> I find the Mahdi recorded in the books of the prophets. There will be no injustice or oppression in his rule.[77]

Muslims over the centuries have followed Ka'b's lead. Some have made a direct comparison between the Mahdi and the rider on the white horse of Revelation:

> For instance the Book of Revelation says: "and I saw and behold a White Horse. He that sat on him ... went forth conquering and to conquer" ... It is clear that this man is the Mahdi who will ride a white horse and judge by the Qur'an (with justice) and with whom will be men with the marks of prostration on their foreheads.[78]

> *Al Mahdi the White Horse Rider* ... This book is a humble attempt by the author to shine the light of Al-Islaam, the Holy Qur'an ... on ... the Book of Revelations. It is my sincere belief that the Holy Scriptures are interconnected and that the Holy Qur'an is the last chapter and the key to understanding all scriptures.[79]

To this day, many Muslims are proud of this portrayal of the Mahdi as the first horseman of Revelation, the rider on the white horse. They see the prophecy of Revelation as confirming their own expectations of the coming of the Mahdi. Rulers of Muslim nations have appropriated this image for themselves. For example, in the 1980's and 90's, the Iraqi dictator Saddam Hussein had numerous murals painted all over Baghdad portraying himself as a Muslim knight on a white horse, doing

---

[77] Ka'b al-Ahbar, quoted in `Ibn Izzat p.15.

[78] `Ibn Izzat p.15.

[79] Hassan Shabazz, *Al Mahdi the White Horse Rider*, lulu.com, 2018, introduction posted on https://books.google.com/books/about/Al_Mahdi_the_White_Horse_Rider.html?id=M 6hoDwAAQBAJ, accessed August 13, 2024.

battle against infidels.[80] He even dedicated the Victory Arch of Baghdad by leading a procession mounted on a white stallion.[81]

Revelation. This section occurs after Satan is cast down to earth. The Lamb of God opens the first of the seven seals of the book of the tribulation (5:8-9 K14). It inaugurates the seven-year period of trials upon the earth. The sound of thunder is the sign that the storm is on its way (6:1).

A white horse appears. Its rider carries a bow, which shows that his intent is to conquer the nations of the world. He receives a glorious crown in anticipation of his victories (6:2).

This is the verse from Revelation so favored by Muslims, who look forward to the coming of their Mahdi.

Later, in 19:11 K38, Jesus Christ will return from heaven to earth at the end of the tribulation. He will also come on a white horse, leading the armies of heaven.

But the rider of the first seal is not Christ. He will be a false prince of peace. He claims to bring order and tranquility to a broken world. He will bring great trouble to all who oppose him.

Who is he really?

We already saw that the *isra'iliyyat* claim him to be the Mahdi.

The Bible does not mention the Mahdi. But it tells us much about the identity of this first rider on a white horse, both in Revelation, and in other books of the Bible.

In the next section, this man will reappear as the *beast* (17:3 K17), with seven heads and ten horns, who carries the woman of Babylon. Together they will rule the world for the first half of the seven years. Later he comes as the beast out of the sea, again with ten horns (13:1 K21), which will represent ten kingdoms. Together they will overthrow the woman and burn her with fire (17:16 K21). The beast then becomes

---

[80] Richardson, p.30.
[81] https://en.m.wikipedia.org/wiki/Victory_Arch, accessed August 13, 2024.

chief ruler. He will be dictator over the second half of the tribulation, a time of continuous war.

Hundreds of years before John's vision, Daniel also had a vision of a beast that had ten horns:

> Daniel 7:19 "Then I desired to know the exact meaning of the fourth beast, which was different from all the others, exceedingly dreadful, with its teeth of iron and its claws of bronze, and which devoured, crushed, and trampled down the remainder with its feet,
> 7:20 and the meaning of the ten horns that were on its head, and the other horn which came up, and before which three of the horns fell, namely, that horn which had eyes and a mouth uttering great boasts, and which was larger in appearance than its associates.
> 7:21 I kept looking, and that horn was waging war with the saints and prevailing against them,"

Looking forward from Daniel's time, this has two future fulfillments. The first was the Roman empire that came a few hundred years after Daniel. The second will be the beast ruling over a revived Roman empire during the tribulation.

In another prophecy, Daniel foresees a man who will come:

> Daniel 9:26b and the people of the prince who is to come will destroy the city and the sanctuary.

This *prince who is to come* also points far ahead to the beast of Revelation.

Another name for the future beast is the *lawless one*. He can only make his appearance after the Holy Spirit stops restraining sin in the world, which happens in conjunction with the rapture of all the true church believers to heaven (see 2 Thessalonians 2:6-8 K13).

The most fitting title of all for the beast is the *antichrist*. John uses this title for this great end-time opponent, as we see from these verses repeated from K05:

> 1 John 2:22 Who is the liar except the one who denies that Jesus is the Christ? This is the antichrist, the one who denies the Father and the Son.

> 4:3 and every spirit that does not confess Jesus is not from
> God; this is the spirit of the antichrist, which you have heard
> is coming, and now it is already in the world.
> 2 John 7 For many deceivers have gone out into the world,
> those who do not acknowledge Jesus Christ as coming in the
> flesh. This is the deceiver and the antichrist.

The antichrist will be the man who pulls off the greatest deception ever. In his arrogance, he will dare to seize the place of Jesus Christ in the universal plan of history. He will mislead many to believe that he is the true deliverer who has returned to earth.

Where does the rider on the white horse – also known as the beast, the prince who is to come, the man of lawlessness, the lawless one, the antichrist – where will he come from? Near the beginning of our timeline, we were told that the beast shall "come up out of the abyss" (17:8 K02). Later we shall see that Satan is the angel of this abyss (9:11 K32). In this way Revelation shows that the antichrist will be the tool and creation of Satan, specially prepared by him to be the supreme ruler of the end-time. He will be Satan's masterpiece, the counterfeit of all that Jesus Christ the son of God claims to be.

Comparison. Many Muslims claim the rider on the white horse of Revelation 6:2 as their own. They believe that only he will bring the proper order of Sharia law to the world. To maintain this belief, they find a way to invalidate almost all the other 403 verses of Revelation. But those verses deserve to be heard, in view of the inner consistency of Revelation, and how its teaching matches the rest of the Bible. It would be better for a Muslim to follow the surah that says "none can change his [Allah's] words" (Surah 6:115), and to recognize that there is no corruption in the Bible. The corruption may well be elsewhere. It would be even better to question whether Allah is the same as the God of the Bible. Perhaps Allah is someone else.

The truth is that the rest of Revelation connects the rider on the white horse with the beast of the tribulation, also known as the antichrist.

Also, followers of Jesus should be careful of jumping to the conclusion that the Hadiths prove the antichrist will be the Mahdi of Islam. As we discussed in K08, God is the only one who knows who the antichrist will be. Satan certainly has prepared alternate candidates at different turns in human history. The Islamic candidate will be one of his strongest, especially since Satan has been influencing Islam for over 1,500 years, and was involved at its founding. As we study more Hadiths, we shall see that their prophecies of the Mahdi's rule intend to replace Revelation's chronology with future events that will be favorable to the imposition of Islam. But it will be God who determines end-time happenings, which will start with the date and time of the rapture. Only then will he allow Satan to have partial control of events, and to raise up the antichrist to be his agent. It may be a favorable time for the Mahdi to come forth as the antichrist. Or the antichrist may come from another ideology that violently opposes Jesus Christ along different lines.

In my time a possible Mahdi seems to be a likely candidate for the antichrist. Whether or not that comes true, our parallel study of the Hadiths alongside God's word in Revelation will shed much light on Satan's deceptions in Islam. If you are a Muslim and are reading this book, please take the truths of Revelation to heart.

K17 :
The woman of Babylon sitting on the beast at the beginning of the seven-year tribulation

: H17
A treaty between Allah's followers and the Romans

17:1‡[K02,K20] Then one of the seven angels who had the seven bowls came and spoke with me, saying, "Come here, I will show you *the judgment of* the great prostitute who sits on many waters."
17:3 And he carried me away in the Spirit into a wilderness; and I saw a woman sitting on a scarlet beast, full of blasphemous names, having seven heads and ten horns.
17:4 The woman was clothed in purple and scarlet, and adorned with gold, precious stones, and pearls, holding in her hand a gold cup full of abominations and of the unclean things of her sexual immorality,
17:5 and on her forehead a name was written, a mystery: "BABYLON THE GREAT, THE MOTHER OF PROSTITUTES AND OF THE ABOMINATIONS OF THE EARTH."
17:15 And he said to me, "The waters which you saw where the prostitute sits are peoples and

[Among the] signs that indicate the approach of the Hour ... a truce between you and *Bani Al-Asfar* (i.e. the Byzantines).[82]

You will make a secure peace with the Romans, then you and they will fight an enemy behind you, and you will be victorious, take booty, and be safe.[83] *(sahih)*

The Prophet said: "There will be four peace agreements between you and the Romans. The fourth agreement will be mediated through a person who will be from the progeny of *Hadhrat Aaron* [Honorable Aaron - the brother of Moses] and will be upheld for seven years." The people asked: "O Messenger of Allah, who will be the *Imaam* [leader] of the people at the time?" The Messenger of Allah said: "He will be from my progeny and will be forty years of age. His face will shine like a star.[84]

---

82 Narrated by `Auf bin Mali, *Sahih al-Bukhari 3176*, Vol. 4, Book 53, Hadith 401, https://sunnah.com/bukhari:3176, accessed May 17, 2024, also see `Ibn Izzat p.44.
83 Narrated by Dhu Mikhbar, *Sunan Abi Dawud 4292*, Book 38, Hadith 4279, quoted in Rahma p.55, see also https://sunnah.com/abudawud:4292, accessed May 17, 2024.
84 Al-Tabarani (10th century hadith compiler), in Ali ibn Abd-al-Malik al-Hindi (16th century Islamic scholar), *Kanz-ul-Aamal* (in Arabic), publisher Dār al-Kutub al-'Ilmīyah, Lebanon, 1998, ed. Mahmud Umar al-Dumyati, Hadith No. 3868, p.268, cited by Muslimapoclyptc (sic), https://www.islamicboard.com/clarifications-about-islam/134273395-mahdi-4.html (in English), February 12, 2009; also referenced in Richardson p.47.

multitudes, and nations and languages.
17:18 The woman whom you saw is the great city, which reigns over the kings of the earth."

'There will come to the people years of treachery, when the liar will be regarded as honest, and the honest man will be regarded as a liar; the traitor will be regarded as faithful, and the faithful man will be regarded as a traitor; and the *Ruwaibidah* will decide matters.' It was said: 'Who are the *Ruwaibidah*?' He said: 'Vile and base men who control the affairs of the people.'[85] *(hasan)*

The Prophet said: 'The people will soon summon one another to attack you, as people when eating invite others to share their dish.' Someone asked: 'Will that be because of our small numbers at that time?' he replied: 'No, you will be numerous at that time: but you will be scum and rubbish like that carried down by a torrent, and Allah will take fear of you from the chests of your enemies and last [*sic*] *wahn* (enervation) into your hearts'. Someone asked: 'What is *wahn*?' The Messenger of Allah replied: 'Love of the world and dislike of death'.[86] *(sahih)*

Then will come a test which is pleasant. Its murkiness is due to the fact that it is produced by a man from the people of my house, who will assert that he belongs to me, whereas he does not, for my friends are only the Allah-fearing. Then the people will unite under a man who will be like a hip-bone on a rib. Then there will be the little black trial which will leave none of this community without giving him a slap, and when people say that it is finished, it will be extended. During it a man will be a believer in the morning and an infidel in the evening, so that the people will be in two camps: the camp of faith which will contain no hypocrisy, and the camp of hypocrisy which will contain no faith. When that happens, expect the antichrist (Dajjal) that day or the next.[87] *(sahih)*

Revelation. The rider on the white horse reappears in a different guise, as the beast who carries the woman of Babylon to power. She is the

---

[85] Narrated by Abu Hurairah, *Sunan Ibn Majah 4036*, Vol. 5, Book 36, Hadith 4036, https://sunnah.com/ibnmajah:4036, accessed May 17, 2024; also referenced in Rahma p.27.

[86] Narrated by Thawban, *Sunan Abi Dawud 4297*, Book 38, Hadith 4284, quoted in Rahma p.28, see also https://sunnah.com/abudawud:4297, accessed May 17, 2024.

[87] Narrated by Abdullah ibn Umar, *Sunan Abi Dawud 4242*, Book 36, Hadith 4230, https://sunnah.com/abudawud:4242, accessed May 17, 2024; also referenced in Rahma p.18.

prostitute, whom we have already encountered in section 17:1 K02. She represents the spirit of empire, originally manifested in Babel, the kingdom of Nimrod. God put a sudden end to it by confusing the world's languages at the tower of Babel.

The spirit of empire came back to power in more kingdoms of the ancient world: Egypt, Assyria, Babylon, Persia, Greece, and Rome. Each of them ruled over Jerusalem at some point. They set the stage for it to be the epicenter for the future empire of the tribulation.

Besides Jerusalem, the Bible also points to Rome as the other epicenter of the end times, or perhaps another city that will be its successor. We know this from Daniel's prophecies of a revived Roman empire. His dream in Daniel chapter 2 was of a statue, the fourth part of which is as strong as iron that crushes (Daniel 2:40). Six hundred years after Daniel was added to the Old Testament, both Jews and Christians recognized his dream's fulfillment in the Roman empire of their time.

Another dream of Daniel's is of beasts, the fourth of which has great iron teeth that breaks things in pieces (Daniel 7:7). But this dream details events that did not come to pass in the ancient Roman empire, as evident from the interpretation that God gave to Daniel for the dream. Instead, the Daniel 7 passage matches up with future events prophesied in Revelation. We can see this if we re-order the verses of Daniel's dream according to Revelation's time sequence:

> Daniel 7:23 "This is what he said: 'The fourth beast will be a fourth kingdom on the earth which will be different from all the other kingdoms, and will devour the whole earth and trample it down and crush it,
> 7:20 and the meaning of the ten horns that were on its head, and the other horn which came up, and before which three of the horns fell, namely, that horn which had eyes and a mouth uttering great boasts, and which was larger in appearance than its associates.
> 7:24 As for the ten horns, out of this kingdom ten kings will arise; and another will arise after them, and he will be different from the previous ones and will humble three kings.
> 7:25 And he will speak against the Most High and wear down the saints of the Highest One, and he will intend to make alterations in times and in law; and they will be handed over to him for a time, times, and half a time.'"

> 7:21 I kept looking, and that horn was waging war with the saints and prevailing against them.
> 7:26 "'But the court will convene for judgment, and his dominion will be taken away, annihilated and destroyed forever,'
> 7:22 until the Ancient of Days came and judgment was passed in favor of the saints of the Highest One, and the time arrived when the saints took possession of the kingdom.
> 7:27 'Then the sovereignty, the dominion, and the greatness of all the kingdoms under the whole heaven will be given to the people of the saints of the Highest One; His kingdom will be an everlasting kingdom, and all the empires will serve and obey Him.'
> 7:18 But the saints of the Highest One will receive the kingdom and take possession of the kingdom forever, for all ages to come.'"

Here is how the Daniel 7 passage matches up with Revelation's prophecies of future events:

- The ten horns of the beast in Daniel 7:20,24 matches up with the ten horns of the beast of Revelation 17:3.
- Daniel's ten horns become ten kings. One of them subsumes three of the others, leaving seven kings (Daniel 7:24). This compares to the seven heads of 17:3.
- Daniel's beast makes war on the saints, and is apparently victorious (Daniel 7:21). This compares with 13:7 K23.
- Then the kingdom will be taken away and he will be judged (Daniel 7:26). This compares with the final defeat of Revelation's beast in 19:20 K40.
- God's saints will then be given possession of the kingdom (Daniel 7:22). This will occur in Revelation 20:4 K43, when the tribulation saints come into the millennial kingdom.
- The saints will possess the kingdom forever and ever (Daniel 7:18,27). This is fulfilled when the saints enter into God's eternal kingdom in 21:3 K47.

This evidence shows that Daniel 7 is describing a different Roman empire, one that is revived during the tribulation. In Revelation this empire will be established by the woman of Babylon, with the help of the antichrist beast.

The woman flaunts her promiscuity, fornication, and adultery. She is so proud of this that she wears a name of mystery on her forehead: "mother of prostitutes and of the abominations of the earth" (17:5). She defies God by promoting sin. She seeks her security elsewhere, in rampant adulteries. She avoids real work by enslaving her victims to serve her.

The woman's forbidden relationship at the outset of the tribulation is with the beast. The vision paints a graphically suggestive picture of her achieving power by sitting on the beast (17:3). Through him, she renews her line of kingdoms. She is dressed as a seductress, holding a golden cup, paid for by those sharing in her temptations (17:4). By her enticements, she achieves a world order at the beginning of the tribulation, and establishes control over many nations, languages and peoples (17:15,18). Her empire makes immorality into a virtue, sees things through a sexual prism, and brings to the masses a stupefying drunkenness that is oblivious to spiritual matters.

Will the woman of Babylon be an actual woman whom we will be able to identify by a physical description, or certain personality traits? The inscription on her forehead may be her actual appearance. But the same woman was mentioned in K02 in conjunction with the six empires that opposed God in the Old Testament. There was no historical female figure to speak of in them, and certainly not one who made her reappearance in each one. The position of political and cultural ruler in those empires was held by a succession of leaders. We can therefore expect that in the tribulation, the woman of Babylon is symbolic, representing one or more top leaders who will be the public face of the revived Roman empire.

Why does the vision speak of a woman of Babylon instead of Rome? Babylon was capital of the Babylonian empire, which was conquered by the Medo-Persians in 539 BCE. The city was never significant after that. Baghdad was founded in 762 CE, 85 km to the north, as the capital of the Islamic Abbasid caliphate. The Babylon of Revelation is likely not referring to Baghdad, nor a future great city that will be rebuilt at its original location.

When John received his vision, Rome was the greatest power on earth. God helped John to shield the churches who received his letter by depicting the leading figure of the future Roman empire as the prostitute of Babylon, instead of as the prostitute of Rome. The use of the word Babylon also ties the tribulation to the series of anti-God empires going back to Babel.

The original Roman empire ruled over the Mediterranean Sea basin, including southern and western Europe, northern Africa, and much of the Middle East up to the borders of Persia. Rome in Italy was its capital for a thousand years. But during the fourth century CE, the capital of the western half was moved to Milan. In the fifth century it shifted to Ravenna. Not long afterwards the western empire fell, in 476.

In 330, Constantinople became capital of the eastern Roman empire, also known as the Byzantine empire. This city was popularly known as the second Rome. It remained capital until 1453, when it was conquered by Ottoman armies. At that time, the Roman empire was finally ended. The city was renamed Istanbul, and was repurposed as the capital of the Ottoman caliphate until 1924. A revived Roman empire will presumably cover much of the same territory.

The end-times capital of the future could be Rome, Brussels, Istanbul, or some other city of the region. It will be the crown jewel of the woman of Babylon, the first city of focus in the geography of the tribulation. The second will be Jerusalem.

Hadiths. The revived Roman empire that is forecast in the Bible is also a theme in many Hadiths. They refer to the Romans as a major player in the end times.

In the previous section H16, the Mahdi made his appearance among the Islamic army of black flags, that has come from distant Khorasan to resolve the three-way civil war that had broken out among Muslims. They have marched to Jerusalem and taken possession of it.

The Mahdi's jurisdiction does not yet extend across the entire world. As a step toward that end, the Mahdi and his followers make a treaty with the Romans, also known as the Byzantines. The purpose of the agreement is to suspend hostilities between the Muslims and the Romans, so that they can jointly fight a common enemy. Together they will be victorious.

In the victory, the Muslim army will take booty. This is a tradition that started with Muhammad.[88] Surah 8 of the Qur'an is devoted to the topic, and is entitled *Al-Anfal*, "the Spoils of War." It describes the Battle of Badr, where Muhammad's forces defeated an army of the polytheistic Quraysh tribe of Mecca, at the beginning of the six-year war between Muhammad and the tribe of his birth. After the victory, he received a revelation which has encouraged jihadists ever since to make war and plunder their defeated enemies:

> And know that out of all the booty that ye may acquire (in war),
> a fifth share is assigned to Allah,- and to the Messenger, and to
> near relatives, orphans, the needy, and the wayfarer. (Surah
> 8:41a)

The Mahdi, during his seven years of ascendancy, will use the seized property and wealth of defeated peoples to compensate his followers. We shall see in H24-H3, after the overthrow of the Romans, booty will be a major engine of the world Islamic economy.

One hadith says that the Muslims will make not one, but four treaties in succession with the Romans. The final one will be negotiated with the help of a Jewish leader, descended from the Aaronic line of priests. The term of the treaty will be for seven years. The Mahdi will be 40 years old when he makes this last treaty.

Historically, Muslim nations have made many treaties with other nations, which the other party believes is a step towards lasting peace. Their example for this is Muhammad. In 628, he signed the treaty of Hudaybiyyah with the Quraysh for a period stipulated to be 10 years. The main provision of the treaty allowed his followers to enter the city and peacefully perform the hajj. The Quraysh scrupulously held to this provision. But less than two years later, after a series of individual killings between the two sides, Muhammad used one such episode to accuse the Quraysh of breaking other terms of the treaty. He returned with an army and took the city of Mecca by surprise. His supporters

---

[88] Shoebat, p.130.

through the centuries argue that he was justified because the Quraysh had violated the treaty.[89]

From this grew three Islamic doctrines.

The first is *hudna*, an Arabic term for a truce for a maximum of ten years. In *The Reliance of the Traveler*, or *Umdat al-Salik*, the classical manual of Islamic jurisprudence composed in the 14th Century, Abu Dawud, a collector of Hadiths, is quoted as saying:

> If Muslims are weak, a truce may be made for ten years if necessary, for the Prophet made a truce with the Quraysh for that long.[90]

A hudna will allow the Muslim state to recover from weakness with a period of calm, allowing it to gain concessions, re-arm, and eventually re-attack the enemy. It is a useful means of facilitating jihad.

The second is *kithman*, a command to deliberately conceal one's beliefs from non-Muslims. This is practiced primarily by Shi'a Muslims. Ja'far al-Sadiq, who ruled Shi'a Islam from 732 to 765 as the sixth of The Twelve Imams, relayed a hadith from Muhammad that supposedly mandated kithman, and commented on it:

> "One who exposes something from our religion is like one who intentionally kills us" - You belong to a religion that whosoever conceals it, Allah will honor him and whosoever reveals it, Allah will disgrace him.[91]

The third is *taqiyya*, which is to conceal belief in Islam when in imminent danger. A synonym for taqiyya would be dissimulation. This doctrine is based on Surah 16:106 of the Qur'an, which was precipitated by the following event recorded in *Dala'il al Imamah*, attributed by

---

[89] *The Myth: The Meccans were the First to Break Their Treaty with Muhammad*, https://www.thereligionofpeace.com/pages/muhammad/hudaibiya.aspx, accessed March 3, 2023.

[90] Shihabuddin Abu al-'Abbas Ahmad ibn an-Naqib al-Misri (1302-1367), *Umdat al-Salik (Reliance of the Traveller)*, translated by Nuh Ha Mim Keller, Amana Publications, 1997, section o9.16, quoted in Shoebat, p. 117.

[91] From *Usul al Kafi*, Twelver Shia hadith collection, compiled by Muhammad ibn Ya'qub al-Kulayni, quoted in Richardson, p. 152; also referenced in Ahmad 'Abdullah Salamah, *Shi'ah Concept of Temporary Marriage (Mut'ah)*, January 1994, http://www.islamicweb.com/beliefs/cults/mutah_book.htm, accessed May 28, 2024.

many[92] to al-Tabari, a ninth century Sunni scholar of early Islamic history and Qur'anic exegesis. The event resulted in a ruling of Muhammad, which he wrote into the Qur'an:

> The non-believers arrested 'Ammar Ibn Yasir and tortured him until he uttered foul words about the Prophet [Muhammad] and praised their gods and idols; and when they released him he went straight to the Prophet. The Prophet said: "Is there something on your mind?" 'Ammar Ibn Yasir said: "Bad news! They would not release me until I defamed you and praised their gods!" The Prophet said: "How do you find your heart to be?" Ammar answered: "Comfortable with faith." So the Prophet said: "Then if they come back for you, then do the same thing all over again." Allah at that moment revealed the verse:[93]

> Any one who, after accepting faith in Allah, utters Unbelief,- except under compulsion, his heart remaining firm in Faith - but such as open their breast to Unbelief, on them is Wrath from Allah, and theirs will be a dreadful Penalty. (Surah 16:106)

This verse from the Qur'an is used by both Shi'a and Sunni jihadists as justification for taqiyya. Ibn Kathir, the 14th century Sunni scholar of the Qur'an, memorably added: "taqiyya is allowed until the day of resurrection."[94]

From this explication of Islamic doctrine, we see that Muslims are encouraged to practice deceit. In fact, they are commanded to do so, given the situation. Deception is justified to gain wealth at the expense of non-Muslims, to murder the enemies of Islam, and to attain the goals of jihad.

The followers of the Mahdi would understand this when he makes the treaty with the Romans, just as Hitler's Nazi followers understood when he made a treaty with his worst ideological enemy – Stalin and the Soviet Union. Hitler did this in 1939 so that he could be free to attack France and Britain. The treaty launched World War II. Less than two years later he attacked the unsuspecting Russians in a surprise invasion.

---

[92] *Is Dala'il al Imamah Authentic?*, https://sjiisme.nl/is-dalail-al-imamah-authentic/, accessed March 4, 2023.
[93] *Al-Taqiyya, Dissimulation Part 1*, https://www.al-islam.org/shiite-encyclopedia/al-taqiyya-dissimulation-part-1, accessed March 4, 2023.
[94] Ibn Kathir, *Tafsir* [Qur'anic commentary], 14th century, on Surah 3:28, quoted in Richardson p.133.

Muhammad, the perfect Muslim, preached hudna, kithman, and taqiyya. He demonstrated how to practice them to expand Islam's domain. But his ultimate guide in all this was the person of Allah.

In the Qur'an, Allah refers to himself as *Khayrul-Makereen* (Surah 3:54, 8:30).[95] Khayrul means best of, and makereen comes from the root m-k-r. In an Arabic dictionary such as Al-Mawrid, m-k-r means to deceive, delude, cheat, double-cross, or delude. Thus, Allah is boasting that he is the "Greatest of all Deceivers."[96]

The Mahdi's treaty with the Romans will be advantageous to Islam. It will be one of hudna, kithman, and taqiyya, and it will be satisfying in the eyes of Allah, the Khayrul-Makereen.

We are told that the face of the Mahdi "will shine like a star." This is a direct echo of the great Jewish deliverer Moses. Whenever Moses met with God in the tabernacle and then went back to speak to his Jewish brethren, the skin of his face shined:

> Exodus 34:34 But whenever Moses went in before the L ord to speak with Him, he would take off the veil until he came out; and whenever he came out and spoke to the sons of Israel what he had been commanded,
> 34:35 the sons of Israel would see the face of Moses, that the skin of Moses' face shone. So Moses would put the veil back over his face until he went in to speak with Him.

The Mahdi's shining face will convince many that he is the awaited one, sent by Allah.

At the time of the treaty agreement with the Romans and Jews, and the establishment of a world government in its wake, the Mahdi and the Muslims have only partial control. A fully Islamic world order is yet to come. In the meantime, the Hadiths describe years of treachery on the part of the *Ruwaybidah.* This unusual word is a diminutive of the word rabidah, meaning lowly, despicable, or worthless, people who are incapable of rising to nobility, lack integrity and possess little more

---

[95] https://wikiislam.net/wiki/Allah,_the_Best_Deceiver_(Qur%27an_3:54), accessed March 5, 2023
[96] Cornelius, *Allah: Truthful Or Deceiver?*, https://www.answering-islam.org/authors/cornelius/makr.html, accessed March 5, 2023.

than a glimmer of religious knowledge. Despite this, they feel empowered to speak out about socio-political affairs.[97]

It is interesting that the Hadiths complain of treachery on the part of the Ruwaybidah, while applauding its use by true Muslims to further the cause of Islam. One of the tools of deception is to falsely accuse your adversary of unjust behavior that you yourself are doing. This puts them on the defensive, and deflects attention from your actions. Islam justifies this kind of mirror accusation with taqiyya.

The leftists of my time condone the same practice. A maxim they will sometimes admit to is: "Accuse your enemy of what you are doing, as you are doing it to create confusion." The above quote has been attributed to Karl Marx, Vladimir Lenin, and Saul Alinsky. Regardless of its origin, mirror accusation is a preferred tool for leftists. The Hadiths predict it will still be a tool of the Romans/Ruwaybidah, who make the end-time treaty with the Mahdi. Perhaps these Romans will be intellectual descendants of the leftists of my day.

All during the truce, the Muslims are warned to be on guard against the Romans, who have their own powerful military. The hadith says they "will soon summon one another to attack." This indicates that the truce will be tense on the Roman side as well, with their army always prepared to launch a preemptive assault.

Another hadith says there "will come a test which is pleasant ... produced by a man from the people of my house." This is a warning to beware Muslims who are co-opted by the Romans. "Then there will be the little black trial," whose details are not spelled out, but which will tempt the Muslims to be double-minded, to act like "a believer in the morning and an infidel in the evening." It will split them into "two camps: the camp of faith which will contain no hypocrisy, and the camp of hypocrisy which will contain no faith."

These warnings will come to pass in the next three sections. They will be connected with the appearance of the great enemy of the Mahdi, the

---

[97] Surkheel Abu Aaliyah, *Muslim Controversialists: Thriving on Fitnah on Social Media,* https://thehumblei.com/tag/who-are-the-ruwaybidah/, accessed March 5, 2023.

Dajjal, who in Muslim eyes will be the antichrist. When they start to happen, "expect the antichrist (the Dajjal) that day or the next."

Comparison. The Romans of the end-time Hadiths, and Revelation's woman of Babylon, both represent a revived Roman empire.

The Christian influence on the original Roman empire and the surrounding areas remained strong for almost 2,000 years. The resulting western civilization slowly matured to encompass all of Europe and the Americas. In the past three hundred years, Asia and Africa also came under its sway.

One of the defining truths of western civilization is the notion that there is such a thing as absolute truth. Universally valid truth is a product of the faithfulness of God, as evidenced by his integrity in the events of the Bible, and in the cohesiveness and internal agreement between all books of the Old and New Testament, whose writing he inspired over a period of 1,500 years. God then sent his son Jesus Christ into the world to be the embodiment of absolute truth:

> John 14:6 Jesus said to him, "I am the way, and the truth,
> and the life; no one comes to the Father except through Me."

Unlike the taqiyya practiced by followers of Muhammad, or the disinformation and propaganda leveraged by Marx and his leftist descendants, Jesus told his followers never to hide their beliefs:

> Matthew 5:14 "You are the light of the world. A city set on a
> hill cannot be hidden;
> 5:15 nor do people light a lamp and put it under a basket, but
> on the lampstand, and it gives light to all who are in the
> house.
> 5:16 Your light must shine before people in such a way that
> they may see your good works, and glorify your Father who
> is in heaven."

In the 20th century, Europe and then North America dispensed with the Christian practices of their ancestors, which were based on the teachings and example of Jesus. Instead, western civilization moved into a post-Christian age. Cultural and political elites dismantled much of the Judeo-Christian foundation. The various Protestant churches and the Roman Catholic church lost their relevance in the culture. Western society dispensed with the Bible and its principles for living.

In the place of the church, a politically correct and false religion has become dominant in Europe and the west. To replace God's ten commandments, an alternate set of commandments has arisen, in the form of thousands of regulations administered by a deep state of unelected bureaucrats, and promoted in all forms of media. They could be boiled down to "anti-commandments" which reward the following behaviors:

- celebration of self, and idolization of celebrity.
- abortion, the murder of the unborn.
- adultery and sexual deviancy.
- lying, often in the guise of disinformation, done in the service of progress (compare with taqiyya in Islam).
- stealing, euphemistically called redistribution of wealth, from people who produce, to privileged ones who take.

These behaviors are grievous sins against God. They go directly against his will for our lives as expressed in his commandments and his written word the Bible. They are deserving of his wrath. But a majority of people are currently devoted to feeding this culture, and enforcing conformity to this system. Personal freedom is sacrificed to the collective will. Anyone who has a personal relationship with Jesus Christ and who follows him as a disciple, is considered a threat to society.

The modern Europe of my time is no longer a set of nation states of Christian heritage distinguished by different languages and national pride. Instead, it has become a polyglot Babylon with migrants from the whole world. There are some left-over descendants that trace their roots to historic churches of centuries past. But most distance themselves from the identity of their ancestors, and have drifted a long way from being true to God's biblical standards of righteousness. Long ago they committed spiritual adultery by diluting any biblical thinking with pure humanism, and they persist in it. Europe and the west have forsaken its Christian underpinning by indulging in moral decay.

They are cementing in place the values of the coming woman of Babylon.

The post-Christian west also proclaims that it is against islamophobia. By this they wish to show solidarity with Muslims. To emphasize this, they marginalize Bible believers, accuse them of hate against Muslims, and justify the persecution of Christians and Jews.

The narrative of anti-islamophobia is bringing about a leftist-Islamic alliance in my time. This is happening even before the rapture, when still present are some believers true to God who remain in the church. But most of the western church has compromised its testimony in the attempt to avoid offending popular notions of globalism and Islam. Other Christians have withdrawn from interaction with the outside world, and no longer try to be God's instruments of common grace to unbelievers. They are not the salt and light to the world that God intended them to be. The church in less affluent countries is holding out somewhat longer.

As you can see, the foundations are already being built that could transition into the revived Roman empire of Revelation or the Hadiths.

Revelation's alliance between the beast and the woman of Babylon, or the Hadiths' armistice between the Mahdi and the Romans, could grow out of this unspoken leftist-Islamic alliance. For both sides, the ultimate stumbling stone is Jesus Christ, the son of God, who died on the cross as a substitute for repentant sinners. They see those who trust in Jesus as their great obstacle toward establishing a new world order.

If the rapture and tribulation happen soon, the current alliance may be formalized in a treaty between the Mahdi, who is the beast or Islamic antichrist, and the woman of Babylon, who symbolizes Europe and the post-Christian west. Both are determined to bring uniformity to the world. Muslims would advocate universal Sharia law to achieve this. The west would instead enforce the spread of permissive culture.

The Hadiths predict a final treaty between the Mahdi and the Romans, for a term of seven years. Through it the leftist-Islamic alliance could proclaim a lasting peace to the Middle East, unequaled in history. The treaty will be mediated by no less than a blood descendant of the Jewish priestly line of Aaron, the brother of Moses. The credit for the treaty will belong to the "prince who is to come" of Daniel:

> Daniel 9:27a And he [the prince who is to come mentioned in
> 9:26b] will confirm a covenant with the many for one week.

In the previous section K16, we saw that this prince who makes the treaty will be the antichrist, known as the beast in Revelation. In the Hadiths he will be the Mahdi.

In the next section, 11:1-2 K18 mentions a rebuilt temple in Jerusalem at the time of the treaty. The Jews will only have control over its inner portion. This would be one of the treaty's provisions.

To make such a definitive treaty, the antichrist or the Mahdi would need the reputation of being moderate, and trusted by most of the world. Israel will then rely on the sworn pledges. The Jews inhabiting Israel at that time will overlook the lessons of the Jews from my day, who are being repeatedly threatened with extermination by Islamists who wish to speed the coming of the Mahdi. But we shall see that after the Jews allow this treaty, God will lift their spiritual blindness.

This unprecedented treaty will probably be what convinces all the nations to swear allegiance to the leftist-Islamic alliance, and come under the jurisdiction of a single world order. The world would fall to the grand deception of the woman adulteress and the Mahdi, the champion of Allah *Khayrul-Makereen*, the "Greatest of all Deceivers." Operating behind the scenes is Satan, the one whom Jesus described as the ultimate deceiver:

> John 8:44b The devil ... was a murderer from the beginning,
> and does not stand in the truth because there is no truth in
> him. Whenever he tells a lie, he speaks from his own nature,
> because he is a liar and the father of lies.

In the Hadiths, the treaty with the Romans will be used to turn against a common enemy that does not recognize the new world order. Some Sunni commentators guess that the enemy will be Shi'as, and Shi'a commentators that it will be Sunnis.[98] Other Muslim commentators speculate that it will be Russia.[99] This would make more sense, since the Romans (Europeans) have been wary of Russia for centuries. Moreover, many Muslims wish for Constantinople to be reestablished as the

---

[98] Furnish, p.41.
[99] Rahma, p.55.

capital of the world caliphate, and the Russians instead want to usurp the role of Constantinople in history by replacing it with Moscow, the third Rome. Or the common enemy could be pockets of resistance among the nations who will not submit to the world order.

In the Bible's end-time accounts, there are two situations involving an unusual alliance facing a common enemy. The first is a Russian-Muslim alliance against Israel, pictured by many Christian commentators in the invasion of Israel from the north described in Ezekiel 38-39. That event will likely happen after the rapture, but before the tribulation. The invasion is defeated by God's supernatural intervention. The second situation is here in Revelation. The common enemy of the beast and the woman of Babylon, whom they will target for destruction, includes those who put their trust in Jesus.

The set of values promoted in the west of my time (and by the future woman of Babylon) includes the irrelevance of any divine being in the things of this world. This premise is blind to the fact that Muslims do not agree with this at all, in fact, violently so. They believe that all things in the world only happen by the will of Allah. Muslims also disagree with some of the leftist anti-commandments, such as those regarding abortion or sexual deviancy. They feel a hidden resentment that they are being leveraged to further a godless agenda. Their Marxist globalist allies of convenience are truly Ruwaybidah in their eyes, lacking in integrity, relying on rhetoric instead of any true religious basis, brazen in their declarations of how to build a just and perfect world.

If this situation extends into the tribulation, the result may well be a sudden breaking of the alliance, the overthrow of the woman of Babylon by the beast, or the unexpected conquering of the Romans by the Mahdi's armies. Such is the prophecy in upcoming sections of our timeline. The antichrist, the master of intrigue, will show his true colors:

> Daniel 11:22b also the prince of the covenant,
> 11:23 after an alliance is made with him he will practice deception, and he will go up and gain power with a small force of people.
> 11:24 In a time of tranquility he will enter the richest parts of the realm, and he will accomplish what his fathers did

not, nor his ancestors; he will distribute plunder, spoils, and
possessions among them, and he will devise his schemes
against strongholds, but only for a time.

K18 :

Preservation of a portion of the nation Israel through the tribulation

: H18

Allah wills three years of famine

12:13 And when the dragon saw that he was thrown down to the earth, he persecuted the woman who gave birth to the male Child. 12:6 Then the woman fled into the wilderness where she had a place prepared by God, so that there she would be nourished for 1,260 days.
12:14 But the two wings of the great eagle were given to the woman, so that she could fly into the wilderness to her place, where she was nourished for a time, times, and half a time, away from the presence of the serpent.
12:15 And the serpent hurled water like a river out of his mouth after the woman, so that he might cause her to be swept away with the flood.
12:16 But the earth helped the woman, and the earth opened its mouth and drank up the river which the dragon had hurled out of his mouth.

Before Dajjal appears there will be three difficult years in which the people will suffer severe famine. In the first year, Allah will command the sky to withhold one third of its rain and the earth to withhold one third of its produce. In the second year, He will command the sky to withhold two thirds of its rain and the earth to withhold two-thirds of its produce. In the third year, he will command the sky to withhold all of its rain, and not a single drop will fall, and the earth to withhold all of its produce, and nothing will grow. All cloven-hoofed animals will die, except those that Allah wills. What will the people live on at that time? *Tahlil, Takbir, Tasbih* and *Tahmid* [there is no God but Allah, Allah is greater, glory to be to Allah, and praise be to Allah]. That will take the place of food for them.[100] *(da'if)*

12:17 So the dragon was enraged with the woman, and went off to make war with the rest of her children, who keep the commandments of God and hold to the testimony of Jesus.
7:1 After this I saw four angels standing at the four corners of the earth, holding back the four winds of the earth so that no wind would blow on the earth, or on the sea, or on any tree.
7:2 And I saw another angel ascending from the rising of the sun, holding the seal of the living God; and he called out with a loud

---

[100] Narrated by Abu Umamah Al-Bahili, *Sunan Ibn Majah 4077*, Vol. 5, Book 36, Hadith 4077, https://sunnah.com/ibnmajah:4077, accessed May 18, 2024; also see `Ibn Azzat p.36.

voice to the four angels to whom it was granted to harm the earth
and the sea,
7:3 saying, "Do not harm the earth, or the sea, or the trees until we
have sealed the bond-servants of our God on their foreheads."
7:4 And I heard the number of those who were sealed: 144,000,
sealed from every tribe of the sons of Israel:
7:5 from the tribe of Judah, twelve thousand were sealed, from the
tribe of Reuben twelve thousand, from the tribe of Gad twelve
thousand,
7:6 from the tribe of Asher twelve thousand, from the tribe of
Naphtali twelve thousand, from the tribe of Manasseh twelve
thousand,
7:7 from the tribe of Simeon twelve thousand, from the tribe of
Levi twelve thousand, from the tribe of Issachar twelve thousand,
7:8 from the tribe of Zebulun twelve thousand, from the tribe of
Joseph twelve thousand, and from the tribe of Benjamin, twelve
thousand were sealed.
14:4 These are the ones who have not defiled themselves with
women, for they are celibate. These are the ones who follow the
Lamb wherever He goes. These have been purchased from mankind
as first fruits to God and to the Lamb.
11:1 Then there was given to me a measuring rod like a staff; and
someone said, "Get up and measure the temple of God and the
altar, and those who worship in it.
11:2 Leave out the courtyard which is outside the temple and do not
measure it, because it has been given to the nations; and they will
trample the holy city for forty-two months."

Revelation. The new world order of the woman of Babylon and the
beast arrives with totalitarian authority. They will target those who
oppose their beliefs and policies. The most vulnerable are Jews.
Unfortunately, the Jewish leaders have forgotten in this most crucial
time to turn to God in heaven. Instead, they are placing their trust in
deceptive promises written into a treaty.

The woman at the beginning of this section is not the woman of
Babylon, but the one who "gave birth to the male Child" (12:13). This is
an obvious reference to the nation of Israel, to which was born God's
promised Messiah, Jesus the Christ. The dragon opposing her is Satan,
who knew of the prophecies that the Messiah would come from the
Jews. Though the evil one expended great efforts to stop this, by God's
plan Jesus was nonetheless born in a manger, died on a cross, rose from
the dead, and ascended alive up to heaven to sit at the right hand of the
Father.

Here at the beginning of the tribulation, Satan once again singles out Israel as his special target for persecution. He does this through his agents the woman of Babylon and the beast.

At the end of this section, the temple in Jerusalem is mentioned (11:1-2). In his vision, John is directed to measure its inner court, also known as the court of the priests (2 Chronicles 4:9). This place includes the Holy Place and the Holy of Holies. That is the area where only the Jewish priests were allowed to enter.

Ever since the last temple was destroyed in 70 CE, many conservative Jews have longed for it to be rebuilt, and the Old Testament sacrificial system to be reestablished. They put their hope in this, instead of putting their faith in the person of Jesus. They refuse to see that God sent Jesus to be the final sacrifice for sin, once and for all time. God desires no more sacrifices.

But at some time before the tribulation, God has allowed the temple to be rebuilt as a place of renewed sacrifices. This is a sign of his favor to the Jews, but not as a means for their salvation. It is given to them in their unbelief, now that the church is gone and Jesus is currently with the church saints in heaven.

The temple of the tribulation becomes a rallying point for many Jews in this terrible time.

Apparently by the terms of the treaty, the outer court of the temple is under the control of the new world government. Gentiles (non-Jews) take advantage of this. They will disrespect the outer court, and the rest of Jerusalem, and will "trample the holy city" (11:2) for the next three and a half years.

The Bible tells us that in these last days, there will be another movement of Jews. Many will realize that blood sacrifices in the temple will not save them. Only by the blood of Jesus, shed on the cross, can anyone be saved from their sins and be reconciled to God. After the church has been raptured to heaven, a great number of Jews will embrace Jesus as their Messiah:

> Romans 11:25 For I do not want you, brothers and sisters, to be uninformed of this mystery—so that you will not be wise in your own estimation—that a partial hardening has

happened to Israel until the fullness of the Gentiles has come
in;
11:26 and so all Israel will be saved; just as it is written:
"The Deliverer will come from Zion, He will remove
ungodliness from Jacob."
11:27 "This is My covenant with them, When I take away
their sins."
11:28 In relation to the gospel they are enemies on your
account, but in relation to God's choice they are beloved on
account of the fathers.

In this section of Revelation, the woman beloved by God flees from the
dragon into the wilderness, where he feeds and protects her for three
and a half years (12:6). This is God's caring for the Jews who turn to
Jesus during the first half of the tribulation. He "seals" twelve thousand
of their new believers from each of the twelve tribes of Israel to become
his special evangelists. There will be 144,000 in total (7:4).[101] God
promises them deliverance from the serpent (12:14), from the
mysterious flood that will be sent by the serpent (12:15-16), and from
the continuous war waged by Satan on those who turn to Jesus (12:17).

The 144,000 will not die during the tribulation. They will be fearless,
despite censorship and persecution. They will be focused, and will avoid
--the sexual temptations offered by the world culture of Babylon (14:4).
Their testimonies about the good news of Jesus will lead many other
Jews to sorrow for their past treatment of Jesus, and to make *Yeshua
HaMashiakh* king of their hearts. God has been waiting for this time to
reward unprecedented numbers of his chosen people with everlasting
life. Zechariah prophesies of this in the Old Testament:

Zechariah 12:8 On that day the Lord will protect the
inhabitants of Jerusalem, and the one who is feeble among
them on that day will be like David, and the house of David
will be like God, like the angel of the Lord before them.
12:10 "And I will pour out on the house of David and on the
inhabitants of Jerusalem the Spirit of grace and of pleading,
so that they will look at Me whom they pierced; and they
will mourn for Him, like one mourning for an only son, and

---

[101] The tribes of Dan and Ephraim are omitted from this listing, perhaps because they
were connected with idolatry in Israel (1 Kings 12:25-33). But Ephraim is covered here
under the tribe of Joseph his father, and Dan is named in the future distribution of land
on the eternal new Earth in Ezekiel 48:2.

they will weep bitterly over Him like the bitter weeping over
a firstborn."

However, only 144,000 Jews, a biblically significant number, are the
sealed ones who will be preserved from death. Many other Jews will
also turn to Jesus, but for this they will die at the hands of the
persecutors. We shall see in K26 they will enter into the martyred
throng of souls in heaven. These victims for Jesus' sake will receive an
eternal reward in the resurrection of the righteous martyrs at the end of
the tribulation (K43).

God will use the 144,000 untouchables of Israel as a channel of witness
to the non-Jews of the world. This would be in keeping with his
purposes for the chosen people. Many gentiles will be disgusted by the
world system put forward by the woman of Babylon, and the alternate
system pushed on them by the beast. They will wonder what happened
to the Christians who disappeared. The truth about the rapture will leak
out. The question will become, "how can I be saved?" The Old
Testament prophet Zechariah prophesied about these 144,000 Jewish
evangelists bringing people to Christ in the end time:

> Zechariah 8:20 "The LORD of armies says this: 'It will yet
> turn out that peoples will come, that is, the inhabitants of
> many cities.
> 8:21 The inhabitants of one city will go to another, saying,
> "Let's go at once to plead for the favor of the Lord, and to
> seek the Lord of armies; I also will go." 8:22 So many
> peoples and mighty nations will come to seek the LORD of
> armies in Jerusalem, and to plead for the favor of the LORD.'
> 8:23 The LORD of armies says this: 'In those days ten people
> from all the nations will grasp the garment of a Jew, saying,
> "Let us go with you, for we have heard that God is with
> you."'"

The witness of the Jewish evangelists will persuade many to follow
Christ, even if it costs them their life.

Hadiths. In the previous section, the Mahdi has achieved a share of
world power by making a treaty with the Romans. But his Muslim
followers are warned to be on guard against these allies, their treachery,
and their temptations. They should see them as precursors of the even

greater treachery and temptations to come, in the person of the Dajjal, who will be the champion of the Jews and new converts to Christianity.

The hadith says that Allah will prepare the people of the world before the Dajjal's coming, by subjecting them to drought and famine. In the timeline of the Hadiths, this happens during the joint rule of the Mahdi and the Romans. The trial stretches for three years. People will be divided in their response. Those who put their trust in Allah and his savior the Mahdi will accept this trial. Their food will be to say "there is no God but Allah, Allah is greater, glory to be to Allah, and praise be to Allah." Others will not do this, but will fall for the material temptations of the Dajjal when he comes. By this trial, the Mahdi and his followers will know who is false toward Allah.

Comparison. In both Revelation and the Hadiths there will be a time of trial before the deliverer of the Jews comes.

Revelation says that the dragon Satan will bring persecution to the Jews (12:13). Satan will create flood conditions upon their land (12:15), and send military forces against them (12:17). He will scheme to withhold food from them (12:6,14), but the result will be that God will provide for them supernaturally. All this occurs before the two witnesses are sent by God to Jerusalem. In the next section, they will defend God's name, and will stand for the Messianic Jewish and the new Jesus-followers among the gentiles.

In the Hadiths, it is Allah, not Shaytan, who arranges for three severe years before the Dajjal comes, years of hunger and drought. Though the hadith does not mention that the Jews are his specific target, the fact that the hunger is connected with the coming of the Dajjal, points to the Jews as the reason why Allah is angry.

This trial of humanity is in keeping with the character of Allah. The 91st of the 99 names of Allah is *Ad-Dharr*, the Distressor.[102] The Arabic root is d-r-r. As a verb it means to harm, or to damage; as a noun, calamity, damage, loss, harm, hurt, bodily affliction, leanness.[103] Thus, Ad-Dhaar

---

[102] *99 Names of Allah (Al Asma Ul Husna)*, https://99namesofallah.name, accessed March 12, 2023.
[103] https://en.m.wiktionary.org/wiki/%D8%B6%D8%B1#Arabic, accessed March 12, 2023.

literally means the causer of harm, the afflicter and creator of suffering. It is also the word used to address vermin and anything nasty.[104] By contrast, the God of the Bible sent his son Jesus to heal the sick, preach to the lost, and raise people from the dead. It is Satan who torments people with calamity, sickness, sin and death.

The food famine sent by Allah in the Hadiths has another counterpart in Revelation. Satan, through the materialism and sexualized culture of the woman, brings a spiritual famine upon the world. Men and women lose their God-consciousness, and are reduced to a plane even lower than the animals.

There are additional comparisons. The time period specified in the hadith, three years, matches the timeline of Revelation. The three years occurs within the first half of the seven-year tribulation, and before the second half or great tribulation. Shortly before the great tribulation, God will send two witnesses to Jerusalem (K19). That is also when the Dajjal is expected (H19).

Revelation sees a re-built temple in Jerusalem, whose outer courts are trashed by gentiles for three and a half years. The Jews are not in a position to compel better treatment for their temple, because they have bound themselves by treaty. This matches what will occur in the Hadiths of the next section. We shall see that the Arabs have gathered in Jerusalem to oppose the workings of the Jews.

---

[104] Shoebat, p. 154.

K19 :
The two witnesses come before the great tribulation begins

: H19
The Dajjal opposes the Mahdi with miracles, but Arabs remain in Jerusalem to fight the false Messiah with the truth

11:3‡K34 And I will grant authority to my two witnesses, and they will prophesy for 1,260 days, clothed in sackcloth.
11:4 These are the two olive trees and the two lampstands that stand before the Lord of the earth.
11:5 And if anyone wants to harm them, fire flows out of their mouth and devours their enemies; and so if anyone wants to harm them, he must be killed in this way.
11:6 These have the power to shut up the sky, so that rain will not fall during the days of their prophesying; and they have power over the waters to turn them into blood, and to strike the earth with every plague, as often as they desire.

Ibn ʿAbbas said, I did not sleep last night at all. They said that the Dajjal and the Mahdi will be alive at the same time. So I did not sleep all night.[105]

The Dajjal would appear in my *Ummah* [community] and he would stay (in the world) for forty – I cannot say whether he meant forty days, forty months or forty years.[106]

There will not be a trial on the earth since Allah disseminated the progeny of Adam, peace be upon him, worse than that of the Dajjal.... If he comes when I am not among you, each man must look out for himself and Allah will take care of every Muslim on my behalf. He will appear from the region between Syria and Iraq and will spread mischief right and left. Oh slaves of Allah, be firm! ... he will appear and say, "I am a Prophet and there is no Prophet after me. I am your Lord," but you will not see your Lord until you die. He is one-eyed and your Lord is not one eyed. Written between his eyes is "Unbeliever" [*kaafir*/infidel]. Every

---

105 Narrated by Ibn ʿAbbas (cousin of Muhammad), in Ibn Kathir, *Tafsir*, cited in ʿIbn Izzat p.21.
106 Narrated by Abdullah b. 'Amr, *Sahih Muslim 2940a*, Book 41, Hadith 7023, https://sunnah.com/muslim:2940a, accessed May 18, 2024; also quoted in ʿIbn Izzat p.32.

believer, whether literate or illiterate, will be able to read it.[107]

Allah is not one-eyed, and behold that Dajjal is blind of the right eye and his eye would be like a floating grape.[108]

Dajjal is blind of left eye with thick hair and there would be a garden and fire with him and his fire would be a garden and his garden would be fire.[109]

The Messenger of Allah … said … if he appears while I am among you, I will contend with him on your behalf, and if he appears when I am not among you, then each man must fend for himself, and Allah will take care of every Muslim on my behalf…. The Dajjal … will command the sky to rain and it will rain, and he will command the earth to produce vegetation and it will do so, and their flocks will come back in the evening with their humps taller, their udders fuller and their flanks fatter than they have ever been …. Then he will pass through the wasteland and will say: "Bring forth your treasures," then go away, and its treasures will follow him like a swarm of bees. Then he will call a man brimming with youth and will strike him with a sword and cut him in two. He will put the two pieces as far apart as the distance between an archer and his target. Then he will call him and he will come with his face shining, laughing.[110] *(sahih)*

Where will the Arabs be on that day? On that day they will be few in number and most of them will be in Jerusalem.[111] *(da'if)*

A group of my community will continue to fight for the Truth and overcome those who resist them until the last of them fights the false Messiah.[112] *(sahih)*

---

[107] Narrated by Abu Umama al-Bahili, quoted in `Ibn Izzat p.33.

[108] Narrated by Ibn Umar, *Sahih Muslim 169 e*, Book 41, Hadith 7005, https://sunnah.com/muslim:169e, accessed May 18, 2024, also in Richardson p.72.

[109] Narrated by Hudhaifa, *Sahih Muslim 2934 a*, Book 41, Hadith 7010, https://sunnah.com/muslim:2934a, accessed May 19, 2024; also referenced in Richardson p.72.

[110] Narrated by Nawwas bin Sam'an Al-Kilobit, *Sunan Ibn Majah 4075*, Vol. 5, Book 36, Hadith 4075, https://sunnah.com/ibnmajah:4075, accessed May 20, 2024; also partially referenced in `Ibn Izzat p.34.

[111] Narrated by Abu Umamah Al-Bahili, *Sunan Ibn Majah 4077*, Vol. 5, Book 36, Hadith 4077, https://sunnah.com/ibnmajah:4077, accessed May 20, 2024; also partially referenced in `Ibn Izzat p.34-35.

[112] Narrated by Mu`adh ibn Jabal, in al-Bukhari, and Muslim, quoted in `Ibn Izzat p.27; see also narrated by Imran ibn Husayn, *Sunan Abi Dawud 2484*, Book 14, Hadith 2478, https://sunnah.com/abudawud:2484, accessed May 20, 2024.

Revelation. God sends two unusual characters onto the scene. In 11:8 K34, their location is specified as the place where Jesus was crucified, which is the holy city of Jerusalem.

Their names are not given. They are only described as two witnesses, and as two prophets (11:10 K34). They will prophesy for 42 months (11:3). We will see them again later in the timeline, toward the close of the second three and a half years (K34). From this we can calculate that they first appear toward the end of the first three and a half years, while the woman of Babylon is still jointly ruling with the beast.

They are likened to two lampstands (11:4). This is because they are a source of shining truth to Jerusalem and the world. They are also called two olive trees. In John's day, olive oil was the preferred fuel for lamps. The olive oil in the witnesses' lamps represents God's Holy Spirit. God has sent them to be his light-bearers during this terrible time of suffering, brought about by the deceit of the dominant godless forces.

There are two of them, because:

> 2 Corinthians 13:1b On the testimony of two or three
> witnesses every matter shall be confirmed.

The two speak truth to authority. The world order cannot tolerate them, and takes extreme action. But God gives them miraculous powers to withstand those who hate them. They have the ability to speak literal flames of fire (11:5). This invokes the memory of the Old Testament prophet Elijah. On two successive occasions the godless king Ahab sent companies of fifty soldiers to arrest him, and twice Elijah called fire from heaven to consume them. The third company approached him with humility, and were spared (2 Kings 1:9-15). The two witnesses demonstrate similar power, which compels many to fear the Almighty God of heaven who sent them.

The future government, if it is anything like the globalist politicians of my day, may claim that it needs the greatest power possible to stop runaway climate change from forever damaging the planet. But only God has such awesome power. He gives the two witnesses the ability to command rains to stop worldwide (11:6a). By this they demonstrate that only God can put forth the awesome energy to quickly change weather systems over thousands of kilometers. This again reminds us of

Elijah, who prayed that Israel would not have rain for three and half years (James 5:17). God answered that prayer. He used Elijah to show the Israelites His power over the false god Baal, whom many had started worshipping. It is interesting that the two witnesses are present for the same length of time as Elijah's trial of drought.

They also have power to turn waters into blood (11:6b). Possibly this happens when soldiers sent against them are struck down at their command, and drown in the sea.

The witnesses also have the ability to send plagues upon the earth (11:6c).

The bloodied waters and the plagues invoke the memory of Moses, the prophet-leader sent by God to free the Israelites from Egyptian slavery under Pharaoh. In response, Pharaoh hardened his own heart, and would not allow the Jews to worship the true God of heaven. God, through Moses, then turned the water of the Nile to blood, and sent upon all of Egypt a series of plagues (Exodus 7-12): of frogs, of gnats, flies, cattle sickness, boils, hail, locusts, and of darkness. The last plague was the death of all the firstborn sons of the Egyptians and firstborn of their cattle. There is circumstantial evidence that many Egyptians, when they saw the power of God against their evil rulers, joined the Israelites in the exodus across the Red Sea to the promised land. They were included in the abundant blessings that God then gave his people. The two witnesses will evoke a similar response.

At the end of his life on earth, Elijah did not die, but was transported up to heaven in a flying chariot. The body of Moses was never found, despite a painstaking search. Centuries later, both came briefly from heaven to earth to be witnesses to the transfiguration (glorification) of Jesus (Matthew 17:1-8). If God has another special mission on earth for their afterlife, it may be that they will be the two witnesses of Revelation, returned to earth to represent him in front of the beast and his followers.

Whether the witnesses are Elijah and Moses, or two new Jewish prophets whom God raises up among the tribulation converts to Jesus, they are a continuous frustration to the woman, the beast, and their government. Their miraculous power attracts great attention, and makes plain the powerlessness of the anti-God authorities who claim to be supreme.

Even the garb of the witnesses points people to God. They are always clothed in sackcloth (11:3). Seeing someone who humbles themself to the extreme of wearing sackcloth, makes people think of their own lack of humility, the need to repent of their sins, and to beg God for forgiveness.

The level of extreme response directed against the witnesses only indicates how successful they are delivering others from the beast and from Satan. They turn many to Christ, the son of God, the giver of life.

Hadiths. The Hadiths expect the Dajjal, the greatest enemy of the Mahdi, to appear after the Mahdi's forces shatter the Roman armies and conquer Constantinople, which allowed the Mahdi to become the preeminent world ruler. They are silent on the Dajjal's activities before then.

But in the previous section, the prelude of three years of famine and drought prior to the Dajjal, suggests that he could start his work right afterward. That would be at a time while the Romans still have joint power with the Mahdi.

At the beginning of the timeline, in H00, we saw the preliminary hadith that warned: "there will not be any tribulation on earth, since the time Allah created the offspring of Adam, that will be greater than the tribulation of Dajjal." In this section, he has arrived, and we have another hadith that gives a similar warning. One more in H00 tells us that the Dajjal is one of the Major Signs of the end.

The Dajjal's full title is *Al-Maseeh Ad-Dajjal*, the Messiah Liar and Deceiver.[113]

He will be the worst trial of the Major Signs, because no one will ever be more successful at tempting people to leave Islam than he. The Hadiths tell that he will remain for forty periods of time, but they wonder whether those are days, months or years. The Mahdi's followers will not sleep at night, knowing that the Dajjal will come sometime during his

---

[113] Smith and Haddad, p.68.

rule. He will first "appear from the region between Syria and Iraq and will spread mischief right and left." When he comes, "each man must fend for himself, and Allah will take care of every Muslim."

The Dajjal will claim to be the final prophet, greater than the Mahdi or even Muhammad. He will work miracles to uphold this claim. He will bring down rain from the sky, and command the earth to grow crops.

He will be blind in the left eye, with the word "unbeliever" written between his eyes, visible to all true Muslims. Their special sight will show them that he cannot possibly be the final prophet. But false Muslims will be fooled.

When the Dajjal comes, the Arabs will be few in number to oppose him. Presumably most of them are occupied elsewhere with finishing the defeat of the Romans, and leading the Muslim community to extend the rule of the Mahdi over areas where the Romans had jurisdiction. Those Arabs that are in the region where the Dajjal is active are concentrated in Jerusalem. This would indicate that the Mahdi regards that holy city, which he conquered and subjected to treaty, as his capital. Jerusalem will be in the grasp of the Mahdi.

Jerusalem (and Damascus, see H24) are much more prominent in Islamic eschatology than Mecca and Medina. This is supported by the hadith of H16, which said that the Mahdi's army from Khorasan would plant their black flags of victory at *Bait al-Maqdis* or "holy house", the Islamic district of Jerusalem.

Bait al-Maqdis covers nearly one sixth of the walled city of Jerusalem, and includes *Al-Haram al-Sharif*, consisting of thirty-five acres of buildings, gardens and famous domes. At its southernmost side is the *Al-Aqsa* mosque, and in the middle the celebrated Dome of the Rock shrine. During the initial years of his prophethood, Muhammad offered his prayers in the divinely ordained direction *(qibla)* of Bait al-Maqdis. However, after constant ridicule by Jewish tribes, Allah directed him to a change in the qibla, from Jerusalem to the Kaaba in Mecca.[114] It has always been the dream of Muslims to occupy Bait al-Maqdis and the

---

[114] Amna Anwaar, https://www.islamicfinder.org/news/history-of-qibla-the-shift-from-bait-ul-maqdas-to-masjid-al-haram/, accessed March 17, 2023.

rest of Jerusalem. This will erase the insults of the Jews which caused Allah to change the qibla.

The Mahdi's jurisdiction over Jerusalem will find another challenger after the demise of the Romans – the Dajjal. The Mahdi's forces will be ready to respond. The hadith says that, though the Muslims may be few at times, a group of them "will continue to fight for the Truth and overcome those who resist them until the last of them fights the false Messiah [the Dajjal]."

Even in my day, many Muslims look forward to the day when their future warriors will fight the Dajjal and his forces. They seek to emulate these Hadiths and the Qur'an, by carrying out violent jihad. They can thus train for Islam to be triumphant in the end time, in preparation for the Mahdi.

Comparison. In both Revelation and the Hadiths, opposition arises against the supreme ruler from a different quarter than his treaty ally. In Islam he is the Dajjal, who poses a greater threat to the Mahdi than the Romans. In Revelation, it is the two witnesses, who are more problematic to the beast than the woman of Babylon. After the witnesses leave the scene in K35, the Lord Jesus Christ will arrive to oppose the beast.

By this close parallel, we see that the Dajjal is the Islamic composite of the two witnesses and Jesus Christ.

The hadith says that the Dajjal will operate for an unknown period of time, either forty days, months or years. Revelation tells us the two witnesses are active for forty-two months, beginning toward the end of the first three and a half years. Forty months is therefore a very good match from the Hadiths, since it is about the period of time that the witnesses take over from the woman of Babylon as the chief obstacle to the antichrist's rule.

In Revelation, the beast will send out forces to Jerusalem. They will try any scheme to limit the two witnesses, and re-interpret the truths that they proclaim. In the Hadiths, it will be the Arabs in Jerusalem, though initially few in number, who stand for the proclamations of the Mahdi against what they perceive as the lies of the Dajjal.

The two witnesses have miraculous power to speak with fire from their mouths, command the rains to stop, turn waters into blood, and send plagues upon the earth. Their intent is to push back on the persecution of the beast and his lieutenants, and to turn suffering people away from the beast toward the true God. The Dajjal will also work miracles. He will call down the rain, and command bountiful crops to grow. No one will be more successful at turning people away from Islam.

The Dajjal will claim to be the final prophet. In Revelation, Jesus Christ will be that one.

This is more proof of the dependence of the Hadiths upon the Bible. Or could it possibly prove the Bible's preeminence?

K20 :

The sins of Babylon subject her to God's wrath

: H20

Seductive women and wealth have their way before the last hour

17:1‡[K02,K17] Then one of the seven angels who had the seven bowls came and spoke with me, saying, "Come here, I will show you the judgment of the great prostitute *who sits on many waters,*
17:2 with whom the kings of the earth committed acts of sexual immorality, and those who live on the earth became drunk with the wine of her sexual immorality,
18:12 [on] cargo of gold, silver, precious stones, and pearls; fine linen, purple, silk, and scarlet; every kind of citron wood, every article of ivory, and every article made from very valuable wood, bronze, iron, and marble;
18:13 cinnamon, spice, incense, perfume, frankincense, wine, olive oil, fine flour, wheat, cattle, sheep, and cargo of horses, carriages, slaves, and human lives."
17:6 And I saw the woman drunk with the blood of the saints, and with the blood of the witnesses of Jesus. When I saw her, I wondered greatly.

The last hour will not come before there is much wealth among you. It will overflow to the point the owner of wealth will be worried about who will accept his *sadaqa* (alms) and until the person to whom he offers it says, No I have no need of it.[115]

A time will come when a man will go about with alms from his gold and will not find anyone to receive it. One man will be seen being followed by forty women dependent upon him on account of the scarcity of men and excess of women.[116]

From among the portents of the Hour are the following: religious knowledge will be taken away; general ignorance (in religious matters) will increase; illegal sexual intercourse will prevail: drinking of alcoholic drinks will prevail. Men will decrease in number, and women will increase in number, so much so that fifty women will be looked after by one man.[117]

---

[115] Abu Huraira, in al-Bukhari and Muslim, quoted in `Ibn Izzat p.63; also narrated by Abu Huraira, *Sahih Muslim 157 d*, Book 5, Hadith 2209, https://sunnah.com/muslim:157d, accessed May 21, 2024.
[116] Narrated by Abu Musa Al-Ash'ari, *Riyad as-Salihin 1825*, Book 18, Hadith 18, https://sunnah.com/riyadussalihin:1825, accessed May 21, 2024; also referenced in `Ibn Izzat p.62-63.
[117] Narrated by Anas, *Sahih al-Bukhari 5231*, Vol. 7, Book 62, Hadith 158, https://sunnah.com/bukhari:5231, accessed May 21, 2024; also referenced in `Ibn Izzat p.63.

18:24 And in her was found the blood of prophets and of saints, and of all who have been slaughtered on the earth.

18:6 Pay her back even as she has paid, and give back to her double according to her deeds; in the cup which she has mixed, mix twice as much for her.

18:7 To the extent that she glorified herself and lived luxuriously, to the same extent give her torment and mourning; for she says in her heart, 'I sit as a queen and I am not a widow, and will never see mourning.'

18:8‡[K21,K25] For this reason *in one day* her plagues will come, *plague and mourning and famine, and she will be burned up with fire; for the Lord God who judges her is strong.*

18:21 Then a strong angel picked up a stone like a great millstone and threw it into the sea, saying, "So will Babylon, the great city, be thrown down with violence, and will never be found again.

18:22 And the sound of harpists, musicians, flute players, and trumpeters will never be heard in you again; and no craftsman of any craft will ever be found in you again; and the sound of a mill will never be heard in you again;

18:23 and the light of a lamp will never shine in you again; and the voice of the groom and bride will never be heard in you again; for your merchants were the powerful people of the earth, because all the nations were deceived by your witchcraft."

There are two types of people of the Fire whom I have not seen: people who have whips like oxtails with which they beat people, and women who are clothed yet naked, with hair piled high like the humps of camels, who are inclined (to evil) and make their husbands inclined towards it. They will not enter the Garden or even smell its scent although its scent can be smelled at such-and-such a distance.[118]

You are like the nations of the tribe of Israel and you will follow their path step-by-step until there is nothing they have that you do not have as well, to the point that people will be approached by a woman and one of them will go to her and lie with her and then returned to his friends and laugh with them.[119]

A man will go to a woman and lie with her in the road or will lift her skirt as the tail of a sheep is lifted. The best and most excellent of people on that day will be those who say, "If you would only conceal yourself behind that wall." In that time such a man will be like Abu Bakr and ʿUmar.[120]

---

[118] Narrated by Abu Harairah, in Muslim, quoted in ʿIbn Izzat p.55; also narrated by Abu Hurairah, *Riyad as-Salihin 1633*, Book 17, Hadith 123, https://sunnah.com/riyadussalihin:1633, accessed May 21, 2024.
[119] Narrated by Ibn Masʿud, in At-Tabarani, quoted in ʿIbn Izzat p.54.
[120] Narrated by Abu Yaʿla, quoted in ʿIbn Izzat p.64.

Revelation. An angel appears to announce the judgment that God will soon send upon the woman of Babylon, the prostitute. She is due punishment because of her persistent wickedness during the first three and a half years of the tribulation, leading the whole world into sin (17:1-2).

Her spiritual heritage goes back to Babel, and the tower its inhabitants built into the sky. It was an audacious attempt to reach heaven without God. The woman's spirit was also present in the great empire kingdoms that spanned the period of the Old Testament (17:9-10 K02). They sought universal dominion over this world, instead of guidance from the Lord Almighty.

The woman of Revelation prefers sexual sin as her mode of ensnaring people. She offers the free love of adultery and promiscuity with no responsibility, and she trades in "human lives" (18:13, perhaps a reference to the modern-day murder industry of abortion).

This lifestyle of sex is sustainable in the context of wealth (17:2). In his vision John saw the most desirable luxuries of his day: precious stones, costly metals, fine fabrics in opulent colors, expensive perfumes and spices, a variety of foods, abundant possessions, and the latest in transportation (18:12-13). You can imagine this multiplied exponentially with the technological advancements of modern times. But materialism becomes an idol. It tends to eclipse all awareness of God, who is the one who makes material blessings possible, and sustains billions of people by them. How easy will it be to dispense with God and indulge in material things and sexual experimentation, under the governance of the woman of Babylon,

All this treasure of Babylon is about to be destroyed with fire (18:8 K21).

The woman promotes any religious systems that accommodate behaviors contrary to God's standards of righteousness. For the woman and her lovers, the entire concept of sin is to be rejected. But her alliance with the beast will be the last of her spiritual affairs. It won't be enduring. We will see that the beast does not adhere to her values, but will enforce his own.

This is the post-rapture world. It will be extremely difficult. By his mercy, God has beforehand evacuated all true Christians who have put their trust in Christ.

In this environment, some who are left come to their senses and realize that the systems of the world are leading them to an eternal doom. They become open to the good news of repentance and forgiveness proclaimed by the 144,000 Jewish evangelists (Zechariah 8:20-23 K18) and the two witnesses. The result is a widespread revival, a spiritual harvest of people whom God will welcome into heaven.

The government of the woman does not tolerate such non-conformists, who undermine the playground-on-earth they wish to build. So they compound their temptations with systematic persecution of these converts. They become "drunk with the blood of the saints, and the blood of the witnesses of Jesus." They execute this oppression with such thorough efficiency, that they will strike fear far and wide (17:6).

But judgment is soon to come upon the woman and the system she represents. The angel of the vision calls on God to pay her back double for all her sins (18:6), to turn her self-glorification into torment and sorrow.

The one who styles herself the world's queen will see destruction in the space of one day (18:8 K21). Babylon will be thrown down, like a great millstone plunged into the sea (18:21). Her sudden end will be like the original Babylon. Its king, Belshazzar, watched the finger of God write words of judgment on the wall. That night the Medo-Persian army swarmed into the city. In less than a day, Babylon met its end (Daniel 5).

When the Babylon of the tribulation falls, the revived Roman empire is finished. Its factories will halt production, designers will stop work, entertainers will lose their audiences, and its luxuries will not be available. The necessities of life will soon become scarce. The world economy will be incapable of supporting all the billions of people in the world.

In the next section we will see who is responsible for this global calamity.

Hadiths. There are some Hadiths looking forward to the end times that also mention opulent wealth, seductive women, and rampant adultery. These are among the trials that descend upon the world before the Mahdi consolidates his authority.

In certain districts, people will be so wealthy that there will be no one to accept their charity *(sadaqa)*. Wine and alcohol, forbidden in the Qur'an, are lawful and ever-present.

There will be a shortage of men, possibly because many are serving in the various armies, or have been killed.

Fornication is permitted and is even encouraged. Woman who are all but naked, entrap the remaining men into open sex, with no shame of Allah or anyone else. Men and women mix freely with no regard to marriage vows. There is no jealousy, no modesty, no fear of Allah. Vileness is perpetuated. The result is moral disintegration and family dysfunction.

At this time, the culture that Muhammad warned against is everywhere. Even Muslim areas are infected with this licentiousness, because of the influence of European colonizers. Muslim writers and thinkers of the end times justify this compromise in the name of progress and advancement. Sharia is not enforced. But true Muslims will combat this corruption, out of zeal for the prohibitions of Allah.[121]

This is the world offered by the Romans, whom the Mahdi has temporarily co-opted to achieve his ultimate goal.

Comparison. These Hadiths are difficult to place in the timeline when only considering other Hadiths. But the account of Revelation helps us to snap them into the proper place of the sequence, and to identify the powers behind these temptations.

In Revelation, the sponsor of this promiscuous culture is the woman of Babylon, the great prostitute. The equivalent power in the Hadiths is the Romans.

The woman is completely different in her opposition to the beast than are the two witnesses (and Jesus Christ who will take their place). The

---

[121] `Ibn Izzat p. 54-55, 64-65.

same could be said of the Islamic version of the end time – the Romans' opposition to the Mahdi is of completely different character than the Dajjal's. The one opponent is godless hedonism, the other is an appeal to the Bible and the triune God that it speaks of. Most Muslim interpreters make the mistake of seeing the end-time Romans and new converts to Jesus as being similar in their outlook against Islam. They are mistaken. The two will be completely different.

The antichrist beast and the Mahdi must deal with both sets of opponents in turn. The first one that he will dispense with will be godlessness, as represented by Europe, North America, and the post-Christian west.

K21 :

The great tribulation begins
with the beast launching
war and the fall of Babylon

: H21

Allah's followers purge out
those who are
compromised, and defeat
the tyrannical rulers

6:3 When He broke the second
seal, I heard the second living
creature saying, "Come!"
6:4 And another, a red horse,
went out; and to him who sat on
it, it was granted to take peace
from the earth, and that people
would kill one another; and a
large sword was given to him.
13:1 And the dragon stood on the
sand of the seashore. Then I saw a
beast coming up out of the sea,
having ten horns and seven heads,
and on his horns were ten crowns,
and on his heads were
blasphemous names.
13:2 And the beast that I saw was
like a leopard, and his feet were
like those of a bear, and his mouth
like the mouth of a lion. And the
dragon gave him his power and
his throne, and great authority.
17:12 The ten horns which you
saw are ten kings who have not
yet received a kingdom, but they
receive authority as kings with
the beast for one hour.
17:13 These have one purpose, and
they give their power and
authority to the beast.
17:16 And the ten horns which you
saw, and the beast, these will hate
the prostitute and will make her

Thou wouldst think they were
united, but their hearts are divided.
(Surah 59:14)

No ruler is appointed but he has
two groups of advisers: A group
which urges him to do good and
tells him not to do evil, and a group
which does its best to corrupt him.
Whoever is protected from their
evil is indeed protected. And he
(the ruler) belongs to the group
that has the greater influence over
him.[122] *(sahih)*

Woe to this community from
tyrannical rulers! How they will kill
and terrorize Allah-fearing people,
except for those who appear to
obey them! Some Allah-fearing
Believers will pretend to cooperate
with them with their tongues but
flee from them in their hearts.
When Allah Almighty wants to
restore the power of Islam, he will
crush every stubborn tyrant.[123]

If there only remained a single day
of this world, Allah would lengthen
that day until a man from the
people of my house was given
control over it. Battles will take
place under his command and
Islam will be victorious.[124]

---

[122] Narrated by Abu Hurairah, *Sunan an-Nasa'i 4201*, Vol. 5, Book 39, Hadith 4206,
https://sunnah.com/nasai:4201, accessed May 22, 2024; also referenced in Rahma p.14
[123] Narrated by Hudhayfa, in Abu Nu`aym and al-Isfahani, quoted in `Ibn Izzat p.26-27.
[124] Narrated by Hudhayfa, in Abu Nu`aym, and in al-Isfahani, quoted in `Ibn Izzat p.27.

desolate and naked, and will eat her flesh and will burn her up with fire.

17:17 For God has put it in their hearts to execute His purpose by having a common purpose, and by giving their kingdom to the beast, until the words of God will be fulfilled.

14:8 And another angel, a second one, followed, saying, "Fallen, fallen is Babylon the great, she who has made all the nations drink of the wine of the passion of her sexual immorality."

18:8‡[K20,K25] For this reason in one day her plagues will come, *plague and mourning and famine,* and she will be burned up with fire; for the Lord God who judges her is strong.

18:11 "And the merchants of the earth weep and mourn over her, because no one buys their cargo any more—

18:14 The fruit you long for has left you, and all things that were luxurious and splendid have passed away from you and people will no longer find them."

18:15 The merchants of these things, who became rich from her, will stand at a distance because of the fear of her torment, weeping and mourning,

18:16 saying, 'Woe, woe, the great city, she who was clothed in fine

The tribes will attack one another and fight until `Aqaba runs with blood.[125]

There will be civil strife *(fitnah)* which will render people deaf, dumb and blind regarding what is right. Those who contemplate it will be drawn by it, and giving rein to the tongue during it will be like smiting with the sword.[126] *(da'if)*

There will emerge people who will recite the Qur'an but it will not go any deeper than their collarbones. Whenever a group of them appears, they should be cut off (i.e. killed) ... until Dajjal emerges among them.[127] *(hasan)*

[Among the] signs that indicate the approach of the Hour ... a truce between you and *Bani Al-Asfar* (i.e. the Byzantines) who will betray you and attack you under eighty flags. Under each flag will be twelve thousand soldiers.[128]

The flourishing state of Jerusalem will be when Yathrib (Medina) is in ruins, the ruined state of Yathrib will be when the Great War *(al-Malhamah al-Kubra)* comes, the outbreak of the Great War will be at the conquest of Constantinople, and the conquest of Constantinople

---

[125] Narrated by `Abdullah ibn `Amr, in al-Hakim, and in Nu`aym ibn Hammad, quoted in `Ibn Izzat p.26.

[126] Narrated by AbuHurayrah, *Sunan Abi Dawud 4264*, Book 36, Hadith 4251, https://sunnah.com/abudawud:4264, accessed May 22, 2024; also referenced in Rahma p.24.

[127] Narrated by Ibn 'Umar, *Sunan Ibn Majah 174*, Vol. 1, Book 1, Hadith 174, https://sunnah.com/ibnmajah:174, accessed May 22, 2024; see also Musnad Ahmad 27767, quoted in Rahma p.26.

[128] Narrated by `Auf bin Mali, *Sahih al-Bukhari 3176*, Vol. 4, Book 53, Hadith 401, https://sunnah.com/bukhari:3176, accessed May 17, 2024, also see `Ibn Izzat p.44.

linen and purple and scarlet, and adorned with gold, precious stones, and pearls.'

18:1 After these things I saw another angel coming down from heaven, having great authority, and the earth was illuminated from his glory.

18:2 And he cried out with a mighty voice, saying, "Fallen, fallen is Babylon the great! She has become a dwelling place of demons and a prison of every unclean spirit, and a prison of every unclean and hateful bird.

18:3 For all the nations have fallen because of the wine of the passion of her sexual immorality, and the kings of the earth have committed acts of sexual immorality with her, and the merchants of the earth have become rich from the excessive wealth of her luxury."

18:4 I heard another voice from heaven, saying, "Come out of her, my people, so that you will not participate in her sins and receive any of her plagues;

18:5 for her sins have piled up as high as heaven, and God has remembered her offenses."

when the Dajjal (antichrist) comes forth.[129] *(hasan)*

The Last Hour would not come until the Romans would land at al-A'maq or in Dabiq. An army consisting of the best (soldiers) of the people of the earth at that time will come from Medina (to counteract them). When they will arrange themselves in ranks, the Romans would say: Do not stand between us and those (Muslims) who took prisoners from amongst us. Let us fight with them; and the Muslims would say: Nay, by Allah, we would never get aside from you and from our brethren that you may fight them. They will then fight and a third (part) of the army would run away, whom Allah will never forgive. A third (part of the army) which would be constituted of excellent martyrs in Allah's eye, would be killed, and the third who would never be put to trial would win and they would be conquerors of Constantinople. And as they would be busy in distributing the spoils of war (amongst themselves) after hanging their swords by the olive trees, the Shaytan (Iblis) would cry: The Dajjal has taken your place among your family.[130]

You have heard about a city, one side of which is on land and the other is in the sea (Constantinople).… The Last Hour would not come unless seventy thousand persons from *Bani Ishaq* would attack it. When they would land there, they will neither fight with weapons nor would shower arrows but would only say: "There is no god but Allah and Allah is the Greatest," and one side of it would fall … and the gates would be opened for them and they would enter therein and, they

---

[129] Narrated by Mu'adh ibn Jabal, *Sunan Abi Dawud 4294*, Book 38, Hadith 4281, https://sunnah.com/abudawud:4294, accessed May 22, 2024; also referenced in Rahma p.68; referenced in `Ibn Izzat p.36.

[130] Narrated by Abu Huraira, *Sahih Muslim 2837*, Book 41, Hadith 6924, https://sunnah.com/muslim:2897, accessed February 18, 2024; also referenced in Rahma p.63-64.

would be collecting spoils of war and distributing them amongst themselves when a noise would be heard saying: Verily, Dajjal has come. And thus they would leave everything there and go back (to confront him).[131]

"Which of the two cities will be conquered first – Constantinople or Rome?" and the Prophet replied: "The city of Heraclius (Constantinople) will be conquered first."[132]

You will attack Arabia and Allah will enable you to conquer it, then you would attack Persia and He would make you to conquer it. Then you would attack Rome and Allah will enable you to conquer it, then you would attack the Dajjal and Allah will enable you to conquer him.[133]

Revelation. It has been three and a half years since the first seal of the scroll was opened, which brought the rider on the white horse. Now in heaven, the Lamb of God opens the second seal. This initiates the second half of the tribulation, known as the great tribulation. The troubles will intensify dramatically. A rider on a red horse comes to earth, and launches full-scale war (6:3-4). Over the next three and a half years, the remainder of the seven seals will be opened. They will be followed one-by-one with the sounding of seven trumpets, and seven bowls pouring out wrath. All this must occur before the second coming of Christ.

The rider on the red horse is the same who came on the white horse (6:2 K16). The rider is not named, but the character of Revelation that has all the attributes of both riders is the beast (13:1-2). Previously he came announcing peace and stability, with treaties and alliances. Now he brings war, drenched in blood. His immediate aim is to do away with his ally, the woman of Babylon. They used each other to gain power (17:3 K17). But he has despised her all along, at times secretly, at other times

---

[131] Narrated by Abu Huraira, *Sahih Muslim 2920 a*, Book 41, Hadith 6979, https://sunnah.com/muslim:2920a, accessed May 22, 2024; also referenced in `Ibn Izzat p.38.

[132] Narrated by Al-Hakim, *Al-Mustadrak, (4/598) no. 8662*, https://qurananswers.me/2016/10/29/sequence-dajjal-arrival/, accessed November 8 2022.

[133] Narrated by Nafi' b. Utba, *Sahih Muslim 2900*, Book 41, Hadith 6930, https://sunnah.com/muslim:2900, accessed May 22, 2024; also referenced in https://qurananswers.me/2016/10/29/sequence-dajjal-arrival/, accessed November 8 2022.

with non-cooperation. His aim has always been absolute supremacy. War is the means to achieve this at this pivotal moment.

John's vision comes around to this event five times, in five different chapters of Revelation, with different details in each one. Since we are following a chronological approach, all the verses about this beginning of the great tribulation are gathered in this section.

The beast comes from the sea. In many Bible passages the sea symbolizes the place of chaos (Psalm 104:6-9, Isaiah 17:12-13, etc), in contrast to God's abode in heaven, the place of peace and tranquility. The beast has seven heads and ten horns, with blasphemous names written on his heads (13:1). He has been maneuvered to world dictatorship by his mentor the dragon (13:2), who also has seven heads and ten horns (12:3 K15). We know the dragon is Satan (see K01).

The evil one has been preparing for this moment for centuries.

The beast is the antichrist.

There is a parallel Old Testament passage that describes the revived Roman empire of the end time. It is in Daniel 7's dream of four beasts, specifically the fourth one, with great iron teeth that breaks in pieces. After the dream, God explained to Daniel the identity of this terrifying character, in these verses repeated from K17:

> Daniel 7:23 "This is what he said: 'The fourth beast will be a fourth kingdom on the earth which will be different from all the other kingdoms, and will devour the whole earth and trample it down and crush it.
> 7:24 As for the ten horns, out of this kingdom ten kings will arise; and another will arise after them, and he will be different from the previous ones and will humble three kings.
> 7:25 And he will speak against the Most High and wear down the saints of the Highest One, and he will intend to make alterations in times and in law; and they will be handed over to him for a time, times, and half a time."

This part of Daniel's dream will be fulfilled by the beast of Revelation. His ten horns are ten kingships, nations that will pledge themselves to the beast. Three of the kingships will be usurped by the beast sometime during his joint rule with the woman, and come under his direct rule

(Daniel 7:24). The seven heads are the remaining kingships. One was the beast's originally, plus six other kings who swore allegiance to the beast and have been secretly scheming with him. All of them despise the prostitute and her ideologies (17:16). The beast has promised the six to be sub rulers with him in a reformatted world government, which he planned after the woman's overthrow (17:12).

The beast has been carefully planning for this hour. His forces coordinate a surprise surgical attack on the government of the woman. All the planning pays off, for the rule of the woman of Babylon is overthrown in the space of just one day (18:8). They kill the woman (or the future government leaders that she represents), and eat the remains in some sort of gruesome ceremony. They burn them, and presumably their capital city, with fire (17:16, 18:8).

Babylon's financial system is brought to its knees. The world economy comes to a sudden halt. Markets and money makers are devastated (18:15-16). The world's idol of wealth cannot save. God judges the political and pseudo-religious system of Babylon because it mandated a world culture of sexual sin at levels never seen before (14:8), a direct affront to God's commandments.

The beast was raised up by Satan. Though the beast hates God, God in his eternal plan gives the domain of Babylon to the beast as judgment upon her (17:17). It is his decree that the spirit of Babylon be destroyed forever (18:21 K20).

The beast opposes Babylon's values for his own reasons. His rule will be dramatically different from the woman's.

Apparently, even in the woman's city of pleasure, there are some who have come to their senses and asked for Jesus to save them. We can deduce this from what God says after Babylon is set on fire – he warns his followers to flee: "come out of her, my people, so that you will not participate in her sins and receive any of her plagues" (18:4). Those who stay will see that Babylon has become a dwelling place for devils (18:2). This ought to be taken literally. The unbelievers who remain, who are totally devoted to the prostitute's lost cause, become demon possessed. This is another divine judgment upon their complete godlessness. They are no better than walking dead. They will be tormented with the full effect of coming plagues, especially the earthquake that will raze their city to the ground (16:18-19 K39).

Hadiths. In section H17, the Mahdi made a truce with the Romans to achieve an equal share of worldwide power. Together they turned against a common enemy. But not all Muslims understand that these actions were an expedient toward the ultimate goal – enforcing Islam upon every single political entity in the world. Like many other Islamic truces, this one was in actuality a hudna truce (see H17), to be revoked when Muslims have gained sufficient advantage. The Mahdi and his allies also exercise taqiyya, or concealment of their complete devotion to Allah, in their delicate dealings with the Romans. This will allow them time to gain needed strength.

The trouble is that many Muslims, even some who advise the Mahdi, see the arrangement with the Romans as worthy of permanent status. They also advocate renewing the historic seven-year treaty with the Jews that has given Muslims jurisdiction over Jerusalem. These compromisers disregard the tyranny over Muslims in regions where the Romans are dominant, and the anti-Islamic culture that the Romans are pushing.

Many Hadiths, and the Qur'an itself, warn against such so-called Muslims. Their devotion to Allah is false. Their hearts are far from the jihadists who rallied to the Mahdi. These weak-willed people are easily corrupted and co-opted by the promises of the Romans.

The Mahdi will not listen to the advice that recommends continued accommodation with the Romans and the Jews. Instead, he will seek the guidance of Allah. The Mahdi will be true to his name as "the rightly guided one." He will rely only on trusted allies who are dedicated solely to Allah.

The compromisers will likely be presidents, prime ministers, and generals of certain Muslim nation states that had autonomous status under the Roman truce and Jewish treaty. The Mahdi begins his takeover with armed battles against these Muslim appeasers and their forces. Civil strife will be rampant. "The tribes will attack one another and fight until [the gulf of] `Aqaba runs with blood." During this time, Jerusalem is flourishing, while "Yathrib (Medina) is in ruins."

(It is difficult to explain how Medina could be in ruins after the coming of the Mahdi. One view is that the Arabic word *kharah* in the hadith, commonly translated as "ruins," is better translated as "desolation." Thus, after the Mahdi's conquest of Jerusalem in H16, Arabs will leave Medina en masse to go to Jerusalem, to help the Mahdi consolidate his rule there. Afterward, Medina is not in actual ruins, but is mostly desolate of human habitation.[134])

After the Muslims have purified their ranks, they accuse the army of the Romans of breaking the truce. They will be said to "betray you [Muslims] and attack you under eighty flags. Under each flag will be twelve thousand soldiers."

But the Mahdi's armies coming from the direction of Medina will spring a military surprise on the Romans, who have gathered their elite troops in Syria. The Mahdi has no further use for them as allies, for by this time they have defeated their joint enemy.

The Romans predicted in the Hadiths are not like the polytheistic Romans who persecuted Christians in the centuries after ʿIsa ibn Maryam. They are much worse. Muslims believe they will be like the Byzantine Romans who converted to Christianity and embraced the false religion of the cross. Or like the Crusaders from Roman Catholic Europe who temporarily evicted the Muslims from Jerusalem during the years 1099–1187 and 1229–1244. The Byzantines and the Crusaders were the main obstacle to the expansion of Islam until 1453, when the Ottoman armies finally conquered Constantinople and made it the rightful seat of the caliphate (see K10). The descendants of these Christians then retreated into their stronghold of Europe.

But after the Ottoman caliphate weakened, Europe and later the United States established a technological and imperial supremacy over large parts of the world, including Muslim areas. Because of the western military superiority, Muslims lost confidence, and were tempted into the mistake of dismantling the Constantinople caliphate in 1924.

---

[134] Rahma pp. 68-69.

The Romans of the end time are the last carriers of this western civilization, based on Byzantine and Catholic Christian roots. They are still the defenders of the cross.

This version of history is the one that drives the Mahdi in his motive to attack and defeat the Romans once and for all, regardless of any agreement with them.

The Romans are not properly prepared. They will regard the attack as a preemptive one against them, in direct violation of the Mahdi's sworn truce. But for followers of the Mahdi, it is the cross-worshipping Romans who have been continuously violating the treaty. They deserve preemptive attack, as Muhammad did to the Quraysh by suddenly ending the treaty of Hudaybiyyah (see H17).

The Islamic Armageddon battle, the *al-Malhamah al-Kubra*, or Greatest Massacre, now takes place. It occurs either at al-A'maq (in southern Turkey near Antakya) or Dabiq (northwestern Syria). Even after the recent purification of Muslim ranks, a third of the Mahdi's army will run away in cowardice. But with all the undependables now gone, the true jihadists who remain will go on to shatter the cream of the Roman army.

They will move on rapidly to easily crush the Roman garrison at Constantinople. Once again, they raise the flag of the *khilafah* (caliphate) there. Among the victorious troops will be 70,000 Jews, the *Bani Ishaq* or sons of Isaac, who converted to Islam after the coming of the Mahdi. The Mahdi will then turn to conquer Persia (Iran) and the remaining parts of Arabia that had eluded his direct rule. His armies then take Rome.

The Mahdi is now victorious over all organized opposition.

At this moment of Islam's greatest success ever, a hadith has Shaytan (Iblis) announcing that the Dajjal will emerge to become the Mahdi's worst adversary. This is the one notable reference where Shaytan appears to be the Dajjal's sponsor (see the section on Main actors of the end-time Hadiths). The Dajjal will tempt many weak-willed Muslims who are left into apostasy against Allah.

Comparison. In 17:10-11 K02 we discussed the six famous empires highlighted in the Old and New Testaments, plus a seventh and eighth that were prophesied to come sometime afterward. We saw how a majority of Christian interpreters see the seventh as the joint kingdom of the woman of Babylon in alliance with the antichrist, and the eighth happening when the beast suddenly defeats the woman's forces to achieve a one-man dictatorship during the second half of the seven-year tribulation.

If the Mahdi prophecies come to pass, a better interpretation is that the eighth kingdom covers the Islamic rule of the Mahdi during the entire seven years, including the time when allied with the Romans, and also after defeating them. The seventh kingdom in this view is the Ottoman caliphate that was abolished in 1924. This will explain the gap in time between seventh and eighth kingdoms suggested by 17:11 K02, which is difficult to account for if the seventh and eighth happen in immediate succession.[135]

This is also supported by the alignment between the Mahdi prophecies of the battle of *al-Malhamah al-Kubra*, and the overthrow of the woman of Babylon to start the great tribulation. This suggests that Satan's best-laid plan for the end time is for the antichrist to rule over a revived Islamic empire.

Most Revelation commentators are Euro-centric, and are not familiar with the historic lands surrounding Israel in the middle east. They have constructed an interpretation which sees the beast and woman of Babylon as two sides of a revived Roman empire. In this view, the beast is the political Babylon. With his allies he leverages the religious Babylon, which is said to be a totally corrupted Roman Catholic church and the papacy in the city of Rome. The ten horns and seven kingships of 13:1, 17:13, 17:16, and Daniel 7:24 are various combinations of European countries, sometimes with reference to the European Union (before 1993 known as the European Community), who come together under the antichrist's leadership to form a centralized world government that erases national boundaries. Midway through the

---

[135] Shoebat p. 321, Richardson pp. 95-96.

tribulation, they overthrow religious Babylon to confiscate all its wealth.[136]

But the Bible has little to say about seven or ten such European countries.

On the other hand, it does have much to say about the ancient lands of Magog, Meshech, Tubal, Persia, Cush (Ethiopia), Put, Gomer, and Togarmah. All eight are called out in Ezekiel 38:1-7, which prophesies their coalition invasion of northern Israel. This attack will likely occur sometime between the rapture and the beginning of the seven-year tribulation. The coalition will be led by a mysterious character named Gog, who could be an appearance of the antichrist a few years before he comes on the white horse:

> Ezekiel 38:1 Now the word of the Lord came to me, saying,
> 38:2 "Son of man, set your face toward Gog of the land of Magog, the chief prince *[rosh]* of Meshech and Tubal, and prophesy against him,
> 38:3 and say, 'This is what the Lord God says: "Behold, I am against you, Gog, chief prince of Meshech and Tubal.
> 38:4 So I will turn you around and put hooks into your jaws, and I will bring you out, and all your army, horses and horsemen, all of them magnificently dressed, a great contingent with shield and buckler, all of them wielding swords;
> 38:5 Persia, Cush, and Put with them, all of them with buckler and helmet;
> 38:6 Gomer with all its troops; Beth-togarmah from the remote parts of the north with all its troops—many peoples with you.
> 38:7 "Be ready, and be prepared, you and all your contingents that are assembled around you, and be a guard for them."

All eight of the ancient lands of Ezekiel have become strongholds of Islam.

Many commentators focus in on the Hebrew word *rosh* for "chief prince" in Ezekiel 38:2. They transpose it to "Russia". But Moscow was

---

[136] For an example of this approach, see https://www.bibleref.com/Revelation/17/Revelation-17-16.html, accessed April 2, 2023.

not founded until 1147, a millennium after Revelation was written. Nowhere else in the Bible is there a pointer to Russia.

In contrast, seven of the eight lands with definite names in Ezekiel were first mentioned in the "table of nations" of Genesis 10 as descendants of Noah. Each went on to create long-lasting nations:

> Genesis 10:1 Now these are the records of the generations of the sons of Noah: Shem, Ham, and Japheth; and sons were born to them after the flood.
> 10:2 The sons of Japheth were Gomer, Magog, Madai, Javan, Tubal, Meshech, and Tiras.
> 10:3 The sons of Gomer were Ashkenaz, Riphath, and Togarmah.
> 10:6 The sons of Ham were Cush, Mizraim, Put, and Canaan.

The geographic location of these peoples is agreed by most scholars to be:[137]

- Magog: either Scythia (northern Caucasus) or Syria
- Meshech: Phrygia (western Turkey)
- Tubal: in eastern Turkey
- Cush: Ethiopia
- Put: Libya
- Gomer: Cappadocia (central Turkey)
- Togarmah: in southeastern Turkey

The one nation not mentioned in Genesis is another extremely ancient land:

- Persia: Iran

All eight of these areas have been Islamic territories for over a thousand years. It should be noted that the list of seven were ruled for centuries by the Ottoman empire (in the case of Ethiopia, ports along the Red Sea coast of Eritrea, which became a separate country from Ethiopia in the late 20th century). The Shi'ite Persians were never subdued by the Ottomans, but fought Shi'a-Sunni wars with them over many centuries with no conclusive victor. The presence of Persia in the listing suggests that the Mahdi will be at last the one to reconcile the Shi'a and the

---

[137] Richardson, pp. 87-92.

Sunni. The list of eight nations can be rounded up to ten, as in the ten horns of Revelation, by considering the supplemental phrase "many peoples are with you" of Ezekiel 38:6.

All this leads to the strong possibility that the allies of the beast who overthrow the woman of Babylon will not be leaders of European Union (EU) countries, but will be Islamic warlords from these different lands. This joins to the other Bible prophecies, and has its grounding in Bible history over millennia of time.

Such an analysis is more convincing than the EU narrative. It also matches the expectation of the Hadiths that the Mahdi will cast off his questionable advisors, and will choose only those who are completely loyal to him. Together they surprise and defeat the Romans.

After the woman's demise, and after Babylon is set on fire by the beast's forces, those who choose to remain become demon possessed. This is a product of the control that Satan has over the dealings of the antichrist. In the Hadiths the people involved would be the Roman citizens who decide to stay in Constantinople or Rome after the Mahdi's armies conquer them. They will be treated no better than the polytheist Quraysh tribe of Mecca that Muhammad subdued. The irony of the future demon possession is that (in the Christian and Jewish view), Muhammad was likely under demonic influence himself when he mistakenly believed that the angel Jibreel was dictating to him the words of the true God of heaven. They were actually the words of Satan, who was rebranding himself as Allah (see K08).

The Hadiths have two main groups of people who will be resistant to the forced conversion to Islam: the Romans, especially those who love the urban life of their capital cities, and Jews. Muslims reflexively regard the future Romans to be defenders of the cross.

In Revelation, the beast will also have two main groups in opposition. They are the Jews once again, and the followers of the woman of Babylon. Let us remember that God helped John protect the early Christians who were reading the account of his vision by portraying the woman as the prostitute of Babylon, which they understood really meant the prostitute of Rome. The future "Romans" who stand by the woman, unlike the Romans of the Hadiths, certainly are not defending the cross. To them, it is most offensive. The woman's system will be a throwback to the original polytheistic Roman empire, obsessed with pleasure and sex, during the period of great Christian persecution of the early centuries CE.

In the Hadiths, after the Romans are defeated, the Dajjal becomes the adversary. There will be many Muslims who are tempted to leave the faith by the promises of the Romans, and then the Dajjal.

There are no other main groups in the Hadiths. Some lesser ones are the unspecified enemy that the Mahdi defeats in temporary alliance with the Romans, and the Hindus, which we will encounter later.

But in Revelation, there is a third main group – new followers of Christ. They are people who have discovered the good news, proclaimed already for thousands of years: that God can forgive them, and that he sent his son Jesus to be the Messiah. He paid the price for their sin by his death on the cross. God will therefore welcome them into heaven. These people have come under conviction that God really does have a perfect standard that they cannot attain, yet he loves them so much that he sent his son to attain it for them. They no longer follow the woman of Babylon and her offers of pleasure, or the Orthodox Jewish leaders and their system of temple sacrifices, or the Hindu gods and their avatars, or Allah who is unapproachable and his prophet Muhammad who is dead and buried.

In the tribulation, many will find Jesus Christ. I am convinced that this will include millions of Muslims. They will hear about him from the 144,000 Jewish evangelists, the two witnesses, from books like this one, and especially from the Bible. Jesus will also appear in their dreams, like he does to hundreds of Muslims in my day.[138]

---

[138] Tom Doyle with Greg Webster, *Dreams and Visions, Is Jesus Awakening the Muslim World?*, Thomas Nelson, Nashville US, 2012.

K22 :

The smoke of Babylon

: H22

The smoke is a painful punishment and an awaited sign

18:9 And the kings of the earth, who committed acts of sexual immorality and lived luxuriously with her, will weep and mourn over her when they see the smoke of her burning,
18:10 standing at a distance because of the fear of her torment, saying, 'Woe, woe, the great city, Babylon, the strong city! For in one hour your judgment has come.'
18:17 For in one hour such great wealth has been laid waste!' And every shipmaster and every passenger and sailor, and all who make their living by the sea, stood at a distance,

Ibn `Abbas said, "I did not sleep last night at all.... They said that a star with a tail had appeared and I feared that the Smoke would spread."[139]

Then watch thou for the Day that the sky will bring forth a kind of smoke (or mist) plainly visible enveloping the people: this will be a Penalty Grievous. (Surah 44:10-11)

18:18 and were crying out as they saw the smoke of her burning, saying, 'What city is like the great city?'
18:19 And they threw dust on their heads and were crying out, weeping and mourning, saying, 'Woe, woe, the great city, in which all who had ships at sea became rich from her prosperity, for in one hour she has been laid waste!'
19:1 After these things I heard something like a loud voice of a great multitude in heaven, saying, "Hallelujah! Salvation, glory, and power belong to our God,
19:2 because His judgments are true and righteous; for He has judged the great prostitute who was corrupting the earth with her sexual immorality, and He has avenged the blood of His bond-servants on her."
19:3 And a second time they said, "Hallelujah! Her smoke rises forever and ever."
18:20 "Rejoice over her, O heaven, and you saints and apostles and prophets, because God has pronounced judgment for you against her."

---

[139] Narrated by Ibn `Abbas, in Ibn Kathir, *Tafsir,* quoted in `Ibn Izzat p.21.

19:4 And the twenty-four elders and the four living creatures fell down and worshiped God who sits on the throne, saying, "Amen. Hallelujah!"

Hadiths. "The smoke" is one of the Major Signs of the end, as we saw in the hadith of H00, and confirmed in the *tafsir* of Ibn Kathir:

> The smoke is one of the awaited signs.[140]

This is a perplexing event that has just one mention in the Qur'an, and little explanation in the Hadiths.

The Qur'an warns that the smoke will be "a penalty grievous." It is something to be greatly dreaded.

The hadith in this section associates the smoke with "a star with a tail," and recognizes that the spreading of the smoke is a fearsome thing. In H15 we saw a tie-in between a star with a luminous tail and the Mahdi. But he should not be regarded as fearsome. All Muslims and even non-Muslims should welcome him. It is therefore confusing why a star with a tail is connected with both the Mahdi and the smoke.

Some of Muhammad's close companions and family members knew that he had spoken of the smoke, and offered some extra detail of their own:

> The smoke is a major sign .... It will rise and cover the whole world. The smoke will affect both the believers and non-believers alike remaining for a period of 40 days and nights. The believers will be affected a little as if suffering from cold, while the smoke will enter the brains of the non-believers and make them unconscious.[141]

> The smoke ... will enter in the ears of the Kuffar [infidels] and the hypocrites and will affect the Muslims like a cold. The whole world will be like a house on fire. It has not happened. It is to happen.[142]

---

[140] Ibn Kathir, *Tafsir*, quoted in `Ibn Izzat p.21.

[141] Hudhayfa b. al-Yaman, companion of Muhammad, recorded by al-Tabari, 9th century expert in Qur'anic exegesis (tafsir), quoted in http://www.inter-islam.org/faith/Majorsigns.html#smoke , accessed April 2, 2023.

[142] Ibn Abbas (cousin of Muhammad), Ibn Umar (companion of Muhammad), Hasan ibn Ali (grandson of Muhammad) and others, recorded by Lawami al-Anwar known as Ibn al-

I have placed the Islamic sign of the smoke at this point of the timeline, because Revelation speaks very specifically of a smoke that will have consequences for the whole world, shortly after a unitary world government is established midway through the seven years.

Revelation. In the previous section, the beast and his allies overthrew the woman of Babylon and set fire to her capital (17:16 K21, 18:8 K21). The megacity is so extensive that it will take much time for the buildings and treasures to be burnt out.

A great cloud of smoke billows above, and starts to spread across the upper atmosphere. The smoke may be so bad that it would affect weather patterns for days or weeks in many parts of the world.

The followers of the woman quickly learn of her downfall, and the fire. They cry out in great agony (18:9-10). Those who believed in Babylon know that their dream of administering an empire is forever finished. Though there were many opportunities, they never repented of their self-idolatry. The godless fruits of pleasure, luxury, and control have come to an end. They are sorry, not for the city, but that the riches of the city will be no more. All those whose livelihood depended on the global economic order are also devastated (18:17-19).

The lingering smoke is the sign of prolonged and irreversible punishment. The time of possible mercy from the Almighty is now in the past.

Jesus said that real treasure is not of this world:

> Matthew 6:19 "Do not store up for yourselves treasures on earth, where moth and rust destroy, and where thieves break in and steal.
> 6:20 But store up for yourselves treasures in heaven, where neither moth nor rust destroys, and where thieves do not break in or steal;
> 6:21 for where your treasure is, there your heart will be also."

Mawsili, 14th century scholar of Shafi'i religious school, https://catchofthedaybooks.com/product/lawami-al-anwar-fi-sharh-sihah-al-ahkbar- , quoted in http://www.inter-islam.org/faith/Majorsigns.html#smoke , accessed April 2, 2023.

There is a crowd of souls in heaven who are observing the smoke. They came to faith in Jesus under the rule of the woman, but were killed during her years of persecution (17:6 K20). When they see the smoke, they rejoice that God has avenged their deaths (19:1-2, 18:20). They are joined by the holy apostles and prophets, and the twenty-four elders (19:4), who represent Christian martyrs of many earlier centuries of persecution (4:4 K14, 5:8-9 K14), resurrected recently in the rapture.

Also present are the four living creatures (19:4), who symbolize different aspects of divine majesty (4:6-9 K14).

The smoke eventually dissipates from the earth, but in the heavenly realm it rises forever and ever (19:3). This is eternal judgment on the woman of Babylon and her spirit of godlessness that sustained many empires. Her empire will never be repeated.

The capital of the revived Roman empire is a smoking ruin. The ensuing events of the great tribulation now focus on Jerusalem. The two witnesses are still very active there. The Jewish temple of the city will soon be targeted for sacrilege by the beast and his chief deputy.

Comparison. The smoke is a major sign of the end time in both the Hadiths and Revelation.

In the Hadiths, a star with a tail is connected with both the Mahdi and the smoke. The Mahdi is to be celebrated, but the smoke is to be feared. The star with a tail thus has mixed connotations.

Revelation casts light on this ambiguity. In 9:1 K15, the end-time star fallen from heaven can be none other than Satan. God cast him down from heaven permanently, after all the believers of the church age were raptured. Within a short time, several years perhaps, Satan raises up the antichrist beast to be his main human agent during the tribulation. After the beast overthrows the woman of Babylon and burns her capital city, the inhabitants who refuse to leave become easy targets for demon possession. That is when the smoke enters the timeline.

Both the smoke and the star fallen from heaven are therefore connected with Satan and the devils. This should be a sobering thought for those who will experience the tribulation. Hopefully Muslims will understand this while they can still change their minds.

K23 :
The supremacy of the beast

13:3 I saw one of his heads as if it had been fatally wounded, and his fatal wound was healed. And the whole earth was amazed and followed after the beast;
13:4 they worshiped the dragon because he gave his authority to the beast; and they worshiped the beast, saying, "Who is like the beast, and who is able to wage war with him?"
13:5 A mouth was given to him speaking arrogant words and blasphemies, and authority to act for forty-two months was given to him.
13:6 And he opened his mouth in blasphemies against God, to blaspheme His name and His tabernacle, that is, those who dwell in heaven.
13:7 It was also given to him to make war with the saints and to overcome them, and authority was given to him over every tribe, people, language, and nation.
13:8 All who live on the earth will worship him, everyone whose name has not been written since

: H23
The supremacy of the Mahdi

The tribes will attack one another and fight until `Aqaba runs with blood. They will turn to the best man of them and say, "Come and let us pledge allegiance to you." He will say, "Woe to you! How many treaties you have broken and how much blood you have shed!" But he will be forced to accept their allegiance. He is the Mahdi on earth and the Mahdi in heaven.[143] *(athar)*

The Mahdi will appear in the latter part of my nation. Allah will grant him rain to bring produce from the earth. He will give out wealth appropriately, cattle will be plentiful, and the nation will become great. He will live as ruler for seven or eight years.[144] *(sahih)*

O Messenger of Allah, why will horses be so cheap? He said: 'They will never be ridden in war again.' It was said to him: 'Why will oxen be so expensive?' He said:

---

[143] `Abdullah ibn `Amr (companion of Muhammad), narrated by Abu Yusuf, in al-Hakim and Nu`aym ibn Hammad, quoted in `Ibn Izzat p.26; also referenced in al-Hafidh Jalal ad-Din as-Suyuti, *al-'Arf al-Wardi fi Akhbar al-Mahdi* (*The Rose Scented Perfume: On the Reports of the Mahdi*), no.168, translated by Bismillahi Rahmani Raheem, Assalamu Alaikum, https://ghayb.com/2019/01/al-arf-al-wardi-fi-akhbar-al-mahdi-by-imam-jalal-ad-din-as-suyuti/, accessed March 11, 2024.

[144] Narrated by Abu Sa'eed Al-Khudri, *al-Mustadrak 'alá al-Ṣaḥīḥayn 8716*, quoted in Abu Amina Elias, *Al-Mahdi, the promised Caliph to lead the Ummah*, September 10, 2019, https://www.abuaminaelias.com/al-mahdi-promised-caliph/; see also Rahma p.12; `Ibn Izzat p.8.

the foundation of the world in the book of life of the Lamb who has been slaughtered.

13:9 If anyone has an ear, let him hear.

13:10 If anyone is destined for captivity, to captivity he goes; if anyone kills with the sword, with the sword he must be killed. Here is the perseverance and the faith of the saints.

'Because all the land will be tilled.[145] *(da'if)*

Wealth will be available to all. A man will stand and say, 'Give to me, Mahdi!' and he will say, 'Take.'[146]

He will be called Mahdi because he will guide (yahdi) to something hidden and will bring out the Torah and Gospel from a town called Antioch.[147] *(da'if)*

The Mahdi will bring out the volumes of the Torah to refute the Jews.[148] *(da'if)*

The Ark of the Covenant will emerge from the Tabariyya Sea (Lake Tiberius) through the efforts of Imam al-Mahdi. It will be placed before him at the Sacred House (either the Holy Ka'aba or Bait al-Maqdis in Jerusalem). When the descendants of Judah (the son of Jacob, the son of Isaac, the son of Abraham) see this (Ark), all except a few will embrace Islam.[149] *(da'if)*

The Prophet said: The Mahdi will be of my stock, and will have a broad forehead and a prominent nose. He will fill the earth with equity and

---

[145] Narrated by Abu Umamah Al-Bahili, *Sunan Ibn Majah 4077*, Vol. 5, Book 36, Hadith 4077, https://sunnah.com/ibnmajah:4077, accessed May 24, 2024; also referenced in `Ibn Izzat p.36.

[146] Narrated by Abu Hurayra, in at-Tabarani, quoted in `Ibn Izzat p.9; also referenced in Ibn Khaldun, *Muqaddimah*, trans. Abdassamad Clarke, October 4, 2022, https://primaquran.com/2022/10/04/hadith-on-imam-mahdi-in-the-light-of-ibn-khaldun/.

[147] Narrated by Ka'b al-Ambar, in Abu Nu`aym, quoted in `Ibn Izzat p.15; also narrated by Imam Muhammad Baqr by way of Jabir Ibn Yazid al-Jo'fi, quoted by Ibn Maymun, August 13, 2017, https://www.shiachat.com/forum/topic/235051638-mahdi-and-the-torah/.

[148] Imam Jalalud-Din As-Suyuti (15th century Egyptian hadith master), *Al-Hawi lil-Fatawi* (in Arabic, collection of *fatwa* legal rulings on Islamic law), *al-Hawi*, https://damas.nur.nu/11282/book/suyuti_al-hawi-lil-fatawi, translated in `Ibn Izzat p.16; also referenced in KL (initials), http://hadithprophesies.blogspot.com/2009/05/imam-mahdi.html, accessed May 25, 2024.

[149] Narrated by Sulaiman ibn Isa, *al-Fitan 1:360#1050*, and Suyuti, *al-Hawi li'l Fatawa II:83*, quoted in Sayyid Ahmed Amiruddin, https://ahmedamiruddin.wordpress.com/2009/05/13/history-of-the-ark-of-the-covenant-an-islamic-perspective/, 2009, accessed July 27, 2024; also referenced in `Ibn Izzat p.16.

justice as it was filled with oppression and tyranny, and he will rule for seven years.[150] *(hasan)*

He will divide the property, and will govern the people by the *Sunnah* of their Prophet and establish Islam on Earth. He will remain seven years.[151] *(da'if)*

He will pave the way for and establish the government of the family of Muhammad... Every believer will be obligated to support him.[152]

The messenger of Allah said, a nation which has me at its beginning, 'Isa ibn Maryam at its end and the Mahdi in between will never be destroyed.[153] *(da'if)*

Revelation. The antichrist, who is the beast of Revelation, has made an end of the woman of Babylon, her influence, and her government. He is now supreme over all the nations (13:7).

In John's apocalyptic vision, when he overthrew the woman, he appeared with seven heads (13:1 K21). We learned in K21 that they represented the beast plus six autonomous rulers that schemed with him against the woman. Here we see that one of the heads is wounded (13:3), likely in the sudden battle with the woman's forces. Out of the seven heads, the death wound is on the one that originally belonged to the beast himself. But he lives on, miraculously. To all appearances, this shows that the beast has divine powers.

The news spreads quickly. People can figure out that the beast has gained supernatural powers because of his devotion to the dragon. In view of this sign and wonder, many are drawn to worship both the beast, and the dragon (13:4). Perhaps they know that the dragon is Satan (as we learned in K01). But even if they do not, it is still great

---

[150] Narrated by AbuSa'id al-Khudri, *Sunan Abi Dawud 4285*, Book 37, Hadith 4272, https://sunnah.com/abudawud:4285, accessed May 26, 2024.
[151] Narrated by Umm Salamah, Ummul Mu'minin, *Sunan Abi Dawud 4286*, Book 37, Hadith 4273, https://sunnah.com/abudawud:4286, accessed May 26, 2024; also referenced in Richardson p.24.
[152] Narrated by Umm Salamah, Ummul Mu'minin, *Sunan Abi Dawud*, Book 36, http://shiastudies.com/en/2423/imam-mahdi-the-universal-leader/, January 25, 2020.
[153] Narrated by Abdullah ibn 'Abbas, in Ahmad ibn Hanbal, Abu Nu'aym, and an-Nasa'l, quoted in 'Ibn Izzat p.8 (see also H16).

blasphemy to worship anyone who has defied the Almighty God in heaven.

The beast basks in this adulation, so much so that he decrees that everyone shall worship him. He decides to be the object of a new world religious system (13:8a).

This religion turns the Bible on its head. The beast is messiah and deliverer, and the dragon takes on the role of God. This reversed religion was prophesied in Daniel's description of a future king, who exalts himself with the help of a "foreign god":

> Daniel 11:36 "Then the king will do as he pleases, and he will exalt himself and boast against every god and will speak dreadful things against the God of gods; and he will be successful until the indignation is finished, because that which is determined will be done.
> 11:37 And he will show no regard for the gods of his fathers or for the desire of women, nor will he show regard for any other god; for he will boast against them all.
> 11:38 But instead he will honor a god of fortresses, a god whom his fathers did not know; he will honor him with gold, silver, precious stones, and treasures.
> 11:39 And he will take action against the strongest of fortresses with the help of a foreign god; he will give great honor to those who acknowledge him and will make them rulers over the many, and will parcel out land for a price."

The new messiah does not choose this moment of victory and consolidation of his power to declare peace on earth. Instead, he starts a campaign of blasphemies. The aim is to discredit the true God, his promises, and the memory of Christians whom God raptured to heaven.

The beast also blasphemes the "tabernacle" (13:6). This refers to the temple rebuilt in Jerusalem by end-time Orthodox Jews to worship God after the pattern of their Old Testament ancestors (11:1-2 K18). The beast profanes the temple despite the seven-year treaty (Daniel 9:27a K17) that he used to gain joint rule with the woman of Babylon. The treaty allowed sole jurisdiction of the temple's separate inner court to the Jews. The blasphemy campaign is the beast's first step to break down this separation. It is also open season to attack Jews and any gentiles who are turning away from the beast to believe in Jesus instead. The next step will be to allow an image of himself to be erected within the inner court, to be worshipped (this will occur in the next section K24).

Jesus prophesied that in the end times the "gentiles" will take full control of Jerusalem:

> Luke 21:24b Jerusalem will be trampled underfoot by the Gentiles until the times of the Gentiles are fulfilled.

This will likely happen when the antichrist abrogates his treaty with the Jews. The gentiles in question are the forces of the beast.

The beast does not limit his activity to Jerusalem. He also sends forces to round up followers of Jesus amongst all the different nations (13:7), and targets them for elimination. God allows many to be overpowered. But their names are "written since the foundation of the world in the book of life of the Lamb who has been slaughtered" (13:8). That verse summarizes God's eternal plan of salvation for his elect. He has ordained from the beginning of time that he would send his son to be the sacrificial lamb. Jesus forfeited his life on the cross for sin, so that sinners belonging to him could be brought to heaven.

Jesus' words in the vision encourages the new converts to endure death. They can do this knowing that those who torment them with sword and murder will have the same done to them (13:10).

Though the beast is at the head of a world government structure, he must use force to sustain it. This is hinted at by 13:8a, which says that *all* that dwell upon the earth, except for those whose names are written in God's book of eternal life, *will* worship the beast. The word *will* speaks to the beast having to compel men and women to worship him. Many will do so only half-heartedly, or will remain defiant in opposition. The beast will continue to war against such opponents (6:8 K25, 9:18 K33). Unfortunately, some of them will also not heed the message of the 144,000 Jewish evangelists for Jesus (Zechariah 8:20-23 K18).

The time allotted for the beast to reign supreme is forty-two months (13:5), the period of the great tribulation. Christ's kingdom of a thousand years upon the earth is yet to come (see K44). The beast's short time is a satanic counterfeit of Christ's coming rule, permitted by

God to help people distinguish good from evil. These evil years will be a time of continuous wars. It will be Christ who brings the wars to an end with his second coming (K38). He will terminate the reign of the beast (19:20 K40).

Hadiths. In section H21, the Mahdi used signs of perceived treachery to accuse the Romans of breaking the treaty. This served as justification for launching the attack that surprised and defeated the Romans in the apocalypse battle of *al-Malhamah al-Kubra*. We saw that before the preemptive strike, he fought with Muslims who wished to continue collaborating with the Romans, in order to purge his ranks. The Mahdi moved on to conquer Constantinople and then Rome.

The lead hadith in the current section says that the collaborators will then send emissaries to the Mahdi. They know their time is up. They will say, "come and let us pledge allegiance to you." He will accept them back, though in his eyes they are also guilty of breaking the treaty.

At the beginning of the seven years, the Mahdi rode to power with the promise that Islamic rule would provide for the material needs of all the earth. Now he sets out to make good on this promise, after permanently defeating his main adversary the Romans, the defenders of the cross. And he has consolidated the Muslims behind him, including the wavering ones. But his promise is only for Muslims who have achieved good standing, plus those who convert to Islam. It is not for infidels.

Allah will now provide an abundance of rain. The ground will bring forth great crops, flocks will multiply, and wealth will be available to all. The Muslim community will grow in number.

In one hadith, Muhammad says that with all the abundance, oxen will be expensive because they will be involved in fully cultivating the earth. More surprising is that horses will be cheap, because "they will never be ridden in war." This is difficult to reconcile with the renewed wars that we shall see against the Dajjal. He will become an even greater opponent against the Mahdi, in both the spiritual and military spheres.

The Mahdi will promote conversions of Jews and Christians to Islam. One thing that will help greatly will be the discovery of ancient manuscripts in Antioch, missing for two thousand years, containing heretofore unknown portions of the Old and New Testaments. The lost books will presumably restore the Bible to a pristine status, prove that the Qur'an is its culmination, and show that all along the Jews and Christians have believed in a false and corrupted Bible. With these lost scriptures, the Mahdi will refute the Jews in their interpretation of the Torah, written by Moses, with the new corrected history of Muslim ancestors. The Mahdi will confirm his authority in these disputed matters with the miraculous discovery of the Ark of the Covenant at Lake Tiberius, lost since the first exile of the Jews to Babylon in 587 BCE. Jews in large numbers will be persuaded and will convert to Islam.

Though the Hadiths that speak of hidden scrolls and the Ark are considered weak *(da'if)*, they are very popular among Muslims, and are a great motivation for them as they look forward to the Mahdi.

Through the imposition of Sharia law, the Mahdi will remove the injustices that have corrupted the world through the influence of non-Islamic ideologies and jurisprudence. Corporal *hudud*[154] punishments for theft, blasphemy, and adultery that are mandated in Sharia, such as stoning, lashing, and amputation, will no longer come under condemnation by an international backlash. Islamic regulations will finally be implemented worldwide. Among them will be the requirement for women to wear veils and be accompanied by male guardians in public places.

The Mahdi's theocratic government will bring all people and all of society to conformance with the will of Allah, by the thorough and consistent enforcement of Sharia. In these efforts, "every believer will be obligated to support him."

Peace will be established by means of wars that extend the reach of the Mahdi's power over pockets of resistance. The ultimate result will be an Islamic peace, through dominance, submission, and stability.

Comparison. Daniel saw into some of the inner workings of the antichrist's end-time regime, in this verse repeated from K17 and K21:

---

[154] Kali Robinson, *Understanding Sharia: The Intersection of Islam and the Law*, Council on Foreign Relations, December 27, 2021, https://www.cfr.org/backgrounder/understanding-sharia-intersection-islam-and-law, accessed April 10, 2023.

> Daniel 7:25 And he [the end-time king] will speak against
> the Most High and wear down the saints of the Highest One,
> and he will intend to make alterations in times and in law;
> and they will be handed over to him for a time, times, and
> half a time.

We are told here that the supreme ruler on earth "will speak against the Most High." This will happen when the beast of Revelation mandates worship of himself instead of the God of heaven. He will "wear down the saints of the Highest One." This will involve persecution of converts to Christ at historically unprecedented levels, unto death.

The antichrist "will intend to make alterations in times and in law." This will happen by instituting a different calendar than the world is accustomed to. Also, a new legal framework will replace the centuries-old laws of western civilization, rooted in the Mosaic law of the Old Testament. The opponents of the beast who turn to Christ "will be handed over to him for a time, times, and half a time." This translates to the beast's exclusive rule for a year (time), plus two years (times), plus half a year (the dividing of time) – perfectly matching the length of time of the great tribulation.

The Mahdi's conquest of the world in the name of Allah would readily fulfill these antichrist prophecies of Daniel 7:25. He "will speak against the Most High." Then he will turn words into action, by tracking down those who believe in the God of the Bible, and by making the biblical doctrine of the trinity punishable by death. The Mahdi also "will intend to make alterations in times and in law." This would be a change from the 365-day Gregorian solar calendar, whose years count forward from the birth of Christ. He will replace it with the 354-day Hijri lunar calendar. This cycle based on the moon is in keeping with the crescent symbol of Islam. Years will be designated AH, counting from the *hijrah* of 622 CE, when Muhammad and his followers migrated from Mecca to Medina and established the first Muslim community *(ummah)*.

He will also abolish western law, whose lineage traces to the ten commandments of the Old Testament (but was terribly corrupted by the precursors of the woman of Babylon over recent decades). In their place the Mahdi will force the imposition of Sharia law worldwide.

The Hadiths promise wealth during this new age of the Mahdi. This is difficult to imagine. Islamic nations have never been known to be engines of economic wealth. This contrasts with capitalism, the product of the Reformed Christian age,[155] which Revelation prophesied in the church of Philadelphia (see K11). The wealth of Muslim nations in recent centuries has not been based on value added, or competitive customer-oriented service, but on the exploitation of natural resources like oil and gas, or the plundering and labor of non-Muslims. It is more realistic that under the rule of the beast/the Mahdi, the merchants of the world will lament for the days of the woman of Babylon/the Romans. She/they presided over the last days of crass materialism, the final and much perverted form of capitalism, which is still capable of tempting people with fabulous wealth.

Moving to spiritual matters, the Hadiths say the Mahdi will bring forth missing scripture and the Ark of the Covenant. By doing this, he claims prerogatives that were thought the exclusive domain of the God of the Bible: the issuing of divine revelation, and the provision of a place of sacrifice where sins can be atoned. This fits Revelation's description of the beast and his blasphemies against the true God (13:5-6).

The Hadiths claim that when the Jews see the Ark, "all except a few will embrace Islam." This is the exact opposite of Revelation. There, the two witnesses, and the 144,000 untouchable evangelists, all of them Jewish, lead many Jews and gentiles away from trusting in an earthly treaty with the evil one, and put their eternal life in the hands of Jesus Christ instead (K18, K19).

One difference between the Hadiths and Revelation is that the antichrist demands worship of himself (13:8a), and the Mahdi does not. Surely Islam does not allow for the worship of any man.

Is this a discrepancy? One could argue that it is not, for three reasons.

First, the Mahdi is recognized as highly exalted in a couple references of this section, and in other Hadiths. One *athar* (words of the companions and followers of Muhammad) says "he is the Mahdi on earth and the Mahdi in heaven." A hadith says "a nation which has me (Muhammad)

---

[155] Max Weber, *Die protestantische Ethik und der Geist des Kapitalismus (The Protestant Ethic and the Spirit of Capitalism)*, 1904.

at its beginning, 'Isa ibn Maryam at its end and the Mahdi in between will never be destroyed."

Second, "the Mahdi will be directed to restore the prophetic caliphate and, as such, is not bound by the letter of Islamic law."[156] Since he "is, by definition, Allah's appointed ruler, he is free to interpret Qur'an, Hadith, and Sharia as he sees fit, disregarding any previous *ijma`*, or scholarly consensus. This means the Mahdi has, in effect, no brakes on his behavior other than his own intellect, personality, and piety."[157]

Third, if the beast of Revelation is the Mahdi of the Hadiths, he does not demand worship until midway through the tribulation, after he has put an end to the woman of Babylon/the Romans, and has gained the sworn allegiance of all Muslims, even those who collaborated. It now becomes quite imaginable for the Mahdi to declare himself the incarnation of Allah, similar to how the infidel Christians view Jesus to the incarnation of God. Behind this scenario one can sense one of Satan's greatest deceptions.[158]

------

[156] Furnish, p. 27.
[157] Furnish, p. 2.
[158] Richardson, pp. 179-184.

K24 :
The false prophet upholds the beast

: H24
ʿIsa ibn Maryam upholds the Mahdi, beheads the infidels, and presides over an idyllic world

13:11 Then I saw another beast coming up out of the earth; and he had two horns like a lamb, and he spoke as a dragon.

13:12 He exercises all the authority of the first beast in his presence. And he makes the earth and those who live on it worship the first beast, whose fatal wound was healed.

13:13 He performs great signs, so that he even makes fire come down out of the sky to the earth in the presence of people.

13:14 And he deceives those who live on the earth because of the signs which it was given him to perform in the presence of the beast, telling those who live on the earth to make an image to the beast who had the wound of the sword and has come to life.

13:15 And it was given to him to give breath to the image of the beast, so that the image of the beast would even speak and cause all who do not worship the image of the beast to be killed.

At this very time that Allah would send ʿIsa ibn Maryam, and he will descend at the white minaret in the eastern side of Damascus wearing two garments lightly dyed with saffron and placing his hands on the wings of two Angels. When he would lower his head, there would fall beads of perspiration from his head, and when he would raise it up, beads like pearls would scatter from it.[159]

The Prophet said: verily ʿIsa ibn Maryam shall descend as an equitable judge and fair ruler. He shall tread his path on the way to *hajj* [pilgrimage] and come to my grave to greet me and I shall certainly answer him![160]

The Hour will not be established until ʿIsa ibn Maryam descends amongst you as a just ruler, he will break the cross, kill the pigs, and abolish the Jizya tax.[161]

So when the sacred months have passed away, then slay the idolaters wherever you find them,

---

[159] Narrated by An-Nawwas b. Samʿan, *Sahih Muslim 2937 a*, Book 41, Hadith 7015, https://sunnah.com/muslim:2937a, accessed May 28, 2024; also referenced in Richardson p.52.

[160] Narrated by Abu Harayra, *Hakim Mustadrak (2:651) #4162*, quoted in Richardson p.53; also partially referenced in Mufti Ebrahim Desai Darul Iftaa, The emergence of Isa, August 29, 2007, https://askimam.org/public/question_detail/15612.

[161] Narrated by Abu Huraira, *Sahih al-Bukhari 2476*, Vol. 3, Book 43, Hadith 656, https://sunnah.com/bukhari:2476, accessed May 28, 2024.

13:16 And he causes all, the small and the great, the rich and the poor, and the free and the slaves, to be given a mark on their right hands or on their foreheads,
13:17 and he decrees that no one will be able to buy or to sell, except the one who has the mark, either the name of the beast or the number of his name.
13:18 Here is wisdom. Let him who has understanding calculate the number of the beast, for the number is that of a man; and his number is six hundred and sixty-six.
14:12 Here is the perseverance of the saints who keep the commandments of God and their faith in Jesus.
20:4‡[K43] *Then I saw thrones, and they sat on them, and judgment was given to them.* And I saw the souls of those who had been beheaded because of their testimony of Jesus and because of the word of God, and those who had not worshiped the beast or his image, and had not received the mark on their foreheads and on their hands; *and they came to life and reigned with Christ for a thousand years.*
14:13 And I heard a voice from heaven, saying, "Write: 'Blessed are the dead who die in the Lord from now on!' " "Yes," says the Spirit, "so that they may rest from their labors, for their deeds follow with them."

and take them captives and besiege them and lie in wait for them in every ambush, then if they repent and keep up prayer and pay the poor-rate, leave their way free to them; surely Allah is Forgiving, Merciful. (Surah 9:5, Shakir translation)

Therefore, when ye meet the Unbelievers (in fight), smite at their necks; At length, when ye have thoroughly subdued them, bind a bond firmly (on them): thereafter (is the time for) either generosity or ransom: Until the war lays down its burdens. (Surah 47:4a)

'Isa ibn Maryam will be a just judge and a just ruler among my nation. He will break the cross, slaughter the pigs, abolish the *jizya* [tax] and charity [*sadaqa*] will be left [abandoned].... Grudges and mutual hatred will disappear and the venom of every venomous creature will be removed, so that a baby boy will put his hand in a snake and it will not harm him, and a baby girl will make a lion run away, and it will not harm her; and the wolf will be among the sheep like their sheepdog. The earth will be filled with peace just as a vessel is filled with water. The people will be united and none will be worshipped except Allah. War will cease and Quraysh will no longer be in power. The earth will be like a silver platter [or, have a silver age], with its vegetation growing as it did at the time of Adam, until a group of people will gather around one bunch of grapes and it will suffice them, and a group will gather around a single pomegranate and it will suffice them. An ox will be sold for such and such amount of money, and a

horse will be sold for a few
dirham.[162] *(da'if)*

The Messenger of Allah said, a nation which has me at its beginning,
'Isa ibn Maryam at its end and the Mahdi in between will never be
destroyed.[163] *(da'if)*

Hadiths. In this section we meet 'Isa ibn Maryam. He will be the
Mahdi's right hand man. There is so much to unpack, so let us break it
into topics.

H1. *'Isa ibn Maryam descends*. The Mahdi arrived at the beginning of
the seven-year end-time period, as the rider on the white horse (H16).
Now his deputy appears on the scene. He is 'Isa ibn Maryam. His
descent from heaven is one of the Major Signs of the end, as given in
the hadith of H00.

In earlier sections we described him. His name in Arabic means Jesus
son of Mary. He is the hope of many Muslims. A survey conducted
among world Muslims in 2012 found that 35% of them believe that 'Isa
is coming soon.[164] They believe he will work with the Mahdi to defeat *al-
Dajjal*, the deceiver or antichrist.

But 'Isa ibn Maryam is quite a different character from Jesus Christ of
the Bible. The Qur'an says 'Isa was never crucified, and never
experienced death. It repudiates the New Testament accounts of his
crucifixion and resurrection. After Allah miraculously delivered 'Isa
from death, he ascended into heaven without ever dying, in a similar
way to Elijah:

> [They were] boasting, "We killed the Messiah, 'Isa Ibn Maryam,
> the messenger of Allah." But they neither killed nor crucified
> him—it was only made to appear so. Even those who argue for
> this (crucifixion) are in doubt. They have no knowledge

---

[162] Narrated by Abu Umamah Al-Bahili, *Sunan Ibn Majah 4077*, Vol. 5, Book 36, Hadith
4077, https://sunnah.com/ibnmajah:4077, accessed May 8, 2023; alternate translations
in brackets from 'Ibn Izzat p.35-36.
[163] Narrated by Abdullah Ibn 'Abbas, in Ibn Hajar al-Haytami (10th century Egyptian
scholar of hadith), *Al-Sawa'iq al-Muhriqah* (see H16), quoted in Ayatollah Sadr al-Din al-
Sadr (d.1953), *Al-Mahdi*, English trans. Jalil Dorrani, Naba Organization, 1994,
https://www.al-islam.org/al-mahdi-sayyid-sadruddin-sadr/chapter-4, accessed May 26,
2024.
[164] Furnish, p..8. The survey was conducted by the Pew Forum on Religion and Public
Life. In Tunisia the number was 67%, Turkey 65%, Iraq 64%, Lebanon 52%.

whatsoever—only making assumptions. They certainly did not kill him. (Surah 4:157, Clear Qur'an)

And when Allah said: O 'Isa, I am going to terminate the period of your stay (on earth) and cause you to ascend unto Me and purify you of those who disbelieve and make those who follow you above those who disbelieve to the day of resurrection; then to Me shall be your return, so I will decide between you concerning that in which you differed. (Surah 3:55, Shakir translation)

After Allah brought him alive to heaven, 'Isa patiently waits to come back to earth, and perform his end-time role.

Muslims believe that unlike the corrupted Christian character who is called Jesus Christ, in no way is 'Isa's role to save people from their sins. It is blasphemy to say that a man can fulfill this function. It is the unknowable domain of Allah alone. 'Isa ibn Maryam is only another one of Allah's prophets. He is outranked by Muhammad, the greatest of them, and the Mahdi, who is the Muhammad of the end time. His special title *al-Maseeh*, or Messiah, does not signify the biblical role of redeeming and delivering people from their sin. It is merely an honorific title of great respect.

The hadith says 'Isa "will descend at the white minaret in the eastern side of Damascus." Then, according to another hadith, he "shall tread his path on the way to hajj." By this pilgrimage to the Kaaba in Mecca, he proves he is a faithful Muslim, and that the Jesus Christ of Christians is an imagined product of their corrupted Bible. Their idea of him is wrong, and keeps them from accepting Allah and Muhammad as his prophet.

At his return, 'Isa becomes the greatest Muslim evangelist ever. He will be the religious leader of the Mahdi's caliphate, and oversees the enforcement of Sharia law. Under his guidance, many willingly convert to Islam. Others are forced to submit. Later in section H34, he will lead the Mahdi's armies victoriously in battle against the Dajjal, who is the main obstacle to the advancement of Islam.

H2. Hatred against Jews and Christians. 'Isa ibn Maryam will be a just ruler. With the justice that he delivers, the hadith says "he will break the cross, kill the pigs, and abolish the *jizya* tax."

Ibn Qayyim al-Jawziyya, the 13th century Islamic theologian and jurisconsult of Damascus, voiced the interpretation of this hadith held by jihadists through all centuries, in his book *Ighatha al-Lahfan* (Helping the Grieved):

> The Muslims are waiting for the descent of the Messiah 'Isa ibn Maryam from heaven, when he will break the crosses, kill the pigs *and kill his enemies among the Jews and the Christians who worship him.*[165] (italics added)

In this widely held view, 'Isa ibn Maryam will forsake his Jewishness. He will also emphatically reject the false notion that he is the head of the Christian religion. To back this up, he cleanses the world of unbelief by killing the Jews and Christians.

This will happen in the most violent manner.

First, let us consider the Jews. By killing his enemies among them, 'Isa ibn Maryam will be following the core teachings of Muhammad.

Why will 'Isa attack the Jews, instead of following the Qur'an's teachings that are favorable toward the Jews? Here are several:

> O Children of Israel! call to mind the (special) favour which I bestowed upon you, and fulfil your covenant with Me as I fulfil My Covenant with you, and fear none but Me. (Surah 2:40)

> O Children of Israel! call to mind the special favour which I bestowed upon you, and that I preferred you to all others (for My Message) (Surah 2:122)

> Indeed, the believers, Jews, Christians, and Sabians—whoever (truly) believes in Allah and the Last Day and does good will have their reward with their Lord. And there will be no fear for them, nor will they grieve. (Surah 2:62, Clear Qur'an)

> We did aforetime grant to the Children of Israel the Book, the Power of Command, and Prophethood; We gave them, for Sustenance, things good and pure; and We favoured them above the nations. (Surah 45:16)

---

[165] Ibn Qayyim al-Jawziyya (13th century Islamic jurisconsult of Damascus), in (Arabic) *Ighatha al-Lahfan* (Helping the Grieved), https://www.albalaghbooks.com/beliefs-and-practices/self-reform/ighathat-al-lahfan-2-volume-set/, translated in 'Ibn Izzat p.12.

The reason is that in the Qur'an many verses seem to contradict one another. In such cases, the Islamic doctrine called *nasik* provides guidance. It states that older revelations that Muhammad received from the angel Jibreel are to be cancelled out *(mansookh)* by newer ones. Many Qur'ans include a chart of cancelled verses, so that the faithful know which ones have been superseded.[166]

The verses above are thus cancelled by others that announce a stark hatred for the Jews:

> The Jews say: "Allah's hand is tied up." Be their hands tied up and be they accursed for the (blasphemy) they utter. Nay, both His hands are widely outstretched: He giveth and spendeth (of His bounty) as He pleaseth. But the revelation that cometh to thee from Allah increaseth in most of them their obstinate rebellion and blasphemy. Amongst them we have placed enmity and hatred till the Day of Judgment. Every time they kindle the fire of war, Allah doth extinguish it; but they (ever) strive to do mischief on earth. And Allah loveth not those who do mischief. (Surah 5:64)

> Of the Jews there are those who displace words from their (right) places, and say: "We hear and we disobey"; and "Hear what is not Heard"; and "Ra'ina"; with a twist of their tongues and a slander to Faith. If only they had said: "We hear and we obey"; and "Do hear"; and "Do look at us"; it would have been better for them, and more proper; but Allah hath cursed them for their Unbelief; and but few of them will believe. (Surah 4:46)

The Jews are also said to start wars and cause general mischief. They have descended to the lowest behavior. Allah was so disgusted by them that he cursed them, and turned them into apes and swine. They are no longer worthy even of being considered as human:

> When in their insolence they transgressed (all) prohibitions, We said to them: "Be ye apes, despised and rejected." (Surah 7:166)

> And well ye knew those amongst you who transgressed in the matter of the Sabbath: We said to them: "Be ye apes, despised and rejected." (Surah 2:65)

> Those who incurred the curse of Allah and His wrath, those of whom some He transformed into apes and swine, those who

---

[166] Richardson pp. 112-113.

> worshipped evil;- these are (many times) worse in rank, and far
> more astray from the even path! (Surah 5:60b)

After Muhammad's death, antisemitism grew over the centuries. The scorn for the Jews far surpasses the specific historical conflicts during his lifetime, for instance, with the Jewish Banu Qurayzah tribe who refused to accept his prophethood, whom Muhammad then slaughtered after a suitable pretext (see K03).

The hatred of Muslims against Jews is more than justified by the Qur'anic scriptures above. In the end time, the Mahdi's nullification of the treaty mediated by the Jews (see H21) opens the door for him to fulfill the will of Allah, once and for all. Islam will finally break through the treachery of countless Jewish agreements. Jews will be made to suffer for all the treaties they extracted from Muslims. They are now marked out for a destiny of absolute and total slaughter. The intention of 'Isa ibn Maryam is to carry out the Mahdi's plan, with a more thorough cleansing of the world from Jews than even Hitler's final solution. That is the prognostication of the Hadiths.

Second, with regards to Christians, the end-time caliphate will not be satisfied with marginalizing Christianity. It will abolish it. The hadith says 'Isa ibn Maryam "will break the cross, (and) kill the pigs." Ibn Qayyim al-Jawziyya adds that he will "kill his enemies among ... the Christians who worship him." Christians, easily identified by the detestable practice of eating pork, will be punished with death. The choice for those who worship the Christ of the Bible will be to either convert to Islam, or to die at the hands of 'Isa ibn Maryam's religious enforcers.

'Isa's actions will bring about the peace that the Mahdi promised, by liquidating any who would challenge his supremacy. Peace through war will characterize the remainder of the Mahdi's seven-year rule.

H3. *Life and death under 'Isa ibn Maryam*. The Hadiths say that 'Isa will do more than "break the cross, (and) kill the pigs." He will also "abolish the *jizya*." This is the tax historically applied to non-Muslims. But it will no longer be applicable, since Christians and Jews are targeted for death. Payment of jizya will no longer excuse their existence.

Their executions will carry out Allah's will. They will be proof that "'Isa ibn Maryam will be a just judge and a just ruler among my nation."

By bringing death to Christians and Jews, 'Isa will bring success and prosperity to Muslims. There will be no greed or coveting. Sheep and camels, oxen and horses, plants and fruit will be in abundance. Presumably so also will be all other material needs and luxuries. *Sadaqa* (voluntary charity) will be abandoned. This tells us that the economy, or more likely the plunder taken as booty from the Jews and Romans/Christians, will be so prolific under the Mahdi that the practice of *sadaqa* will no longer be needed.

The animal kingdom itself will be transformed. None of the creatures will be menacing any longer. Children will play with snakes and lions, and wolves will not harm sheep. The new world will be purged of all infidels and polytheists. This would include present day versions of the ancient Quraysh idolaters of Mecca – like Hindus, and of course all Christians. After they are done away with, the caliphate will have perfect peace and harmony. Only Allah will be worshipped.

The glorious age that will come upon the earth is described in the hadith as "a silver age." This is the suitable place to requote the hadith that says: "a nation which has me [Muhammad] at its beginning, 'Isa ibn Maryam at its end and the Mahdi in between will never be destroyed."

H4. Beheading of Infidels. Islam's preferred method of dealing with unyielding infidels is to execute them. Undoubtedly, this will also be true under the regime of the Mahdi and 'Isa ibn Maryam. The practice can be traced to the perfect man, the prophet Muhammad, who gave the directive of Surah 9:5, known as "the verse of the sword." It says to "slay the idolaters wherever you find them." Based on this command, the overwhelming majority of Muslim scholars up to the present day teach that Muslims are allowed to fight unbelievers. They are even to seek them out, force them to submit to Allah, and if they do not, to kill them.

The preferred method of execution is beheading. This is given in Surah 47:4, which says, "when ye meet the Unbelievers (in fight), smite at their necks; At length, when ye have thoroughly subdued them, bind a bond firmly (on them) … until the war lays down its burdens." Ibn Kathir, a still-respected Qur'anic commentator of the fourteenth century, attempted to clarify this verse:

> [Guide] the Believers to what they should employ in their fight against the idolaters. Allah says, "So when you meet those who disbelieve [in battle], smite their necks, which means when you fight against them, cut them down totally with your swords. "Until you have fully defeated them" meaning you have killed and utterly destroyed them. This is referring to the prisoners of war whom you have captured.[167]

But Muhammad did not say to behead only enemy soldiers captured as prisoners of war. His own example was to order the beheading of civilians, including women and children.

According to the ancient biography (*sirat*) of Muhammad Ibn Ishaq, *after* the prophet had already defeated and subdued the polytheistic Quraysh tribe of Mecca (see H17), he directed that their combatants and civilians – men, women, and children – be beheaded:

> Then they [the Quraysh] surrendered and the apostle *(the prophet Muhammad)* confined them in Medina. Then the apostle went out to the market of Medina [which is still its market today] and dug trenches in it. Then he sent for them and struck off their heads in those trenches as they were brought out to him in batches…. They were six hundred or seven hundred in all, though some put the figures as high as eight hundred or nine hundred. This went on until the apostle made an end to them.[168]

Later, Ibn Ishaq describes how Muhammad ordered the beheading of four hundred Jews.[169]

Though these two mass beheadings are not recorded in the Qur'an, they are in Muhammad's authoritative and ancient biography. The actions of the perfect man are the model for all faithful Muslims to follow.

---

[167] Ibn Kathir, *Tafsir*, on Sura 47:4, https://www.alim.org/quran/tafsir/ibn-kathir/surah/47/4/, accessed May 6, 2023; also referenced in Richardson p.133.
[168] Ishaq, Ibn, *Sirat Rasul Allah -The Life of Muhammad*, A. Guillaume, translator, Oxford University Press, 1955, p. 464; also quoted in https://en.m.wikipedia.org/wiki/Battle_of_the_Trench, accessed July 29, 2024.
[169] Ishaq, Ibn, p. 752.

Islam therefore engenders a culture where the killing and beheading of non-Muslims is acceptable. To this day, Muslim jihadists feel no obligation to treat their prisoners by the Geneva convention, or any other standard of leniency, even if they make a written agreement to do so (see the discussion of *taqiyya*, or concealment of Islamic belief, in H17).

In my day, the ISIS movement (Islamic State of Iraq and Syria) has tried to solidify its claim to reestablish the caliphate by performing mass beheadings of non-combatant Christians. They relay them by video feed in real time on Internet social media platforms, for the whole world to see. Through these beheadings, they reinforce their literalist Islamic credentials, win over young Muslims to their cause, and provoke western "Christian" countries into deploying ground troops against them. This leads to more cycles of violence, which results in greater notoriety for ISIS, and more recruits to their cause. The aim is to inaugurate the end time, and induce the appearance of the Mahdi. Their methods have spread to Muslim countries far beyond the Middle East. The result is that Christians are the most persecuted group in majority Muslim countries.[170]

News of this persecution against Christians is largely suppressed in non-Muslim countries that favor globalism and statism. This is done to appease Muslims, in the hope that jihadists won't be provoked to violence in western countries.

It is a worrying concern that in countries they control, these same globalists and statists are applying persecution in softer forms against Christians. This is a precursor to the treaty of unholy alliance between the end-time "Romans" and the Mahdi (H17).

The Mahdi and his deputy 'Isa ibn Maryam will be fully justified in emulating Muhammad and in obeying the words of the Qur'an. They will follow the example of many generations of jihadists, and the teachings of Islam through all the centuries. Their goal will be the beheadings of millions of Jews, Christians, and any other non-Muslims who do not convert. Nevermore will there be any who oppose Allah.

---

[170] Furnish, p. 34.

Revelation. The four topics of the Hadiths regarding the return of the Islamic 'Isa have parallels in Revelation's account of the false prophet. He comes on the scene to be the beast's copartner (13:11-12). Revelation also dwells on two more topics: the mark of the beast, and the number of the beast.

R1. *The false prophet does great wonders.* This secondary character is described as another beast, who comes out of the earth (13:11). But we will see him in future sections under a different name, in verses 16:13 K38, 19:20 K40, and 20:10 K45. There he is identified as *the false prophet*. His title of "prophet" tells us that he will be a religious figure. He speaks as a dragon, which identifies him as a mouthpiece of that greater dragon, Satan (12:9 K15). Thus, his prophecies and admonitions will be "false," because they cast aspersions on the true God of the Bible.

John in his vision sees this other beast as having two horns, like a lamb (13:11). In the Old Testament, God commanded that a lamb be slaughtered as a blood sacrifice by every Jewish family at the yearly Passover observance, to atone for their sins before him. The false prophet's appearance as a lamb is a deception. He pretends to deliver people from the obligation that their sins be paid for before God. Unlike Jesus, the false prophet certainly does *not* offer himself up for the sins of the people. Instead, he means for the people of the tribulation to be indebted forever to him for evading God's righteous requirements.

The false prophet works signs and wonders, "he even makes fire come down out of the sky to the earth in the presence of people" (13:13). But the false prophet is definitely second to the beast in authority, and is loyal to him in all his actions.

R2. *Sacrilege of the temple.* Whenever people see the miraculous healing of the beast's fatal wound, they are convinced of his almost-divine powers. He displays it proudly. His deputy the false prophet calls fire down from heaven to prove his divinity (13:12-13).

The false prophet takes further advantage of the awe of the people. He commands that an image of the beast be made into a kind of statue. After it is put into position, the false prophet dazzles the whole world by giving life to the image (13:14). To all appearances this is another miraculous act, equal to God originally forming the first man Adam from dust and giving him life (Genesis 2:7).

This last miracle is totally compelling to most people. In their amazement, they join in worshipping the image. It becomes the religious centerpiece of the tribulation. People worldwide channel their spirits toward the image, and the one it represents.

The image of the beast will be the *abomination* that causes desolation, prophesied by Daniel:

> Daniel 9:27 And he [the prince who is to come] *will confirm a covenant with the many for one week,* but in the middle of the week he will put a stop to sacrifice and grain offering; and on the wing of abominations will come the one who makes desolate, *until a complete destruction, one that is decreed, gushes forth on the one who makes desolate.*
> 12:11 And from the time that the regular sacrifice is abolished and the abomination of desolation is set up, there will be 1,290 days.

The phrase "in the middle of the week" points to soon after the midpoint of the tribulation, when worship of the image will replace the God-given temple rites of sacrifice and offering (Daniel 9:27). In the Old Testament, they were performed by the Jewish priests to atone for the sins of the people. But the priests of the tribulation have been ejected from the temple, as part of the abrogation of the treaty by the beast.

The image of abomination is the most audacious counterfeit object of worship. We can deduce from Daniel that the image will be placed inside the holy temple itself, as a maximum statement of defiance against the holy God of the Bible. At the time John received this vision, there was already a precedent for such an abomination. In 167 BCE, the Greek king Antiochus IV Epiphanies desecrated the temple in Jerusalem, by setting up an altar to Zeus, and sacrificing a pig upon it. He also slaughtered a great number of the Jews, sold others into slavery, outlawed the practice of circumcision, required Jews to sacrifice to pagan gods and eat pig meat. But Antiochus did not enter a covenant with Israel for seven years. So his was only a partial foreshadowing of the end-time events.

The false prophet's sacrilege will be compounded when the beast's followers take full control of the city and the temple.

The apostle Paul also looked ahead to this event. He foresaw that the main actor, whom Revelation labels as the beast, will be none other than the man of lawlessness, the antichrist. His intention will be to exalt himself above God:

> 2 Thessalonians 2:3 No one is to deceive you in any way! For it will not come unless the apostasy comes first, and the man of lawlessness is revealed, the son of destruction,
> 2:4 who opposes and exalts himself above every so-called god or object of worship, so that he takes his seat in the temple of God, displaying himself as being God.

R3. *Persecution and death under the beast and the false prophet*.

Not everyone will worship the image, however. Under the regime of the great tribulation, the attack on Christ-believers will eclipse anything seen in history.

The false prophet commands that those who do not pay homage be killed (13:15).

Jesus warned all his followers to prepare for such a time:

> Matthew 24:9 "Then they will hand you over to tribulation and kill you, and you will be hated by all nations because of My name."

Church history records numerous periods of persecution resulting in the death of many Christ-followers. They occurred from time to time in certain countries, but not in others. The difference during the great tribulation will be that "you will be hated by all nations because of My name." The word *all* tells of the global nature of the persecution. It points ahead to the global empire established by the beast.

The heavenly Father watches from on high. He sees those who are targeted for death, all because they have decided against the beast and turned to Jesus to save them. God knows their new-found faith, and their new commitment to please him and obey his commandments (14:12).

R4. *Martyrdom of Jesus' followers*. The persecution will be intense. John in his vision sees great numbers of new believers "beheaded because of their testimony of Jesus and because of the word of God" (20:4). Widespread death and famine will be the result, in this and the next section of the timeline. The consequence will be the *desolation* of the world, triggered by the abomination of God's holy temple.

Jesus confirmed to his twelve disciples that the abomination of desolation will come as a marker of the end times. They recorded his prediction in the gospels. He warned the Jews of the future Jerusalem not to seek any arrangement with the false prophet. Instead, they must flee. If they do so, Jesus promises to save them:

> Matthew 24:15 "Therefore when you see the abomination of desolation which was spoken of through Daniel the prophet, standing in the holy place— let the reader understand—
> 24:16 then those who are in Judea must flee to the mountains.
> 24:17 Whoever is on the housetop must not go down to get things out of his house.
> 24:18 And whoever is in the field must not turn back to get his cloak.
> 24:19 But woe to those women who are pregnant, and to those who are nursing babies in those days!
> 24:20 Moreover, pray that when you flee, it will not be in the winter, or on a Sabbath."
> 24:30 And then the sign of the Son of Man will appear in the sky, and then all the tribes of the earth will mourn, and they will see the Son of Man coming on the clouds of the sky with power and great glory.
> 24:31 And He will send forth His angels with a great trumpet blast, and they will gather together His elect from the four winds, from one end of the sky to the other.

Those who flee the abomination in faith, and nevertheless meet their death, will be gathered with the elect. They will live after death. After their beheading, in section K43 we shall see verse 20:4 again. The martyrs will be sitting on magnificent heavenly thrones prepared by God at the end of the great tribulation. They will share in judging their persecutors, and themselves will receive God's favorable judgment, bestowed at the cost of Christ's sinless life.

Their further reward will be to receive glorified bodies. They shall then return to earth to reign with Christ in his millennial kingdom (K44).

In the last verse of this section, an angel encourages believers facing impending death and beheading in the great tribulation, with the beautiful words "blessed are the dead who die in the Lord from now on" (14:13).

Jesus spoke of this future of all his followers in these two verses of Matthew:

> Matthew 7:14 For the gate is narrow and the way is constricted that leads to life, and there are few who find it. 5:10 "Blessed are those who have been persecuted for the sake of righteousness, for theirs is the kingdom of heaven."

R5. *Mark of the beast*. Another innovation of the false prophet in John's vision is the infamous mark of the beast (13:16-17).

When the beast rode the red horse (6:4 K21) to seize supreme power from the woman of Babylon (17:16 K21), the rich economy of the world grounded to a sudden halt (18:14 K21). He ramps up the persecution against the new believers into outright war upon them, and upon any other pockets of opposition (13:7-8 K23).

The plunder of these wars may satisfy the beast's closest followers, but cannot sustain billions of people. Shortages of basic necessities will be the result, with inevitable rationing. We shall see in the next section (K25) that famine and death are coming to the wider population, even to those who worship the beast.

Rationing has been used by many tyrants as a tool of war to keep their subjects under control. This is what the false prophet will do, acting as deputy to the beast. In his portfolio as minister of religion and worship, he will prioritize rationing according to loyalty. Those who swear allegiance to the beast are branded with a mark "on their right hands or on their foreheads" (13:16). Many people who earlier were not convinced that the beast was worthy of worship, will now reluctantly do so, if only to gain the mark. That way they can have access to precious goods and services. "No one will be able to buy or to sell, except the one who has the mark, either the name of the beast or the number of his name" (13:17). (We will talk about the number of the beast in the next subsection).

Those who still refuse the mark of the beast are assumed to be followers of Christ. They will be easily identified, because they do not display the mark. It is conceivable that angry crowds will be whipped up to kill them, saving the beast's forces from doing the job.

The hidden aim is to do away with every single Christ-follower. After this is fully accomplished, they believe prosperity will return. The beast and the false prophet will then somehow cement an everlasting paradise upon the earth. Their insane logic is that Christians are to blame for the troubles of the world. They will follow in the footsteps of many governments that have targeted Christians through the centuries, only to find total failure in the end.

R6. *Number of the beast: 666*. The mark of the beast is just one display of loyalty. The other is to show the number of the beast (13:17). "The number is that of a man; and his number is six hundred and sixty-six." (13:18).

Why 666, and not some other number? A common answer is that it represents some historical figure who best fits the description of the antichrist. He will be the model for the future beast, who will come back in his name. A way to determine who will come back is to use *gematria*, the practice of coding numbers into words. This is a technique that traces back to ancient languages such as Hebrew and Greek. Before the advent of the decimal system, people used letters from their alphabets to also stand for numbers. If given a number as a starting point, it can be transposed back into letters, hopefully revealing meaningful words, or the name of a key person.

Using this method and Hebrew values for letters, 666 is written as קסר נרון, transliterated as Qsr Nrwn. This is said to be Nero,[171] one of the emperors of the Roman empire. In 64 CE, Nero set fire to his own capital city, blamed the Christians for it, and burned them on crosses as punishment. In this interpretation, a new Nero will reestablish the

---

[171] Peter Goeman, *The Mark of the Beast, 666, and Nero (Rev 13:18),* August 1, 2020, https://petergoeman.com/the-mark-of-the-beast-666-and-nero-rev-1318/.

Roman empire as beast of the tribulation. Then he will persecute the believers on a far more massive scale.

Gematria can also be interpreted in terms of acronyms. The number 666 in Roman numerals is DCLXVI, which could be the Latin acronym *Domitius Caesar Legatos Xti Violenter Interfecit* - which translates roughly to "the emperor Domitian violently killed the ambassadors of Christ."[172] Domitian persecuted the Christians of the Roman empire during his rule from 90 to 96.

Another person that may reappear in a revived Roman empire from such a 666 analysis is Vespasian. Nero sent him to Israel in 66 to bring the Jews under full submission to Rome. His son Titus finished the task, and destroyed the Jewish temple in the year 70. For the rest of the church age, there was no temple. Vespasian went on to be emperor.

A different spin is that perhaps many of the scenes of Revelation are symbolic of events that have already occurred in the past, in the age of the person who represents 666. Certain popes, and of course Hitler, have been found to fit that model.

As you can see, gematria is a very subjective approach that can lead into almost any direction.

A much better interpretation is to read that 666, "the number ... of a man" (13:18), means the number of *all mankind*. This comes from seeing the number six in the Bible as representing men and women in their rebellion, imperfection, sin, and weakness. Consider these key passages of the Bible:

- The sixth day of the creation week is when Adam and Eve were created, the ancestors of all mankind (Genesis 1:26-31).
- Six days of the week are set aside for man to labor (Exodus 20:9).
- Six hundred years was Noah's age when God flooded the whole earth, as judgment upon the wickedness of all its inhabitants (Genesis 7:6,11).

---

[172] *The Mystery of the Book of Revelation: Which Roman Emperor is the Antichrist?*, March 18, 2015, https://www.educationalcoin.com/the-mystery-of-the-book-of-revelation-which-roman-emperor-is-the-antichrist/.

- The sixth commandment is "You shall not murder" (Exodus 20:13, Deuteronomy 5:17).
- At the sixth hour (Hebrew time, meaning six hours after dawn) during Christ's crucifixion, there was darkness over the world (Matthew 27:45).[173]
- Six hours is the length of time that Jesus suffered on the cross (Mark 15:25, Matthew 27:46-50).

The three sixes of 13:18 is the number of sinful man three times over. Thus, the number of the beast is a counterfeit trinity. Sinful man in triplicate substitutes for the holy trinity, the divine three-in-one – God the Father, God the Son, and God the Holy Spirit.

The first member of the 666 trinity is Satan. Ever since his fall (Ezekiel 28:15 K01), he has schemed to sideline God and take permanent control over the pinnacle of creation – the earth – and all men and women who dwell in it.

The second of the 666 trinity is the beast. Satan has recruited this mortal man to be the antichrist, the messiah alternative to Jesus.

The third member of the tribulation 666 is the false prophet. He is another mortal, who substitutes for the Holy Spirit. The false prophet believes he can prove his credentials by showy miracles in front of masses of people.

The true trinity of the Bible is Father, Son, and Holy Spirit. Jesus the son did miracles, but refused to do them to prove his divinity. We see this for example in this passage from Mark:

> Mark 8:11 And the Pharisees came out and began to argue with Him, demanding from Him a sign from heaven, to test Him.
> 8:12 Sighing deeply in His spirit, He said, "Why does this generation demand a sign? Truly I say to you, no sign will be given to this generation!"

Jesus promised the Holy Spirit would come to take his place before he went to the cross:

---

[173] *How Long was Jesus on the Cross,* https://www.gotquestions.org/Jesus-on-the-cross.html, accessed September 16, 2022.

> John 16:13 But when He, the Spirit of truth, comes, He will
> guide you into all the truth; for He will not speak on His
> own, but whatever He hears, He will speak; and He will
> disclose to you what is to come.
> 16:14 He will glorify Me, for He will take from Mine and will
> disclose it to you.

After Jesus ascended into heaven, the Holy Spirit descended upon the newly born church on the day of Pentecost (Acts 2:1-4). He is the third person of the Godhead. He comes to live in the heart of every believer. But unlike the false prophet, he operates secretly without conspicuous display:

> 1 Corinthians 3:16 Do you not know that you are a temple of
> God and that the Spirit of God dwells in you?

The Holy Spirit is our helper in times of trouble:

> John 14:16 I will ask the Father, and He will give you another
> Helper, so that He may be with you forever;
> 14:17 the Helper is the Spirit of truth, whom the world
> cannot receive, because it does not see Him or know Him;
> but you know Him because He remains with you and will be
> in you.

The Holy Spirit prays for us:

> Romans 8:26 Now in the same way the Spirit also helps our
> weakness; for we do not know what to pray for as we
> should, but the Spirit Himself intercedes for us with
> groanings too deep for words;
> 8:27 and He who searches the hearts knows what the mind
> of the Spirit is, because He intercedes for the saints
> according to the will of God.

The Holy Spirit is divine, but the false prophet is not. The beast's deputy does not care to provide comfort or prayer. He cannot bring peace into our hearts.

The number 666 falls three times short of the biblically perfect number seven:

- God rested on the seventh day after creating the universe
  (Genesis 1; 2:1-2).

- God granted the seventh day as a day of rest for all men (Exodus 20:9-11).
- Every seventh year, the Old Testament Israelites were to cancel all the debts they had made with each other (Deuteronomy 15:1-2).
- Jesus taught we should forgive each other seventy-seven times (Matthew 18:21-22).
- On seven occasions, Jesus healed on the Sabbath day (Mark 1:21-28, 29-31, 3:1-6, Luke 13:10-17, 14:1-6, John 5:1-18, 9:1-16).
- As Jesus was hanging on the cross, he spoke seven times in his agony (Luke 23:34, 23:43, John 19:26-27, Matthew 27:46, John 19:28, 30, Luke 23:46).[174]
- Jesus used seven metaphors for himself in the gospel of John. He is the bread of life (John 6:35), light of the world (John 8:12), the door to salvation (John 10:9), the good shepherd (John 10:11), the resurrection and the life (John 11:25-26), the way, the truth, and the life (John 14:6), and the vine (John 15:5).

To conclude, 666, the number of the beast, represents Satan leading men and women in one last effort to create a world without God. During the great tribulation, the hatred of fallen man against God is branded three times over, with man's number.

Comparison.

C1. *'Isa ibn Maryam compared with the false prophet*. Both 'Isa in the Hadiths and the false prophet in Revelation come on the scene to become the chief assistant of their superior, the Mahdi or the beast, to whom they are completely devoted.

Both 'Isa and the false prophet are delegated the responsibility of enforcing religious conformance in the new world order. 'Isa begins this by performing the hajj pilgrimage to the Kaaba. From there he goes on to be the greatest advocate ever for Allah and Islam. The false prophet

---

[174] Dolores Smyth, *What Is the Biblical Significance of the Number 7?*, January 31, 2020, https://www.christianity.com/wiki/bible/what-is-the-biblical-significance-of-the-number-7.html.

begins by performing incredulous miracles that capture the imagination of millions.

Both 'Isa and the false prophet are prophets. 'Isa is revered as both a past and future prophet of Islam. He is subordinate in standing to Muhammad, the founder and greatest prophet of Islam, and to the Mahdi, the future deliverer. The false prophet is also revered as a prophet because of his miracle working. But Revelation labels him as "false," because he opposes the things of the true God of heaven. This aligns him with the false prophets of the Bible, who proclaimed words they said were from Almighty God, but in reality led people away from him. The false prophet does the same, with the object of capturing the souls of people. His goal is for them to serve him and the beast instead.

Many Muslims have never questioned the core Islamic belief that the biblical account of Jesus Christ contains much falsehood. They take for granted that the Muslim Jesus, 'Isa ibn Maryam, will be the completely true Jesus who will come back in the end time.

But the parallels between 'Isa and the false prophet of Revelation are a much more compelling match. They suggest that Jesus Christ is really who the Bible says he is.

C2. *Hatred against Jews and their temple*. The Hadiths celebrate the idea that 'Isa ibn Maryam "will kill his enemies among the Jews." This will be the culmination of centuries of righteous antisemitism, fully justified by the example of Muhammad and the teachings of the Qur'an.

In Revelation, the false prophet doubles down on his miracles by bringing the living image of the beast inside the holy temple of the Jews. He eagerly sets forth this abomination that causes desolation. It is the opening of the official campaign to eradicate the Jews of the tribulation, along with any who have come to faith in Christ.

Lurking behind these actions against Jews, in both Revelation and the Hadiths, is Satan's ancient hatred for the Jews.

From the day God gave Jacob the name Israel (Genesis 35:10) and selected his descendants to be his chosen people, Satan has not rested from his attacks on them. Throughout the Bible, and afterward, he has used human rulers to persecute and kill Jews.

Pharaoh ordered all male Hebrew newborn to be slaughtered (Exodus 1:15-22). Haman attempted to have all the Jews of the Medo-Persian empire killed (Esther 3:8-9). The Greek king Antiochus Epiphanies laid siege to Jerusalem, in which countless Jews were killed (Daniel 8:23-25, 1 Maccabees 1-6, Josephus). Titus, son of Vespasian, besieged Jerusalem and leveled the temple, in the process killing 1.1 million Jews (Josephus). In the last two thousand years, various Islamic and supposedly Christian nations have targeted Jews for persecution. We cannot forget Hitler's Nazi Germany, which killed six million Jews, and the Islamic terrorists of recent decades, for whom Jews are the chief target.

The history of the Jews over millennia, and how God has preserved his chosen people despite their unbelief, is proof that Satan exists. He is their worst enemy.[175]

The future actions of the Mahdi, 'Isa, and their followers follow in this line of history. They are mirrored not just in Revelation, but also in the prophecy of Daniel 9:26b that we saw in section K16. Back then, at the beginning of the tribulation, the beast came as the rider on the red horse. He will be Daniel's "prince who is to come":

> Daniel 9:26b the people of the prince who is to come will destroy the city and the sanctuary.

This anticipates the future temple to be built in Jerusalem. The antichrist with a large band of followers will ruin it and lay waste to the city.

The Hadiths echo Daniel's prophecy. 'Isa Ibn Maryam will lead the followers of the Mahdi to "break the cross, kill the [Christian] pigs," and kill his enemies among the Jews as well. It is likely they will devastate the Jewish quarter of Jerusalem and desecrate the temple in the name of Allah. They will regard the rebuilt temple as a direct competitor to Islam's holiest site, the Kaaba in Mecca. It is therefore worthy of sacrilege and destruction.

Muslims will revere 'Isa Ibn Maryam, because to them he is the *maseeh* (messiah, or Christ) sent by Allah back to earth. But the true Jesus of

---

[175] Richardson, pp.115-117.

the New Testament warned his disciples and all future believers of such false christs who would come:

> Luke 21:8 And He said, "See to it that you are not misled; for many will come in My name, saying, 'I am He,' and, 'The time is near.' Do not go after them."

If it is in God's sovereign plan that the Mahdi will be the antichrist, then 'Isa ibn Maryam would be the false prophet of Revelation. He will claim the name of Christ. He will deceive many.

It is terribly ironic that the Qur'an mentions portions of the Old Testament as holy books that were given to the Jews by Allah: the *Taurat* (Torah) revealed to *Musa* (Moses), and the *Zabur* (Psalms) revealed to *Dawud* (David). Yet after Muhammad came, Allah cursed the Jews for all eternity.

The true God of the Bible did not curse the Jews forever when most of them refused Jesus as the messiah. Many of them were complicit with his death on the cross. When they disobeyed God, he did not turn against them, but kept his promises to Moses and David. And he has brought many Jews to belief in Jesus in the last two thousand years.

Unlike Allah and Satan, God does not curse groups of people in this life. Instead of cursing the Muslims who argue with the idea that God has a son, Jesus has appeared to thousands of them in their dreams.[176] When they meet Jesus, they know that he loves them and forgives them.

Allah does not surprise with such forgiveness. He is unpredictable. If he favored the Jews, and then cursed them centuries later, might he do the same with Muslims even before the Mahdi comes?

C3. *Life and death under 'Isa ibn Maryam and the false prophet.* The Hadiths and Revelation both agree that the vast majority of Christians and Jews will forfeit their lives in the end time.

'Isa will "kill his enemies among the Jews and the Christians *who worship him.*" This paraphrase of the hadith given above by Ibn Qayyim emphasizes that 'Isa knows he is not divine. Allah alone is to be

---

[176] Tom Doyle with Greg Webster, *Dreams and Visions: Is Jesus Awakening the Muslim World?*, Thomas Nelson, Nashville US, 2012.

worshipped. In the Muslim view, Christians and Jews who confuse 'Isa with the divine Jesus of the Bible continue to be deceived. They refuse to give up this blasphemy, even in the face of death. They are therefore deserving of their punishment at the hands of 'Isa, the Mahdi, and their forces.

The false prophet, 'Isa's counterpart in Revelation, likewise seeks out those who do not worship according to his demands. He will "cause all who do not worship the image of the beast to be killed." (13:15). Those who refuse the mark of the beast, and his number upon their foreheads or hands, will lose their lives.

Jesus prophesied that there will come a time when those who kill Christians will believe they are pleasing God:

> John 16:2b an hour is coming for everyone who kills you to
> think that he is offering a service to God.

There have been many enemies of Christians throughout the centuries who have persecuted them unto death: the polytheists of the Roman empire, nature worshippers of barbarian tribes, Buddhists and Hindus in Asia, animists in Africa, and communists in many countries. But none of them follow a monotheistic religion. None of them did so in the name of God, or to please a single figure whom they regarded as God.

The one exception to this has been Muslims. There are countless accounts, since the time of Muhammad, of Muslims killing Christians in the name of their one god, Allah. In the Hadiths, the Mahdi's followers believe they will be pleasing Allah. He will reward them for carrying out his death sentence against the infidels.

In Revelation, the "God" who will be pleased is Satan. It is not evident from John's vision that the followers of the beast and the false prophet realize that Satan is the one inspiring their actions. The true God certainly is not pleased. His response to these murders will be a series of punishments upon the empire of the beast: widespread famine with continuing deaths (K25), heavenly omens and a great earthquake (K27), hail, fire, and blood (K29), darkening of the heavens (K31), and more.

Such divine retributions against the actions of the Mahdi and 'Isa are nowhere to be found in the Hadiths.

Instead, the hadith that begins "'Isa ibn Maryam will be a just judge" transitions seamlessly to the mass executions of Christians and Jews, then to a resulting idyllic world that is almost a paradise for Muslims. "A baby boy will put his hand in a snake and it will not harm him, and a baby girl will make a lion run away, and it will not harm her; and the wolf will be among the sheep like their sheepdog. The earth will be filled with peace just as a vessel is filled with water."

These words are an echo of Isaiah, written by that Jewish prophet thirteen centuries before Muhammad:

> Isaiah 11:6 And the wolf will dwell with the lamb, And the leopard will lie down with the young goat, And the calf and the young lion and the fattened steer will be together; And a little boy will lead them.
> 11:7 Also the cow and the bear will graze, Their young will lie down together, And the lion will eat straw like the ox.
> 11:8 The nursing child will play by the hole of the cobra, And the weaned child will put his hand on the viper's den.
> 11:9a They will not hurt or destroy in all My holy mountain.

Isaiah's words will come true in Revelation. But the fulfillment will not occur in the middle of the beast's rule. We must wait until the end of the great tribulation. Then we shall see Jesus Christ return to earth (in K38), and make an end of the beast (K40). Afterward, Jesus will reign over the much-perfected world that Isaiah describes. There will be a thousand years of justice and peace (K44), and not just the seven years of the Hadiths.

This millennial kingdom of Christ is also prophesied by Isaiah:

> Isaiah 11:2 The Spirit of the Lord will rest on Him, The spirit of wisdom and understanding, The spirit of counsel and strength, The spirit of knowledge and the fear of the Lord.
> 11:3 And He will delight in the fear of the Lord, And He will not judge by what His eyes see, Nor make decisions by what His ears hear;
> 11:4 But with righteousness He will judge the poor, And decide with fairness for the humble of the earth; And He will strike the earth with the rod of His mouth, And with the breath of His lips He will slay the wicked.
> 11:5 Also righteousness will be the belt around His hips, And faithfulness the belt around His waist.

> 16:5 A throne will be established in faithfulness, And a judge
> will sit on it in trustworthiness in the tent of David;
> Moreover, he will seek justice, And be prompt in
> righteousness.

Are Isaiah and Revelation the true words of the Almighty, or is it the Hadiths? Which one is corrupted?

C4. *Martyrdom of believers in Christ*. The Hadiths agree with Revelation 20:4 that beheading will be the method used to execute Christians during the end-time period. How significant is this agreement? Is it an indicator that the Mahdi will be the antichrist of the Bible?

Over the centuries, biblical prophecy interpreters have imagined various countries that the antichrist would originate from. Up until recent times, most of these countries employed beheading as a method of execution.

But the practice of beheading has been gradually abolished around the world. It is almost universally regarded as a cruel and barbaric form of execution. In Britain it was formally abolished in 1747, France in 1792 (replaced by the guillotine), Denmark 1892, Japan end of the nineteenth century (replaced by hanging), Sweden 1903, Norway 1905, Germany 1938, China shortly after takeover by communists in 1949 (replaced by shooting). All the European countries that previously used beheading have abolished the death penalty entirely.

The exception to all this are Muslim nations. At the time I write this, beheading is lawful in Iran, Qatar, Yemen, and other countries. Saudi Arabia uses public beheading as the punishment for murder, rape, drug trafficking, sodomy, armed robbery, apostasy, sorcery and certain other offenses. In 2018, Saudi Arabia publicly beheaded 136 men and 3 women for murder, armed robbery, terrorism and drug offences.[177]

The fact that only Islamic nations utilize beheading has become significant as we get closer to the end times.

---

[177] *Execution by beheading (decapitation)*,
http://www.capitalpunishmentuk.org/behead.html, accesed May 6, 2023.

Is it noteworthy that in John's vision he saw that the saints of the tribulation were beheaded for their faith, and not killed by some other method? The answer is yes. During the time that Jesus walked on earth, when John was one of his twelve foremost disciples, he knew that John the Baptist was beheaded for his faith at the order of the tetrarch Herod Antipas (Matthew 14:6-10). He also knew that the apostle Paul was beheaded in Rome by Nero in 67. That was three years after Paul was imprisoned on the false charge that he was a Christian ringleader who helped set fire to Rome. Paul wrote 2 Timothy while waiting for his death.

When John received the vision of Revelation, he undoubtedly knew that he was the last of the apostles still alive. Word had spread that all the other apostles were killed by methods other than beheading. This included crucifixion, piercing by spear, stabbing, stoning, clubbing, and burning. Also, according to these orally-transmitted traditions, John himself avoided execution when he escaped unhurt after being cast into boiling oil in Rome.[178]

Yet, despite all these different modes of execution that would have been familiar, God shows John that the martyrs of the tribulation are put to death specifically by beheading. John does not recount them dying by any of the other methods experienced by the apostles.

The words of Jesus in Matthew 24:9 (see R3 above) tell us that the end-time persecution and martyrdom will be global, and that the governing authority will demand death for Jesus-followers. The Mahdi, 'Isa ibn Maryam, and the worldwide Islamic caliphate of the end time fit these predictions. An alternate religious system could also conceivably arise that would kill large numbers of Christians. But only Islam employs beheading as its preferred method of execution. It is mandated in its holy scripture, and in the actions of its founder.

Beheading is thus a nexus between the Hadiths and Revelation. It suggests that Islam is trying to rewrite the prophecies of the God of the Bible, so that the cause of Allah will be victorious.

---

[178] Ken Curtis, *What Happened to the Twelve Apostles*, April 28, 2010, https://www.christianity.com/church/church-history/timeline/1-300/whatever-happened-to-the-twelve-apostles-11629558.html.

C5. *Mark of the beast compared with Islamic displays of allegiance*.
There has been much speculation on what the mark of the beast will be.
A lot of this thinking involves technologies that globalists could use to
control the world population, with the goal of establishing a unified
world government. Here are some proposed schemes in my recent time,
which may seem ridiculous and outdated by the time you read this:

- credit cards
- biometric identification
- RFID microchip implants
- smartphone apps
- social credit scoring
- cryptocurrency tokens
- vaccine passports
- quantum dots

A person who accepts the mandated control will receive government
services. Those who do not will be shamed and ostracized.

During the tribulation, the technologies available may be far more
advanced. It is therefore premature to fear any single one of the above
methods. However, in aggregate they do show a trend toward the
establishment of a world order.

Such a technologically oriented system is quite conceivable in the first
half of the tribulation, during the time when the woman of Babylon
tempts the world with materialism and self-indulgence (see K20). But
the mark of Revelation is not the mark of the prostitute. It is the mark
of the beast. Midway through the tribulation, the beast overthrows the
woman, and her technology-driven economy comes to a sudden halt
(K21). Could this mean that the mark will *not* be technological in
nature?

In Islam, the Hadiths are silent on the topic of any special mark that
distinguishes the Mahdi's followers and qualifies them for favor.
However, ever since the time of Muhammad, Muslims have displayed
visible marks of allegiance on their person. Many jihadists wear arm
badges and headbands that show Islamic mottos, creeds, words, and
symbols. Favorite words on headbands are "No God but Allah,

Muhammad is his messenger." A popular symbol is the crescent of Islam inscribed with "The Islamic Organization."[179]

Muhammad taught that displaying a badge of allegiance to Allah will literally outweigh all of one's sins:

> Indeed Allah will distinguish a man from my *ummah* [nation] before all of creation on the Day of Judgment. Ninety-nine scrolls will be laid out for him, each scroll is as far as the eye can see, then He will say: 'Do you deny any of this? Have those who recorded this wronged you?' He will say: 'No, O Lord!' He will say: Do you have an excuse?' He will say: 'No, O Lord!' So He will say: 'Rather you have a good deed with us, so you shall not be wronged today." Then He will bring out a badge (or card, *Bitaqah*); on it will be: "I testify to *La Ilaha Illallah*, and I testify that Muhammad is His servant and Messenger." He will say: 'Bring your scales.' He will say: 'O Lord! What good is this badge next to these scrolls?' He will say: 'You shall not be wronged.' He said: 'The scrolls will be put on a pan (of the scale), and the badge on (the other) pan: the scrolls will be light, and the badge will be heavy, nothing is heavier than the Name of Allah.'[180] *(sahih)*

The Mahdi's armies and supporters will eagerly display their marks of allegiance, thereby assuring their acceptance before Allah on judgment day. This can be done with no technological infrastructure at all. For such a mark to fulfill the vision of Revelation, it only needs to be worn on the right hand or on the forehead (13:16). This is already common for jihadist warriors.

C6. *Number of the beast vs the Islamic trinity.* We saw above that 666, the number of the beast, is the number of sinful man in triplicate. It represents three counterfeits of the Father, the Son, and the Holy Spirit. Their imitators in the great tribulation will be Satan, the beast, and the false prophet.

The Hadiths don't speak of the triple number, or any other special number. But there happens to also be a triple number of major

---

[179] Shoebat, p. 376.
[180] Narrated by 'Abdullah bin 'Amr bin Al-'As, *Jami` at-Tirmidhi 2639*, Vol. 5, Book 38, Hadith 2639, https://sunnah.com/tirmidhi/40/34, accessed May 8, 2023; also referenced in Shoebat, p. 377.

protagonists in the end-time caliphate. They are Allah, the Mahdi, and 'Isa ibn Maryam.

Let's compare the ruling threesome of the great tribulation with those of the Hadiths.

First are the Mahdi and the beast (the antichrist). Both present themselves as the messiah of the end time. But they purposely do not mimic Jesus Christ, the Messiah sent from heaven, who went to the cross to save his followers from their sins. Instead, the Mahdi and the beast transform the world into their own image. This is their model of messiahship.

Second are 'Isa and the false prophet. Their task is to serve their chief as deputies. Their aim is to bring a sense of security to their followers. 'Isa does this by hunting down Christians and Jews. After their demise he oversees a worry-free idyllic world, powered by plunder. The false prophet does it by performing incredible miracles that strike awe into the minds of people. Those who are not impressed he pursues unto death. The false prophet then presides over a scarce war economy by favoring those who accept the mark of the beast.

The kind of security offered by the end-time caliphate and the great tribulation, is the security sought by the deceived or the desperate.

But the eternal security offered by God comes when he sends his Holy Spirit to make a home in the heart of a new believer. The Spirit gives comfort, and assurance of unbreakable relationship with God. He operates secretly, without conspicuous display:

> 1 Corinthians 3:16 Do you not know that you are a temple of God and that the Spirit of God dwells in you?

> Isaiah 57:15 For this is what the high and exalted One Who lives forever, whose name is Holy, says: "I dwell in a high and holy place, And also with the contrite and lowly of spirit In order to revive the spirit of the lowly And to revive the heart of the contrite."

Jesus Christ and the Holy Spirit are fully divine, as members of the trinity. The Mahdi and 'Isa are not, but are nevertheless treated by their followers as if they had minor god status. For instance, we saw in

H23 that the Mahdi is not bound by the letter of Islamic law. He can act as he sees fit, as a semi-divine potentate. This is an echo of ancient Rome, when the pagan subjects of that empire regarded their emperors as gods, ruling on behalf of the gods in heaven. The subjects of the Mahdi will similarly regard him as the all-powerful one who rules in the name of Allah. His followers might knowingly or unknowingly give him the worship that is meant for Allah alone.

Similar to the Mahdi, 'Isa is another godlike man. According to Islamic belief, he never died, but evaded the cross and was transported to heaven. His arrival back to earth as a two-thousand-year-old man will give him semi-divine prerogatives among the Islamic faithful, perhaps even more so than the Mahdi.

Mahdi and 'Isa are created beings. They can only have partial divinity, different in their essence from Allah. By contrast, Jesus Christ, the true God-man, is not a created being. He has been with God the Father through all eternity:

> Hebrews 7:3 Without father, without mother, without genealogy, having neither beginning of days nor end of life, but made like the Son of God, he remains a priest perpetually.

Finally, the third and highest in the ruling threesome of the end-time Hadiths is Allah. He is the God who is absolutely and utterly alone. The Islamic doctrine for this is called *tawhid*. It is not merely one of many tenets of Islamic belief. Tawhid is a non-negotiable commandment.[181]

The doctrine of tawhid is at the core of Wahhabism, the fundamentalist branch of Sunni Islam. Its founder, al-Wahhab (d. 1792), focused so much on the unity of Allah, that others referred to his followers as *muwahhidun*, or unitarians. He denounced other notions of Allah as heretical innovation, or *bid'ah*. Al-Wahhab was also dismayed at the widespread laxity in following traditional Sharia law.[182]

Just as adherence to tawhid is the most important commandment, the greatest sin is *shirk*. Shirk is idolatry, expressed in worship of other

---

[181] Richardson, p. 105.
[182] Austin Cline, *Origins and Doctrines of Wahhabism, Islam's Extremist Sect*, March 24, 2018, https://www.learnreligions.com/wahhabism-and-wahhabi-islam-250235.

gods. It is regarded as a sin greater than murder, rape, child molesting, or genocide. Whereas those sins can be outweighed by works pleasing to Allah, the sin of shirk is unforgivable. Many fatwas, or Islamic legal opinions, have ruled that shirk is the utmost sin. Here is such a fatwa recent to my day:

> *Kufr* [not believing in Allah and His Messenger] and *Shirk* are interrelated. Every *Kafir* [infidel] is a *Mushrik* [polytheist, someone who associates partners with Allah] because he has associated Shaytan with Allah.[183]

The most heinous shirk imaginable is to believe that Jesus Christ is divine, the son of God, the three-in-one (see H05).

Unlike the God of the Bible, who through his son Jesus seeks personal relationship with lost sinners, Allah is not personal. A human being cannot have a relationship with him.[184] The Qur'an teaches that Allah is the transcendent creator. He is all-powerful. He knows all people and all things, but people cannot know him. Many Muslims believe he has pre-arranged all our thoughts, words and deeds, both for good and for evil. He is far more judgmental than gracious. He also has fatalistically determined each person's eternal destiny. That is why Muslims frequently say, *in sha'Allah*, "if Allah wills it."[185]

The Islamic trinity of Allah, the Mahdi, and 'Isa is very different from the biblical three-in-one. The Father, Son, and Spirit are equal persons. They are also one God in one essence. This is a mystery beyond our full comprehension.

I will close this section by mentioning that, while Allah is the third protagonist in Islam's end time, the third member of Revelation's 666 trinity is none other than Satan.

---

[183] *Fatwa No: 384118*, fatwa Date:1-10-2018, https://www.islamweb.net/en/fatwa/384118/the-terms-kafir-and-mushrik-are-interchangeable, accessed April 21, 2023.
[184] https://114chambers.wordpress.com/2016/01/08/is-allah-personal-impersonal-or-none-of-the-above/, accessed May 10, 2023.
[185] Rob Phillips, https://oncedelivered.net/2007/12/20/yahweh-the-god-of-the-bible-vs-allah-the-god-of-the-koran/, December 20, 2007.

K25 :
Famine and death upon a fourth of men under the beast's rule

: H25
The Dajjal curses enemies or blesses followers by his miracles

18:8‡[K20,K21] For this reason *in one day* her plagues will come, plague and mourning and famine, *and she will be burned up with fire;* for the Lord God who judges her is strong.

6:5 When He broke the third seal, I heard the third living creature saying, "Come!" I looked, and behold, a black horse, and the one who sat on it had a pair of scales in his hand.

6:6 'When He broke the third seal, I heard the third living creature saying, "Come!" I looked, and behold, a black horse, and the one who sat on it had a pair of scales in his hand.

6:7 When the Lamb broke the fourth seal, I heard the voice of the fourth living creature saying, "Come!"

6:8 I looked, and behold, an ashen horse; and the one who sat on it had the name Death, and Hades was following with him. Authority was given to them over a fourth of the earth, to kill with sword, and famine, and plague, and by the wild animals of the earth.

Another aspect of the trial brought by the Dajjal is that he … will pass by a people who will deny him, and all their animals will die. He will pass a people who believe him, and he will command the sky to rain in the earth to flourish, so that on that very evening their herds will become very fat and large but their flanks distended and their udders full of milk.[186]

If anyone memorizes ten verses from the beginning of Surat al-Kahf, he will be protected from the trial of Dajjal (antichrist).[187] *(sahih)*

---

[186] Narrated by Abu Sa`id al-Khudri, quoted in `Ibn Izzat p.34; similarly in hadith reference # 5 Muslim, # 1 3 IbnMajah, quoted in Shaykh Mufti Muhammad Shafiz, *Signs of Qayamah and Arrival of Maseeh*, trans. Rafiq Abdur Rehman, publisher Daryl Isha'at, Karachi Pakistan, 2000, https://archive.org/stream/SignsOfQayamahAndArrivalOfMaseeha.sByShaykhMuftiMuh ammadShafi/SignsOfQayamahAndArrivalOfMaseeha.sByShaykhMuftiMuhammadShafir. a_djvu.txt, accessed May 30, 2024.

[187] Narrated by Abu al-Darda', *Sunan Abi Dawud 4323*, Book 38, Hadith 4309, https://sunnah.com/abudawud:4323, accessed February 4, 2024., also see https://www.quranclick.com/benefits-and-virtues-of-reciting-surah-al-kahf, accessed February 4, 2024.

Revelation. After the overthrow of Babylon, the beast and his six closely allied kings consolidated political and military power into their hands (K21). But, in the previous section, they were unable to bring the peace and well-being they promised. Instead, war begets war. The rationing system based on the mark of the beast merely determines who will first succumb to the famine that quickly spreads across the world. The awful hunger is heralded by the opening of the third seal of Revelation's scroll (see 5:1 K00). It reveals a rider on a black horse. He carries aloft the scales of scarcity (6:5-6). Jesus' followers are already scapegoats for the famine, because they refused the mark of the beast and its privilege of buying and selling (13:17 and 20:4 in K24). This diverts everyone's attention from the true cause of the famine. It is in reality a man-inflicted situation, permitted by God as judgment upon Babylon and those who inherit her remains (18:8).

In the vision, the fourth seal is opened soon afterward. It reveals a rider on a ashen horse, who brings death (6:7-8).

Famine and death have been inseparable throughout history. With this wave of deaths, the abomination of 13:15 K24 now gives way to *desolation*:

> Daniel 9:27 *And he will confirm a covenant with the many for one week, but in the middle of the week he will put a stop to sacrifice and grain offering;* and on the wing of abominations will come the one who makes desolate, until a complete destruction, one that is decreed, gushes forth on the one who makes desolate.

A fourth part of all people die in these calamities of famine and war (6:8). This is at least 25% of the world's population, billions of men, women, and children. Among them are many who have realized their allegiance to the woman or the beast was wrong. Instead, they now trust their eternal lives to Christ. There are more among the dead who opposed the beast for other reasons. Still others are civilian victims of war.

During this great tribulation, God allows Satan to reach another height of power. Satan does not bring peace and tranquility. Even if he were able, he is unwilling to do so. Instead, it is a time of continuous war, famine and death. Though he uses various intermediaries to tempt men and women to forsake God, his real goal is to do away with as many billions of them as possible. If he is successful, he and his legions of fallen angels will never be threatened by those created in the image of God and of Christ (Genesis 1:27). Satan can then sideline God, and achieve his ultimate goal of becoming effective ruler of the universe.

Hadiths. In the previous section H24, Allah sent 'Isa ibn Maryam from heaven back to earth. 'Isa cemented the Mahdi's empire, by organizing the concerted effort to slay all infidels, including Jews and Christians. At the same time, he carries out his duties as "a just judge and a just ruler" to all Muslims. For them he ushers in a silver age of plenty. Even the animals will stop fearing their predators. "The wolf will be among the sheep like their sheepdog. The earth will be filled with peace just as a vessel is filled with water. The people will be united and none will be worshipped except Allah."

Despite this, in upcoming sections the wars of the Mahdi will continue. For example, in H33 we shall see "battles will take place under his command and Islam will be victorious."

The Hadiths are a dialectic of simultaneous war and peace. How can this be?

The answer lies with the chief end-time enemy of the Mahdi and 'Isa ibn Maryam: the Dajjal. So far in our Hadiths timeline, deduced by reconciling with the vision of Revelation, we saw that "before Dajjal appears there will be three difficult years in which the people will suffer severe famine" (H18). He then took advantage of the hunger to (H19) "appear in my community and he would stay for ... forty days, forty months or forty years." He then attracts many weak people, who cannot cope with food shortages, by (H19) "command(ing) the sky to rain and it will rain, and he will command the earth to produce vegetation and it will do so." We already discussed how these earlier events regarding the Dajjal will likely occur during the time of the temporary alliance between the Romans and the Mahdi.

We also saw that after the Mahdi turns against the Romans and savages their army, that (H21) it will be at "the conquest of Constantinople when the Dajjal (antichrist) comes forth." He will no longer be a secondary character. The Dajjal will displace the Romans as the Mahdi's foremost enemy.

Now that 'Isa has come on the scene (H24), the hadith in our current section H25 tells us that the Dajjal will ramp up his temptations. In this way he gains new followers around the world. He will bring trouble to "people who will deny him, and all their animals will die." But he will benefit those "who believe him, and he will command the sky to rain in the earth to flourish, so that on that very evening their herds will become very fat and large but their flanks distended and their udders full of milk."

Though the rule of the Mahdi and 'Isa brings about the silver age, the unwanted presence of the Dajjal requires ongoing war until he is destroyed.

In the second hadith of this section, Muhammad gave the future Muslims a simple antidote against the temptations of the Dajjal. It is to memorize the first ten verses of Surah 18 of the Qur'an, Surah al-Kahf:

> Surah 18 Praise be to Allah, Who hath sent to His Servant the Book, and hath allowed therein no Crookedness
> 18:2 (He hath made it) Straight (and Clear) in order that He may warn (the godless) of a terrible Punishment from Him, and that He may give Glad Tidings to the Believers who work righteous deeds, that they shall have a goodly Reward
> 18:3 Wherein they shall remain for ever
> 18:4 Further, that He may warn those (also) who say, "Allah hath begotten a son"
> 18:5 No knowledge have they of such a thing, nor had their fathers. It is a grievous thing that issues from their mouths as a saying what they say is nothing but falsehood
> 18:6 Thou wouldst only, perchance, fret thyself to death, following after them, in grief, if they believe not in this Message
> 18:7 That which is on earth we have made but as a glittering show for the earth, in order that We may test them - as to which of them are best in conduct
> 18:8 Verily what is on earth we shall make but as dust and dry soil (without growth or herbage)
> 18:9 Or dost thou reflect that the Companions of the Cave and of the Inscription were wonders among Our Sign
> 18:10 Behold, the youths betook themselves to the Cave: they said, "Our Lord! bestow on us Mercy from Thyself, and dispose of our affair for us in the right way!"

The key verse to always dwell on is Surah 18:4. It gravely warns against the idea of God having a son. To believe in that will result in one's eternal doom (see H05).

The fact that Muhammad connects these ten verses with the Dajjal shows that the Dajjal will masquerade as this odious son of God. He is therefore to be opposed with all levels of violence.

In the Hadiths it is interesting that both 'Isa and the Dajjal display miraculous powers. 'Isa descends from heaven. The Dajjal does miracles to materially advance his followers. Each one also brings calamity on their enemies. They are not merely men who have risen to positions of high influence. Each is actually linked to a spiritual overworld – one of good, the other of evil. In the Hadiths, 'Isa is regarded as supremely virtuous, for he enforces the will of Allah. The Dajjal is strikingly wicked. He champions the cause of the intransigent infidels among the Christians and the Jews.

Comparison. In Revelation, the great famine begins soon after the beast overthrows the woman of Babylon, at the midpoint of the seven years. It is the product of the beast's policies, permitted by God Most High as a judgment upon rebel humanity. The followers of Jesus are blamed for exacerbating the shortages. They are put to death in large numbers.

In the Hadiths, a great end-time famine already occurred in the three years before the Dajjal arrived. The famine was at Allah's command, to test the faith of his people (H18). It happened during the time of the Mahdi's military alliance of convenience with the Romans.

In this section, the Dajjal has come on the scene. He becomes an object of alternative faith that opposes Allah. He curses those who curse him, and miraculously causes their animals to die. Thus, he brings famine upon some who are committed to following the Mahdi. In the Hadiths the Dajjal becomes the scapegoat for hunger that is caused by others.

The Mahdi has defeated the Romans, and now has the Dajjal as his chief adversary. The Muslims then launch a new series of wars against the Dajjal's followers and other pockets of opposition. It seems that the Mahdi is absolved of any responsibility for famine, because hunger is not mentioned in the Hadiths of future sections. Only the material well-being of his people is described. But undoubtedly both hunger and death will be a product of these wars. Famine that is caused by the wars of the Mahdi serves as a false flag operation that discredits the Dajjal even more.

In Revelation, the Christians are the scapegoat. In the Hadiths, it is the Dajjal, who is defender of Christians and Jews. In this way the Hadiths are a pale reflection of the Bible.

The Hadiths offer the strange character of the Dajjal as an object of alternative faith that opposes Allah. In Revelation, instead of trusting the beast, up to the very end God still offers all men and women the opportunity to put their faith in Jesus Christ. Jesus promised this to everyone past, present, and future:

> Matthew 5:6 "Blessed are those who hunger and thirst for righteousness, for they will be satisfied.
> 5:10 "Blessed are those who have been persecuted for the sake of righteousness, for theirs is the kingdom of heaven."

K26 :

The martyrs' plea for retribution

6:9 When the Lamb broke the fifth seal, I saw underneath the altar the souls of those who had been killed because of the word of God, and because of the testimony which they had maintained;

12:11 And they overcame him [the accuser] because of the blood of the Lamb and because of the word of their testimony, and they did not love their life even when faced with death.

6:11 And a white robe was given to each of them; and they were told that they were to rest for a little while longer, until the number of their fellow servants and their brothers and sisters who were to be killed even as they had been, was completed also.

7:9 After these things I looked, and behold, a great multitude which no one could count, from every nation and all the tribes, peoples, and languages, standing before the throne and before the Lamb, clothed in white robes, and palm branches were in their hands;

7:10 and they cried out with a loud voice, saying, "Salvation belongs to our God who sits on the throne, and to the Lamb."

7:11 And all the angels were standing around the throne and around the elders and the four living creatures; and they fell on their faces before the throne and worshiped God,

7:12 saying, "Amen, blessing, glory, wisdom, thanksgiving, honor, power, and might belong to our God forever and ever. Amen."

6:10 and they cried out with a loud voice, saying, "How long, O Lord, holy and true, will You refrain from judging and avenging our blood on those who live on the earth?"

7:13 Then one of the elders responded, saying to me, "These who are clothed in the white robes, who are they, and where have they come from?"

7:14 I said to him, "My lord, you know." And he said to me, "These are the ones who come out of the great tribulation, and they have washed their robes and made them white in the blood of the Lamb.

7:15 For this reason they are before the throne of God, and they serve Him day and night in His temple; and He who sits on the throne will spread His tabernacle over them.

7:16 They will no longer hunger nor thirst, nor will the sun beat down on them, nor any scorching heat;

> 7:17 for the Lamb in the center of the throne will be their
> shepherd, and will guide them to springs of the water of life;
> and God will wipe every tear from their eyes."

Hadiths. Now that 'Isa ibn Maryam has come back to earth to be the chief proselytizer for Islam, the only substantial opposition ahead will come from the Dajjal. The Hadiths set their compass on war and world submission to Islam. They ignore the signs that Allah may not be the true God, or that 'Isa may not be who he claims to be. Thus, we will see silence from the Hadiths over the next several sections.

Revelation. The main actors in the previous sections were the beast and the false prophet. At their instigation, the persecution and killings of believers reaches the greatest level ever known.

But now they lose control of events. Instead, in the upcoming sections our Father God reacts in a series of supernatural judgments

John's vision shifts to heaven, and the opening of the fifth seal. A stream of people is arriving there, whose blood was shed. He sees their souls under the heavenly altar (6:9). This is reminiscent of the Old Testament blood sacrifices, which were poured out under the altar of the temple in Jerusalem.

The church saints are already in heaven, having arrived after the rapture (5:9-10 K14). Unlike the new arrivals, they have more than their souls – they have been given glorified bodies and are enjoying eternal life. One of the twenty-four elders, who represent the church (4:4 K14), wonders out loud, where did this stream of victims come from (7:13)? He then answers his own question.

The new arrivals are the martyrs of the tribulation. They were killed for refusing to follow the beast (12:11). Though they have died in body, they are alive after death in soul. In this bodiless existence, they are given ethereal white robes to wear (6:11). The purity and spotlessness of this garb is indicative of their standing before God. He no longer sees them as sinners, because they put their faith in Christ. He sees them white as snow.

Many of the dead are Jews, the beast's favorite targets, beyond the 144,000 whose lives were specially safeguarded by God (7:3-4 K18). But the majority are gentiles, from all the other nations (7:9). Together they are thankful that God has given them white garments of grace. They join in a song of praise to God and to his Lamb sacrificed on their behalf, the Lord Jesus Christ (7:10-12). By his blood shed on the cross, he has washed away their sins, forever (7:14). The death he died brings life to sinners, as promised in many biblical passages such as this one:

> Romans 5:8 But God demonstrates His own love toward us,
> in that while we were still sinners, Christ died for us.
> 5:9 Much more then, having now been justified by His blood,
> we shall be saved from the wrath of God through Him.

The martyrs, their sins forgiven and forgotten, now have rest. They are honored before God, and gladly serve him continually (7:15). They will never thirst or hunger again (7:16), free of the fears and threats of the tribulation. Jesus is in their midst, and will wipe away their tears (7:17).

God is a righteous God who forgives those who repent of their rebellion against him. But the martyrs know that he also judges those who take pleasure in their wickedness. Having just come from the world that has declared war against God, they cry out for God to not wait any longer, but to avenge their deaths, and to punish the persecutors who are still operating on earth (6:10).

They now become heavenly witnesses, as more victims of the tribulation continue to join them. They will see God unleash his irresistible wrath upon their tormentors.

God signals retribution with heavenly omens and earthquake

> 6:12 And I looked when He broke the sixth seal, and there
> was a great earthquake; and the sun became as black as
> sackcloth made of hair, and the whole moon became like
> blood;
> 6:13 and the stars of the sky fell to the earth, as a fig tree
> drops its unripe figs when shaken by a great wind.
> 6:14 The sky was split apart like a scroll when it is rolled up,
> and every mountain and island was removed from its place.
> 6:15 Then the kings of the earth and the eminent people, and
> the commanders and the wealthy and the strong, and every
> slave and free person hid themselves in the caves and among
> the rocks of the mountains;
> 6:16 and they said to the mountains and the rocks, "Fall on
> us and hide us from the sight of Him who sits on the throne,
> and from the wrath of the Lamb;
> 6:17 for the great day of Their wrath has come, and who is
> able to stand?"

Revelation. The tribulation so far has seen wars, famine, death, and martyrdoms. They give lie to the glittering promises of the new world order that was set into motion by the woman of Babylon (now overthrown), the beast, and his deputy the false prophet.

But now, in response to the martyrs' plea for retribution, God becomes a direct actor in the events of the tribulation. John sees this in his vision with the opening of the sixth seal (6:12). God makes the first in a series of punishments upon the antichrist beast and his followers.

The sixth seal opens to an awesome and cosmic response. God miraculously interrupts the routine behavior of the sun, the moon, and even the remote stars (6:12-14). On the earth he calls forth an earthquake that moves all mountains and islands (6:12,14).

This awesome display of God's unquestionable power over his creation is only a precursor to other actions of judgment that God will initiate: the seventh seal, the seven trumpets and the seven bowls.

The unbelievers flee to safety "in the caves and among the rocks of the mountains" (6:15) – men and woman, rich and poor, the powerful and the powerless. These shelters might be underground bunkers very familiar to modern technological societies under conditions of war. They know instinctively that it is the God in heaven, and not the god of their imagination or the god they have legislated out of existence, who is now bringing calamity upon them for their wrongdoing.

They do not beg for mercy, but only cry out bitterly, "who is able to stand?" (6:17). They can only seek death as their escape. But these people will learn, as all of us someday will, that death does not result in the termination of our existence. Instead, rebels against God will spend body and soul in hell for all eternity.

These events in the sky and on earth are only preliminaries, and do not immediately result in loss of life. That will come with more judgments in the days and months to come. Together they will make up God's great day of wrath (6:17).

K28 :
Silence in heaven before the wrath of God

> 8:1 When the Lamb broke the seventh seal, there was silence in heaven for about half an hour.
> 8:2 And I saw the seven angels who stand before God, and seven trumpets were given to them.
> 8:3 Another angel came and stood at the altar, holding a golden censer; and much incense was given to him, so that he might add it to the prayers of all the saints on the golden altar which was before the throne.
> 8:4 And the smoke of the incense ascended from the angel's hand with the prayers of the saints before God.
> 8:5 Then the angel took the censer and filled it with the fire of the altar, and hurled it to the earth; and there were peals of thunder and sounds, and flashes of lightning and an earthquake.
> 8:6 And the seven angels who had the seven trumpets prepared themselves to sound them.

Revelation. The seventh seal is opened, revealing a complete silence in heaven (8:1). It is reminiscent of the stillness in a courtroom just before the foreman of the jury pronounces the verdict.

It is interesting that a prolonged silence was not God's immediate answer to the fifth seal, when the martyrs pleaded for retribution against their murderers (6:9-10 K26). He chose first to get the attention of everyone on earth with the cosmic omens and the earthquake of the sixth seal (6:12 K27).

Only after those omens, does he follow up with the silence of the seventh seal. After one-half hour of stillness, it gives way to a scene of heavenly angels with seven trumpets of judgment (8:2,6).

In the Bible, trumpets are featured on many critical occasions. Before God called Moses to the top of Mount Sinai to receive the ten commandments, a trumpet was sounded (Exodus 19:19-20). At God's command, the sound of trumpets brought down the walls of Jericho (Joshua 6:20). The sounding of the trumpet of God across the world signals the rapture of the church believers into heaven (1 Thessalonians 4:16).

The seven trumpets of Revelation will be no less critical.

As the angels are given the trumpets, another angel stands before the heavenly altar with a golden censer (8:3). At the end of its swinging chains is a metallic firepot with burning incense inside. In the Bible, incense is so significant to God that he directed Moses to mix a special blend of four spices that he would accept for worship: stacte, onycha, galbanum, and frankincense (Exodus 30:34). The Jewish priests of the Old Testament used only censors with this incense blend in their temple worship (Leviticus 16:12-13). Later, the Christians of the early centuries developed a liturgical form of worship that had elements of Jewish temple worship. It included the use of censers by priests. This liturgy persists in the Eastern Orthodox church of my day.

The perfumed mixture of incense distributes a fragrant aroma, with a wafting smoke. It is a picture of prayers rising up to heaven, a reminder that God regards the prayers of his children as a sweet-smelling perfume to the Lord.

But this angel in heaven is not making the typical prayer offering with his censer. Instead, he hurls it, filled with fire, down to the earth. The result is peals of thunder, rumblings, flashes of lightning, and an earthquake – all signs of further judgment (8:5). More responses are to come from the Almighty, in answer to the pleas of the tribulation martyrs (8:4).

K29 :
God sends hail, fire, and blood

> 8:7 The first sounded, and there was hail and fire mixed with blood, and it was hurled to the earth; and a third of the earth was burned up, and a third of the trees were burned up, and all the green grass was burned up.
> 8:8 The second angel sounded, and something like a great mountain burning with fire was hurled into the sea; and a third of the sea became blood,
> 8:9 and a third of the creatures which were in the sea and had life, died; and a third of the ships were destroyed.

Revelation. The seven seals have been opened. Now an angel blasts the first of the seven trumpets (8:7).

Hail and fire fall from the sky. This is not a localized issue – vegetation around the world is affected. A third of the trees are burnt up. So are a third of all grasses. Such hail would doubtless catch many men, women, children, and animals in the open, resulting in many injuries, the shedding of blood, and even death. This would explain how the hail gets mixed with blood (8:7). It is reminiscent of the plague of hail and fire upon the Egyptians, the seventh plague that God inflicted on them before he extricated the Jewish people from their slavery (Exodus 9:18-26).

This punishment will draw people's attention to the way they take plant life for granted. Plants and trees are truly a gift from God that sustains the animal kingdom, and all humanity, whether they are believers or unbelievers. Without them, life on earth is not sustainable.

Another angel blasts the second trumpet (8:8). With that sound, something like a great mountain plunges into the sea. Perhaps it is a flaming asteroid from outer space, tens or hundreds of kilometers in diameter, whose orbit was coordinated in advance by the God who stands over space and time.

The falling mountain also wreaks havoc. A third of all ships are destroyed, a third of the seas turn to blood, and a third of all sea creatures die (8:8-9). This reminds us of the first plague upon the

Egyptians, when the waters of the Nile river were turned into blood (Exodus 7:14-24).

K30 :
God sends wormwood

> 8:10 The third angel sounded, and a great star fell from heaven, burning like a torch, and it fell on a third of the rivers and on the springs of waters.
> 8:11 The star is named Wormwood; and a third of the waters became wormwood, and many people died from the waters because they were made bitter.

Revelation. Another mighty angel sounds the third trumpet, which heralds a special star. It falls from heaven upon the waters of the earth (8:10). It is not likely to be a normal star, but a comet or meteoroid whose orbit God arranges to intersect with that of earth. Its special composition results in the poisoning of a third part of all rivers and springs, and makes them unfit for drink or irrigation (8:11). The result would be a great scarcity of clean water, and the death of millions of creatures.

The poisoned waters are said to become *wormwood*, an unusual and poisonous plant with a bitter taste. Wormwood is a medicine when taken in small quantities. But in higher doses, it acts like a hallucinogen, becomes toxic, and can result in death.

Here in the great tribulation, God brings punishment through the fallen star that also shares the name "Wormwood."

This event has a parallel in the bitter waters that Moses and the Israelites encountered at Marah, during their wilderness wandering after God freed them from Egypt. When they cried out, God directed Moses to take a special log. When he cast it into the water, the water became sweet (Exodus 15:22-25).

The bitter waters turned sweet foreshadowed God's ultimate grace and forgiveness to rebel sinners, when he sent his son Jesus to die on the cross in payment for our sins.

Even during the trials of the great tribulation, like the wormwood trial of bitter waters, Jesus offers the gift of eternal life to all who cry out for relief and forgiveness.

K31 :
God darkens the heavens

> 8:12 The fourth angel sounded, and a third of the sun, a third
> of the moon, and a third of the stars were struck, so that a
> third of them would be darkened and the day would not
> shine for a third of it, and the night in the same way.
> 8:13 Then I looked, and I heard an eagle flying in midheaven,
> saying with a loud voice, "Woe, woe, woe to those who live
> on the earth, because of the remaining blasts of the trumpet
> of the three angels who are about to sound!"

Revelation. The fourth trumpet sends an even greater trial upon the earth, through the ripping apart of the heavenly cosmos. The light of the sun, moon, and stars – so dependable and mundane – is interrupted by the direct intervention of Almighty God. Those who believe that the universe is a random mistake will be forced to recant. They will have to recognize the profound wisdom of King David:

> Psalm 19:1 The heavens tell of the glory of God; And their
> expanse declares the work of His hands.

As in the first three trumpets, the trial of the fourth trumpet affects a third of things that are vital to the world (8:12). A third of the sun's rays, a third of the moon's reflections, and a third of the stars are darkened. The daytime will go dark for a third of the time. The night will turn into the blackness of the blind for a third of its time.

Those who say these events are impossible and should be interpreted symbolically do not know the power of God. He is the one who created the universe out of nothingness:

> Genesis 1:1 In the beginning God created the heavens and the
> earth.

The one who created the space-time laws of physics can suspend them where and when he will.

The theme of three continues in John's vision in 8:13. An eagle flies through the heavens. He calls out a curse of three woes upon the rebels on earth. They will soon regret their prideful disobedience with even more trials that are coming from the God of heaven.

273

K32 :
Satan unleashes the demons from their confinement to torment unbelievers for five months

: H32
People desire death in the midst of the great trials

9:1‡[K15] Then the fifth angel sounded, and I saw a star from heaven *which had fallen to the earth;* and the key to the shaft of the abyss was given to him.
9:2 He opened the shaft of the abyss, and smoke ascended out of the shaft like the smoke of a great furnace; and the sun and the air were darkened from the smoke of the shaft.
9:3 Then out of the smoke came locusts upon the earth, and power was given them, as the scorpions of the earth have power.

This world will not end before a man passes by a grave and rolls on it and says, "O would that I were in the place of this person in the grave! The *deen* is nothing but affliction."[188]

The time has almost come when a funeral will pass by a group of people in a market and a man will see it and shake his head and say, "O would that I were in his place!" he was asked, "O Abu Dharr, is that because of something terrible?" He said, "Yes."[189] *(athar)*

9:4 They were told not to hurt the grass of the earth, nor any green thing, nor any tree, but only the people who do not have the seal of God on their foreheads.
9:5 And they were not permitted to kill anyone, but to torment for five months; and their torment was like the torment of a scorpion when it stings a person.
9:6 And in those days people will seek death and will not find it; they will long to die, and death will flee from them!
9:7 The appearance of the locusts was like horses prepared for battle; and on their heads appeared to be crowns like gold, and their faces were like human faces.
9:8 They had hair like the hair of women, and their teeth were like the teeth of lions.
9:9 They had breastplates like breastplates of iron; and the sound of their wings was like the sound of chariots, of many horses rushing to battle.

---

[188] Narrated by Abu Hurarya, quoted in ʻIbn Izzat p.65; see also narrated by Abu Huraira, *Sahih Muslim 157 L*, Book 41, Hadith 6948, https://sunnah.com/muslim:157L, accessed July 16, 2023.
[189] Abu Dharr al-Ghifari (fourth or fifth person converting to Islam), quoted in ʻIbn Izzat p.65.

9:10 They have tails like scorpions, and stings; and in their tails is their power to hurt people for five months.
9:11 They have as king over them, the angel of the abyss; his name in Hebrew is Abaddon, and in the Greek he has the name Apollyon.

Revelation. After the martyrs' plea for retribution in K26, God in his anger has responded with four trumpets. They announced plagues on natural objects: the trees and grasses, the seas, the rivers and springs, and the lights of heaven.

The next two trumpets announce plagues directly on men and women.

We already saw verse 9:1 in K15, after the rapture of the church to heaven, and the withdrawal of the Holy Spirit's favor from the world. At that time, the "star from heaven which had fallen to the earth," namely Satan, was permanently evicted from heaven. He was then allowed a much freer rein amongst his many followers on earth.

Now the rest of 9:1 comes to pass. It is the fifth trumpet judgment. The effects are so extreme, that in the next section (9:12 K33) they are called a *woe*, a great calamity upon mankind. It is the first of the three foretold woes (8:13 K31) that will befall them.

God gives Satan even greater control over his followers, by giving him the key to the *abyss*. In keeping with a faithful and literal approach to scripture, this should not be treated as a purely symbolic or mythical place. A careful study of the Bible will lead to a much deeper understanding of what takes place.

When the pit opens, smoke comes forth that obscures the sun and pollutes the air (9:2). Then locusts suddenly appear (9:3). They bring to mind the locust plague that God sent upon Egypt to consume its grain fields, in punishment for its enslavement of the Israelites (Exodus 10:4-19).

But these locusts of Revelation are not insects that swarm and multiply exponentially by consuming standing grain. They are demons. We can deduce this by connecting the Greek word for "the abyss" (9:2), *abyssos*, with another verse where it is found in the New Testament, Luke 8:31. It is at the end of the passage describing how Jesus encountered the demoniac man who was possessed by a legion (several thousand) of evil spirits. Those demons begged him not to send them to the *abyssos*. It seems they were aware that many other demons were already imprisoned there. How could that be the case?

Jude 6-8 hints at a group of demons, Satan's accomplices, that were imprisoned long ago:

> Jude 6 And angels who did not keep their own domain but abandoned their proper dwelling place, these He has kept in eternal restraints under darkness for the judgment of the great day,
> 7 just as Sodom and Gomorrah and the cities around them, since they in the same way as these angels indulged in sexual perversion and went after strange flesh, are exhibited as an example in undergoing the punishment of eternal fire.
> 8 Yet in the same way these people also, dreaming, defile the flesh, reject authority, and speak abusively of angelic majesties.

The "eternal restraints under darkness for the judgment of the great day" mentioned here equates to the abyss of Luke and Revelation. Jude compares its occupants to the sexually deviant sinners of Sodom and Gomorrah (Jude 7), and also to the Romans of Jude's day who indulged in sexual orgies (Jude 8).

The connection between demons and sexual experimentation takes us to the following strange passage in Genesis, where some demons, charitably called "sons of God," managed to have intercourse with earthly women to give rise to a line of human giants:

> Genesis 6:4 The Nephilim were on the earth in those days, and also afterward, when the sons of God came in to the daughters of mankind, and they bore children to them. Those were the mighty men who were of old, men of renown.

The best-known Nephilim with the genes of this line appeared over 1,300 years later. He was the giant Goliath, slayed by the youthful David (1 Samuel 17:32-50), who was to become king of Israel.

From the passage in Jude, it seems that even before the flood, God punished the multitude of demons involved in producing the line of the Nephilim. He imprisoned them in the abyss. They have been waiting the day when Satan their chief would free them, so that once again they could afflict humans.

God permits the demons to torment people, but not to kill them (9:4-5). The torment involves severe pain, like the stings of scorpions (9:10).

The name of the demons' leader is *Abaddon* in Hebrew, or *Apollyon* in Greek (9:11). Both mean destroyer, another title for Satan. Though sometimes Satan appears through a human character such as the false prophet (13:13-15 K24, 16:13 K38, 19:20 K40, 20:10 K45), or as an angel of light (2 Corinthians 11:14), his true nature as hater of men and women is now seen.

The effects of a normal scorpion sting may last a couple of days. But this scourge continues for five whole months (9:5). The locusts and scorpions are described in 9:7-10 in nightmarish terms. This suggests an affliction that is at the extreme level of demonic possession.

The followers of the beast and false prophet are so tormented, that they wish to commit suicide. But surrounding forces prevent them from doing so (9:6).

Only the followers of Jesus will be safe, those who are protected and sealed by God (9:4). They are safeguarded from demonic influence by the shield of faith in Christ.

Comparison. The Hadiths have been silent for quite a long portion of the Revelation timeline. We last heard from them in H25. Back then they forecast that after the coming of ʿIsa ibn Maryam to assist the Mahdi in the subjugation of the world for Islam, the only substantial opposition ahead will come from the Dajjal.

Revelation has provided many missing gaps that are vital to a true understanding. The martyrs, whom the Mahdi and ʿIsa's forces have killed because of their faith in the son of God, have come in their souls before the Almighty God of heaven (K26). He responded with a series of supernatural judgments. In this latest one, he has allowed Satan to unleash all his demon allies to torment the followers of the beast and the false prophet.

Hadiths. As we have seen, it is challenging to unravel Revelation in terms of a cohesive timeline, but not impossible. The end-time Hadiths defy such an analysis. There are too many of them that are disjointed one from another when trying to line them up in chronological order. Careful scholars of Islamic eschatology are forced to admit this. For example, according to Smith and Haddad:

> The attempt to impose an order and a structured sequence on the events of the eschaton has been, as we have seen, a somewhat arbitrary one. To a limited extent Islam, or at least Islamic tradition, has found such an ordering to be necessary even though it is noticeably absent from the Qur'an. From another perspective, however, it is clear that many of the issues around which the eschatological story has been woven do not necessarily relate to any given sequence of occurrences.[190]

The Hadiths given in this section offer a case in point. They speak of a terrible juncture in time when many people will pass by graves or funeral caskets, and wish they were in them, instead of enduring a widespread affliction. They will desire death instead of trial.

These Hadiths are difficult to assign to the time before universal judgment, because in Islamic eschatology, both the good and the evil will be resurrected. The grave will not offer a way to avoid judgment before Allah.

However, the time framework of Revelation suggests a meaning behind these otherwise obscure Hadiths. They are much better placed here in the chronology, instead of near the time of final judgment. Satan and the demons, who have been a behind-the-scenes influence on Muhammad, Islam, the Mahdi, and the ersatz 'Isa ibn Maryam, now take full possession of their followers.

Ibn Battal Al-Qurtubi, the 13th century Andalusian Sunni Hadith scholar, was an expert on the subject of death. He drew on the authority of the Qur'an and the Hadiths. His view of this end-time scene gives insight as to why the great trials have reached a new extreme:

> The people in the graves will be envied, and death will be desired when the great trials appear. That is due to fear of the

---

[190] Smith and Haddad, p.83.

end of the world on account of the prevalence of falsehood, the corruption of its people, and the appearance of disobedience and evil.[191]

---

[191] Ibn Battal Al-Qurtubi, *al-Tadhkirah fī Aḥwāl al-Mawtà wa-Umūr al-Ākhirah (Reminder of the Conditions of the Dead and the Matters of the Hereafter)*, quoted in ʿIbn Izzat p.65.

K33 :
The four evil angels gather armies that slay another third of men

: H33
The Mahdi's armies continue battle

9:12 The first woe has passed; behold, two woes are still coming after these things.

9:13 Then the sixth angel sounded, and I heard a voice from the four horns of the golden altar which is before God,

9:14 saying to the sixth angel who had the trumpet, "Release the four angels who are bound at the great river Euphrates."

9:15 And the four angels, who had been prepared for the hour and day and month and year, were released, so that they would kill a third of mankind.

9:16 The number of the armies of the horsemen was two hundred million; I heard the number of them.

9:17 And this is how I saw in my vision the horses and those who sat on them: the riders had breastplates the color of fire, of hyacinth, and of brimstone; and the heads of the horses are like the heads of lions; and out of their mouths came fire and smoke and brimstone.

[Hudhaifa bin Al-Yaman asked the Messenger of Allah] will there be any evil after that good? "Yes, there will be some people who will invite others to the doors of Hell, and whoever accepts their invitation to it will be thrown in it (by them)." … What do you order me to do if such a thing should take place in my life? "Adhere to the group of Muslims and their Chief." If there is neither a group (of Muslims) nor a chief (what shall I do)? "Keep away from all those different sects, even if you had to eat [cling to] the root of a tree, till you meet Allah while you are still in that state."[192]

The tribes will attack one another and fight until `Aqaba runs with blood.[193]

There are two groups of my *Ummah* whom Allah will free from the Fire: The group that invades India, and the group that will be with 'Isa bin Maryam.[194] *(hasan)*

Abu Hurayrah narrated that the Prophet mentioned India one day

---

[192] Narrated by Hudhaifa bin Al-Yaman, *Sahih al-Bukhari 3606*, Vol. 4, Book 56, Hadith 803, https://sunnah.com/bukhari:3606, accessed June 1, 2024; alternate translation in brackets from `Ibn Izzat p.40.

[193] Narrated by `Abdullah ibn `Amr, in al-Hakim, and Nu`aym ibn Hammad, quoted in `Ibn Izzat p.26; also referenced in Abu Rahma, https://qurananswers.me/2017/07/03/will-caliphate-return-before-the-mahdi/, July 3, 2017, accessed June 1,2024.

[194] Narrated by Thawban, *Sunan an-Nasa'i 3175*, Vol. 1, Book 25, Hadith 3177, https://sunnah.com/nasai:3175, accessed June 1, 2024; also referenced in Rahma p.72.

9:18 A third of mankind was killed by these three plagues, by the fire, the smoke, and the brimstone which came out of their mouths.
9:19 For the power of the horses is in their mouths and in their tails; for their tails are like serpents and have heads, and with them they do harm.
9:20 The rest of mankind, who were not killed by these plagues, did not repent of the works of their hands so as not to worship demons and the idols of gold, silver, brass, stone, and wood, which can neither see nor hear nor walk;
9:21 and they did not repent of their murders, nor of their witchcraft, nor of their sexual immorality, nor of their thefts.

and said: An army from amongst you will attack India and Allah will grant them victory until they put the leaders of Sindh in chains. Allah will forgive them their sins; they will depart when they depart and when they do so they will find the Messiah, son of Maryam, in Syria.[195] *(da'if)*

The Messenger of Allah promised us that we would conquer India, so if I am martyred I will be among the best of the martyrs, and if I return then I am Abu Hurayrah the freed (protected from Hellfire).[196] *(da'if)*

If there only remained a single day of this world, Allah would lengthen that day until a man from the people of my house was given control over it. Battles will take place under his command and Islam will be victorious.[197]

Revelation. In the previous section, the fifth trumpet released the demons (9:1-6 K32). It was the first woe (9:12). But relief by death was not permitted. Now another angel blows the sixth trumpet (9:13), which becomes the second woe (11:14 K36). With it God removes the bounds that had been restraining four evil angels. They had been been confined to the area around the Euphrates river in the Middle East (9:14-15).

---

[195] Musnad Ishaq b. Rahawayh 537, Nu'aym b. Hammad's Kitai al-Fitan 1576, quoted in Rahma p.72; also narrated by Abu Hurayrah, quoted in https://islamqa.info/en/answers/145636/hadith-about-the-conquest-of-india, accessed June 1, 2024.
[196] Narrated by Abu Hurairah, quoted in https://islamqa.info/en/answers/145636/hadith-about-the-conquest-of-india, accessed June 2, 2024; also narrated by Abu Hurairah, *Sunan an-Nasa'i 3174*, Vol. 1, Book 25, Hadith 3176, https://sunnah.com/nasai:3174, accessed June 2, 2024.
[197] Narrated by Hudhayfa, in Abu Nu`aym, and al-Isfahani, quoted in `Ibn Izzat p.27; also partially narated by Abdullah ibn Mas'ud, *Sunan Abi Dawud 4282*, Book 37, Hadith 4269, https://sunnah.com/abudawud:4282, accessed June 1, 2024.

A golden altar in heaven is the backdrop of God's action. It illustrates that God continues to answer the prayers of the martyred believers (6:10 K26).

The four evil archangels use their freedom to inspire the formation of the largest army ever known. It consists of "two hundred million" fighters (9:16). Such manpower can only be gathered across a region of hundreds or thousands of kilometers. The monstrous scale is only conceivable if the armies are rapidly formed from volunteers, equipped from large inventories of manufactured weapons that are on hand. They are likely whipped into a frenzy to fight alongside a small professional core of soldiers.

The fantastic imagery of this army in John's vision in 9:17-19 could be his way of portraying military weaponry that will appear centuries into his future. What he saw would be incomprehensible to the understanding of anyone who was alive at the time of the Roman empire.

In God's overarching plan over time and space, the vast armies have been appointed for this moment (9:15). They come into being in the intensely militaristic world of the beast.

The armies face great resistance. This is a world at war, with forces of the beast and the false prophet opposed by myriad pockets of resistance. Counter-armies of various warlords would also be in play, some of them previous allies of the woman of Babylon, others who only pretended to support the one-world government of the tribulation period.

In the battles that ensue, a third of all people die (9:15,18). Many of the victims are civilians, some of them converts to Christ, others who stick to their own ideologies. When added to the previous famine and death upon a fourth of men under the beast's rule (6:8 K25), the godless world of the tribulation has brought death to at least 50% of the earth's population. The only more devastating time in history was the worldwide flood of Noah's day, which left just eight survivors. That was also God's expression of wrath upon a world that had almost totally forsaken him.

But here in the tribulation, many are still alive. God continues to give them opportunity to turn away from the beast or their own leaders, and to come to him instead. Jesus will be returning soon.

This is yet another time that God permits destruction to a *third*. Previously we saw devastation of the third part of trees (8:7 K29), of the sea (8:8 K29), of all ships (8:9 K29), of the rivers (8:10-11 K30), and of the light of the sun, moon, and stars (8:12 K31).

With this theme of thirds, God is mocking the number of the beast, 666. That number misses the mark by a third. The thirds emphasize the futility of the beast's ambition to be absolute king over the world.

When Jesus comes, he will add the third back. He will rule for much longer than three and a half or seven years. He will be the true righteous king for 1,000 years, the perfect period of fulfillment (K44). After that, he will rule for all eternity (K47).

Despite the bloodshed and death, most who survive do "not repent of their murders, nor of their witchcraft, nor of their sexual immorality, nor of their thefts." They would rather follow in the path of Satan, the beast, and their proponents (9:20-21).

Hadiths. In section H24, when ʿIsa ibn Maryam came from heaven back to earth to assist the Mahdi in creating a worldwide Islamic domain, the Hadiths prophesied that there would be an idyllic time of plenty. We were told that ʿIsa "will break the cross, slaughter the pigs ... grudges and mutual hatred will disappear ... the earth will be filled with peace just as a vessel is filled with water. The people will be united and none will be worshipped except Allah. War will cease ... the earth will have a silver age."

From the Hadiths in our current section, it seems that the killings of the Christians and Jews were not fully adequate to establish the peace of a silver age. The promised harmony must be continually enforced by military means.

When one of Muhammad's followers asked, "will there be any evil after that good?", he replied that there will still be those who reject Islam. They will prefer the doors of hell to Allah. They will overpower Muslims who come one-by-one to oppose them, and will hurl them into those doors. Their violence will tempt Muslims to weaken their faith.

Entire groups or sects of Muslims may be so tempted. Muhammad warns that amongst such pockets of evil that remain, each Muslim should make sure to "adhere to the group of Muslims and their Chief," who will be the Mahdi. Group solidarity is the key to their salvation. If a Muslim finds himself isolated amidst the unbelievers, or in a Muslim sect that is compromised, he should flee all their temptations, "even if you had to [cling to] the root of a tree, till you meet Allah."

We met compromising Muslims earlier in H21. There they were advising the Mahdi not to break his treaty with the Romans. When the Mahdi rejected their counsel, and brought his army against the Romans, they were among the third of the Mahdi's army who fled the scene of battle.

After the Mahdi becomes supreme, any Muslim sects who do not whole-heartedly follow his direction are also worthy of elimination. His armies will wipe out their resistance. The hadith that we saw in H21 and H23 is therefore also applicable here: "The tribes will attack one another and fight until `Aqaba runs with blood."

The Jews and the Christians are the main targets of the Mahdi for extinction.

But he will not ignore the *kuffar* (infidels) of other religions or ideologies. Among them will be the Hindus of India. As someone who grew up in trade, Muhammad[198] had knowledge of them, for Arabic traders had dealings with India across the Arabian Sea even before the seventh century.[199] From other traders he would have learned that the polytheism of the Hindus was even worse than that of his own Arabian countrymen. This was totally repugnant to him, the messenger of the true God Allah. He devoted some of his thought to the Hindus. The

---

[198] *Muhammad: The Trader,* no author or date, https://www.soundvision.com/book/muhammad-the-trader, accessed July 23, 2023.
[199] *Who were the Ancient Arab Sea Traders?,* https://www.nabataea.net/explore/travel_and_trade/who-were-the-ancient-arab-sea-traders/, accessed July 23, 2023.

angel Jibreel must have explained what Allah had in store for them during the future time of the Mahdi.

A number of Muhammad's oral sayings regarding the end-time Muslim wars in India have been recorded in the Hadiths. Two of them are given in this section.

In these Hadiths, Muhammad promises automatic acceptance at the end-time judgment seat of Allah to everyone who fights in the army of ʿIsa ibn Maryam, and also to those who fight in India. He promises that the army attacking India will be victorious. They will bring it into the domain of Islam. Afterward, those warriors will join ʿIsa's army in Syria. This would be in time for his major push against the Dajjal, the most persistent enemy of the Mahdi.

Comparison. Revelation numbers the massive army called forth by the four evil archangels at 200 million. But it is silent as to why an army is the means used to slay a third of the world's population. Why not something less bloody like plague, famine, or forced labor in gulags? What governments typically use to bring an unarmed population into subjection are secret police, informers, government agents, community activists, so-called health advocates, but not armies.

The fact that an army of such massive proportions is raised indicates that there is widespread opposition to the beast during the great tribulation, and that this opposition has access to advanced armaments.

The Hadiths do not speak to the size of the Mahdi's armies, but they do speak of his ongoing wars. Once again, this is indicative of widespread and armed opposition to the Mahdi during his supposedly silver age. The fact that India is called out as one arena of battle gives a clue that the Mahdi's forces deployed must be numbered in the tens of millions.[200] Only such a gigantic force could completely vanquish a population of a billion Hindus, and keep them in submission.

---

[200] "A recent Rand Corp. study by military analyst James Quinlivan concluded that the bare minimum ratio to provide security for the inhabitants of an occupied territory, let alone deal with an active insurgency, is one to 50." in Stephen Budiansky, *Proven Formula for How Many Troops We Need*, May 9, 2004, https://www.washingtonpost.com/archive/opinions/2004/05/09/a-proven-formula-for-how-many-troops-we-need/5c6dbfc9-33f8-4648-bd07-40d244a1daa4/.

India and Hinduism are not mentioned in Revelation, or anywhere else in the Bible. But the main religions that were founded in India – Hinduism and Buddhism – point people far away from the three-in-one true God of the Bible. Satan inspired these religions centuries before Jesus was born in Israel, and before any of the New Testament books were written. In Hinduism, the concept of a single god is replaced by many gods. Life after death in either heaven or hell is replaced with a vicious cycle of rebirths. The quest of Hindus is to achieve spiritual liberation from them. In Buddhism, the soul is meant to break through the sham realities of this world to the liberation of nothingness.

Islam is a much newer religion than Old Testament Judaism, Hinduism, Buddhism, or faith in Christ. Satan inspired the founding of Islam after John wrote the book of Revelation, which completed the canon of the Bible. It took time for Satan to thoroughly digest the prophecies set forth in it, and to come up with his own plan. Some five centuries later, he countered by inspiring the formation of yet another religion - Islam. This time he did not offer a multiplicity of gods, or a goal of nothingness, but a unipolar god named Allah, who could not possibly have a son who paid for our transgressions, or a holy spirit that dwells among his followers.

Satan would then take pleasure in seeing the children of his different religions hate and destroy each other.

In the end times, India would very logically be one of the greatest pockets of resistance to the Mahdi's/beast's rule, since radical Muslims and Hindus have always detested one another. Perhaps India swore allegiance to the worldwide government headed by the woman of Babylon when she was allied with the beast, and kept a large measure of autonomy in the process. But with the downfall of the woman/the Romans, the beast/Mahdi consolidated power by asserting supremacy over religion. That would absolutely infuriate Hindus. With their large degree of military self-sufficiency, India would present a major challenge for the beast/Mahdi to subjugate it.

Much the same could be said of China, though it is not mentioned anywhere in Revelation or the Hadiths. The authoritarian leaders of China keep to their own ideology. They have historically been known to maximize their powers, and of negotiating careful agreements that they would then interpret to their own convenience. With a large and capable military to back them up, China would be difficult for the beast/Mahdi to keep in compliance.

The Hadiths' emphasis on force for achieving Islamic victory conforms to the precedent set forth in Revelation. The main difference between the two is that Revelation focuses on the death of one third of all people. Though these deaths come at the hands of the beast's army, at a spiritual level they are a punishment from God in response to mankind's abject godlessness, both among the supporters of the beast and his opponents. In contrast, the Hadiths do not speak of the numbers of the dead. Their focus is on Muslim group solidarity in the face of challenges to their faith by opponents, among whom are other groups of Muslims who are not dependable in their allegiance to the Mahdi.

We shall see in Revelation that the beast will ultimately fail in having all people worship him. But in the Hadiths, the Mahdi will be successful in bringing the world under the command of Allah and Islam.

K34 :
Satan kills the two witnesses

11:3‡[K19] "And I will grant authority to my two witnesses, and they will prophesy for 1,260 days, clothed in sackcloth."
11:7 When they have finished their testimony, the beast that comes up out of the abyss will make war with them, and overcome them and kill them.
11:8 And their dead bodies will lie on the street of the great city which spiritually is called Sodom and Egypt, where also their Lord was crucified.
11:9 Those from the peoples, tribes, languages, and nations will look at their dead bodies for three and a half days, and will not allow their dead bodies to be laid in a tomb.
11:10 And those who live on the earth will rejoice over them and celebrate; and they will send gifts to one another, because these two prophets tormented those who live on the earth.

: H34
ʿIsa ibn Maryam seeks out and kills the Dajjal

There will be no part of the earth left that he [the Dajjal] does not enter and prevail over, except for Makkah and Al-Madinah, for he will not approach them on any of their mountain paths, but he will be met by angels with unsheathed swords, until he will stop at the red hill at the end of the marsh. Then Al-Madinah will be shaken with its people three times, and no hypocrite, male or female, will be left, all will come out to him. Thus it will be cleansed of impurity just as the bellows cleanses the iron of dross. And that day will be called the Day of Deliverance.[201] *(da'if)*

Ad-Dajjal will come to Medina and find the angels guarding it. So Allah willing, neither Ad-Dajjal, nor plague will be able to come near it.[202]

The Dajjal will appear while the *deen* is half asleep. Then ʿIsa the son of Maryam will descend and will call out at dawn, "O people! What prevents you from going out against this loathsome liar?" ... When they have prayed the *Subh* prayer, they will attack the Dajjal. When the liar sees him, he will

---

[201] Narrated by Abu Umamah Al-Bahili, *Sunan Ibn Majah 4077*, Vol. 5, Book 36, Hadith 4077, https://sunnah.com/ibnmajah:4077, accessed June 2, 2024; also narrated by Abu Saʿid al-Khudri, quoted in ʿIbn Izzat p.34.
[202] Narrated by Anas bin Malik, *Sahih al-Bukhari 7134*, Vol. 9, Book 88, Hadith 248, https://sunnah.com/bukhari:7134, accessed June 2, 2024; also referenced in Richardson p.74.

melt away as salt melts in
water.[203]

The Dajjal would appear in my *Ummah* [community] and he would stay
(in the world) for forty - I cannot say whether he meant forty days,
forty months or forty years.[204]

I heard the Messenger of Allah say: A section of my people will not
cease fighting for the truth and will prevail until the day of
resurrection. He said: 'Isa ibn Maryam would then descend and their
commander [the Mahdi] would invite him to come and lead them in
prayer, but he would say: No, some amongst you are commanders
over some. This is the honour from Allah for this *Ummah.*[205]

The time of prayer shall come and then 'Isa Ibn Maryam would
descend and would lead them. When the enemy of Allah (the Dajjal)
would see him ... Allah would kill them by his ('Isa's) hand and he
would show them their blood on his lance (the lance of 'Isa ibn
Maryam).[206]

He ['Isa Ibn Maryam] would then search for him (the Dajjal) until he
would catch hold of him at the gate of Ludd and would kill him.[207]

Their leader will lead them in prayer. When he has finished, 'Isa will
say: "Open the gate." So they will open it and behind it will be Dajjal
with seventy thousand Jews, each of them carrying an adorned sword
and wearing a greenish cloak. When Dajjal looks at him, he will start to
melt as salt melts in water. He will run away, and 'Isa will say: "I have
only one blow for you, which you will not be able to escape!" He will
catch up with him at the eastern gate of Ludd, and will kill him. Then
Allah will defeat the Jews, and there will be nothing left that Allah has
created which the Jews will be able to hide behind, except that Allah
will cause it to speak - no stone, no tree, no wall, no animal ... except

---

[203] Narrated by Jabir ibn `Abdullah, *Musnad* of Ahmad ibn Hanbal, quoted in `Ibn Izzat
p.32.
[204] Narrated by Abdullah b. 'Amr, *Sahih Muslim 2940a*, Book 41, Hadith 7023,
https://sunnah.com/muslim:2940a, accessed May 18, 2024; also quoted in `Ibn Izzat
p.32.
[205] Narrated by Jabir b. 'Abdullah, *Sahih Muslim 156*, Book 1, Hadith 293,
https://sunnah.com/muslim:156, accessed June 2, 2024; also referenced in Richardson
p.53.
[206] Narrated by Abu Huraira, *Sahih Muslim 2897*, Book 41, Hadith 6924,
https://sunnah.com/muslim:2897, accessed June 2, 2024; also referenced in Richardson
p.75.
[207] Narrated by An-Nawwas b. Sam`an, *Sahih Muslim 2937 a*, Book 41, Hadith 7015,
https://sunnah.com/muslim:2937, accessed June 2, 2024; also referenced in `Ibn Izzat
p.27.

that it will say: "O Muslim slave of Allah, here is a Jew, come and kill him!"[208]

Revelation. It has been three and a half years (11:3) since the two witnesses appeared (see section K19), to challenge the people of the tribulation to repent and turn back to God. They started their ministry before the woman of Babylon was betrayed and overthrown by the beast. Their base of operation is described as Sodom and Egypt, which were places of opposition to the true God in the Old Testament. But this same place is also described as the city where Jesus was crucified (11:8), none other than Jerusalem. The equivalence made between Sodom, Egypt, and Jerusalem shows how far from God the inhabitants of the city have gone, under the rule of the beast and the false prophet.

The witnesses are fearless in the face of wickedness and unbelief. They know their time is short, and that they will share the suffering that Jesus endured when he came to Jerusalem two thousand years ago. They came to testify about him. He is the only one who can save people from the trials that have come as a consequence of their own fatal choices.

The two witnesses command respect, because they speak truth. They confirm the truth, at least in some people's eyes, by the miracles that God works through them: speaking fire to consume those sent against them (11:5 K19), stopping the rain, and bloodying the waters (11:6 K19). Because of their example, many turn from the beast and the false prophet. They now profess Christ, during a time when all the powers of the world are determined to obliterate his name forever.

But now the government's military power has expanded exponentially. 200 million armed men have spread out from the area of the Euphrates (9:16 K33). They are waging total war on all opponents, whether they are new believers in Christ, or long-time and secret adherents of other ideologies and religions.

With a third of all people meeting their end in the recent wars (9:18 K33), it is intolerable to the government that the two witnesses have

---

[208] Narrated by Abu Umamah Al-Bahili, *Sunan Ibn Majah 4077*, Vol. 5, Book 36, Hadith 4077, https://sunnah.com/ibnmajah:4077, accessed May 29, 2024; similar narration by Umm Sharik bint Abi Bakr, quoted in 'Ibn Izzat pp.34-35.

not yet met the same fate. But God has put a protective hedge around them. We have seen that they cannot be harmed by any mortal man.

Only the direct intervention by Satan can overcome them. He is equally distressed by their opposition to the fulfillment of his plans. After rising from the abyss (11:7), and leading the devils who had been imprisoned there to do their worst upon the earth (9:2-5 K32), Satan turns his attention to taking out the two witnesses once and for all.

God has his own plan. Surprisingly, he does not stand in Satan's way, but allows him to overcome the witnesses and kill them both (11:7).

The reaction among most onlookers is unmitigated glee. There is such contempt for the witnesses on the part of the beast's government that they are not even allowed a proper burial. Their dead bodies are left to lie in the street (11:8).

In our age of instant and global electronic media, it would be an easy thing for the government of the beast to take advantage of the occasion. It would be a perfect vehicle to spread their mantra of unstoppable world domination.

Great numbers of people, in Jerusalem, and undoubtedly billions more online via Internet, rejoice over the demise of the witnesses. They do so in the many languages of the world (11:9). They make merry, and shower each other with gifts (11:10).

The story does not stop here. God will soon show that his power is made perfect in weakness (2 Corinthians 12:9).

Before turning to the Hadiths, it is instructive to point out that the desecration of dead bodies is acceptable in few religions. One of them is Islam. "The practice of displaying the dead bodies of enemies or criminals in public places is a distinctly Islamic practice and is still done to this day."[209]

Hadiths. The Mahdi and 'Isa ibn Maryam have made great progress in cleansing the long-awaited Islamic world from Jews, Christians, Hindus, and wavering Muslims. But their great enemy, the Dajjal, is still alive. We last saw him in section H25, tempting people away from Allah with

---

[209] Shoebat, p. 180.

miracles. His goal is to confuse the faith of people. In the time of extreme war and want, he offers rain and sustenance. But he brings plague on those who steadfastly oppose him, and causes their animals to die.

In our current section we learn that the Dajjal will range across the whole world. "There will be no part of the earth left that he does not enter." The hadith goes on to say he will "prevail over" the whole world, except for the holiest cities of Islam, Mecca and Medina. By the will of Allah, they will be protected from the rampages of the Dajjal. Islamic angels will confront him there with unsheathed swords. The cities will expel those who succumb to his temptations, leaving a zone of 100% permanent loyalty to the Mahdi. This day of purification will be called the Day of Deliverance.

The Dajjal "will appear while the deen is half asleep."

The word *deen* has several meanings in the Qur'an and the Hadiths.[210] One is to receive reward or punishment. A second is submission, obedience, service or slavery. In this interpretation, deen means to humble oneself before Allah, and no one else. We saw that application of the word in H32. There, many of the faithless regarded the humility of deen as a burdensome affliction instead of a privilege. Rather than serve Allah, and suffer the accompanying trials caused by Allah's enemies, they sought death.

Here in H35, we see the third meaning for deen: sovereignty, power, lordship, kingship, or rulership. The Dajjal probes for weakness in this quality of deen as practiced in the Islamic society under the Mahdi, and takes advantage wherever he can. Muslims of the end times need to stand together in solidarity against him. They will find that 'Isa ibn Maryam is the gifted leader they can depend on for guidance in their struggles with the Dajjal.

The events prophesied by Muhammad that come next can be deduced by harmonizing the remaining Hadiths of this section.

---

[210] Abul A'la Al-Mawdudi, *Islam and the Meaning of Deen*, https://www.newmuslim.net/islam-and-the-meaning-of-deen/, accessed August 8, 2023.

The second of the five pillars of Islam[211] obligates Muslims to pray five times a day, at set times. The Mahdi and 'Isa his deputy will assemble their armies for such times of prayer. These prayers will be added to those of millions of Muslims regarding their enemy the Dajjal, and will now reach a crescendo. Allah will answer at one of their dawn prayers.

The time of dawn as the setting of Allah's response is especially significant. The dawn prayer is the first daily prayer, known as the *fajr*[212] or *subh*.[213]

> The time just before sunrise is the best time to pray. It is the time in which Allah descends to the first heaven in a manner befitting him, and grants the prayers of his believing servants who are awake. [214]

'Isa has just recently descended from heaven, and appeared first in Damascus to assist the Mahdi (H24). The Hadiths narrate what is prophesied to happen next.

In front of his armies, the Mahdi will invite 'Isa to come and lead them in prayer, but 'Isa will defer to his superior to begin the prayers. This despite 'Isa being the religious leader of Islam during the silver age. 'Isa indicates that he is only a servant and subordinate of the Mahdi. Only when his chief is finished does 'Isa lead them in prayer. He will do so with a call to all faithful Muslims, in words that will be magnified in their effect.

---

[211] The five pillars of Islam are: the profession of faith (the *shahada*), the five daily prayers (*salat*), alms-giving (*zakat*), fasting during Ramadan (*saum*), and pilgrimage to Mecca (*hajj*), in Elizabeth Macaulay, https://www.khanacademy.org/humanities/ap-art-history/introduction-cultures-religions-apah/islam-apah/a/the-five-pillars-of-islam, accessed August 7, 2024.

[212] *What is the importance of time for prayer (salah)?*, https://questionsonislam.com/article/what-importance-time-prayer-salah, accessed August 8, 2023.

[213] *Difference between Subh and Fajr Prayer*, https://islamqa.info/en/answers/79345/difference-between-subh-and-fajr-prayer, accessed August 8, 2023.

[214] *Significance of sunrise/dawn in Islam?*, comment by unnamed author, 2021, https://www.reddit.com/r/islam/comments/q6mh0l/significance_of_sunrisedawn_in_islam/, accessed August 8, 2023.

Muhammad prophesies that 'Isa will now lay down the challenge to the Muslim force: "What prevents you from going out against this loathsome liar?" He will command the gate to be opened. Seen through it will be the Dajjal with 70,000 Jews, all carrying swords and wearing crowns.

But the crowns of the Jews will provoke the Mahdi's forces. When they have finished praying, they will attack. The army of Jews will scatter in panic. The Dajjal will look at 'Isa, and will melt in fear as salt melts in water. He also will flee.

The jihad waged over the last 1,500 years finally reaches its fulfillment. The unbroken line of Muslim warriors who followed the example of Muhammad, and continue to fight for the Truth, finally achieve their culminating victory, when the last of them fights the false Messiah under the leadership of 'Isa.

The Jews will be desperate to find places to hide, but even inanimate objects will cry out against them. The stones, trees, and walls will point them out to the pursuing Muslims, and will say, "here is a Jew, come and kill him!"

And so, Muslims will once and for all defeat the Jews.

In the mayhem of this massacre, 'Isa ibn Maryam will seek out the Dajjal, and will thrust him through with his lance. The spot where he catches the false Messiah will be at the Ludd Gate in Palestine. It is common Islamic belief that this gate is in the city of Lod, 15 km southeast of Jerusalem.

The death of the Dajjal will be to the credit of these fighters of the future. On them and their jihadist predecessors will rest the laurels of eternity that will rightly be theirs. The Islamic community of the present time and ages past yearns for this day.

Comparison. The two witnesses are unlike the Dajjal in many ways. Their deaths occur differently. Their base of operations is not the same, either – the two witnesses are in Jerusalem, while the Dajjal will range across the whole world.

But there are a number of similarities. This is evident in an even-handed comparison, even though the Hadiths push their own distinct narrative that draws Muslims away from the testimony of Revelation.

The first similarity is that both Revelation and the Hadiths predict a religious and political framework that extends itself worldwide during the end times. After the beast broke his alliance with the woman of Babylon and overthrew her, the two witnesses came to prominence as the beast's main enemy. Similarly, after the Mahdi broke his truce with the Romans and defeated them, the Dajjal became the leader of opposition to him. The two witnesses and the Dajjal are the primary competition to the dictatorship they oppose for the hearts and minds of people across the world.

Second, miracles are a common tool for both. God empowers the witnesses to speak fire to consume those sent against them (11:5 K19), to stop the rain, and to turn waters to blood (11:6 K19). People can readily perceive that it is the true God of heaven who is the power behind these miracles. Through them they become open to the good news proclaimed by the witnesses. Many are thus emboldened to turn away from the anti-God system of the beast and the false prophet. They put their faith in Christ instead.

The Dajjal is also a miracle worker. He performs miracles for the well-being of his followers the Jews and Christians. But he inflicts plagues on those who reject him.

Third, the 200-million-man army of Revelation compares with the Mahdi's main army, now supplemented by portions of another large army available after subduing India in H33. In that section we speculated that this vast army, with numbers never seen before, could only be formed swiftly from volunteers. This fits the pattern of flash jihadist armed groups raised in rapid time, in response to agitation by imams and mullahs against severe insults to Islam.

Fourth, the massacre of the Dajjal's Jewish army of 70,000 by this army of the Mahdi, compares to the martyrs of Revelation, who fall victim to the beast's armies of persecution and extermination.

Fifth, in Revelation as well the Hadiths, the armies of the dictatorship are unable on their own to stop the activity of the two witnesses and the Dajjal. God has put a hedge around the witnesses. We have seen that they cannot be harmed by any mortal man. In the case of the Dajjal, it takes two Islamic angels wielding otherworldly swords to fend him off from Mecca and Medina.

Death comes to them only by supernatural agency. It takes the power of Satan to kill the two witnesses (11:7). In the case of the Dajjal, he meets his end at the hands of 'Isa ibn Maryam. He seems to be a mortal man, the deputy of the Mahdi. But who is 'Isa, really? Muslims claim him to be the one who was sentenced to the cross in Jerusalem two thousand years ago, but whom Allah spirited away to heaven, and provided a replacement to die in his place. In this view, 'Isa never experienced death long ago, and did not age afterward. After he returns to earth, and is successful in killing the Dajjal, we shall see in H44 that he will finally die a natural death. This begs the question, by whose supernatural power does he exist, deathless, in heaven for over two thousand years? Is it by this power that he will kill the Dajjal?

In the Islamic understanding, the Dajjal is the champion of the Jews. This automatically makes him an Islamic type of Satan. But in the Bible, Satan's primary focus was not to champion the Jews, but to stop them from giving birth to the promised messiah, whom he knew would be the incarnation of the divine son of God. Satan sought to kill all the Jews, if only he could prevent the coming of Christ to earth. It is quite the change in the Muslim version of the end times for an Islamic Satan to be the hope of the Jews. The Dajjal as placeholder for Satan draws attention away from the one who truly holds the role of the evil one in the Hadiths.

Another of the great ironies of Islamic belief is that Muslims agree with Jews on the person of Jesus Christ. Many Muslims cannot get past the Islamic doctrine that God is wholly one. They regard it as unforgivable to believe that he has a divine son. But they should reflect on the fact that most Jews, whom they hate the most, have the same belief. Two thousand years ago the Jews appealed to this doctrine to justify the crucifixion of Jesus Christ.

These various truths are obscured in the Hadiths. They are all parts of Satan's elaborate deception, planned by him carefully for centuries. In the teachings of Islam, they are presented as something different, with plausible deniability.

What is the Hadiths' message to Muslims of the end times? They are admonished to stand together in solidarity against the Dajjal. This is because Allah does not care to know them personally as individuals. Their acceptance before him depends on their solidarity with the Muslim community, the *ummah*.

But the message of the two witnesses to Muslims, and to all people, is that they can know God personally, because he knows them and loves them. The true God of the Bible draws each of his children to himself. He knows them by name. Jesus his son seeks out every lost sheep and brings him or her home. God then seals his relationship with his chosen ones by sending the Holy Spirit to live in their hearts.

What is the outcome of the demise of the Dajjal versus that of the two witnesses? The death of the Dajjal seals the victory of the Mahdi for Islam. No more challenge will be made. But for the beast, we will see in the next section that the death of the two witnesses brings him only within grasp of world domination, but no further. He does not achieve complete victory. That is because the witnesses point to someone beyond themselves, Jesus Christ the son of God, who has promised to come again. Now that they are dead, his return is imminent. He will shatter the imposing edifice of a military world that the beast and false prophet have constructed.

K35 :
God resurrects the two witnesses

: H35
The Dajjal is identified by his power to resurrect and must be opposed

11:11 And after the three and a half days, the breath of life from God came into them, and they stood on their feet; and great fear fell upon those who were watching them.

11:12 And they heard a loud voice from heaven saying to them, "Come up here." And they went up into heaven in the cloud, and their enemies watched them.

11:13 And at that time there was a great earthquake, and a tenth of the city fell; seven thousand people were killed in the earthquake, and the rest were terrified and gave glory to the God of heaven.

One man will say to the Dajjal, "I testify that you are the same Dajjal whose description was given to us by the messenger of Allah, may Allah bless him and Grant him peace." The Dajjal will say to the people, "If I kill this man and bring him back to life again, will you doubt my claim?" They will say, "No." Then the Dajjal will kill that man and bring him back to life. That man will say, "Now I am even more certain of your identity than I was before." The Dajjal will want to kill him but will be unable to do so.[215]

He [the Dajjal] will say to a Bedouin: "What do you think, if I resurrect your father and mother for you, will you bear witness that I am your Lord?" He will say: "Yes." Then two devils will appear to him in the form of his father and mother and will say: "O my son, follow him, for he is your Lord."[216] *(da'if)*

Revelation. The bodies of the two witnesses have been lying in the street in Jerusalem. No one has taken steps to bury them. The beast's followers have been rejoicing that these enemies will no longer challenge their consciences. They rest in the thought that the killings and persecutions will bring on an optimal world.

---

[215] Narrated by Abu Sa'id al-Khudri, *Sahih Muslim 2938 a*, quoted in `Ibn Izzat p.31; also in Book 41, Hadith 7017, https://sunnah.com/muslim:2938a, accessed June 3, 2024.
[216] Narrated by Abu Umamah Al-Bahili, *Sunan Ibn Majah 4077*, Vol. 5, Book 36, Hadith 4077, accessed June 3, 2024; also referenced in Richardson p.73.

But three and a half days after the death of the witnesses, an event occurs which has only taken place once before in history – their resurrection. It is quickly followed by ascension into heaven.

The other time this happened was two thousand years ago, when Jesus Christ died, crucified on a rough Roman cross. The four different gospel accounts of the New Testament go on to explain that on the third day after death, his friends and disciples discovered that his tomb was empty (see for example John 20:1-18). Jesus had been resurrected from the dead by the power of God. Hours later, they met Jesus, now with a glorified deathless body, instead of the natural body that we all know (Luke 24:39). Yet they recognized that it was the same Jesus whom they had followed for three years, confirmed by the wound marks in his hands from the nails that had held him to the cross (John 20:24-29).

For forty days Jesus stayed with them (Acts 1:3). He explained the fulfillment of prophecies about him in the Old Testament (Luke 24:44-49), and the trials that awaited them in years to come (John 21:18-19). The disciples now understood his mysterious words from earlier:

> John 11:25 Jesus said to her, "I am the resurrection and the
> life; the one who believes in Me will live, even if he dies,
> 11:26 and everyone who lives and believes in Me will never
> die. Do you believe this?"

There were numerous eyewitnesses of the resurrected Christ. On one occasion, five hundred people were with him (1 Corinthians 15:6). Then, on the fortieth day, Jesus gathered his twelve disciples. Before their eyes, he rose up into the sky and disappeared beyond the clouds. This was his ascension into heaven (Acts 1:9-11).

The two witnesses, prior to their death, were preaching the gospel message of the Christ: that God has definite standards of righteousness for us to live by, and that no one deserves heaven because each of us are in rebellion against him. Despite this, God provided his son Jesus as a substitute to those who repent. He invites us to trust in him for our salvation:

> Romans 5:8 But God demonstrates His own love toward us,
> in that while we were still sinners, Christ died for us.

Now, three and a half days after the death of the witnesses, they follow in Christ's footsteps. God raises their dead bodies from the street, and breathes life into them again. Their putrefying bodies are transformed into perfect, glorified bodies.

Great fear grips all who have been watching and mocking their deaths (11:11). They now realize that there is a God in heaven who has performed this resurrection, and that he will soon punish them for the evil they have done.

God then raises the two up into the sky. Their enemies see this as it happens (11:12). The witnesses then transition from the heavenly clouds into heaven itself. There they join all those of the church who, before the tribulation began over six years earlier, had received glorified bodies and were raptured into the heavenly presence of God.

The eyewitness spectators of the killings and resurrection are in Jerusalem. They had hated the two witnesses with venom. They would not even give them the courtesy of a burial after watching them be murdered. They make a first circle of unbelievers. There is a second and much wider circle – billions of people who likely have been viewing the events in real time via cyberspace.

God is not done. He is not satisfied just to display his power to resurrect the dead. Within an hour of the witnesses' ascension, God gets the attention of both circles. He sends an earthquake upon Jerusalem (11:13). A tenth of the city is leveled straightaway. Seven thousand are killed. Fear of God's impending wrath now intensifies, as people in Jerusalem and across the world see that he is sending punishment.

Against their will, those watching unwillingly give "glory to the God of heaven" (11:13). Their mortal fear drives them to admit that God is God. At least some of them now understand that the beast and his mentor Satan cannot sustain a world devoid of God.

Hadiths. In the previous section, the Dajjal met his end at the hands of 'Isa ibn Maryam. But since we are now on the topic of bodily resurrection, it is helpful to quote Hadiths that predict that the Dajjal will raise people from the dead.

In the hadith of H25, the Dajjal had power to command the sky. He brought rain for those who believed in him, so that their livestock would flourish. But he brought death to the animals of those who denied him.

The Dajjal's greatest miracles involve bringing people back to life. This is something that even the Mahdi or 'Isa ibn Maryam are not said to do.

However, the two instances of resurrection given here involve questionable circumstances. In the first, the Dajjal tries to convince some Muslims to follow him by killing one, and then immediately bringing him back to life. This only convinces them that he is a charlatan with evil intentions. The Dajjal then seeks to kill the man a second time. In reward for the man's allegiance, Allah protects him.

In the second event, the Dajjal is again manipulative. He tries to convince a Bedouin Arab to believe in him by offering to bring his parents back from the dead. But when he does so, the hadith explains that they are really two devils who merely simulate the appearance of the father and mother.

These Hadiths are teaching to always beware of the Dajjal. He is a false miracle worker. The resurrections that he performs are only illusions meant to entice people. The Dajjal does not and cannot give life to people, for "Allah alone can give life and cause to die."[217]

Comparison. The Dajjal of the Hadiths is a garbled echo of the Bible's 'Isa al-Maseeh, more widely known as Jesus Christ. We can know Jesus in a pure and uncorrupted way by reading the accounts of his life, death, and resurrection in the New Testament. They were written by multiple independent authors, who told of their own encounters with Jesus. They also related the eyewitness testimony of hundreds of people.

During this ministry to Israel two thousand years ago, Jesus raised three people from the dead:

- Jairus' daughter (Mark 5:22-23,35-43)
- the young man at Nain (Luke 7:12-17)

---

[217] 'Ibn Izzat p.31.

- Lazarus (John 11:38–45)

In all three events, Jesus acted from the most genuine of motives. There is no inkling of manipulation.

But like the Muslims who came six hundred years later, the Jewish Pharisees of Christ's day refused to believe that he was the messiah, the divine son of God. They also held to their doctrinal position of the absolute oneness of God. God cannot possibly be a trinity. This despite indisputable evidence of Christ's perfect goodness, divine power, and his intimate relationship with God the Father. Like the Hadiths in the case of the Dajjal, the Pharisees accused Christ of performing miracles and resurrections by the power of Satan:

> Matthew 12:24 But when the Pharisees heard this, they said, "This man casts out demons only by Beelzebul the ruler of the demons."

It is blindness and folly to say that Jesus hides evil intensions under the cover of good. His character comes out in all the gospel letters. He loves and cares for all different kinds of people: of low standing and high, Jews and gentiles, rulers, lepers, prostitutes, tax collectors, soldiers, mothers, fathers, and children. His teachings are wise beyond measure. His miracles and healings help people. His blessings are for a lifetime and beyond. Only the bitter could say that he does all this by the power of Satan.

Under such an accusation, Jesus did not become angry, but answered with words of wisdom:

> Matthew 12:25 And knowing their thoughts, Jesus said to them, "Every kingdom divided against itself is laid waste; and no city or house divided against itself will stand.
> 12:26 And if Satan is casting out Satan, he has become divided against himself; how then will his kingdom stand?
> 12:27 And if by Beelzebul I cast out the demons, by whom do your sons cast them out? Therefore, they will be your judges."

When his disciples were exposed to the consistent character and teaching of Jesus, his sinless life and his miracles, they came to believe that he was the son of God. They had seen him raise people from the dead back to their previous state. These were incredible feats which showed that the power of God worked through Jesus.

Those raised went on to live great lives of faith. They eventually died a second time, this time with the assurance that they will be raised again into the heavenly realm.

When the disciples saw the resurrected Jesus, after he died on the cross to pay for their sins, he met them in a glorified body. They instinctively recognized it was an eternal one. The heavenly Father was showing that his son Jesus shares all the attributes of his divinity. God raised his only begotten son as the first fruits from the dead, to pave the way for future resurrections of all who ever lived. Those who trust in Jesus will be raised in glory to eternal life, in fellowship with him. Those who do not will live in eternal torment, away from the presence of the Lord.

Angels announce seven coming plagues of divine wrath

11:14 The second woe has passed; behold, the third woe is coming quickly.

11:15 Then the seventh angel sounded; and there were loud voices in heaven, saying, "The kingdom of the world has become the kingdom of our Lord and of His Christ; and He will reign forever and ever."

11:16 And the twenty-four elders, who sit on their thrones before God, fell on their faces and worshiped God,

11:17 saying, "We give You thanks, Lord God, the Almighty, the One who is and who was, because You have taken Your great power and have begun to reign.

11:18 And the nations were enraged, and Your wrath came, and the time came for the dead to be judged, and the time to reward Your bond-servants the prophets and the saints and those who fear Your name, the small and the great, and to destroy those who destroy the earth."

11:19 And the temple of God which is in heaven was opened; and the ark of His covenant appeared in His temple, and there were flashes of lightning and sounds and peals of thunder, and an earthquake, and a great hailstorm.

14:14 Then I looked, and behold, a white cloud, and sitting on the cloud was one like a son of man, with a golden crown on His head and a sharp sickle in His hand.

14:15 And another angel came out of the temple, calling out with a loud voice to Him who sat on the cloud, "Put in Your sickle and reap, for the hour to reap has come, because the harvest of the earth is ripe."

14:16 Then He who sat on the cloud swung His sickle over the earth, and the earth was reaped.

14:17 And another angel came out of the temple which is in heaven, and he also had a sharp sickle.

14:18 Then another angel, the one who has power over fire, came out from the altar; and he called with a loud voice to him who had the sharp sickle, saying, "Put in your sharp sickle and gather the clusters from the vine of the earth, because her grapes are ripe."

15:1 Then I saw another sign in heaven, great and marvelous, seven angels who had seven plagues, which are the last, because in them the wrath of God is finished.

15:5 After this I looked, and the sanctuary of the tent of witness in heaven was opened,

> 15:6 and the seven angels who had the seven plagues came
> out of the temple, clothed in linen, clean and bright, and
> their chests wrapped with golden sashes.
> 15:7 And one of the four living creatures gave to the seven
> angels seven golden bowls full of the wrath of God who lives
> forever and ever,
> 15:8 And the temple was filled with smoke from the glory of
> God and from His power; and no one was able to enter the
> temple until the seven plagues of the seven angels were
> finished.

Hadiths. In section H34, the Islamic chronology of the end time reached its goal of worldwide submission to Allah, with the satisfying killing of the Dajjal. There is no longer a substantive opposition to the Mahdi's caliphate. The silver age, that began when ʿIsa ibn Maryam joined the Mahdi, proceeds unimpeded. As described in H24-H3, Muslims will live in a world where they are prosperous and uniformly submissive. They will have all the benefits of a master race.

Comparison. In Revelation, we have reached the third woe (11:14). It is introduced by an angel sounding the seventh and last trumpet (11:15).

You will recall that the first woe was at the fifth trumpet. The people of the tribulation were tormented with demons, but were left alive (9:3-6 K32). The second woe was at the sixth trumpet. A third of the world's population were killed by the beast's army of 200 million men (9:16,18 K33). These two woes were instigated by Satan.

The Hadiths had their own versions of the first two woes. In H32, many people desired their deaths in a misguided effort to evade judgment before Allah. In H33, the Mahdi and ʿIsa raised great armies to subdue Christians, Jews and Hindus.

The third woe has no analog in the Hadiths. This is because it is directly instigated by the true God of heaven. Satan is powerless to counteract the upcoming series of events.

Revelation. The third woe and seventh trumpet come in answer to the murders of the two witnesses (11:7 K34) and their miraculous resurrection (11:11 K35). With the trumpet are heard loud voices from heaven. They announce that the kingdom of the world has become the kingdom of our Lord God and of his Christ (11:15). The end of the tribulation is rapidly approaching.

Earlier in the great tribulation, a throng of souls in heaven who had been martyred to that point cried out to God for retribution (6:10 K26). His response was the judgments of the seven trumpets (K29-K33, K36).

Now after the death and resurrection of the two witnesses, the scene has again shifted to heaven. There the raptured church believers, led by the twenty-four chief elders (4:4 K14), have been watching the latest carnage on earth. The terrible events are compelling them to bring worship and prayer before God (11:16).

They are appealing on behalf of the new believers who are being targeted daily among the nations of the new world order. The elders' plea is for God to act directly. They ask that he strike down the killing bands. And that he quickly convene his judgment seat, to reward the martyrs with eternal life (11:18).

We shall see that God will grant their requests in stages. The last stage will be to give the martyrs glorified bodies of resurrection. That will happen following the second coming of Christ, in 20:4 K43. Before then, God will send the plagues of the seven bowls (K37-K39). But before all those things, God gives the raptured saints a view of the heavenly temple (11:19). They see the fabled ark of the covenant, lost after the destruction of the last temple in Jerusalem in 70 CE. It contains the ten commandments, written by the finger of God on two tablets of stone. They are a forewarning of God's coming wrath upon those on earth who are violating those commandments. The scene is not a peaceful one. It is accompanied by lightning and thunder, an earthquake, and great hail.

Seated on a cloud above the temple comes one identified as *the son of man*. He is crowned in gold (14:14). This can be none other than Jesus Christ. He has been in heaven since he briefly came to earth and raptured the church saints to heaven, to save them the ordeals of the tribulation. "Son of man" was his favorite way to refer to himself during his ministry on earth two thousand years ago. This title linked him with the people that he came to save. He used the title in other contexts: in reference to his future return at his second coming (which will come in

K38), and in his prophecy of the sheep and goats judgment (which will happen shortly thereafter in K42):

> Matthew 25:31 "But when the Son of Man comes in His glory, and all the angels with Him, then He will sit on His glorious throne.
> 25:32 And all the nations will be gathered before Him; and He will separate them from one another, just as the shepherd separates the sheep from the goats."

In his place upon the cloud, Christ is holding a sharp sickle. He now swings it across the earth (14:16). This starts the reaping of men. This is part of the harvest judgment that he prophesied to his disciples would happen at the end of the age:

> Matthew 13:36 Then He left the crowds and went into the house. And His disciples came to Him and said, "Explain to us the parable of the weeds of the field."
> 13:37 And He said, "The one who sows the good seed is the Son of Man,
> 13:38 and the field is the world; and as for the good seed, these are the sons of the kingdom; and the weeds are the sons of the evil one;
> 13:39 and the enemy who sowed them is the devil, and the harvest is the end of the age; and the reapers are angels.
> 13:43 Then the righteous will shine forth like the sun in the kingdom of their Father. The one who has ears, let him hear."

The good seed of Matthew 13:38 and the sheep of Matthew 25:32 are those who come to faith during the tribulation. They will shine in God's kingdom. At the end of the seven years God will commend them in the judgment of the righteous (20:4 K43), and will usher them into the millennial kingdom.

But the weeds of Matthew 13:38 and the goats of Matthew 25:32 will be cast into fire. They will be the unbelievers who survive the seven years of the tribulation, yet refuse Christ's offer of salvation all the way to its end. In the upcoming harvest judgment, they will be put to death for their sins (2:27 K42). After the thousand years of the millennium that follows, they will be resurrected in their souls, and cast into the lake of fire (20:15, 21:8 K46).

The harvest is not immediate, however. Another angel comes forward with his own sickle (14:17). He is asked to thrust it down to earth (14:18). He will do so in 14:19 K38.

Seven more angels now come forward with seven bowls. Each contains a plague to be released (15:1,5-8) upon the rebels of the tribulation. The bowls express the totality of God's wrath. Later, when Christ finally makes his reappearance upon the earth, the harvest will continue. The unbelievers of the armies of the beast shall suffer bloodshed on a historic scale (19:15 K38, 14:20 K40).

With the casting down of the sickles from heaven to earth, the upcoming bowl plagues of Revelation now play out.

K37 :

The first five plagues: God sends boils, blood on the sea and waters, heat, darkness

: H37

The last hour will not come before time contracts

16:1 Then I heard a loud voice from the temple, saying to the seven angels, "Go and pour out on the earth the seven bowls of the wrath of God."
16:2 So the first angel went and poured out his bowl on the earth; and a harmful and painful sore afflicted the people who had the mark of the beast and who worshiped his image.

The hour shall not be established until time is constricted, and the year is like a month, a month is like the week, and the week is like the day, and the day is like the hour, and the hour is like the flare of the fire.[218] *(sahih)*

16:3 The second angel poured out his bowl into the sea, and it became blood like that of a dead man; and every living thing in the sea died.
16:4 Then the third angel poured out his bowl into the rivers and the springs of waters; and they became blood.
16:5 And I heard the angel of the waters saying, "Righteous are You, the One who is and who was, O Holy One, because You judged these things;
16:6 for they poured out the blood of saints and prophets, and You have given them blood to drink. They deserve it."
16:7 And I heard the altar saying, "Yes, Lord God, the Almighty, true and righteous are Your judgments."
16:8 And the fourth angel poured out his bowl upon the sun, and it was given power to scorch people with fire.
16:9 And the people were scorched with fierce heat; and they blasphemed the name of God who has the power over these plagues, and they did not repent so as to give Him glory.
16:10 And the fifth angel poured out his bowl on the throne of the beast, and his kingdom became darkened; and they gnawed their tongues because of pain,

---

[218] Narrated by Anas bin Malik, *Jami` at-Tirmidhi 2332*, Vol. 4, Book 10, Hadith 2332, https://sunnah.com/tirmidhi:2332, accessed June 3, 2024; also referenced in Abu Amina Elias, *Hadith on Signs: Time passes quickly before the Hour*, August 31, 2021 https://www.abuaminaelias.com/dailyhadithonline/2021/08/31/time-passes-rapidly/, accessed September 11, 2023.

16:11 and they blasphemed the God of heaven because of their pain and their sores; and they did not repent of their deeds.

Hadiths. The hadith of this section speaks of a future time when events take place so rapidly that time itself seems to compress. According to al-Suyuti, a 15th century *muhaddith* (hadith master):

> It was said that this is in fact literal, and that the hours of day and night will grow shorter when the onset of the Hour is at hand. And it was said that it is metaphorical, and that what is meant is that days will pass quickly and the barakah (blessing) will be removed from all things, even from time…. And there are other opinions as well. And Allah knows best.[219]

A common Islamic interpretation is that this will occur during the time that precedes Allah's final judgment (H46).[220] But an alternate view is "that will happen in the time of the Mahdi or ʿIsa or both."[221]

Comparison. The hadith does not spell out the blessings that will be removed during these most hectic days. The interpretation that this will happen during the days of the Mahdi and ʿIsa should lead us to consider their counterparts in Revelation – the beast and the false prophet – and the events that will so quickly transpire near the end of their rule. We shall see that time will indeed seem to compress.

Revelation. The true God of heaven now directly intervenes in the world of the beast.

The angels pour out the first five bowls in rapid fire. Each one results in a plague upon the whole earth. They are therefore distinct from the trumpet judgments, which affected only a third of things (see K29, K30, K31, K33). They are also different from the seal judgments, which took time to succeed each other. The plague judgments proceed swiftly one after another. The followers of Christ are nowhere mentioned. It seems that they are supernaturally protected.

---

[219] https://islamqa.info/en/answers/34618/one-of-the-signs-of-the-hour-is-that-time-will-pass-more-quickly, accessed September 11, 2023.
[220] http://inthenameofallah.org/The%20Hour%20OR%20%20Judgement%20Day.html, accessed September 11, 2023.
[221] ʿIbn Izzat p.20.

The action is occurring towards the close of the great tribulation, possibly packed into a period of just weeks.

The first plague sends sores or boils (16:2) on the skin of everyone who took the mark of the beast and worshipped his image (13:15-17 K24). They are tormented with great pain, but John does not see them dying in his vision. Perhaps they are spared from death to await what comes next.

The second bowl is poured upon all the waters of the seas, and turns them into blood. This causes all the creatures of the oceans to die (16:3). The third bowl is poured upon the rivers and fresh water springs of the earth. They also become blood (16:4). A world of waters turned to blood certainly cannot sustain life for long.

The blood of the second and third bowls is an appropriate forewarning to those complicit in the deaths of the tribulation martyrs (16:5-7). God will soon put each of them on trial for the blood they have shed (see K42).

The fourth bowl is poured upon the sun. It flares up and sends a sudden wave of heat upon the earth. The unbelievers are scorched with fire (16:8), but again, death seems not to touch them. Though they know that the plagues are sent by God, they refuse to repent of their ways. Instead, they curse the Almighty (16:9).

These events, and many others in Revelation, should not be dismissed as being mere allegory. If they are, they and most of Revelation can be treated as fantasy. But they can be explained by God miraculously intervening in the normal workings of the cosmos. The God who created all things in six days, and the laws that govern them, can act upon the universe as he wishes.

The target of the fifth bowl is the nerve center of the tribulation. The angel pours it onto the throne of the beast. As a consequence, the godless world that the beast has carefully planned is plunged into darkness (16:10-11). His supporters are reduced to gnawing their tongues in pain and distress. Though they see the catastrophic demonstrations of judgment against them, they still do not repent of their evil. They curse God instead. They are confirmation that the heart of the godless is desperately wicked (Jeremiah 17:9).

They need God to change their hearts. It starts with a person confessing their sin before the Father. He can then cleanse them by the blood that his son Jesus shed on the cross:

> 1 John 1:9 If we confess our sins, He is faithful and righteous, so that He will forgive us our sins and cleanse us from all unrighteousness.

The bowl plagues of Revelation are reminiscent of the plagues that God inflicted on Pharaoh and his kingdom of Egypt. Those plagues opened the gateway to freedom across the Red Sea for the Israelites, his chosen people.

In the future time of John's vision, the boils, the blood, and the darkness will extend to more than one kingdom. They will afflict the whole world. The plagues of the bowls will ultimately gain freedom for all the believers of the tribulation.

K38 :

The second coming of Christ, and the sixth plague: the battle of Armageddon

: H38

One army conquers Jerusalem, the earth swallows another before it reaches Mecca

16:12 The sixth angel poured out his bowl on the great river, the Euphrates; and its water was dried up, so that the way would be prepared for the kings from the east.

16:13 And I saw coming out of the mouth of the dragon, and out of the mouth of the beast, and out of the mouth of the false prophet, three unclean spirits like frogs;

16:14 for they are spirits of demons, performing signs, which go out to the kings of the entire world, to gather them together for the war of the great day of God, the Almighty.

16:16 And they gathered them together to the place which in Hebrew is called Har-Magedon [Armageddon].

17:14 These will wage war against the Lamb, and the Lamb will overcome them because He is Lord of lords and King of kings; and those who are with Him are the called and chosen and faithful.

16:15 "Behold, I am coming like a thief. Blessed is the one who stays

[Armies carrying] black flags will come from Khorasan. No power will be able to stop them and they will finally reach Bait al-Maqdis [in Jerusalem] where they will erect their flags.[222] *(da'if)*

Surely black flags will appear from the Khorasan until the people (under the leadership of this flag) will tie their horses with the olive trees between Bait-e-Lahya and Harasta (names of places in Jerusalem).[223]

"An army will invade the Ka`ba and when the invaders reach Al-Baida', all the ground will sink and swallow the whole army." I said, "O Allah's Messenger! How will they sink into the ground while amongst them will be their markets (the people who worked in business and not invaders) and the people not belonging to them?" The Prophet replied, "all of those people will sink but they will be

---

[222] Sunan al-Tirmidhī 2269, as quoted in Mohammed Ali Ibn Zubair Ali, *Signs of Qiyamah*, New Delhi, Abdul Naeen, 2004, p.42, cited in Richardson p.27; also see narrated by Abu Hurairah, *Jami` at-Tirmidhi 2269*, Vol. 4, Book 7, Hadith 2269, https://sunnah.com/tirmidhi:2269, accessed June 3, 2024; also quoted in Abu Amina Elias, *Are hadith of the black flags of al-Mahdi authentic?* October 2, 2014, https://www.abuaminaelias.com/hadith-black-flags-al-mahdi/.

[223] Nuaim Ibn Hammad (9th century hadith compiler), *Kitab Al-Fitan* https://daiyah.fandom.com/wiki/Hadith_of_black_flags, accessed March 16, 2023.

awake and keeps his clothes, so that he will not walk about naked and people will not see his shame.”

resurrected and judged according to their intentions."[224]

19:11 And I saw heaven opened, and behold, a white horse, and He who sat on it is called Faithful and True, and in righteousness He judges and wages war.

1:7 Behold, He is coming with the clouds, and every eye will see Him, even those who pierced Him; and all the tribes of the earth will mourn over Him. So it is to be. Amen.

19:12 His eyes are a flame of fire, and on His head are many crowns; and He has a name written on Him which no one knows except Himself.

19:13 He is clothed with a robe dipped in blood, and His name is called The Word of God.

19:16 And on His robe and on His thigh He has a name written: “KING OF KINGS, AND Lord OF LORDS.”

19:14 And the armies which are in heaven, clothed in fine linen, white and clean, were following Him on white horses.

19:19 And I saw the beast and the kings of the earth and their armies, assembled to make war against Him who sat on the horse, and against His army.

19:15‡[K42] From His mouth comes a sharp sword, so that with it He may strike down the nations, *and He will rule them with a rod of iron;* and He treads the wine press of the fierce wrath of God, the Almighty.

19:17 Then I saw an angel standing in the sun, and he cried out with a loud voice, saying to all the birds that fly in midheaven, “Come, assemble for the great feast of God,

19:18 so that you may eat the flesh of kings and the flesh of commanders, the flesh of mighty men, the flesh of horses and of those who sit on them, and the flesh of all people, both free and slaves, and small and great.”

14:19 So the angel swung his sickle to the earth and gathered the clusters from the vine of the earth, and threw them into the great wine press of the wrath of God.

19:21 And the rest were killed with the sword which came from the mouth of Him who sat on the horse, and all the birds were filled with their flesh.

Revelation. The great hope of the New Testament is that the risen Christ will someday return to earth, as he promised many times to his

---

[224] Narrated by `Aisha, *Sahih al-Bukhari 2118*, Vol. 3, Book 34, Hadith 329, https://sunnah.com/bukhari:2118, accessed September 13, 2023.

disciples. This finally happens with the pouring out of the sixth bowl, and is directly connected with the infamous battle of Armageddon.

Jesus came to earth briefly before the tribulation, when he descended from the clouds in the rapture (K13). At that time the church saints who had died were resurrected, and joined those of the church who were still alive. Together they accompanied Jesus back to heaven. But at his second coming, his stay on earth will be permanent. Unlike after the rapture, there will be no doubt from anyone that he has come back to earth. His descent from the clouds this time cannot be misinterpreted.

The second coming of Jesus is the hallmark event of John's entire vision. We can say this because Revelation circles around to add details about it in five separate passages: in chapters 1, 14, 16, 17, and 19. I have sorted them into the most plausible chronological order in our present section.

At his return, Christ is immediately faced with the forces of Satan and the beast. Their army pivots to confront him. The stage is set for the battle of Armageddon.

What do we know about this great army that stands in his way? The epicenter where it is recruited is the Euphrates river. In John's vision, that army is called to action after the angel pours out the contents of the sixth bowl onto the Euphrates, and causes its waters to dry up (16:12).

Earlier, after the sixth trumpet, the Euphrates was also featured. At that time the four territorial spirits of the surrounding region kicked off the rapid formation of the unprecedented 200-million-man army (9:14,16 K33). In the wars that followed, a third of all the earth's inhabitants lost their lives (9:15 K33).

But that is not enough to satisfy Satan, that hater of humanity. Now, with the sixth bowl, unclean spirits come out of the mouth of Satan (in the vision seen as a dragon), the mouth of the beast and the mouth of the false prophet, who are agents of Satan. The three spirits resemble frogs (16:13). They perform wonders that motivate the army, or perhaps elite troops within it, to move westward towards Israel. It is not clear whether the army is part of the earlier 200 million men, or is a new army raised up for the final battle.

The commanders of the force are undoubtedly closely allied with the beast. They are called "kings from the east." Their eastward location would be with respect to the most important site of the great tribulation, Jerusalem. It would then be logical that these kings will be from the Euphrates region east of Jerusalem: from Syria, Turkey, Iraq and Iran, and perhaps more regions further east. They are joined by "kings of the entire world," who bring more detachments (16:14). The various kings would have autonomous rule over their areas of jurisdiction. But they all act within the beast's world government, and are subservient to him. This is a government structure like that of the original Roman empire.

This massive army of the kings of the earth (19:19) concentrates its final campaign on God's holy land of Israel. In John's vision, he is not given to see them attacking and ravaging Jerusalem. But in the Old Testament, Zechariah prophesied that will happen:

> Zechariah 14:1 Behold, a day is coming for the Lord when the spoils taken from you will be divided among you.
> 14:2 For I will gather all the nations against Jerusalem to battle, and the city will be taken, the houses plundered, the women raped, and half of the city exiled, but the rest of the people will not be eliminated from the city.

In Zechariah, the Lord God of heaven is the one said to gather all the nations against Jerusalem. Considering what occurs next, it is better understood that God in his sovereign power over all, has ordained that the beast will gather his international armies to ravish Jerusalem. God allows this so that afterward the armies will concentrate their elite units in the vicinity of the Jezreel valley, north of Jerusalem. This place is better known as Armageddon (16:16).

The cream of the beast's armies come to Armageddon for a final showdown. Surely the beast knows that he has provoked the Lord God of heaven by ransacking his holy city of Jerusalem. Nevertheless, the beast expects to prevail, by the quantity of his fighting men, and the quality of their fanatic devotion to their leader.

But their opponent will not be like any other army that has appeared before. It is an army from heaven. At its head is a Lamb, who amazingly is also the lord of lords and king of kings. He is Jesus the son of God

(17:14). He cries out: "behold, I am coming like a thief" (16:15). This is the second coming of Christ, long awaited, and much yearned for by many generations of believers.

Those who come to faith during the tribulation, and who become familiar with the word of God, will not be surprised. They will be aware of the prophecies of Christ's return seven years after the woman of Babylon and the beast establish their government over all the earth. But the minds of the beast and his followers are held captive by their own wishful thinking, and their determination to nullify the prophecies of the Bible. The appearance of the true Jesus does not fit their expectations. For them, he comes unexpectedly and unwanted, like a thief.

Christ comes riding on a white horse (19:11). The beast did the same seven years earlier (6:2 K16). But he was a false messiah. This new rider is not a pretender. He is sent by God the Father on high, to destroy those who attempt to be god in his place.

Jesus is not alone. He comes at the head of a great heavenly army, also riding white horses. They are wearing fine linen garments, in blazing white, showing they are without sin before the Almighty (19:14).

Does Jesus' army consist of angels? Or are they the believers whom Jesus recently raptured, now in their glorified bodies?

They will most likely be angels, from the evidence of two passages elsewhere in the Bible:

- Jude 14-15, which speaks of the second coming of Christ, uses the Greek word *hagias* for the saints that descend from heaven with him:

  > Jude 14 It was also about these people that Enoch, in the seventh generation from Adam, prophesied, saying, "Behold, the Lord has come with many thousands of His holy ones [*hagias*],
  > 15 to execute judgment upon all, and to convict all the ungodly of all their ungodly deeds which they have done in an ungodly way, and of all the harsh things which ungodly sinners have spoken against Him."

In the New Testament, hagias refers specifically to holy angels, in Mark 8:38, Luke 9:26, Acts 10:22, Revelation 14:10 (K42). It does not refer to human believers. Lol

- Revelation 20:4 (K43), which describes the people who are given entrance into the millennial kingdom that follows Christ's second coming, mentions only those who became believers during the tribulation. It does not include any who came down with Jesus from heaven. If they were in Jesus' army, they would have to experience sin once again during the millennial kingdom. That would be contrary to God's promise that once they came to heaven, they would never again see sin and death.

The most consistent biblical interpretation therefore is that the raptured saints stay in heaven during Christ's second coming and his millennial kingdom. They will come back to earth when it is reconstituted as the new earth, in 19:7-8 K48.

The two armies now face each other. This will be the crowning battle of all ages – the battle of earthly kings (19:19) against the heavenly king of kings (19:16). Christ the lord of lords has been sent by his Father on high to bring the wrath of God upon a world of godless nations.

Zechariah's prophecy supports what happens next:

> Zechariah 14:3 Then the Lord will go forth and fight against those nations, as when He fights on a day of battle.

The beast's massed armies finally face an opponent that they cannot defeat militarily. The battle is over before it is even fought.
A single sword of stunning power appears out of the mouth of Christ, the lead rider on the white horse (19:15). The armies of the beast are immediately rendered powerless by the shockwave of defeat that comes upon them. The result is their prompt and utter destruction (19:21).

This battle of Armageddon was introduced by an angel pouring out the sixth bowl. Let us recall that seven plagues, corresponding to the seven bowls, were announced by angels two sections ago in K36. Near the close of that section, in 14:17-18 K36, one of them called upon a special angel, who was outside the heavenly temple, to use the sickle that he held to execute God's judgment. At the close of the Armageddon battle, this judgment occurs. The angel who had been waiting now signals the scavenger birds of the air to come and feast on the flesh of the beast's army (19:17-18). The angel then swings his sickle down from heaven across the earth (14:19). The sickle gathers the flesh of the rebel horde for the winepress of the wrath of God. What was the greatest of armies is now a mass of dead carcasses (19:21).

Comparison with H34 ('Isa ibn Maryam seeks out and kills the Dajjal). To summarize, immediately after his second coming, Jesus Christ leads an army from heaven to defeat the beast's armies. In the days that follow, he will begin his rule as king for a thousand years on earth. After that he will continue his reign, this time forever, over a new heaven and a new earth.

The Hadiths see much different activities for 'Isa ibn Maryam, their version of Jesus Christ. We saw in the earlier section H34, that 'Isa ibn Maryam led an army that pursued the Dajjal's forces, composed of 70,000 Jews. Afterward, 'Isa personally killed the Dajjal.

In a future section (H44), we shall see that after forty or perhaps forty-five years, 'Isa ibn Maryam shall die a natural death.

But Jesus Christ or 'Isa al-Maseeh of the Bible lives forever. He also freely gives everlasting life to everyone that the Father has given to him:

> John 17:1 Jesus spoke these things; and raising His eyes to
> heaven, He said, "Father, the hour has come; glorify Your
> Son, so that the Son may glorify You,
> 17:2 just as You gave Him authority over all mankind, so that
> to all whom You have given Him, He may give eternal life.
> 17:3 And this is eternal life, that they may know You, the
> only true God, and Jesus Christ whom You have sent.
> 17:4 I glorified You on the earth by accomplishing the work
> which You have given Me to do."

This very real 'Isa al-Maseeh of the Bible is definitely not the same person as the imagined 'Isa ibn Maryam of the Hadiths. 'Isa ibn Maryam is said to spurn his background as a Jew and forsakes all Christians who have called upon his name for two thousand years. But the real Jesus Christ, who in his first coming came to seek and save the lost, will fulfill his promise to come back in his second coming. At the battle of Armageddon, he will bring an end to those determined rebels who regard him as the embodiment of evil, and as the obstacle to their schemes for world domination.

Comparison with H16 (Allah sends the Mahdi for a seven-year glorious age). Many analysts have noted that the kings of the east, who lead their armies to Revelation's battle of Armageddon (16:12,16), find a remarkable parallel with the Hadiths' prophecy of armies carrying black banners also coming from the east, more specifically the region of Khorasan. Two Hadiths from section H16 are given at the top of this section to highlight this parallel. The bearers of the banners ride with the Mahdi to Jerusalem to impose an Islamic world order.

The regions east of Jerusalem are the common aspect of this parallel. Revelation foresees the region of the Euphrates as the recruiting center for the armies raised up for the deciding battle against God and his son. This compares with Khorasan in the Hadiths, further east of the Euphrates, which includes parts of Afghanistan. This is not surprising, since in my day Afghanistan is a model for jihad that inspires the millions of Muslims in the Euphrates region to armed jihad as well.

The challenging aspect of this parallel is that if the antichrist (or beast) of Revelation will eventually be the Mahdi of Islam, his confederates from Khorasan made their appearance at the beginning of the Mahdi's silver age of seven years, not at its end.

But there is one hadith that is more precisely aligned in the seven-year timeline with the battle of Armageddon and the second coming of Christ. We shall discuss it next.

Hadiths. The final hadith in our current section prophesies an army that is miraculously wiped out on the way to the holiest site of Islam, the Kaaba in Mecca. When this invading army reaches Al-Baida', the desert area between Mecca and Medina, "all the ground will sink and swallow the whole army." The souls of these enemies of Islam are then set aside, for special punishment before Allah at his day of judgment.

Comparison with H38 (One army conquers Jerusalem, the earth swallows another before it reaches Mecca). This final hadith describes a supernatural end to a great army that opposes the Mahdi. It comes into focus as Islam's chronological counterpart to Revelation's battle of Armageddon. We see this by comparing it with the miraculous defeat of the beast's armies, after they have ravaged Jerusalem and reached the plains of Armageddon. Shortly after the second coming of Christ, they are destroyed by the sword proceeding from the mouth of Jesus. The army headed to Mecca in the Hadiths also meets its end in a miraculous manner.

Which prophecy will come true of a massive army meeting its end by the means of a divine power? The account of Revelation is decidedly more coherent in this regard than the fragmented account of the Hadiths. The strength of its prophecy is convincing that the final battle of Armageddon will happen near Jerusalem, not Mecca.

K39 :

The seventh plague: the physical destruction of Babylon

: H39

Allah causes the earth to swallow up the fornicators

16:17 Then the seventh angel poured out his bowl upon the air, and a loud voice came out of the temple from the throne, saying, "It is done."
16:18 And there were flashes of lightning and sounds and peals of thunder; and there was a great earthquake, such as there had not been since mankind came to be upon the earth, so great an earthquake was it, and so mighty.
16:19 The great city was split into three parts, and the cities of the nations fell. Babylon the great was remembered in the sight of God, to give her the cup of the wine of His fierce wrath.
16:20 And every island fled, and no mountains were found.
16:21 And huge hailstones, weighing about a talent each, came down from heaven upon people; and people blasphemed God because of the plague of the hail, because the hailstone plague was extremely severe.

If a woman removes her clothes in a house other than her husband's, she tears down the veil between herself and Allah. If she puts on perfume for anyone other than her husband, it is fire and disgrace for her. When fornication is made lawful and after this wine is drunk and musical instruments played, Allah will be jealous in His Heaven and will say to the earth, "Make them tremble!" If they repent and stop, then all will be well. Otherwise it will crash down with them.[225]

People among my nation will drink wine, calling it by another name, and musical instruments will be played for them and singing girls (will sing for them). Allah will cause the earth to swallow them up, and will turn them into monkeys and pigs.[226] *(hasan)*

Revelation. We have reached the last bowl. The seventh angel pours it into the air (16:17). Prior to it, the sixth bowl brought doom, but only to the armies of the beast. This seventh one affects everyone, across the

---

[225] A'isha (Muhammad's third wife), in al-Hakim, quoted in `Ibn Izzat p.64; also partially narrated by Abu Al-Malih Al-Hudhali, *Jami` at-Tirmidhi 2803*, Vol. 5, Book 41, Hadith 2803, https://sunnah.com/tirmidhi:2803, accessed June 3, 2024.
[226] Narrated by Abu Malik Ash'ari, *Sunan Ibn Majah 4020*, Vol. 5, Book 36, Hadith 4020, https://sunnah.com/ibnmajah:4020, accessed June 3, 2024; also referenced in `Ibn Izzat p.63-64.

world, with the greatest earthquake ever known (16:18). Not just one, but all the fault lines of the world shift simultaneously.

The only time this previously occurred was possibly at the inception of Noah's flood, described in detail in the first book of the Bible, in Genesis 7-8. In my day there are creation scientists who believe that God used coordinated earthquakes to unloose reservoirs of water from deep underground, which combined with atmospheric changes that released rain from a watery canopy that enveloped the earth in the antediluvian age. The result was 40 days of non-stop rain everywhere, and water covering every square kilometer of land.[227] The climate and continents that are familiar to everyone today are products of this event, lost to the mists of time, but known to us from the Bible.

The post-Armageddon earthquakes are equally devastating. Islands and mountain ranges disappear completely (16:20). Monstrous hail formed of congealed ice bits falls from the sky. John is told that each hailstone is one talent in weight (16:21), which is near 50 kilograms. That would make them half a meter in diameter.

These earthquakes destroy all the major cities of the world. But most who survive are not chastened. Instead, they utter curses and blaspheme God.

With these quakes, the city of Babylon comes back into the vision. It was the capital city of the woman of Babylon's world order during the first half of the seven-year tribulation, before her ally the beast treacherously overthrew her, and shifted the focus to Jerusalem. In K17, we saw that the Babylon of John's vision was likely the capital of Europe at the beginning of the tribulation. Candidates for this city would therefore be Rome, Istanbul (Constantinople), Brussels, or some other European city.

Three-and-a-half years ago, the beast and the ten kings allied with him overthrew the government in Babylon and set fire to the city (17:16 K21, 18:9 K22). It became the habitation of devils (18:2 K21). Though these were actions by Satan that increased the power of the beast, they were also permitted by God in punishment for the sins that the woman

---

[227] Bodie Hodge, https://answersingenesis.org/bible-timeline/biblical-overview-of-the-flood-timeline/, accessed October 23, 2023.

of Babylon promoted across the world: promiscuity, fornication, and adultery (14:8 K21). Now, at the close of the tribulation, God gives Babylon the final "cup of the wine of His fierce wrath." The earthquakes split what remains of the city into three disconnected parts (16:19). The once glorious capital of all the earth is physically destroyed. Those who did not flee earlier meet a terrifying end.

Why does the physical destruction of Babylon occur three-and-a-half years after it was set on fire in section K22, back at the time of the second seal? The event is placed here in the timeline because the chronology of Revelation is best explained by the seven seals, seven trumpets, and seven bowls being in consecutive order. The other events of the vision wrap around the seals, trumpets, and bowls. Since the seventh bowl signals the end of the beast's rule and the end of the tribulation, the earthquakes that dismember Babylon are delayed until this time. Whereas the overthrow and burning of the city were done by the beast, under the instigation of Satan, its total destruction is the direct action of God.

Hadiths. In section H20, before the Mahdi defeated the Romans to achieve world dominion for Islam, we saw Hadiths that described the decadence of the Roman society. Seductive women had power over the male sex, and easy wealth lured humanity into spiritual deadness.

In our present section we have two Hadiths that prophesy Allah himself taking direct action against these gross idolaters. He will command the ground to tremble and crash down against women who are no better than prostitutes, and against men who share in their wine and music. The earth will swallow them up, because of their persistent subhuman ways. They will be monkeys and pigs in Allah's sight, no better than Jews and Christians.

Besides Allah, the other new actor in these Hadiths compared with H20 is the earth itself. Allah "will say to the earth, make them tremble!" He "will cause the earth to swallow them up."

Let us recall that among Islam's Major Signs of the end are the three landslides, in the east, the west, and in Arabia, as given in the hadith of H00.

The 15th century Egyptian hadith scholar Ibn Hajar al-Asqalani commented that landslides are not rare, and for them to be cited as a Major Sign, their occurrence in the end time would have to be of much greater severity. They would affect far greater numbers of people than usual landslides do. But Muslim scholars have noted that there are no other Hadiths that clearly provide additional detail.[228]

The Hadiths in this section may indirectly be speaking of the Major Sign landslides worldwide. If so, Allah uses them to bring sudden death to the fornicators.

Comparison. After the beast overthrew Babylon and burned it with fire, God brings an absolute end to the city with the great earthquake. After the Mahdi defeated the Romans, whose loose morals repulsed him, Allah brings judgment on fornicators and revelers by landslides and the earth swallowing them up. In this way Revelation lines up with the Hadiths.

In the Hadiths, Allah is totally pleased with the Mahdi. In the next section we shall see in Revelation that the opposite is true – God reserves even greater punishment for the beast compared with what he metes out to Babylon. Though the city was a breeding ground for sin and rebellion against God, the beast is worse. He is the pretender who seeks to take the place of the son of God. His goal is to sideline God the Father to irrelevance. He is the tool of Satan. He is the antichrist.

---

[228] Jamaal Al-Din Zarabozo, *Three Landslides: The last major Sign of the Day of Judgment – 7*, https://www.arabnews.com/news/452712, May 24, 2013.

K40 :
The final defeat of the beast and his armies

: H40
ʿIsa ibn Maryam and the Muslims will kill the remaining Jews

19:20 And the beast was seized, and with him the false prophet who performed the signs in his presence, by which he deceived those who had received the mark of the beast and those who worshiped his image; these two were thrown alive into the lake of fire, which burns with brimstone. 14:20 And the wine press was trampled outside the city, and blood came out from the wine press, up to the horses' bridles, for a distance of 1,600 stadia.

The last hour would not come unless the Muslims will fight against the Jews and the Muslims would kill them until the Jews would hide themselves behind a stone or a tree and a stone or a tree would say: Muslim, or the servant of Allah, there is a Jew behind me; come and kill him; but the tree *Gharqad* would not say, for it is the tree of the Jews.[229]

Revelation. The beast has lost the battle of Armageddon. He has lost the greatest army that was ever mustered. He has also lost all the cities that swore allegiance to him, destroyed by the coordinated earthquakes.

Evidently the beast and his deputy the false prophet attempt one last escape to some place of safety. But they fail in that also. Instead, the army from heaven that came down with Christ takes them prisoner. It takes angelic power to subdue them, because they are more than flesh and blood. They are empowered by Satan. They are the last gasp of the evil spirit of empire that has been distracting people away from the true God ever since the tower of Babel (K02).

These military and religious leaders of the great tribulation now meet their final end. They are cast into the eternal lake of fire, burning with sulfur (19:20). They will be the first two inhabitants of that gruesome

---

229 Narrated by Abu Huraira, *Sahih Muslim 2922*, Book 41, Hadith 6985, https://sunnah.com/muslim:2922, accessed June 5, 2024; also quoted in Richardson p.42.

place – hell. This fulfills the destiny of destruction, planned for them by God before time even began (17:8 K02).

Satan will follow them, but not until a thousand years into the future, at the end of Christ's millennial kingdom on earth (20:10 K45). Satan will be joined by the souls of unbelievers who did not ask for forgiveness from God during their time on earth. Until the end, Satan will refuse to believe the destiny prophesied for him throughout the Bible. He will always believe that he can find a flaw in the plan, so that he can sideline God to an irrelevant corner of the universe.

With the demise of the beast and the false prophet, and their armies shattered, the ground is covered with dead bodies for the space of 1600 stadia (14:20) or 320 km in all directions from Armageddon. They are spread over the entire land of Israel and beyond. The image in John's vision is of a winepress of monstrous dimensions, pressing the blood of grapes until it becomes a torrent. The blood of the dead soldiers splatters as high as the bridles of the horses they rode. Such is the effect of the sharp sickle wielded by the angel of judgment at the close of the Armageddon battle (14:19 K38).

The seven seals, seven trumpets, and seven bowls are now completed. The final plague is one of blood. It is a fitting close for the seven-year age of godless terror parading as heaven on earth.

Hadiths. When ʿIsa ibn Maryam descended from heaven to join the Mahdi in enforcing Islam across the world, he began the final end-time campaign to slay the infidels. First and foremost among them were the Jews. We learned that from the Hadiths in section H24. Muslim hatred for Jews is unbending. It is based on the example set by Muhammad, and is ordered by Allah in the Qur'an.

Later, in a hadith from section H34, the Mahdi's great army defeated the army of 70,000 Jews, and ʿIsa ibn Maryam killed the Dajjal.

Now, in the current section, there is another hadith that does not speak of ʿIsa nor the Dajjal, but only that the last hour will not come until Muslims seek out Jews and exterminate them. This hadith implies that the targets will be Jews outside the 70,000-man army, and may occur sometime after the death of the Dajjal. It is the last showdown between the Jews and the Muslims. It is the culmination of Islam's dream, and fulfills Allah's great command to finally make Jews an extinct species.

This hadith speaks of a tree named *Gharqad*. This Arabic word is only found in this and similarly worded Hadiths.[230] The etymology of the word gives no solid indication of an actual variety of tree. It is apparently a tree of safety for Jews, that Muslims should take special care to counteract. Behind such a tree a Jew might hide and not be revealed.

Muhammad relayed this important information about the mysterious Gharqad tree to the future Muslims of the Mahdi's time. His purpose was to warn them that the hunting down of Jews would not be easy after the Dajjal's demise. They should not become complacent. The Jews would use the Gharqad as a last ditch means of sorcery to evade Allah's judgment upon them.

Some Muslims of my time believe there is a clandestine effort by the Israeli government to plant thousands of Gharqad trees, in preparation for the final retreat of the Jews in the face of the inevitable Islamic victory.

Comparison. In the Hadiths, the crowning event of the Mahdi's rule is the final extermination of the Jews, so hated by Allah above all other peoples.

Behind the scenes of this eradication of Jews is God's sworn enemy, Satan. For him, Islam is the most useful tool toward this end. If Muslims can make an end of the Jews once and for all, those who are God's chosen people, Satan believes he can "extend his existence to rule this world and postpone his eternal judgment by God."[231]

Revelation has a strong parallel to this. After the antichrist beast turned against the woman of Babylon to achieve world dictatorship (K21), "it was also given to him to make war with the saints and to overcome them, and authority was given to him over every tribe, people, language, and nation" (13:7 K23). We have already seen how the beast and the false prophet hunted down new followers of Jesus to solidify their rule.

---

[230] *Gharqad*, https://en.m.wikipedia.org/wiki/Gharqad, accessed November 4, 2023.
[231] Shoebat p. 170.

In the Hadiths, no more is heard of Jews and Christians after this last massacre. The Mahdi finishes his time of rule basking in the glory of uniform Islamic predominance. But in Revelation, the antichrist's overwhelming power is suddenly reversed by the return of the true Christ from heaven. He puts an end to the beast's evil rule, and relegates him and the false prophet to the eternal flames of the lake of fire. We shall see in sections to come that he will also save his people to eternal life.

Both the beast and the Mahdi are relentless in their quest to kill Jews and Christians. No doubt the beast, when faced with Jesus coming down from heaven to face him, gives further orders to continue the roundup of God's people. It will be reminiscent of when Hitler's armies were being rolled back to Berlin, yet he continued to divert precious resources to ramp up the killing of Jews in gas chambers. Likewise, in the midst of all the Mahdi's wars, he and 'Isa will give orders to prioritize the killing of Jews and Christians.

In both accounts, God's people will find refuge in a way that will confound their pursuers. In the Hadiths it will be by Gharqad trees. A comparison with the tribulation events of Revelation hints at the biblical parallel for this tree: the cross of Calvary, upon which Christ died. All who take refuge in that cross will follow Jesus into eternal life:

> 1 Peter 2:24 and He Himself brought our sins in His body up on the cross, so that we might die to sin and live for righteousness; by His wounds you were healed.

K41 :
An angel offers the message of the everlasting gospel one last time

> 14:6 And I saw another angel flying in midheaven with an
> eternal gospel to preach to those who live on the earth, and
> to every nation, tribe, language, and people;
> 14:7‡[K42] and he said with a loud voice, "Fear God and give
> Him glory, because the hour of His judgment has come;
> worship Him who made the heaven and the earth, and sea
> and springs of waters."

Hadiths. Muhammad did not quote the book of Revelation verbatim in any of the Hadiths. However, Muslims are inspired by some of its imagery, as they look forward to the Mahdi's complete victory over all foes of Islam. Along these lines, the modern writer ibn `Izzat writes:

> Ka'b al-Ahbar said: "I find the Mahdi recorded in the books of the prophets."

> [then commentary by ibn `Izzat] For instance the Book of Revelation says: "then I looked and saw a man standing on the mount Sion, and with him a hundred forty and four thousand, having his name and his father's name written in their foreheads."[232]

These words capture the spirit of the Hadiths that speak of Islam's future fulfillment. It envisions a man standing on Mount Zion, the site of the Old Testament temple of Jerusalem that had been turned to rubble by the Roman army in 70 CE. It is a special place for Islam as well, the place upon which the Muslim caliphate built the Dome of the Rock in 691. The man is pictured is the Mahdi, standing in triumph over the mount. With him are 144,000 warriors for Islam, having his name and the name of Allah written on their foreheads.

This is a vision of the future triumph that many Muslims aspire to. It is a fitting conclusion to the Mahdi's long string of victories, and is a capstone to the glory of his rule.

---

[232] `Ibn Izzat p.15.

Comparison. Ibn `Izzat claims to quote a passage from Revelation. But his is not a quotation or a translation. It is a scene he and other Muslims have built in their imaginations, based on the 144,000 men specially called in verse 7:4 (see K18).

In their view, the 144,000 are those chosen by the Mahdi and Allah to celebrate the complete and total obliteration of their enemies. They extol the demise of the Dajjal, the hunting down of Christians and Jews, and the dominance of Islam which will never again be disputed. The warriors wear the name of Allah. They do not dare question why Allah is not there in person to commend them. The distance between them and Allah is unbridgeable, and cannot possibly involve a personal relationship with him.

But this picture conveniently ignores the entire context of the passage in K18. Revelation carefully explains that the 144,000 were raised up at an early point of the tribulation, and not at its conclusion. They certainly did not wear the name of Allah on their foreheads. They are counted from the sons of Israel, and not from the ranks of Islamic warriors.

They were Jews.

The 144,000 were raised up by the God of the Bible. He gave them a seal of some highly unusual sort, which safeguarded them from tribulation disasters upon the earth, the seas, and the trees (7:3 K18). As explained in that section, this seal apparently guaranteed their lives through to the end of the tribulation, allowing them to be fearless advocates for Christ. They made him known to the multitudes of rebels and the confused who were following them.

In Revelation, a celebration is coming, which will be far greater than what ibn Izzat spoke of. It will celebrate the events of the previous section – the demise of the beast and the false prophet, who are the counterparts to the Mahdi and `Isa ibn Maryam.

But first, there is one last invitation to God's enemies, to be followed by punishment of those who refuse it.

Revelation. God in heaven is finished with the seven bowls. With them he has poured out his seven plagues.

The verses of chapter 14 that surround 14:6-7 of our current section, are in a particularly turbulent part of John's vision. They flash backward and forward through many disjointed parts of the future chronology.

The prior verse, 14:5, will occur in K43, when the 144,000 are ushered into the millennial kingdom. The following verse, 14:8, is the announcement that Babylon is fallen. That happened at the midpoint of the tribulation, in section K21. Verse 14:9-11 will come in the next section, K42. They tell us that the haters of God who have survived the seven years of tribulation will meet their punishment by death.

But in the verses of our current section, the apostle John sees a very hopeful thing that will happen. An angel flies across all the heavens to warn of the upcoming punishment (14:7). He also shouts out one last hope, the life-saving message of the everlasting gospel (14:6).

I have chosen to place these verses here in K41, before the impending judgment of the next section. Those who hear the message know that the elite army of the beast has met its demise. They have seen Jesus come down from heaven to earth in his second coming. They cannot dispute the power and majesty of Christ, whose name is above all names. This location within the timeline is fitting with the great forbearance and loving kindness of our Father God, even after the defeat of these same rebels in the battle of Armageddon.

This is the first and only time that the word *gospel* is found in Revelation.

Most people who lived through the tribulation have heard the gospel. The 144,000 Jews, who were sealed by God to be his special servants (7:3-4 K18), in all likelihood brought this message to the four corners of the earth. This despite the world government's endeavors to stop them.

If not from the 144,000, the gospel was heard from the testimony of the two witnesses (11:3-6 K19). Paradoxically, their message probably was relayed with the aid of the world government's propaganda arm. It would have gone out through that agency's efforts to discredit the witnesses, to anyone who still had a soft heart. The gospel gained even more notoriety by their murder and subsequent resurrection (11:7-10 K34, 11:11-13 K35).

This angel who circumnavigates the earth now brings the gospel message one last time to anyone who still has not heard, offering to turn them from death to life.

What is the gospel?

The Hebrew word for gospel is *besora*, meaning "good news." During Jesus' first coming to Israel, this is the word that the disciples frequently heard when he spoke to them in the Hebrew language. The similar word in Arabic is *beshara*, which is also a popular name for baby boys and girls. The Greek word is *euangelion*. That is the word found in the original language of the Bible, when the New Testament writers translated what Jesus said to the larger Greek-speaking audience of their time.

Before the time of Jesus, the typical application of the words besora, beshara, and euangelion was to convey good news of victory in battle.

But Jesus chose this word to convey much better news. He is victorious as God's son over sin and death.

By his victory, Jesus gives forgiveness of sin to anyone who requests it with a sincere heart. He gives freedom from shame and guilt. Jesus then becomes your representative before his Father in heaven. He can approach the Father as your substitute, because he is God's son, and he paid the price for your sin. He took the blame that you deserve when he died for you on the cross. By his holiness, he presents a new you before the Father.

You will be a renewed person. Jesus promises to put you on the way to heaven, and to live rightly before God in the here and now. He does this by sending the Holy Spirit to live in your heart.

By this free gift from Christ, you are allowed to claim the Father as your own Father. When you die, he will gladly receive you into his heavenly presence to live eternity with him. While we are still in this life on earth, those who receive this gift by faith become messengers of this good news to others.

Accepting the gospel involves not just faith, but repentance. The Jesus of the Bible asks you to humble yourself, and recognize that on your own, you cannot possibly meet God's standards of holiness. Your sins against God and against other people – sins that you do intentionally, out of habit, or following the ways of the world around you – can only be overcome by God's renewing work within you. He chooses to give you life, not because of anything you have done, or what he foresees you will do in future, but because of his love for you. Jesus explained this in his most memorable summary of the gospel:

> John 3:16 "For God so loved the world, that He gave His only Son, so that everyone who believes in Him will not perish, but have eternal life."

The gospel path to eternal life is spelled out in the following verses from the Bible's book of Romans, popularly known as the Roman road:

> Romans 3:23 For all have sinned and fall short of the glory of God,
> 6:23 For the wages of sin is death, but the gracious gift of God is eternal life in Christ Jesus our Lord.
> 5:8 But God demonstrates His own love toward us, in that while we were still sinners, Christ died for us.
> 10:9 If you confess with your mouth Jesus as Lord, and believe in your heart that God raised Him from the dead, you will be saved.

According to the gospel, if you accept this gift, your relationship with Jesus and obedience to him will bring you a joy that will increase. Christ will walk alongside you and be with you, no matter what trials you have in this life. This includes the horrific trials of the tribulation.

Here at the end of the seven years, God sends his angel to offer this forgiveness to those who least deserve it. Those who accept will be the few last ones that will be saved from hell. This is reminiscent of Jesus hanging on the cross, yet offering salvation to the thieves crucified next to him. One mocked him. But to the other whose heart was changing he said: "Today you will be with me in paradise" (Luke 23:43).

Looking on in derision will be Satan, the foremost opponent of God and his son. Now that the beast and false prophet are defeated and have been cast into the eternal lake of fire, Satan is the greatest loser in the gospel. The other eternal losers are the great majority of people who choose to follow the lies that Satan sewed in their hearts, instead of the God who can change hearts. We shall see that after the upcoming glorious kingdom of a thousand years, they will join the beast, the prophet, and Satan, in the lake of fire.

K42 :

K42 :
The live unbelievers do not survive the end of the great tribulation

: H42
The dead Christians and Jews will be remembered for their false religion

14:7‡[K41] *And he said with a loud voice, "Fear God and give Him glory, because the hour of His judgment has come; worship Him who made the heaven and the earth, and sea and springs of waters."*

And there is none of the People of the Book [Christians and Jews] but must believe in him before his death; and on the Day of Judgment he will be a witness against them. (Surah 4:159)

2:27 And he shall rule them with a rod of iron, as the vessels of the potter are shattered, as I also have received authority from My Father.

12:5‡[K05] *And she gave birth to a Son, a male,* who is going to rule all the nations with a rod of iron; *and her Child was caught up to God and to His throne.*

19:15‡[K38] *From His mouth comes a sharp sword, so that with it He may strike down the nations,* and He will rule them with a rod of iron; *and He treads the wine press of the fierce wrath of God, the Almighty.*

14:9 Then another angel, a third one, followed them, saying with a loud voice, "If anyone worships the beast and his image, and receives a mark on his forehead or on his hand,

14:10 he also will drink of the wine of the wrath of God, which is mixed in full strength in the cup of His anger; and he will be tormented with fire and brimstone in the presence of the holy angels and in the presence of the Lamb.

14:11 And the smoke of their torment ascends forever and ever; they have no rest day and night, those who worship the beast and his image, and whoever receives the mark of his name."

20:1 Then I saw an angel coming down from heaven, holding the key of the abyss and a great chain in his hand.

20:2 And he took hold of the dragon, the serpent of old, who is the devil and Satan, and bound him for a thousand years;

20:3‡[K45] and he threw him into the abyss and shut it and sealed it over him, so that he would not deceive the nations any longer, *until the thousand years were completed; after these things he must be released for a short time.*

Revelation. The last offer to turn back to God is come and gone. But many who received the mark of the beast (14:9) refused the offer. They would rather stay true to the beast and his ownership over them, even though they have seen him relegated to the lake of fire (19:20 K40).

These unchastened people, who caused the death of billions, must now die for their crimes. The God of heaven is their ultimate judge. He has standards that he will not set aside. His loving kindness does not extend to those who scorn the offer of salvation that Jesus made for them on the cross.

The first step in this direction is that an angel forces them to bow down in worship to God (14:7). They will drink the wine of his wrath from the cup of his anger. The wine is undiluted (14:10) – this time his anger is unrestrained by mercy and grace.

The second step is to meet the one who holds the rod of iron. He is Christ.

John sees the rod at three different points of his vision: in the prophecy to the church of Thyatira (2:27, see K09), in the vision of Christ's incarnation and ascension (12:5, see K05), and in the battle of Armageddon (19:15, see K38). All three repeat these words about the rod almost verbatim: he will rule all the nations with a rod of iron.

Many say that the rod symbolizes an absolute government during the thousand-year kingdom (see K44), which will compel people to observe the righteous standards of God.

The chronological method leads to a different analysis. I believe that Christ uses the rod, not to *rule* the citizens of his thousand-year kingdom, but to issue a *ruling* of punishment, before starting the kingdom. Like a judge in a courtroom, he pronounces sentence upon those who still follow the antichrist. There are multitudes of them left over from all the various nations.

Since these rebels reject repentance, the most extreme of punishments is mandated by God's holy standards. Otherwise, they would remain alive to challenge all the premises of the millennial kingdom at its very inception.

The sentence is immediately carried out. This act is signaled by these words: "he shall rule them with a rod of iron, as the vessels of the potter are shattered" (2:27). The co-conspirators of the tribulation now meet their death.

But we know from other portrayals of death in the Bible it will not be the end for them. Their souls will be taken to the holding place of Hades (Luke 16:23). There they will wait until the close of the millennium, when they will receive their eternal judgment. At that time they will be cast into the lake of fire, the fire of hell. We are told this in 14:10, which anticipates the lake of fire of verses 20:15 and 21:8 in K46.

The fire will be everlasting (14:11). When they are sent there, they will rejoin the false prophet, and the beast, whom they worshipped.

The physical death at the end of the tribulation, followed later by spiritual death in the eternal lake of fire, is the realization in two parts of Christ's parable of the weeds of the field:

> Matthew 13:38 and the field is the world; and as for the good seed, these are the sons of the kingdom; and the weeds are the sons of the evil one;
> 13:39 and the enemy who sowed them is the devil, and the harvest is the end of the age; and the reapers are angels.
> 13:40 So just as the weeds are gathered up and burned with fire, so shall it be at the end of the age.
> 13:41 The Son of Man will send forth His angels, and they will gather out of His kingdom all stumbling blocks, and those who commit lawlessness,
> 13:42 and they will throw them into the furnace of fire; in that place there will be weeping and gnashing of teeth.

It is also fulfilled in his prophecy of the sheep and the goats:

> Matthew 25:32 And all the nations will be gathered before Him; and He will separate them from one another, just as the shepherd separates the sheep from the goats;
> 25:33 and He will put the sheep on His right, but the goats on the left.
> 25:41 "Then He will also say to those on His left, 'Depart from Me, you accursed people, into the eternal fire which has been prepared for the devil and his angels;
> 25:42 for I was hungry, and you gave Me nothing to eat; I was thirsty, and you gave Me nothing to drink;
> 25:43 I was a stranger, and you did not invite Me in; naked, and you did not clothe Me; sick, and in prison, and you did not visit Me.'

> 25:44 Then they themselves also will answer, 'Lord, when
> did we see You hungry, or thirsty, or as a stranger, or naked,
> or sick, or in prison, and did not take care of You?'
> 25:45 Then He will answer them, 'Truly I say to you, to the
> extent that you did not do it for one of the least of these, you
> did not do it for Me, either.'
> 25:46 These will go away into eternal punishment, but the
> righteous into eternal life."

The physical death of the wicked corresponds to the gathering of the weeds, and to the separation of the goats from the sheep. Their eternal death matches up with the burning of the weeds, and to the goats being cast into the fire.

Such is the fate of those who will follow the beast into hell.

Later in John's vision, he sees another punishment that occurs at the end of the tribulation, in verses 20:1-3. The guilty one this time is Satan, who was allowed free reign during the seven years. He appears in these verses as the serpent, reminding us that he deceived Adam and Eve, and tempted them into their original sin which has plagued all humanity ever since. He also appears as the dragon, which links him to the beast, the false prophet, the woman of Babylon, and their confederates. Satan inspired them all to corrupt the souls of billions during the tribulation.

God sends an angel especially equipped to overcome Satan. This will probably be the great archangel Michael, whom God commissioned earlier to lead the other angels, when they expelled Satan and the devils permanently from heaven before the rapture (12:7 K15).

This time the angel has a great chain in his hand. With it he binds Satan with such force that there is no possible way to escape, even for the cunning one.

The angel is also equipped with the key to the abyss. We encountered this pit earlier, as the prison that held many demons, until God allowed Satan to release them during the great tribulation. For five months they tormented men and women who had not taken refuge in Christ. That took place in the judgment of the fifth trumpet (9:1 K32).

This time the pit is adding to its population instead of subtracting. The angel casts Satan into the pit and uses the key to lock it. He then seals the pit. The seal would make it immediately evident if any tampering occurs to try to release the prisoners inside.

Satan is the one mentioned as being bound and thrown into the pit. Presumably, all the other devils are sent there as well, because there will be no sign of their activity on earth during the thousand-year millennial kingdom in section K44. As punishment, Satan is imprisoned for those thousand years within the pit. He will not be allowed to deceive men and women during that time.

Note that God does not yet send Satan to his final doom in the lake of fire, where he will join the beast and the false prophet who are already there (19:20 K40). Instead, the imprisonment will give Satan one final chance to repent of his ways. During his incarceration, he will undoubtedly know of the glories of the millennium. He will lament how he failed to dethrone God.

We shall see in K45 that God will release Satan from the pit, and give him one last opportunity to redeem himself.

Qur'an. The remaining Jews have been hunted down by the Islamic forces. They have met their deaths (H40). In the eyes of Muslims, it was richly deserved.

But death will not offer them the relief of non-existence.

The surah from the Qur'an at the top of our section refers to these "People of the Book." This label evidently groups the Jews and Christians together. It says that each of them will believe in ʿIsa ibn Maryam "before his death." Muslim scholars have debated whether this is speaking of the death of ʿIsa, which will happen in H44, or the deaths of the Jews and Christians. The text lends itself to both meanings. If we accept the second one, the verse would be understood to mean this: none of the People of the Scripture will die without first believing in ʿIsa.[233] Somehow at their impending deaths, they will realize that the

---

[233] *Surah an-Nisa Ayat 159 (4:159 Quran) with Tafsir,* https://myislam.org/surah-an-nisa/ayat-159/, accessed December 8, 2023.

text of their Bible has been corrupted to the core. They have been worshipping a God of their imaginations, and his false son Jesus Christ.

The Jews who denied 'Isa ibn Maryam, claiming to have killed and crucified him, will be faced with the fact that 'Isa did not die. Instead, he is a messenger who has always been devoted to Allah. His message is the truth.

But this realization before their deaths will not bring them acceptance by Allah. The surah further explains that when their souls come before Allah for final judgment, 'Isa will be their chief accuser.[234] There will be no divine power from their holy writings to rescue them. They will have no way to avoid being resurrected to hell.

One of the earliest authorities on the Jews and Christians in the end times was Ahmad ibn Hanbal, the ninth century Muslim jurist, theologian, and ascetic. He compiled a most important Sunni hadith collection, the *Musnad*.[235] Ibn Hanbal also wrote *Kitab Az Zuhd*, the Book of Abstinence. Though it is not a collection of Hadiths, it contains traditions going back to Muhammad and his Companions.[236] In the Zuhd, Ahmad ibn Hanbal writes this:

> **They are those who flee with their religion. They will be gathered with 'Isa the son of Maryam on the Day of Resurrection.[237]**

The best understanding of this is that the Jews and Christians will find no safety in their religions. They will be condemned by 'Isa before Allah at the day of judgment.

---

[234] *Surah an-Nisa' (Women) 4:159*,
https://www.quran-wiki.com/ayat-4-159-anNisa, accessed December 8, 2023.
[235] https://en.m.wikipedia.org/wiki/Ahmad_ibn_Hanba, accessed December 8, 2023.
[236] Seifeddine-M, *Kitab az-Zuhd Of Imam Ahmad (rahimahullah)*, January 16, 2012,
https://www.muftisays.com/forums/12-virtues/6487-kitab-azzuhd-of-imam-ahmad-rahimahullah.html.
[237] Ahmad b. Hanbal (9th century Sunni jurist and theologian), *Kitab Az Zuhd (Book of Abstinence)*, ISBN: 9773720233, p.236, accessed December 4, 2023,
https://kitaabun.com/shopping3/zuhd-imam-ahmad-hanbal-arabic-only-p-2338.html, quoted in Rahma p.17.

Comparison. I have made the case that Christ wields his rod of iron to prevent the unrepentant from entering into his glorious millennial kingdom. This will be accomplished by the sentence of death. This is the surest interpretation that takes into account the entire timeline of Revelation.

The Hadiths also speak of the deaths of all oppositionists, this time those who oppose the Mahdi and 'Isa ibn Maryam, especially Jews and Christians. But those deaths are not carried out in the manner of a legal tribunal before a divine personage. Instead, the armies of the Mahdi hunted down the remaining People of the Book one-by-one, and murdered them, whether they were previously uniformed soldiers in the Dajjal's army, or civilian women, children, and elderly. This occurred in section H40.

In both the biblical and Islamic end-time narratives, there is a lengthy time separation between the physical deaths of these individuals, and their spiritual deaths at the day of resurrection before God or Allah. In both, the destiny of these enemies will be hell.

But only in the Bible is Satan identified as the main inspiration behind the human rebellion against the Almighty. He is singled out for a punishment peculiar to him: to be bound with a chain, and cast into the abyss. In comparison, though the Qur'an has Allah cursing Iblis, chief of the shaytans, shortly after the creation of Adam (Surah 38:74-85), Iblis is mentioned in connection with the Dajjal only tangentially (see H21). Long after the Dajjal's demise at the hands of 'Isa Ibn Maryam, Iblis then reappears when the Yajuj and Majuj (Gog and Magog) people descend upon the world (H45). Allah waits until then to punish Iblis, at the day of judgment. I will revisit this topic when we consider the final resting place of Satan in sections K45 and H46.

K43 :
The still-living believers and resurrected tribulation martyrs ushered into the millennial kingdom after judgment of the righteous

: H43
How happy are those who join the Mahdi, but woe to those who oppose him

14:1 Then I looked, and behold, the Lamb was standing on Mount Zion, and with Him 144,000 who had His name and the name of His Father written on their foreheads. 14:2 And I heard a voice from heaven, like the sound of many waters and like the sound of loud thunder, and the voice which I heard was like the sound of harpists playing on their harps.

The Mahdi will emerge when there is hopelessness and despair about there being any escape. How happy is the one who joins him and is one of his helpers! Woe to the one who opposes him and resist him![238]

14:3 And they sang a new song before the throne and before the four living creatures and the elders; and no one was able to learn the song except the 144,000 who had been purchased from the earth.

14:5 And no lie was found in their mouths; they are blameless.

15:2 And I saw something like a sea of glass mixed with fire, and those who were victorious over the beast and his image and the number of his name, standing on the sea of glass, holding harps of God.

15:3 And they sang the song of Moses, the bond-servant of God, and the song of the Lamb, saying, "Great and marvelous are Your works, Lord God, the Almighty; Righteous and true are Your ways, King of the nations!

15:4 "Who will not fear You, Lord, and glorify Your name? For You alone are holy; For all the nations will come and worship before You, For Your righteous acts have been revealed."

20:4‡[K24] Then I saw thrones, and they sat on them, and judgment was given to them. And I saw the souls of those who had been

---

[238] Abu Ja`far Muhammad ibn Ali (10th century Persian Shi'te Islamic scholar), quoted in `Ibn Izzat p.25; also quoted in Mari' bin Yusuf Karami Hanbali (17th century Islamic jurisprudence scholar, Cairo), *Fawaid Fawaid al-Fikr fil Mahdi al-Montazar*, cited in Harun Yahya, https://www.harunyahya.info/en/books/the-prophet-jesus-as-and-hazrat-mahdi-will-come-this-century/chapter/part-2-characteristics-of-hazrat-mahdi-as-in-the-hadiths-5-20-signs-of-the-appearance-of-hazrat-mahd, 2010, accessed June 5, 2024.

beheaded because of their testimony of Jesus and because of the word of God, and those who had not worshiped the beast or his image, and had not received the mark on their foreheads and on their hands; and they came to life and reigned with Christ for a thousand years.
20:5‡ *The rest of the dead did not come to life until the thousand years were completed.* [K46] This is the first resurrection.

Hadiths. After centuries of inferiority and despair, Islam has achieved the worldwide dominance promised by Muhammad. The Mahdi has brought the long-awaited silver age. Islamic scholars, who had the early compilations of Hadiths, imagined how happy the future Muslims would be who followed the Mahdi with all their hearts.

Though the quote at the top of this section is not a hadith, these words of the 10th century Persian Shi'ite Islamic scholar Abu Ja`far Muhammad ibn Ali summarize the expectations of all Muslims, based on the Hadiths that peer into the end times. The followers of the Mahdi will look with pleasure upon the suffering they have inflicted on the Christians and Jews. These menaces to Allah's supremacy will never again tempt anyone with their heresies.

Revelation. The people who entered into the period of the tribulation had only vague memories of the Christians who had been taken away to heaven in the rapture (K13). But even without them, and despite the overwhelming surveillance and indoctrination exercised by the government of the beast, by now many people have come to their senses. Perhaps the horrors of tribulation have driven them to self-examination. They realized they were complicit in rebellion against the holy God. Therefore, they repented of their sins against him, and against others. They have accepted the grace of God, and put their trust in Jesus his son.

By taking this route, they became enemies of the new world order. We saw that many were hunted down and killed, with the name of Jesus on their lips, or with Jesus in their hearts. Many were beheaded (20:4, see also K24-C4). But God knows each of the martyrs by name. He claims them as his own. He separates the dead believers from the other dead victims of the tribulation, as in Jesus' parable of the sheep and the goats:

> Matthew 25:32 And all the nations will be gathered before
> Him; and He will separate them from one another, just as
> the shepherd separates the sheep from the goats;
> 25:33 and He will put the sheep on His right, but the goats
> on the left.

As God's sheep, their souls have already been received before God in heaven. There they cried out for justice on behalf of other believers still on earth (6:10 K26). The raptured church saints added their own pleas, petitioning God to resurrect these martyred souls, and to welcome them into his kingdom (11:16,18 K36). The martyrs are the elect that Jesus promised would be gathered from the four winds of heaven:

> Matthew 24:31 And He will send forth His angels with a
> great trumpet blast, and they will gather together His elect
> from the four winds, from one end of the sky to the other.

God now answers these prayers.

He brings on "the first resurrection" of Revelation (20:5) – granting them perfect, deathless, glorified bodies. They live again (20:4), with all the fullness of life.

The church saints who were similarly resurrected at the rapture (1 Thessalonians 4:15-17 K13) will see this, and will rejoice.

Now that the tribulation martyrs are resurrected, they must come one-by-one before the judgment throne of God. This requirement applies to every single person who ever lived:

> Romans 14:10b For we will all appear before the judgment
> seat of God.
> 14:11 For it is written: "As I live, says the Lord, to Me every
> knee will bow, And every tongue will give praise to God."
> 14:12 So then each one of us will give an account of himself
> to God.

There has already been the judgment of the church believers immediately after the rapture (K13). After the millennium, there will be more believers who will be resurrected and judged (20:11-12 K46). But this moment at the end of the seven years is when the tribulation martyrs will come before God.

The throne of the Almighty is the most fearful place to come before. Those who do so alone cannot avoid the awful wrath that is due their sins. They are reminded of this by the sea of glass that surrounds the judgment throne, mingled with fire (15:2). The glass is symbolic of God's glory, the fire of his standard of absolute perfection.

But for believers, Jesus the Lamb of God will be there (14:1). He advocates for each of them personally before the Father.

Though each one's account of his or her life is very different, what is common to all is that they have trusted Jesus, God's only begotten son, to stand for them. They recognize that they deserve only condemnation for their pattern of sinful actions. But they have turned their lives over to Jesus Christ. They are willing to be crucified as he was:

> Galatians 2:20 I have been crucified with Christ; and it is no longer I who live, but Christ lives in me; and the life which I now live in the flesh I live by faith in the Son of God, who loved me and gave Himself up for me.

Such will be the judgment of the sheep who died during the tribulation.

They will now be rewarded with thrones of their own. With them they will reign with Christ as his helpers for the millennial kingdom (20:4). In order to co-rule with the deathless one, they too will have glorified bodies, completely sinless and spotless in nature.

But their persecutors, who just prior to this event were punished with death (2:27, 12:5, 19:15, all in K42), will have to wait the thousand years before they receive resurrected bodies (20:5 K46). Their eternal destiny will be very different. They will be the goats that Jesus spoke of. Their appearance one-by-one before the Almighty will happen at the great white throne judgment (20:11-12 K46). Jesus will not be standing with them. God's verdict of their lives will result in the worst eternity.

The different destinies for people who died during the tribulation is summarized in the following words, spoken by Jesus to his disciples during his first coming:

> Matthew 25:34 "Then the King will say to those on His right, 'Come, you who are blessed of My Father, inherit the kingdom prepared for you from the foundation of the world.'

> 25:41 "Then He will also say to those on His left, 'Depart
> from Me, you accursed people, into the eternal fire which
> has been prepared for the devil and his angels;
> 25:46 These will go away into eternal punishment, but the
> righteous into eternal life.'"

The tribulation martyrs will not be the only ones to enter the millennial kingdom. Its citizens will also include all the new believers still alive at the end of the tribulation.

The most fruitful group among these survivors are the 144,000 Jews for Jesus who were sealed with God's name on their foreheads (14:1). He specially preserved them from death (7:3-4 K18). They had dedicated themselves to be pure in his sight (14:5). Now they celebrate their God and protector with a song of redemption (14:3). They stand with the Lamb on Mount Sion, overlooking Jerusalem with great anticipation of his kingdom (14:1). Since they are still alive, they will enter into the kingdom in their natural bodies.

A much larger group will be the rest of the new believers, some of them Jews but probably mostly gentiles. They are the ones who rejected the mark of the beast (15:2), and refused to worship him (20:4 K24). They heard the gospel message of salvation, perhaps from one of the 144,000, or the words of the two witnesses (11:3-6 K19), or from friends or family. When they did, they turned to Christ. Some of them did so at the last minute, when the angel flew over the whole earth proclaiming the everlasting gospel (14:6 K41). These Jews and gentiles will be the nations that will worship God in Jerusalem during the millennium, as prophesied by Isaiah:

> Isaiah 2:2 'Now it will come about that In the last days The
> mountain of the house of the Lord Will be established as the
> chief of the mountains, And will be raised above the hills;
> And all the nations will stream to it.
> 2:3 And many peoples will come and say, "Come, let's go up
> to the mountain of the Lord, To the house of the God of
> Jacob; So that He may teach us about His ways, And that we
> may walk in His paths." For the law will go out from Zion
> And the word of the Lord from Jerusalem.

Here at the outset of the millennium, all these various peoples join in a song celebrating their redemption. They are overjoyed that God in his mercy set them free from their sin and the awful world of the beast. Theirs is reminiscent of the song of Moses, which the Jews sang after God parted the Red Sea and delivered them from Pharaoh's army into the promised land (15:3).

Several prophecies in the Hebrew scriptures indicate that the millennial kingdom will also welcome those who lived during the Old Testament period, who trusted their eternal salvation to the future Messiah promised by God. Most of them are Jewish. The key prophecies that predict this are from Ezekiel and Isaiah:

> Ezekiel 37:9 Then He said to me, "Prophesy to the breath, prophesy, son of man, and say to the breath, 'The Lord God says this: "Come from the four winds, breath, and breathe on these slain, so that they come to life." ' "
> 37:10 So I prophesied as He commanded me, and the breath entered them, and they came to life and stood on their feet, an exceedingly great army.
> 37:11 Then He said to me, "Son of man, these bones are the entire house of Israel; behold, they say, 'Our bones are dried up and our hope has perished. We are completely cut off.'
> 37:12 Therefore prophesy and say to them, 'This is what the Lord God says: "Behold, I am going to open your graves and cause you to come up out of your graves, My people; and I will bring you into the land of Israel.
> 37:13 Then you will know that I am the Lord, when I have opened your graves and caused you to come up out of your graves, My people.
> 37:14 'And I will put My Spirit within you and you will come to life, and I will place you on your own land. Then you will know that I, the Lord, have spoken and done it," declares the Lord.' " '

> Isaiah 11:11 'Then it will happen on that day that the Lord Will again recover with His hand the second time The remnant of His people who will remain, From Assyria, Egypt, Pathros, Cush, Elam, Shinar, Hamath, And from the islands of the sea.
> 11:12 And He will lift up a flag for the nations And assemble the banished ones of Israel, And will gather the dispersed of Judah From the four corners of the earth.
> 11:16 And there will be a highway from Assyria For the remnant of His people who will be left, Just as there was for Israel On the day that they came up out of the land of Egypt.

Ezekiel 37:11, Ezekiel 37:12, and Isaiah 11:12 all specifically name "Israel" as the group that will be gathered to God at some far distant end-time event. Ezekiel 37:10-14 adds the additional detail that, at that time, these people will be raised from the dead.

The most consistent literal interpretation sees these passages as describing the resurrection of Old Testament messianic believers, just before the beginning of the millennial kingdom. They would then come before the throne of God in favorable judgment. Then they will enter the kingdom with glorified bodies and sinless natures. They will assist Christ in his reign alongside the tribulation martyrs, who will also be present in perfect bodies.

Unfortunately, many Jews who lived before Christ's first coming, counted on their circumcision or their good works to be their automatic ticket to eternal life in heaven. In doing so, they disrespect the coming *Yeshua HaMashiakh*. The apostle Paul recognized that these men and women were actually seeking the approval of others like themselves, instead of seeking God's heart:

> Romans 2:28 For he is not a Jew who is one outwardly, nor
> is circumcision that which is outward in the flesh.
> 2:29 But he is a Jew who is one inwardly; and circumcision
> is of the heart, by the Spirit, not by the letter; and his praise
> is not from people, but from God.

God will wait until the end of the millennium to deal with these prideful Old Testament Israelites, at the great white throne judgment (K46). Both Ezekiel and Daniel prophesied that such Jews would be separated from the true believers:

> Ezekiel 20:34 "I will bring you out from the peoples and
> gather you from the lands where you are scattered, with a
> mighty hand and with an outstretched arm and with wrath
> poured out;
> 20:35 and I will bring you into the wilderness of the peoples,
> and there I will enter into judgment with you face to face.
> 20:36 Just as I entered into judgment with your fathers in
> the wilderness of the land of Egypt, so I will enter into
> judgment with you," declares the Lord God.
> 20:37 "I will make you pass under the rod, and I will bring
> you into the bond of the covenant;
> 20:38 and I will purge from you the rebels and those who
> revolt against Me; I will bring them out of the land where

> they reside, but they will not enter the land of Israel. So you will know that I am the Lord."

> Daniel 12:2 And many of those who sleep in the dust of the ground will awake, these to everlasting life, but the others to disgrace and everlasting contempt.

All those who will experience the joys of the millennium are now present. They will share the kingdom with their king, the Lord Jesus Christ, the son of God.

Comparison. In the previous section, we saw the punishment of those who rejected the end-time messiah of the world, Jesus Christ in Revelation, or the Mahdi in the Hadiths. In the present section, we see the reward that is bestowed upon that messiah's supporters.

The reward that Muslims expect is exceeding happiness for a time. They will take pleasure in the Mahdi's final victories. They will rest as they contemplate the misery that their historic adversaries, the Jews and Christians, now experience.

On the other hand, the reward described in Revelation is far greater than a personal feeling of achievement. It is pronounced upon each of the tribulation followers of Jesus, from the mouth of God himself, as they appear one-by-one before his throne for judgment. The 144,000 Jewish believers, whom he sealed shortly after the tribulation began (7:4 K18), receive special commendation. But all the other millions who turned to follow Christ, also receive acclamation for their faith. God praises them, personally and directly. The frightful dread of judgment is thus transformed into a beautiful event, which cements their standing as children of the living God, and brothers and sisters of his son, Jesus Christ.

In the Hadiths and the Qur'an, Allah makes no such appearance to his warriors. They cannot hope for absolute assurance of their continued standing before him. Instead, even after the Mahdi's dominion is fully established, they must continue to strive in their life of jihad until their last breath. They will always stand in a position of dread of the distant one, who by his nature is wholly other and aloof.

In our current section, the further reward of the tribulation martyrs is to be resurrected from the dead, and to be granted their own thrones.

From them they will assist Christ in administering the upcoming millennial kingdom.

The further reward of the Muslim followers of the Mahdi is to experience the final years of his caliphate, before he dies. That will occur in the next section.

K44 :
The millennial kingdom

: H44
The earth is blessed by the Mahdi's rule, then he dies

20:6‡[K46] Blessed and holy is the one who has a part in the first resurrection; over these the second death has no power, but they will be priests of God and of Christ, and will reign with Him for a thousand years.

The inhabitants of the heavens and the inhabitants of the earth will be pleased with him [the Mahdi] and such plants will be produced by the earth that the living will wish the dead come back to life (when they see the security, happiness, and the blessing of the earth and the might of Islam.) That will last for about seven or eight years.[239]

Glad tidings to you of the Mahdi.... He will fill the earth with justice as it was filled with oppression. The dwellers of the heavens and the earth will be pleased with him. He will distribute wealth with fairness and will fill the hearts of the Muslim nation with joy; his justice will be sufficient for them so much so that an announcer will state: 'If anyone is in need, come to me (the Mahdi)'.... The Mahdi will remain in this condition for six, seven, eight, or nine years and after that, there will be no good in life.[240]

Allah would reveal to 'Isa these words: I have brought forth from amongst My servants such people against whom none would be able to fight [Yajuj and Majuj]; you take these people safely to [the mountain] Tur. And then Allah would send Yajuj and Majuj and they would swarm down from every slope.[241]

---

[239] Narrated by Abu Sa`id al Khudri, in at-Tabarani and Abu Nu`aym, quoted in `Ibn Izzat p.26; also partially narrated by Abu-Saeed al-Khudri in Musnad Ahmad, quoted in *Major Signs before the Day of Judgement*, http://www.inter-islam.org/faith/Majorsigns.html, accessed June 8, 2024.

[240] *Musnad Ahmad 10333*, quoted in Rahma p13; also partially narrated by Al-Hakim, quoted in Ustaz Abdassamad Clarke, https://primaquran.com/2022/10/04/hadith-on-imam-mahdi-in-the-light-of-ibn-khaldun/, accessed June 8, 2024.

[241] Narrated by An-Nawwas b. Sam`an, *Sahih Muslim 2937 a*, Book 41, Hadith 7015, https://sunnah.com/muslim:2937a, accessed June 8, 2024; also quoted in Abu Rahma, *Who and where are the Yajuj and Majuj (Gog and Magog)? Has their barrier been broken?*, March 4, 2016, https://qurananswers.me/2016/03/04/who-and-where-are-the-gog-and-magog/#_ftn8, accessed January 16, 2024.

> **The Prophet said: There is no prophet between me and him, that is,
> 'Isa..... He will destroy the antichrist and will live on the earth for forty
> years and then he will die. The Muslims will pray over him.**[242] *(sahih)*

> **'Isa ibn Maryam will descend to the earth, get married and have
> children. He will live for 45 years and will then pass away. He will be
> buried with me in my grave. 'Isa and I will stand up from one grave on
> the Day of Qiyamah between Abu Bakr and 'Umar.**[243] *(da'if)*

Hadiths. Islam became the worldwide system of government in section
H21. That happened after the Mahdi's victory over the Romans in
Islam's version of the final Armageddon battle, the *al-Malhamah al-
Kubra*. The Dajjal then rose to become a pernicious irritant, and led
many astray into his false religion. But in H34, the Mahdi's deputy, 'Isa
ibn Maryam, led the jihadist forces to corner the Dajjal. They killed him
at the Ludd gate not far from Jerusalem. This was followed by the final
operation to eradicate the remaining Jews and Christians, and any
other remaining organized opposition (H40).

Even during the time when the Mahdi was consolidating his rule, the
Hadiths speak of the material abundance, equity, and justice that he
brought to the Muslims who were loyal to him. We saw descriptions of
this fantastic prosperity in section H23, after the Mahdi established his
supremacy, and section H24, when his lieutenant 'Isa started
administering the idyllic Islamic world.

We now come to the last years of the end-time caliphate.

The Hadiths that speak to this time are few in number. But they are
effusive in their praise of the Mahdi's glorious rule, in the few years left
of his life. The earth will produce abundantly, above and beyond the
needs of all who remain. There will be security and happiness as never
before. The might of Islam will be on ever present display. The
oppression that other nations exercised over Muslims will become a
memory of the past. Wealth will be distributed in fairness according to
Islamic governance, and Islamic justice will bring contentment to all

---

[242] Narrated by Abu Hurayrah, *Sunan Abi Dawud 4324*, Book 38, Hadith 4310,
https://sunnah.com/abudawud:4324, accessed June 8, 2024; also referenced in
Richardson p.58.
[243] Moulana Suhail Motala, *A narration regarding 'Isa*,
https://islamqa.org/hanafi/hadithanswers/120112/a-narration-regarding-isa-alayhis-
salam/, accessed October 19, 2023.

true believers. Security and happiness will characterize the remaining years of the Mahdi's rule.

It is sad to think that the Mahdi will only be human. The Hadiths tell us that he will die at the end of the seven years, perhaps after eight or nine.

After the Mahdi's death, 'Isa ibn Maryam will take on his duties. Unfortunately, the Hadiths are silent on the disposition of the Muslim community, the *ummah*, during the time when 'Isa is alone without the Mahdi.

At some time during his rule, Allah will have 'Isa prepare a small group of Muslims who are found to be worthy, to survive the upcoming world takeover by the Yajuj and Majuj (Gog and Magog) people. The Yajuj and Majuj will be the topic of the next section, H45. 'Isa will take the group to the mountain Tur to safeguard them from the arrival of the marauding bands of Yajuj and Majuj. Despite the fact that Yajuj and Majuj will be a plague to many Muslims, only some of them will be in safety at the special mountain.

Then 'Isa ibn Maryam also dies. But he does not pass away until forty years after returning to earth to assist the Mahdi in establishing the *khilafah*. A weak (*da'if*) hadith has his death occurring after forty-five years. In the meantime, he will get married and have children. Perhaps that occurs at the mountain Tur.

Comparison. According to Islamic teaching, Allah sent someone else to take 'Isa ibn Maryam's place on the cross. The substitute willingly died, in the process somehow deceiving the experienced Roman soldiers that crucified him, and all the Jewish onlookers. Soon afterward, 'Isa was transported up to heaven without dying a natural death. He lived there for two thousand years. After Allah sent him back to earth to be the Mahdi's deputy, his life became mortal again. Now, forty years after the Mahdi's appearance, and thirty-three years after the Mahdi's death, 'Isa ibn Maryam dies, leaving a wife and children.

His counterpart in the Bible, Jesus Christ or 'Isa al-Maseeh, had eyewitnesses who saw him crucified. These people knew him intimately. They met him again three days later when he was resurrected from the dead. They immediately recognized that he was the same Jesus whom they saw die on the cross. But Thomas, one of the twelve apostles, doubted their story:

> John 20:24 But Thomas, one of the twelve, who was called Didymus, was not with them when Jesus came.
> 20:25 So the other disciples were saying to him, "We have seen the Lord!" But he said to them, "Unless I see in His hands the imprint of the nails, and put my finger into the place of the nails, and put my hand into His side *[where the soldier pierced him with a spear to confirm his death]*, I will not believe."
> 20:26 Eight days later His disciples were again inside, and Thomas was with them. Jesus came, the doors having been shut, and stood in their midst and said, "Peace be to you."
> 20:27 Then He said to Thomas, "Place your finger here, and see My hands; and take your hand and put it into My side; and do not continue in disbelief, but be a believer."
> 20:28 Thomas answered and said to Him, "My Lord and my God!"
> 20:29 Jesus said to him, "Because you have seen Me, have you now believed? Blessed are they who did not see, and yet believed."

This first-hand account helped convince centuries of Christians to share the words of Thomas. For them Jesus is also "my Lord and my God."

Forty days later, the apostles and disciples saw him ascend into heaven. This is the same Jesus who promised to return. He did so at the battle of Armageddon (19:11 K38). It is also the same Jesus who now comes to sit on the throne of the millennial kingdom.

The hadith says that "the living will wish the dead come back to life, when they see the security, happiness, and the blessing of the earth" during the rest of the Mahdi's seven-year tenure. When comparing with the Bible's account of Christ's thousand-year kingdom on earth, the irony is that Muhammad's wish will come true. But it will be for Christ-followers instead of Muslims. In the previous section we saw that God already brought the dead tribulation martyrs and Old Testament saints back to life, so that they could share in the blessings of Christ's kingdom, alongside those who survived the seven years.

Revelation. The Bible mentions a literal thousand-year end-time period in only one place: Revelation chapter 20. But there it is repeated six times in six consecutive verses, 20:2 through 20:7. This repetition helps snap into focus several Old Testament prophecies, mostly in Isaiah, but also from Ezekiel, Zechariah, and the Psalms. Revelation helps us to see that those prophecies apply to a time that comes before eternity, and not to eternity itself. I will discuss them below.

We dealt with 20:2-3, which described the binding of Satan, in K42. His imprisonment freed the world from the action of evil spirits, and set the proper conditions for the millennial kingdom to flourish. In K43 we covered 20:4 and 20:5b: the resurrection of the tribulation martyrs, and the promise that they would rule with Christ for the thousand years. In the next section K45 20:7, we will see that at the end of the thousand years, Satan will be released from the abyss. Then in K46 20:5a, the wicked dead will be resurrected after the thousand years, so that they can appear before the judgment throne of God.

Our current section has the remaining verse, namely 20:6. It spells out that Christ's reign on earth will last the one thousand years. This is far superior to the tribulation kingdom of the antichrist, which lasted only seven years.

Implicit in the sequence of events is that the survivors of the tribulation will find themselves accepted as citizens of the new kingdom. This is because they accepted Christ as their savior. They will be in their natural bodies. Therefore, they can still expect death and resurrection, and they will still sin against the Almighty. But as believers, they are forever forgiven because of their faith.

Verse 20:6 does not mention those survivors, but it does call out those entering the millennium in glorified bodies. These are the beneficiaries of the "first resurrection" that happened after Christ's return and the battle of Armageddon. Among them will be the tribulation martyrs and resurrected Old Testament saints, as discussed in K43. They cannot die again in the "second death" (20:6), which unbelievers will experience when they are cast into hell at the end of the millennium (20:15, 21:8 K46). Instead, during the thousand years these glorified ones will be priests of God and of Christ (20:6). They will rule with Jesus (20:4-5 K43). They will help him administer the kingdom. In Jerusalem some of the resurrected Old Testament Jewish saints will serve as priests in the millennial temple, to be discussed below.

The deathless saints in glorified bodies will have the most amazing interaction with those like you and me who will live during the millennium in their natural bodies. The glorified ones will be shepherds to the mortals, and evangelists to their children born during the millennium. The only precedent for this is after Jesus was resurrected. He appeared in his glorified body among his disciples for forty days. In the millennium this other worldly dynamic will be normal.

Revelation gives no details regarding what life will be like during the millennium. But Isaiah was prophesying about this kingdom when he wrote down these words from God, eight centuries before John's vision:

> Isaiah 65:20 "No longer will there be in it an infant who lives only a few days, Or an old person who does not live out his days; For the youth will die at the age of a hundred, And the one who does not reach the age of a hundred Will be thought accursed."

This describes the amazing longevity of life among the survivors of the tribulation and the children born to them during the millennium. It will be comparable to life expectancies before Noah's flood. Then it was common for people to live seven, eight, or even nine hundred years, as recorded in Genesis 5. Perhaps the regular interactions of the mortals with the immortals in their glorified bodies increases their life spans dramatically. It also will help that Satan is imprisoned in the abyss (20:3 K42), and that all the devils are sidelined. They will not be present to promote the creation of new pathogens that would kill people.

This next verse speaks of child-bearing in this future age:

> Isaiah 65:23 "They will not labor in vain, Or give birth to children for disaster; For they are the descendants of those blessed by the Lord, And their descendants with them."

This will reverse one of the curses that God pronounced on Eve and all her future daughters, after she and Adam led the human race into the path of sin:

> Genesis 3:16a To the woman He said, "I will greatly multiply Your pain in childbirth, In pain you shall deliver children."

In the future kingdom, child bearing will not be painful. And the children born to these mothers will be exposed to fewer temptations than the world has ever known.

I am writing to you from the church age. In my time, the kingdom of God is his invisible spiritual reign in the hearts of believers. They carry the principles of his kingdom into the world, by acting as salt and light to those around them. The millennial kingdom promises to be much more. God will not only act invisibly in and through the lives of his followers, he will rule visibly in the person of his son, the lamb, come to live on earth:

> Isaiah 16:1 Send the tribute lamb to the ruler of the land,
> From Sela by way of the wilderness to the mountain of the
> daughter of Zion.

Christ the king will reign from Mount Zion, which is Jerusalem:

> Isaiah 2:2 Now it will come about that In the last days The
> mountain of the house of the Lord Will be established as the
> chief of the mountains, And will be raised above the hills;
> And all the nations will stream to it.
> 24:23b For the Lord of armies will reign on Mount Zion and
> in Jerusalem, And His glory will be before His elders.

The entire world will be his kingdom:

> Psalm 2:6 "But as for Me, I have installed My King Upon
> Zion, My holy mountain."
> 2:7 "I will announce the decree of the Lord: He said to Me,
> 'You are My Son, Today I have fathered You.
> 2:8 "Ask it of Me, and I will certainly give the nations as
> Your inheritance, And the ends of the earth as Your
> possession."

Jesus will rule with wisdom. His judgments from day to day will bless the meek of the earth. He will reprove the wicked tendencies that arise in sinful hearts among mortal individuals:

> Isaiah 11:2 The Spirit of the Lord will rest on Him, The spirit
> of wisdom and understanding, The spirit of counsel and
> strength, The spirit of knowledge and the fear of the L ord.
> 11:3 And He will delight in the fear of the Lord, And He will
> not judge by what His eyes see, Nor make decisions by what
> His ears hear;

> 11:4 But with righteousness He will judge the poor, And
> decide with fairness for the humble of the earth; And He will
> strike the earth with the rod of His mouth, And with the
> breath of His lips He will slay the wicked.
> 11:5 Also righteousness will be the belt around His hips, And
> faithfulness the belt around His waist.
> 16:5 A throne will be established in faithfulness, And a judge
> will sit on it in trustworthiness in the tent of David;
> Moreover, he will seek justice, And be prompt in
> righteousness.

There will be no war, or any armed strife between peoples. This will
fulfill the wishes of pacifists for the first time in human memory:

> Isaiah 2:4 And He will judge between the nations, And will
> mediate for many peoples; And they will beat their swords
> into plowshares, and their spears into pruning knives.
> Nation will not lift up a sword against nation, And never
> again will they learn war.

There will be profound peace and mutual esteem between gentiles and
Jews. Antisemitism will be a thing of the past. God's chosen people, the
children of Israel, will be given a favored place. Gentiles also will receive
manifold spiritual blessings, and will give honor to the Jewish followers
of Jesus:

> Isaiah 14:1 When the Lord has compassion on Jacob and
> again chooses Israel, and settles them on their own land,
> then strangers will join them and attach themselves to the
> house of Jacob.
> 49:22 This is what the Lord God says: "Behold, I will lift up
> My hand to the nations And set up My flag to the peoples;
> And they will bring your sons in their arms, And your
> daughters will be carried on their shoulders.
> 60:14 "The sons of those who afflicted you will come bowing
> to you, And all those who despised you will bow down at the
> soles of your feet; And they will call you the city of the Lord ,
> The Zion of the Holy One of Israel.
> 60:15 "Whereas you have been forsaken and hated With no
> one passing through, I will make you an object of pride
> forever, A joy from generation to generation.
> 60:16 "You will also suck the milk of nations, And suck the
> breast of kings; Then you will know that I, the Lord, am your
> Savior And your Redeemer, the Mighty One of Jacob."

There will be great material abundance. Isaiah describes it in the context of his time, the eighth century BCE:

> Isaiah 30:23 Then He will give you rain for your seed which you will sow in the ground, and bread from the yield of the ground, and it will be rich and plentiful; on that day your livestock will graze in a wide pasture.
> 30:24 Also the oxen and the donkeys that work the ground will eat seasoned feed, which has been winnowed with shovel and pitchfork.
> 35:1 The wilderness and the desert will rejoice, And the desert will shout for joy and blossom; Like the crocus
> 35:2 It will blossom profusely And rejoice with joy and jubilation. The glory of Lebanon will be given to it, The majesty of Carmel and Sharon. They will see the glory of the Lord, The majesty of our God.
> 65:21 "They will build houses and inhabit them; They will also plant vineyards and eat their fruit.
> 65:22 "They will not build and another inhabit, They will not plant and another eat; For as the lifetime of a tree, so will be the days of My people, And My chosen ones will fully enjoy the work of their hands."

Even the animals of the earth will be changed for the better. They will not fear one another. There will be no predators. The state of nature in the garden of Eden, before Satan brought sin to the human race, will be reestablished:

> Isaiah 11:6 And the wolf will dwell with the lamb, And the leopard will lie down with the young goat, And the calf and the young lion and the fattened steer will be together; And a little boy will lead them.
> 11:7 Also the cow and the bear will graze, Their young will lie down together, And the lion will eat straw like the ox.
> 11:8 The nursing child shall play over the hole of the cobra, and the weaned child shall put his hand on the adder's den.
> 11:9a They will not hurt or destroy in all My holy mountain.

Isaiah also mentions a holy place in Jerusalem where people of the world will come to make offerings, both Jews and gentiles:

> Isaiah 66:20 "Then they shall bring all your countrymen from all the nations as a grain offering to the Lord, on horses, in chariots, in litters, on mules, and on camels, to My holy mountain Jerusalem," says the Lord, "just as the sons of

> Israel bring their grain offering in a clean vessel to the house
> of the Lord."

This points to the continued presence of the temple of Jerusalem,
which was desecrated during the tribulation (11:1-2 K18), but is now
purified and glorious.

The prophet Ezekiel describes this temple at great length, in seven
consecutive chapters of his book (Ezekiel 40-46). Its priests will likely be
the resurrected Old Testament Jewish believers from the line of Aaron,
who entered into the thousand-year kingdom (20:6). The glory of the
Lord will come again to fill this temple, as it did at the inauguration of
the first temple by King Solomon:

> Ezekiel 43:4 And the glory of the Lord entered the house by
> way of the gate facing east.
> 43:5 And the Spirit lifted me up and brought me into the
> inner courtyard; and behold, the glory of the Lord filled the
> house.

A river that promotes life will flow from the temple, according to both
Ezekiel and Zechariah:

> Ezekiel 47:1 Then he brought me back to the door of the
> house; and behold, water was flowing from under the
> threshold of the house toward the east, for the house faced
> east. And the water was flowing down from under, from the
> right side of the house, from south of the altar.
> 47:12 And by the river on its bank, on one side and on the
> other, will grow all kinds of trees for food. Their leaves will
> not wither and their fruit will not fail. They will bear fruit
> every month because their water flows from the sanctuary,
> and their fruit will be for food and their leaves for healing.
>
> Zechariah 14:8 And on that day living waters will flow out of
> Jerusalem, half of them toward the eastern sea and the other
> half toward the western sea; it will be in summer as well as
> in winter.

The priests will make daily sacrifices:

> Ezekiel 46:13 "And you shall provide a lamb a year old
> without blemish as a burnt offering to the Lord daily;
> morning by morning you shall provide it."

But these sacrifices will be different in their character than those performed in the Old Testament temple. That is because Christ's sacrifice on the cross fulfilled God's requirement for atonement once and for ever. This is made clear in the New Testament book of Hebrews, written to explain why Christ willingly died for us:

> Hebrews 10:11 Every priest stands daily ministering and offering time after time the same sacrifices, which can never take away sins;
> 10:12 but He, having offered one sacrifice for sins for all time, sat down at the right hand of God,
> 9:28 so Christ also, having been offered once to bear the sins of many, will appear a second time for salvation without reference to sin, to those who eagerly await Him.

Ezekiel and Hebrews can both be taken literally, if we regard the millennial sacrifices as looking back to Christ's death on Calvary, while the Old Testament sacrifices looked forward to the cross.

The citizens of the millennium who live in their natural bodies will still sin and still die. The temple is there to remind them of their need for repentance, and also reminds them that Jesus has already paid the price to redeem them from their sins.

Though the material blessings will be great, the spiritual life of the millennium will be greater:

> Isaiah 11:9b For the earth will be full of the knowledge of the Lord As the waters cover the sea.
> 11:10 Then on that day The nations will resort to the root of Jesse, Who will stand as a signal flag for the peoples; And His resting place will be glorious.
> 2:3 And many peoples will come and say, "Come, let's go up to the mountain of the Lord, To the house of the God of Jacob; So that He may teach us about His ways, And that we may walk in His paths." For the law will go out from Zion And the word of the Lord from Jerusalem.

More people than ever in history will live by the Holy Spirit, and will dedicate themselves to Jesus Christ, God's son:

> Isaiah 32:15 Until the Spirit is poured out upon us from on high, And the wilderness becomes a fertile field, And the fertile field is considered as a forest.

32:16 Then justice will dwell in the wilderness, And
righteousness will remain in the fertile field.
32:17 And the work of righteousness will be peace, And the
service of righteousness, quietness and confidence forever.
32:18 Then my people will live in a peaceful settlement, In
secure dwellings, and in undisturbed resting places.
44:3 For I will pour water on the thirsty land And streams on
the dry ground; I will pour out My Spirit on your offspring,
And My blessing on your descendants;
44:4 And they will spring up among the grass Like poplars
by streams of water.
44:5 This one will say, 'I am the Lord's'; And that one will
call on the name of Jacob; And another will write on his
hand, 'Belonging to the Lord,' And will give himself Israel's
name with honor.

K45 :
Rebellion of Gog and Magog at the end of the millennium

: H45
The sun rises from the west, the beast of the earth comes forth, Yajuj and Majuj overwhelm the believers, and a cold wind kills the rest of them

20:3‡[K42] *and he threw him into the abyss and shut it and sealed it over him, so that he would not deceive the nations any longer,* until the thousand years were completed; after these things he must be released for a short time.
20:7 When the thousand years are completed, Satan will be released from his prison,
20:8 and will come out to deceive the nations which are at the four corners of the earth, Gog and Magog, to gather them together for the war; the number of them is like the sand of the seashore.
20:9 And they came up on the broad plain of the earth and surrounded the camp of the saints and the beloved city, and fire came down from heaven and devoured them.
20:10 And the devil who deceived them was thrown into the lake of fire and brimstone, where the beast and the false prophet are also; and they will be tormented day and night forever and ever.

Allah most high has placed in the west for repentance a gate with a breadth of seventy years' journey, and it will not be locked as long as the sun does not rise in its direction. That agrees with Allah's words, 'On the day that certain of the signs of your Lord come, a soul which has not believed before will not be benefited by believing in them' [quoting Surah 6:158][244]

I heard the Messenger of Allah say: The first of the signs to appear will be the rising of the sun in its place of setting and the coming forth of the beast against mankind in the forenoon. Whichever of them comes first will soon be followed by the other.[245] *(sahih)*

And when the Word is fulfilled against them (the unjust), we shall produce from the earth a beast to (face) them: He will speak to them, for that mankind did not believe with assurance in Our Signs. (Surah 27:82)

---

[244] Narrated by Safwan b. 'Assal, *Mishkat al-Masabih 2345*, Book 9, Hadith 118, https://sunnah.com/mishkat:2345, accessed January 23, 2024.
[245] Narrated by Abu zur'ah, *Sunan Abi Dawud 4310*, Book 38, Hadith 4296, https://sunnah.com/abudawud:4310, accessed January 16, 2024.

The Beast [Dabbat al-ard] will emerge and will have with it the seal of Sulaiman bin Dawud [Solomon son of David] and the staff of Musa bin 'Imran [Moses]. It will make the faces of the believers shine with the staff, and will mark the noses of the disbelievers with the seal, until the inhabitants of a cluster of houses will gather together; then one will say 'O believer!' And to another 'O disbeliever.'[246] *(da'if)*

"Woe to the Arabs, from the Great evil that is nearly approaching them. Today a gap has been made in the wall of Yajuj and Majuj like this." (Sufyan illustrated this by forming the number 90 or 100 with his fingers.) It was asked, "Shall we be destroyed though there are righteous people among us?" The Prophet said, "Yes, if evil increased."[247]

Abu Hurairah, from the Prophet, regarding the 'barrier': "They excavated each day, until when they are just about to penetrate it, their leader says: 'Go back so that you can penetrate it tomorrow!'" He said: "But Allah makes it return just as it was, until their appointed time, when Allah ordains to send them upon the people, and their leader says: 'Go back so you can penetrate it tomorrow, if Allah wills.' So he makes this exception."[248] *(sahih)*

Until after Yajuj and Majuj have broken loose from the barrier, swarming down from every hill. (Surah 21:96, Clear Qur'an)

The Prophet said: "The people will continue performing the Hajj and 'Umrah to the Kaaba even after the appearance of Yajuj and Majuj." Narrated Shu`ba extra: The Hour (Day of Judgment) will not be established till the Hajj (to the Kaaba) is abandoned.[249]

The people will return to their own lands and will be confronted with Yajuj and Majuj people, who will: "swoop down from every mound." They will not pass by any water but they will drink it, (and they will not pass) by anything but they will spoil it. They (the people) will beseech

---

[246] Narrated by Abu Hurairah, *Sunan Ibn Majah 4066*, Vol. 5, Book 36, Hadith 4066, https://sunnah.com/ibnmajah:4066, accessed June 8, 2024; also referenced in Ahmad b. Hanbal (9th century Sunni jurist and theologian), *Musnad II, 491*, quoted in Khashif Ali, *The Dabbat al-ard (Beast of the Earth) in Quran and Hadith*, https://wordofprophet.com/dabbat-al-ard/, July 25, 2023, accessed January 16, 2024.
[247] Narrated by Zainab bint Jahsh, *Sahih al-Bukhari 7059*, Vol. 9, Book 88, Hadith 181, https://sunnah.com/bukhari:7059, accessed January 16, 2024.
[248] Narrated by Abu Rafi', *Jami` at-Tirmidhi 3153*, Vol. 5, Book 44, Hadith 3153, https://sunnah.com/tirmidhi:3153, accessed January 16, 2024.
[249] Narrated by Abu Sa`id Al-Khudri, *Sahih al-Bukhari 1593*, Vol. 2, Book 26, Hadith 663, https://sunnah.com/bukhari:1593, accessed June 8, 2024; also quoted in Abu Rahma, *Who and where are the Yajuj and Majuj (Gog and Magog)? Has their barrier been broken?*, March 4, 2016, https://qurananswers.me/2016/03/04/who-and-where-are-the-gog-and-magog/#_ftn8, accessed January 16, 2024.

Allah, and I will pray to Allah to kill them. The earth will be filled with their stench.[250] *(sahih)*

Yajuj and Majuj people will … spread throughout the earth, and the Muslims will flee from them until the remainder of the Muslims are in their cities and fortresses, taking their flocks with them. They will pass by a river and drink from it, until they leave nothing behind, and the last of them will follow in their footsteps and one of them will say: 'There was once water in this place.' They will prevail over the earth, then their leader will say: 'These are the people of the earth, and we have finished them off.[251] *(hasan)*

Then Allah would send cold wind from the side of Syria that none would survive upon the earth having a speck of good in him or faith in him but he would die, so much so that even if some amongst you were to enter the innermost part of the mountain, this wind would reach that place also and that would cause his death…. Only the wicked people would survive and they would be as careless as birds with the characteristics of beasts. They would never appreciate the good nor condemn evil. Then Shaytan would come to them in human form and would say: Don't you respond? And they would say: What do you order us? And he would command them to worship the idols but, in spite of this, they would have abundance of sustenance and lead comfortable lives.[252]

Revelation. At the end of the thousand years, Satan is allowed out of the abyss (20:3,7). But his imprisonment has not changed his attitude. He has spent his time planning one more attempt to dethrone the living God. He will raise another army like that of the beast during the tribulation.

Whom can he attract to his cause, amidst the peaceful and almost perfect world of the millennial kingdom? His recruits will have to come from among those born to the survivors of the tribulation. These descendants did not experience the terrors of the beast, the woman of Babylon, and the false prophet. Under those extreme conditions, their fathers and mothers cried out to Christ to save them.

---

[250] Narrated by 'Abdullah bin Mas'ud, *Sunan Ibn Majah 4081*, Vol. 5, Book 36, Hadith 4081, https://sunnah.com/ibnmajah:4081, accessed January 16, 2024.
[251] Narrated by Abu Sa'eed Al-Khudri, *Sunan Ibn Majah 4079*, Vol. 5, Book 36, Hadith 4079, https://sunnah.com/ibnmajah:4079, accessed January 28, 2024.
[252] Narrated by 'Abdullah b. 'Amr, *Sahih Muslim 2940a*, Book 41, Hadith 7023, https://sunnah.com/muslim:2940a, accessed January 16, 2024.

But there will be fifty generations born during the millennium who will know nothing of such trials. They will live longer lives, and will greatly outnumber the first tribulation generation. Large numbers of them will be tempted in their sinful nature to demand something better than Christ sitting on the world's throne in Jerusalem. And they have not invited him to sit on the throne of their hearts. These are the secret rebels who will succumb to the new temptation offered by Satan. They will join him in attacking God and his people in force.

The truth of the sinner is that even under the most ideal circumstances imaginable, we may reject God in favor of the sin that appeals to us. Afterward, many of us refuse God's grace and new life in Christ. The Bible speaks to this:

> John 3:19b the Light has come into the world, and people
> loved the darkness rather than the Light; for their deeds
> were evil.

Those who love darkness more than light are setting their own course into an unknown eternity. We shall see in the next section (K46) that their works will result in their doom.

The people who are deceived and join in with Satan will be from many different nations, "at the four corners of the earth." Together they will comprise "Gog and Magog" (20:8). That label invokes the memory of the nation of Magog, and its prince Gog, leader of a coalition of seven nations invading Israel from the north (Ezekiel 38:2-16): Magog, Meshech, Tubal, Gomer, Togarmah, Persia, Cush (Ethiopia), and Put (Libya). That invasion is another scheme of Satan's, prophesied in Ezekiel 38-39. It will likely occur in the brief period that occurs between the rapture and the tribulation, over a thousand years earlier than the rebellion here at the end of the millennium.

Magog is also mentioned in Genesis 10:2 as one of the sons of Japheth, and grandson of Noah.

It is significant that Gog and Magog reappear here at the end of the millennium. Perhaps they are two leaders whom Satan recruited from the children of the millennium, or collective titles for the rebellion. In either case, they are Satan's trademark for trouble. God allows this test for the children of the millennium. Those with true faith will confirm their devotion to Jesus by standing against the rebellion, which involves yet another false trinity: Satan, Gog, and Magog.

John sees that the new Gog and Magog is a vast army, "the number of them is like the sand of the seashore" (20:8). Even here in the distant future, Satan prefers war to accomplish his goals. The army comes up to Jerusalem "the beloved city," and surrounds the outnumbered camp of believers there (20:9).

But God intervenes. He sends a fire from heaven that devours the army of Gog and Magog. And he deals with Satan, too. This time it is not a matter of imprisonment. The chief of deceivers is cast into the lake of fire, for all eternity. He joins the beast and the false prophet, who have already been in the lake for a thousand years (19:20 K40). The devils who follow Satan will certainly share his fate. He will never again tempt God's people. Instead, he will be tormented day and night for ever and ever (20:10). He will never again have opportunity to sideline the God of the universe.

Hadiths. After the deaths of the Mahdi and ʿIsa ibn Maryam, an unspecified time passes. The caliphate of the silver age will evidently quickly decompose without their leadership. A remnant of worthy Muslims has been brought to safety to the mountain Tur by ʿIsa, where they will be safe from the upcoming terrible events. The Hadiths are silent as to this group's future fate.

Then three of the Major Signs of the end times will happen. They are given in the hadith of H00, and mentioned in many others:

- The sun will rise from the west.
- The beast of the earth will crawl out of the ground.
- Yajuj and Majuj (Gog and Magog) will break out of their imprisonment.

A fourth sign will also take place:

- Allah will send a cold wind.

Let us cover each of these.

The rising of the sun from the west will be first. Allah will engineer this fantastic cosmic miracle and somehow reverse the motion of the earth.

This event definitively closes the age of repentance. From this time forth, even if someone were to journey a lifetime of seventy years to reach the western gate of repentance, he will find it locked. He will be flatly rejected entry into paradise, because of any faults he commits after the gate was closed. Those who remain on earth will have to live a life of perfection in response to the remaining trials.

Coupled with this event, the beast of the earth, *Dabbat al-ard*, will crawl out of the ground. Most interpreters agree that this creature will not be human, yet he will have the ability to speak. He will admonish the unbelievers for their lack of devotion to Allah. Muslims will not be exempt, because we have seen that many who are outwardly practicing as Muslims are hypocritical in their faith.

To prove his authority, the *Dabbat* will carry the staff of Moses, which is well known from the Qur'an.[253] He will also be holding the legendary seal of Solomon,[254] a ring which bears the Jewish mark of the six-pointed star of David. With it he will go to and fro through the world, marking the noses of each unbeliever. By this the beast shows that these reprobates will be counted alongside the hated Jews in the resurrection. It is amazing that many of them were accepted by the Mahdi and ʿIsa ibn Maryam, and fought in their armies to kill Christians and Jews. Yet these will be deemed unworthy.

The third of the Major Signs of this time will involve *Yajuj* and *Majuj*, Arabic for the Hebrew Gog and Magog. They will break out of their imprisonment, ravage the earth, and kill all believers in their way.

Some Hadiths mention Yajuj and Majuj as two individuals, others have them as tribes descended from them. But most portray them as the unbelieving mass of humanity who will be counted as belonging to Yajuj and Majuj. They will ultimately be cast into hellfire by Allah (see H46).

Their origins trace back to the days of Noah. He had three sons who came with him aboard the ark: Sam, Ham, and Yafith. The descendants of Sam are the Arabs, the Persians, and the Romans. The descendants of

---

[253] For example Surah 26:63.
[254] *Testament of Solomon*, unknown author and date, https://archive.org/stream/jstor-1450398/1450398_djvu.txt, p.16, accessed January 28, 2024.

Ham are Sudan, Barbar, and Kibbutz. The descendants of Yafith are the Turks, Sakaliba, and Yajuj and Majuj.[255]

The early activities of Yajuj and Majuj are mentioned in the Qur'an in Surah 18, known as Surah al-Kahf, the story of the Cave. It tells of a good ruler named Zul-Qarnain. In his travels he came across a group of people who asked for help to stop the tribes of Yajuj and Majuj from despoiling their land:

> They pleaded, "O Zul-Qarnain! Surely Yajuj and Majuj are spreading corruption throughout the land. Should we pay you tribute, provided that you build a wall between us and them?" He responded, "What my Lord has provided for me is far better. But assist me with resources, and I will build a barrier between you and them. Bring me blocks of iron!" Then, when he had filled up the gap between the two mountains, he ordered, "Blow!" When the iron became red hot, he said, "Bring me molten copper to pour over it." And so the enemies could neither scale nor tunnel through it. He declared, "This is a mercy from my Lord." (Surah 18:94-98a, Clear Qur'an)

Zul-Qarnain helped by building a barrier wall and imprisoning the peoples of Yajuj and Majuj behind it. They have miraculously stayed alive there for thousands of years, waiting for the death of the Mahdi, the rising of the sun in the west, and the beast of the earth to appear. Yajuj and Majuj have been busy, though. A hadith describes how they have been fruitlessly excavating the wall to try to break out.

But now, with Allah's permission, they make a final penetration, and escape into the world. Apparently, their place of confinement was in mountainous terrain, for they are said to "swarm down from every slope."

Despite Yajuj and Majuj being released, Muslims will continue their hajj and `umrah (non-hajj) pilgrimages to Mecca. This indicates that Yajuj

---

[255] *Mustadraku Alas Sahihain Lil Hakim, 6429,* quoted in *Yajuj and Majuj in Islam? The origin and end of this mysterious nation,* September 22, 2021, https://muslimguiding.com/yajuj-and-majuj-islam/.

and Majuj's attack would be gradual and in stages, and will not immediately stop all travel to Mecca.[256]

But eventually the Yajuj and Majuj will overwhelm the remaining true believers. They will devastate the earth, and drink all the waters. "The earth will be filled with their stench." They will kill all believers in their way. Presumably, they will look to eliminate those who do not have the mark of the Dabbat.

Finally, they reach the point when their leader declares: "These are the people of the earth, and we have finished them off."

After the Yajuj and Majuj have taken their course, all true believers who somehow eluded them – everyone with even the smallest measure of human-kindness or faith – will die as the result of a cold wind sent across the earth by Allah. Only the wicked will remain.

At this point Shaytan (Iblis) finally arrives on the scene, in human form. He will command the wicked ones who are left to worship the idols. Shaytan will give them abundance of sustenance and comfortable lives. Among them will be many who regarded themselves as Muslims, and even based their religion on a pledge of allegiance to the Mahdi. They now pledge themselves to their new provider.

Comparison. What Muslim could possibly endure after the sun rises in the west, when repentance will no longer be allowed them? It will be impossible to prove oneself worthy, even by a journey of seventy years seeking acceptance. This contrasts with the end of the millennium in Revelation, when Satan puts out his temptations to secret rebels of the heart to join his rebellion. Each man and woman will have to decide – whether to follow the desires that Satan has stoked inside them, or to repent of them and seek God's forgiveness. Unlike Allah, the grace of God will still be available to those who turn back to Christ the king in repentance.

The battle-hardened veterans of the wars of the Mahdi, who are still alive when Yajuj and Majuj come after them, are now abandoned by

---

[256] Abu Rahma, *Who and where are the Yajuj and Majuj (Gog and Magog)? Has their barrier been broken?*, March 4, 2016, https://qurananswers.me/2016/03/04/who-and-where-are-the-gog-and-magog/.

Allah to their deaths. The safe route to the mountain Tur is no longer available, and the gate of repentance is closed. They know from the Hadiths that they will not be able to withstand Yajuj and Majuj, and that Allah will finish them off with the cold wind. This will be the most bitter pill to swallow for those who fought to the end for the Mahdi.

By contrast, in Revelation God takes an enormous interest in the veterans who turned away from the antichrist beast during the tribulation, and then fought against him. He forgives those who survived, and resurrects those who were killed, inviting both into the blessings of the millennium (see K43). Here at the end of the millennium, he does not leave those who trusted him to their own devices, but defends them against Satan, Gog and Magog (20:9).

It is remarkable that Dabbat al-ard, who then comes out to place a mark on the millions of unworthy people, will do so with the six-sided star of the ring of Solomon. The ring is unknown in either the Old or the New Testament, or in the Islamic versions of them: the Taurat, Zabur, or Injil (see the section "Sacred texts" above). The ring is actually a legend that first found its way into writing in the pseudepigraphic (extra-biblical) letter known as *Testament of Solomon*, written after the end of the first century CE by an unknown author.[257] Muhammad and some Arabs of the seventh century were a bit familiar with this letter. It tells a fanciful story of Solomon receiving the magic ring from the archangel Michael, which he then used to gain control of demons all the way up to Beelzebub himself.

We can tell that Muhammad was impressed by the story of the ring and its great powers, since he spoke the Hadiths that depict the beast of the earth wearing the ring. When the angel Jibreel told him of the ring and its reappearance at the end of time, Muhammad made sure to make it known among his followers. The star of David marking those destined for destruction is an added twist that has tantalized Muslims ever since.

It is notable that Muhammad regarded the Testament of Solomon as equal in truth to passages of the Old and New Testament (those that he did not find objectionable). The Christians of the early centuries were not swayed by such personal preferences. Instead, they grappled with

---

[257] https://en.m.wikipedia.org/wiki/Testament_of_Solomon, accessed January 28, 2024.

the various writings to isolate those that were the pure word of God. They strove to understand what was difficult by reconciling scripture with scripture. In the process, they rejected dozens of faulty letters such as the Testament of Solomon, as interesting as they might be. Such writings are not to be found in the Bible.

Like the Hadiths, Revelation also talks of marking a multitude of people. The people who willingly received the mark of the beast during the tribulation (13:16-17 K24) are those who believe in him. The Jesus-followers and others who did not accept the mark were targeted for death by the beast's armies (13:15 K24, 20:4 K24). In our current section of Hadiths, we see that a mark also ends up protecting people from death. Ironically, it is the unbelievers and double-minded Muslims who are marked with Solomon's seal. With this seal of unbelief, they stay alive, at least temporarily. Those without the mark are targeted for death by Yajuj and Majuj and the cold wind from Allah, while those with the mark stay alive and pledge themselves to Shaytan.

Gog and Magog have different origins in the two accounts. In Revelation, when Satan returns at the end of the thousand years, he recruits a vast army from scratch by appealing to the discontented among the children of the millennium (20:8). That army is a parallel to the Gog and Magog that invaded Israel from the north shortly before the tribulation. In the Hadiths, Yajuj and Majuj are entire tribes loosed from their imprisonment. Their goal is not to recruit people, but to seek out and kill all true Muslim believers. Nevertheless, along the way, their numbers are dramatically increased. In the next section we will see that out of all humanity, 999 out of a thousand people will be counted as belonging to Yajuj and Majuj. For their lack of devotion, the extra people will be punished in the same way as the Yajuj and Majuj people who broke through the restraining wall.

In Revelation, Gog and Magog's army comes up to Jerusalem, and surrounds the outnumbered camp of believers there (20:9). Then, before they have the chance to achieve victory, they are consumed by fire from heaven. The wicked are destroyed. The only people left are true believers in Christ. In the Hadiths, the peoples of Yajuj and Majuj outnumber and overwhelm all the remaining true Muslim believers. Any that might be left are finished off by the cold wind. The only people surviving are the wicked, and Shaytan comes to claim them. In the next section those wicked will be bold enough to challenge heaven itself. But they will be no match for the last of the Major Signs. At that time, Shaytan will be thrown headlong into hell

In Revelation, Satan is one of the major antagonists opposing God. He is the one imprisoned for a thousand years (20:1-3 K42), and then released to recruit the armies of Gog and Magog in the final rebellion (20:3, 7-8).

In the Hadiths' version of the end times, it is Gog and Magog, or Yajuj and Majuj, who have been imprisoned, in their case for many thousands of years. Shaytan is a secondary character. He works by way of his primary agent, the Dajjal (H19, H25, H34). But Shaytan himself has been absent the entire time of the Mahdi's silver age, the lifetime of ʿIsa, the removal of repentance from the world, and the Yajuj and Majuj eradicating anyone left having any human kindness. After the cold wind, he finally makes his appearance on earth. He does so in human form (in imitation of the incarnation of Jesus the son of God) to make clear that he owns the evil people who remain. He grants them comfortable lives in return for their complete subservience and worship. It is not a coincidence that in the next section, they will be punished in the final judgment.

K46 :
Resurrections after the millennium, then judgment at the great white throne

: H46
Yajuj and Majuj assault heaven, the last Major Sign, and the final judgment of the Last Hour

20:5‡[K43] The rest of the dead did not come to life until the thousand years were completed. *This is the first resurrection.*

20:6‡[K44] *Blessed and holy is the one who has a part in the first resurrection;* over these the second death *has no power, but they will be priests of God and of Christ, and will reign with Him for a thousand years.*

20:13 And the sea gave up the dead who were in it, and Death and Hades gave up the dead who were in them; and they were judged, each one of them according to their deeds.

20:11 Then I saw a great white throne and Him who sat upon it, from whose presence earth and heaven fled, and no place was found for them.

2:26 The one who overcomes, and the one who keeps My deeds until the end, I will give him authority over the nations;

2:28 and I will give him the morning star.

20:12 And I saw the dead, the great and the small, standing before the throne, and books were opened; and another book was opened, which is the book of life; and the dead were judged from

Yajuj and Majuj people … their leader will say …. 'Now let us fight the people of heaven!' Then one of them will throw his spear towards the sky, and it will come back down smeared with blood. And they will say: 'We have killed the people of heaven.' While they are like that, Allah will send a worm like the worm that is found in the noses of sheep, which will penetrate their necks and they will die like locusts, one on top of another. In the morning the Muslims will not hear any sound from them, and they will say: 'Who will sell his soul for the sake of Allah and see what they are doing?' A man will go down, having prepared himself to be killed by them, and he will find them dead, so he will call out to them: 'Be of good cheer, for your enemy is dead!' Then the people will come out and let their flocks loose, but they will not have anything to graze on except their flesh, and they will become very fat as if they were grazing on the best vegetation they ever found.'[258] *(hasan)*

And (the people) will beseech Allah and I will pray to Allah, then the sky will send down rain that will carry them (Yajuj and Majuj)

---

[258] Narrated by Abu Sa'eed Al-Khudri, *Sunan Ibn Majah 4079*, Vol. 5, Book 36, Hadith 4079, https://sunnah.com/ibnmajah:4079, accessed January 28, 2024.

the things which were written in the books, according to their deeds.

20:15 And if anyone's name was not found written in the book of life, he was thrown into the lake of fire.

21:8 But for the cowardly, and unbelieving, and abominable, and murderers, and sexually immoral persons, and sorcerers, and idolaters, and all liars, their part will be in the lake that burns with fire and brimstone, which is the second death.

20:14 Then Death and Hades were thrown into the lake of fire. This is the second death, the lake of fire.

and throw them in the sea.[259] *(sahih)*

The Last Hour would not come until a person would pass by a grave of another person and he would say: wish it had been my abode.[260]

The Last Hour … will not come until you see ten signs … at the end of which fire would burn forth from the Yemen, and would drive people to the place of their assembly.[261]

The truest of word is the Book of Allah and best of guidance is the guidance of Muhammad. The worst of things are those that are newly invented; every newly-invented thing is an innovation and every innovation is going astray, and every going astray is in the Fire.[262] *(sahih)*

On that Day We shall let the people loose to surge like waves on one another. The trumpet will be blown and We shall assemble the mankind all together. (Surah 18:99, M. Farook Malik translation)

Then the mountains will turn to dust and the earth will be stretched out like a hide.[263] *(sahih)*

All that is on earth will perish, but will abide (for ever) the Face of thy Lord,- full of Majesty, Bounty and Honour. (Surah 55:26-27)

---

[259] Narrated by 'Abdullah bin Mas'ud, *Sunan Ibn Majah 4081*, Vol. 5, Book 36, Hadith 4081, https://sunnah.com/ibnmajah:4081, accessed January 16, 2024.

[260] Narrated by Abu Huraira, *Sahih Muslim 157 k*, Book 41, Hadith 6947, https://sunnah.com/muslim:157k, accessed June 9, 2024; also referenced in Rahma p.66.

[261] Narrated by Hudhaifa b. Usaid al-Ghifari, *Sahih Muslim 2901 a*, Book 41, Hadith 6931, https://sunnah.com/muslim:2901a, accessed June 9, 2024; also referenced in Rahma p.144.

[262] Narrated by Jabir bin 'Abdullah, *Sunan an-Nasa'i 1578*, Vol. 2, Book 19, Hadith 1579, https://sunnah.com/nasai:1578, accessed February 4, 2024.

[263] Narrated by 'Abdullah bin Mas'ud, *Sunan Ibn Majah 4081*, Vol. 5, Book 36, Hadith 4081, https://sunnah.com/ibnmajah:4081, accessed January 16, 2024.

One of the specific signs mentioned in Tradition is: there will be a call from heaven to all the people of the earth and everyone will hear it in their own language and people responsible for Innovations will be transmogrified.[264]

(After the cold wind) the trumpet would be blown .... then Allah would send or he would cause to send rain which would be like dew and there would grow out of it the bodies of the people. Then the second trumpet would be blown and they would stand up and begin to look (around). Then it would be said: O people, go to your Lord, and make them stand there. And they would be questioned. Then it would be said: Bring out a group (out of them) for the Hell-Fire. And then it would be asked: How much? It would be said: Nine hundred and ninety-nine out of one thousand for the Hell-Fire.[265]

The Prophet said, "On the day of Resurrection Allah will say, 'O Adam!' Adam will reply, '*Labbaik* (here I am) our Lord, and *Sa'daik* (at your service).' Then there will be a loud call (saying), Allah orders you to take from among your offspring a mission for the (Hell) Fire.' Adam will say, 'O Lord! Who are the mission for the (Hell) Fire?' Allah will say, 'Out of each thousand, take out 999.' ... whereupon the Prophet said, "From Yajuj and Majuj nine-hundred ninety-nine will be taken out and one from you. You Muslims (compared to the large number of other people) will be like a black hair on the side of a white ox, or a white hair on the side of a black ox, and I hope that you will be one fourth of the people of Paradise." On that, we said, "Allahu-Akbar!" Then he said, "I hope that you will be) one-third of the people of Paradise." We again said, "Allahu-Akbar!" Then he said, "(I hope that you will be) one-half of the people of Paradise." So we said, Allahu Akbar."[266]

The Prophet said, "I looked at Hell and saw that the majority of its inhabitants were women."[267]

[For, on that Day,] To those straying in Evil, the Fire will be placed in full view. And it shall be said to them: 'Where are the (gods) ye worshipped besides Allah? Can they help you or help themselves?' Then they will be thrown headlong into the (Fire),- they and those straying in Evil, and the whole hosts of Iblis together. (Surah 26:91-95)

---

[264] `Ibn Izzat p.18; also partially referenced in https://www.islam.org.hk/hy/signsofthelastday/science_and_technology.html, accessed June 9, 2024.

[265] Narrated by 'Abdullah b. 'Amr, *Sahih Muslim 2940a*, Book 41, Hadith 7023, https://sunnah.com/muslim:2940a, accessed January 29, 2024.

[266] Narrated by Abu Sa`id Al-Khudri, *Sahih al-Bukhari 4741*, Vol. 6, Book 60, Hadith 265, https://sunnah.com/bukhari:4741, accessed January 28, 2024.

[267] Narrated by `Imran bin Husain, *Sahih al-Bukhari 3241*, Vol. 4, Book 54, Hadith 464, https://sunnah.com/bukhari:3241, accessed April 7, 2024.

> And verily, Hell is the promised abode for them all. To it are seven gates: for each of those gates is a (special) class (of sinners) assigned. (Surah 15:43-44)

> Death would be brought on the Day of Resurrection. in the form of a white-colored ram.... Then it would be made to stand between the Paradise and the Hell.... It would be said to the inmates of Paradise: Do you recognize this? They would raise up their necks and look towards it and say: Yes, it is death. Then it would be said to the inmates of Hell-Fire: Do you recognize this? And they would raise up their necks and look and say: Yes, it is death. Then command would be given for slaughtering that and then it would be said: O inmates of Paradise, there is an everlasting life for you and no death. And then (addressing) to the inmates of the Hell-Fire, it would be said: O inmates of Hell-Fire, there is an everlasting living for you and no death.[268]

Hadiths. At the close of the previous section (H45), the people of Yajuj and Majuj overwhelmed the true Muslims, and devastated the earth. Anyone who had a trace of human kindness then fell victim to the cold wind sent by Allah. That left the field completely open to Shaytan (Iblis). He appeared in human form to lay claim to all the wicked, who were the only ones remaining. We shall see that they will be counted with the Yajuj and Majuj in Allah's final judgment.

In the present section, the Yajuj and Majuj do not rest on their laurels. They are not satisfied to merely possess the earth. Their leader will say "Now let us fight the people of heaven!" They are foolish enough to think that they can defeat heaven by firing weapons into the air: "One of them will throw his spear towards the sky, and it will come back down smeared with blood." Based on that, they rejoice: "We have killed the people of heaven." They really think they have killed Allah and everyone in heaven.[269]

But their victory is a delusion. Allah sends worms that multiply rapidly, and plague all the Yajuj and Majuj. They die in the severest agony of pain. "In the morning the Muslims will not hear any sound from them."

---

[268] Narrated by Abu Sa'id, *Sahih Muslim 2849 a*, Book 40, Hadith 6827, https://sunnah.com/muslim:2849a, accessed March 9, 2024.
[269] Medi1Saif *(sic)*, https://islam.stackexchange.com/questions/65482/who-does-gog-magog-kill-in-the-sky, March 3, 2021.

The Muslims referred to could be those who, some years earlier, were led into safety to the mountain Tur by ʿIsa ibn Maryam (in H44).

A different hadith has some Muslims appealing for relief to Allah against the Yajuj and Majuj. He responds by unleashing fierce rains that sweep the Yajuj and Majuj into the sea.

The two different prophecies of their demise might actually supplement each other. Conceivably they will first fall prey to a pandemic of worms, and then meet their death by drowning in the sea, all while the small band of Muslims watch from their place of safety.

The next hadith tells that "the Last Hour would not come until a person would pass by a grave of another person and he would say: wish it had been my abode." This can apply to the current situation. As the Yajuj and Majuj die one by one, their pitiful hope is that death would mean total annihilation and nothingness. Then they would not have to face the judgment of the Last Hour before Allah, which they instinctively know is coming. But their wishes will not help them avoid the judgment.

Then "the trumpet will be blown," and the last of the Major Signs of the end times will occur. It was the last one given in the hadith of H00: the fire that burns forth from the Yemen. This implies that a massive fire will begin in Yemen, which over time will extend over the earth.

The fire will reveal innovations of men and women that are repugnant to Allah. It will also purify the world from them. These innovations are of various categories. Some constitute blatant disbelief. Others are sinful, but do not come under the heading of disbelief. Others are disliked.[270] "The worst of things are those that are newly invented," that is, beyond the dictates of the Book of Allah.[271] All these innovations will disappear into the fire. Islam will, once and for all, be cleansed from the innovations that had crept into it, and distorted the pristine principles of the faith.

---

[270] https://islamqa.info/en/answers/237360/is-every-innovation-bidah-worse-and-more-serious-than-every-major-sin, accessed February 7, 2024.
[271] Sayyid Sa'eed Akhtar Rizvi, https://www.al-islam.org/understanding-karbala-sayyid-saeed-akhtar-rizvi/how-imam-hasan-and-imam-husayn-saved-islam, accessed February 7, 2024.

The spreading fire will start the process of driving people "to the place of their assembly." This is apparently a reference to Allah's judgment seat. Surah 18:99 says, "on that day we shall let the people loose to surge like waves on one another."

At this time, "the mountains will turn to dust and the earth will be stretched out like a hide." This is the final cataclysm *(fana')*. It will be the extinction of all living beings, even the angels, at the hands of the angel of death. Allah then commands the angel of death to do away with himself, so that all creatures would experience death.[272] As Smith and Haddad explain:

> Many traditional eschatological descriptions develop an elaborate vision of this ultimate desolation of the earth and all living creatures. The *Kitab ahwal al-qiyama*[273] describes Allah as commanding the angel of death to annihilate the oceans, the mountains, [and] the earth, despite their sad limitations…. Finally Allah commands that because of his word, all souls will taste death; even the angel of death himself must die, and so he does.[274]

Another call from heaven now occurs. In response, all people of all languages who are responsible for any innovations "will be transmogrified." This refers to the resurrection of questionable Muslims. But since the *fana'* describes the death of all living beings, the resurrection must not only include all dead infidels, but also all true Muslims who were careful to avoid innovations. The process is pictured for us: "Allah would … send rain which would be like dew and there

---

[272] Zulkifli Mohammad al-Bakri, *The Death of Angels*, https://maktabahalbakri.com/444-the-death-of-angels/, June 15, 2022, citing interpretation of Surah 55:26-27 by Ibn Abbas, cousin of Muhammad, considered greatest author of *tafsir* commentaries on the Qur'an.

[273] *Kitab ahwal al-qiyama* (*Book of the Phases of Resurrection*) is an anonymous text translated from Arabic into German by M. Wolff, Rabbi of the Jewish congregation in Gothenburg, as *Muhammedanische Eschatologie*, Leipzig: F. A. Brockhaus, 1872, according to https://archive.org/stream/imamalghazalienglish/ThePreciousPearlAl-jamiAl-durrahAlFakhirahByImamGhazali_djvu.txt, https://www.encyclopedia.com/philosophy-and-religion/bible/bible-general/eschatology, and https://www.quran-earlyislam.com/Muhammedanische-Eschatologie, accessed March 16, 2024.

[274] Smith and Haddad, p.71, citing J. McDonald, *The Day of Resurrection*, Islamic Studies, 5 (1966), p.148, which quotes Abu al-Layth al-Samarqandi, Sunni Hanafite jurist and Quran commentator, who lived during the second half of the 10th century.

would grow out of it the bodies of the people. Then the second trumpet would be blown and they would stand up and begin to look (around)."

"And they would be questioned." This is from another portion of Sahih Muslim 2940a, a most prophetic hadith, which we have already encountered in H19, H34, and H45.

What will be Allah's criteria for judgment? That is the anxious question in the hearts of all Muslims. As Smith and Haddad explain, the issue of crucial concern to Islam is the nature of good and bad deeds, *al-salihat* and *al-masiyat*. The dividing line between them is obedience, or the lack of it. Failure to obey the divine prescriptions will be punished, just as obedience to them will be rewarded.

But Muslim theologians have trouble delineating which deeds are bad enough to send someone to hell. Most recognize a distinction between grave sins and lesser sins, but they don't agree on the separation between them.

Regardless of this, the Muslim is certain that there is one unpardonable sin, for which the pain of the fire is assured. It would be a refusal to testify to the *tawhid* of Allah. From section H24-C6, we learned that tawhid is the doctrine that Allah is the God who is absolutely and utterly alone. Closely associated with this is the sin of *shirk* (idolatry). The worst form of shirk is to worship Jesus Christ as another god, who is somehow subsumed into a higher God that is structured. The absolute unforgiveability of tawhid and shirk may be the only point on which Muslim teachers have completely agreed over the centuries.[275]

This Islamic belief traces back to Muhammad himself. He is said to have taught that the greatest sin is shirk. Below it comes the killing of one's child and treating parents in an inhuman way. Further below comes adultery and bearing false witness (though *taqiyya*, which is to conceal belief in Islam when in imminent danger, might actually be rewarded, see H17). Another tradition cites the prophet as having enumerated several deadly sins: shirk, magic, murder, robbing orphans, usury, apostasy, and slander against faithful women.

---

[275] Smith and Haddad, p.22.

How will these acts of obedience and disobedience be measured? Allah will use the great *mizan*, or balance, on the day of judgment.[276]

Three elements might alleviate Allah's judgment on each person that comes before him: his mercy, human repentance, and intercession.

First, Allah is *al-Rahman al-Rahim*, the Merciful and Compassionate. He is the one who can forgive all sins except shirk (Surah 4:48).

Second, the Qur'an frequently mentions repentance (*tawba*), from the perspectives of both the individual sinner who repents, and Allah who accepts his repentance. However, last minute repentance made on one's deathbed is not effectual. On the contrary, it will result in a severe punishment.[277]

Third, some passages in the Qur'an leave room for the possibility of intercession, which is intervention by another on the sinner's behalf. This may be exercised by Allah himself. Also authorized to intercede on occasion are angels (Surah 53:26), true witnesses (Surah 43:86), and those who have made a covenant with Allah (Surah 19:87).[278]

The Muslim should strive for a pure faith (*iman*) in their hearts. That may convince Allah to be merciful, and earn his or her entrance into paradise. We covered the five constituent elements of iman in section H00 (Surah 2:177): faith in Allah, in his angels, in his messengers, in his books, and in the Last Day or day of judgment.[279]

Besides iman, one cannot be a true Muslim outside of the community (*ummah*, see H02, H24-C5). The ummah is the vehicle for individual salvation. Participation in the collective life of the ummah is vital in the balance. By doing so, a person can make progress toward perfection, which might also gain him or her entrance into paradise.[280]

Despite all these mitigating factors, the Hadiths tell us that the end result of the questioning will be overwhelmingly negative. "'Who are the mission for the (Hell) Fire?' Allah will say, 'Out of each thousand, take

---

[276] Smith and Haddad, p.23.
[277] Smith and Haddad, p.24-25.
[278] Smith and Haddad, p.26.
[279] Smith and Haddad, p.27.
[280] Smith and Haddad, p.29.

out 999.'" With these numbers, the Hadiths predict scant mercy from Allah. During his lifetime, Muhammad reiterated that at the final judgment: "from Yajuj and Majuj nine-hundred ninety-nine will be taken out and one from you. You Muslims (compared to the large number of other people) will be like a black hair on the side of a white ox, or a white hair on the side of a black ox." Allah will count 999 of each thousand of humanity to be no better than the evil ones of Yajuj and Majuj.[281]

This is devastating, especially since only decades before this, the Mahdi and 'Isa ibn Maryam had brought all the inhabitants of the earth into the glorious domain of a world-wide Islamic government. It is also a warning to the 25% of the world's population (at the time I write this book) who count themselves as Muslims.[282] The final judgment will determine that the overwhelming number of Muslims have been false or inadequate throughout the centuries.

After saying these words, which were inspired by Allah, Muhammad was aghast. He wished out loud that this stark ratio would be changed. Instead of one thousandth, may it be one quarter, or one third, or even better, one half of mankind to be saved from the hell fire. In the end, his listeners could only say, *Allahu Akbar*, "Allah is greatest."

The Hadiths also tell us that the majority of the 999 will be women. However, the exact proportion of women to men is not given.

What is the ultimate fate of Shaytan, known as Iblis? In the section on Main actors of the end-time Hadiths, I mentioned that in the Qur'an, Surah 38:85, Allah promised to someday "surely fill up hell with you and whoever follows you from among them, all together." Surah 26:91-95 is the fulfillment of this fate. After the death and resurrection of all creatures, Allah will pronounce judgment on all those human beings counted as lost due to their grievous error – as well as "the whole hosts of Iblis together." Whereas Allah will extend a small measure of slight

---

[281] Abu Rahma, *Who and where are the Yajuj and Majuj (Gog and Magog)? Has their barrier been broken?,* https://qurananswers.me/2016/03/04/who-and-where-are-the-gog-and-magog/, March 4, 2016.
[282] https://en.m.wikipedia.org/wiki/List_of_religious_populations, accessed February 17, 2024.

and uncertain mercy to those identifying as Muslims, he will extend none to Iblis and the shaytans. *Allahu Akbar.*

Surah 15:43-44 of the Qur'an describes *jahannam* (hell) as having seven gates, each for its appointed class. Based upon this surah, among Islamic theologians in the centuries after Muhammad,

> the idea developed that the (hell) Fire consists of seven layers, each descending one an abode of increasing torment …
>
> the purgatorial fire [*jahannam*] for Muslims;
> the flaming fire [*laza*] for Christians;
> the raging fire [*hutama*] for Jews;
> the blazing fire [*sa 'ir*] for Sabaeans;
> the fierce fire [*jahim*] for the Magi;
> the scorching fire [*saqar*] for idolaters;
> and the abyss [*hawiya*] for hypocrites.[283]

Finally, a white-colored ram will be brought forth. It will be recognized as death itself by all those who just passed through the judgment. Some of them will be in paradise, but most of them will be in hell. They will all be told that "there is an everlasting living for you and no death." This reiterates that eternal existence awaits all. Those in hell will not be able to escape it by another death, either in terms of nothingness, or annihilation.

Scattered throughout the Qur'an are details on the tortures of hell:

> Its flames crackle and roar (Surah 25:14) *[misquoted, it is actually S 25:12]*, it has fierce, boiling waters (Surah 55:44), scorching wind, and black smoke (S 56:42-43); it roars and boils as if it would burst with rage (S 67:7-8). The people of hell are sighing and wailing, wretched (S 11:106), their scorched skins are constantly exchanged for new ones so they can taste torment anew (S 4:45) *[actually 4:46]*, they drink festering water and though death appears on all sides they cannot die (S 14:16-17), people are linked together in chains of 70 cubits (S 69:30-32) wearing pitch for clothing and fire on their faces (S 14:50), boiling water will be poured over their heads, melting their insides as well as their skins, and hooks of iron will drag them back should they try to escape (S 22:19-21). To these terrifying details the Hadiths could only add more elaboration and more specifics.[284]

---

[283] Smith and Haddad, p.85.
[284] Smith and Haddad, pp.85-86.

Revelation. We have reached the end of the thousand-year kingdom. It is time for God's final judgment, upon all those who have not yet come before him. (Already judged and welcomed into heaven are those of the "first resurrection" which occurred at the end of the tribulation in 20:5 K43, made up of the tribulation martyrs and Old Testament believers. Also in heaven are the church believers who were resurrected and raptured before the tribulation, in K13).

A throng of colossal dimensions is now gathered. The vast majority of this crowd are the non-believers who ever lived. During their lifetimes, most of them did not seek God. Others refused his offer of salvation. The souls of all these people have been waiting in the intermediate location of *hades* (20:13). To prepare them for the judgment throne and for eternal existence afterward, God gives each one a resurrected body (20:5).

Revelation does not mention the final judgment of the believers who lived during the millennium. Evidently, they are resurrected and come before God at this time.

Now, with all human beings gone from the world, the entire physical creation is extinguished: "from [God's] presence earth and heaven fled, and no place was found for them" (20:11). Time itself is suspended.

This is the cosmic dissolution by fire that was prophesied by Peter:

> 2 Peter 3:10 But the day of the Lord will come like a thief, in which the heavens will pass away with a roar and the elements will be destroyed with intense heat, and the earth and its works will be discovered.

A great white throne appears, beyond space and time (20:11). We know that Jesus Christ sits on it, from this prophecy in the book of Matthew:

> Matthew 25:31 "But when the Son of Man comes in His glory, and all the angels with Him, then He will sit on His glorious throne."

Before this white throne, books are opened, which record the events of every person's life (20:12). Christ, with his authority as the son of God, will judge each one by what they had done (20:13):

> Romans 14:10b For we will all appear before the judgment seat of God.
> 14:11 For it is written: "As I live, says the Lord, to Me every knee will bow, And every tongue will give praise to God."
> 14:12 So then each one of us will give an account of himself to God.

What account will people give of their lives before God? They might believe their reliance on a religion or ideology will be sufficient for this moment. Perhaps their belief system has taught that bad works will be outweighed because they disputed Christ being the son of God, or helped to persecute Christians that followed him. Or maybe they lived a noncommittal life, and believe that their friends can explain that they are relatively good. In both cases, they are saying that God should be satisfied by the measure of their works.

But the God of the Bible does not measure works with a balance. He measures them on a scale. Even one sinful work that registers on the scale will result in your doom, because "all have sinned and fall short of the glory of God" (Romans 3:23). Your sinful works will be weighed according to God's perfect standard of righteousness, as expressed in the ten commandments (Exodus 20:3-17):

1. You shall have no other gods before me.
2. You shall not make for yourself a carved image.
3. You shall not take the name of the LORD your God in vain.
4. Remember the Sabbath day, to keep it holy.
5. Honor your father and your mother.
6. You shall not murder.
7. You shall not commit adultery.
8. You shall not steal.
9. You shall not bear false witness against your neighbor.
10. You shall not covet.

In his life on earth, Jesus never broke any of these commandments, not even in thought.[285] Only he is qualified to pay the penalty of sin on behalf of others.

The non-believers who died at the end of the tribulation put their hope in the woman of Babylon, or the beast, or perhaps a lesser leader who attempted to operate autonomously during the seven years, or in themselves. The woman and the beast both opposed Christ. Though they disagreed with each other, each one gloried in their own system of anti-commandments. By them they justified killing those who did not comply.[286]

The throng of non-believers will unfortunately also include Old Testament Jews who claim they acceptably followed God's law. The prophet Ezekiel prophesied that God would not allow these prideful Israelites into his millennial kingdom. Neither will they be allowed entrance to the new earth that is coming. This contrasts with those Old Testament Jews who put their trust in God's promised Messiah (K43):

> Ezekiel 20:38 and I will purge from you the rebels and those
> who revolt against Me; I will bring them out of the land
> where they reside, but they will not enter the land of Israel.
> So you will know that I am the Lord.

God sees all these self-justifying people as what they really are, by thought if not in deed: the cowardly, the faithless, the detestable, murderers, the sexually immoral, sorcerers, idolaters, and liars (21:8).

But the followers of Jesus come before his throne humbly. They know that they are unworthy to gain heaven based on the merits of their works. Their appeal is based on something else entirely – faith. The object of this faith is the one sent by God, the one who did the greatest work of all time:

> John 6:28 Therefore they said to Him, "What are we to do, so
> that we may accomplish the works of God?"
> 6:29 Jesus answered and said to them, "This is the work of
> God, that you believe in Him whom He has sent."

---

[285] Dave Johnson, *Jesus and the Ten Commandments*, March 4, 2018, https://christchurchvaldosta.org/sermon-jesus-ten-commandments-march-4-2018/.
[286] In the case of the woman see for example 17:2, 18:13, 18:23 in K20. For the beast and false prophet, see 13:4, 7-8, 10 in K23 and 13:12, 14 in K24.

Eternal life in heaven is granted, not to those who seem to have earned it, but to those who place their faith in the Christ. He sacrificed his blameless life on the cross to pay for their sins:

> John 15:13 Greater love has no one than this, that a person will lay down his life for his friends.

In addition to the long stream of people being judged before the white throne, there are also observers. They include the church saints. They have been living in heaven for at least one thousand plus seven years since the time they were raptured and resurrected (K13). Also observing are the tribulation martyrs and Old Testament believers. They have been on earth for a thousand years in glorified bodies, assisting Christ in governing the millennial kingdom (20:6 K44). They made their testimonies of faith at the post-tribulation judgment (20:4 K43). Joining them in watching are the millennial believers who have just been resurrected. We can surmise that they have already given their accounts of faith, and judged favorably.

All these observers are granted the privilege of being Christ's assistants, as the non-believers are tried and consigned to punishment (2:26). This privilege was part of the promise that Jesus made much earlier in John's vision (K09). He made it not just to the church of Thyatira, but to believers of all ages. Another reward they will receive is to be granted "the morning star" (2:28). This description usually refers to Venus when it appears before the dawning of a new day. But we will learn in 22:16 K50 that this morning star is Jesus himself. After he presides over the white throne judgment, the new heaven and new earth will be the dawn of eternity.

The godless are now judged. This completes Christ's prophecy that speaks of the separation of the goats, which began to be fulfilled in K43:

> Matthew 25:32 And all the nations will be gathered before Him [the Son of man]; and He will separate them from one another, just as the shepherd separates the sheep from the goats;

The verdict upon the wicked is shame, damnation, and everlasting contempt:

> Daniel 12:2 And many of those who sleep in the dust of the
> ground will awake, these to everlasting life, but the others to
> disgrace and everlasting contempt.

> John 5:28 Do not be amazed at this; for a time is coming
> when all who are in the tombs will hear His voice,
> 5:29 and will come out: those who did the good deeds to a
> resurrection of life, those who committed the bad deeds to a
> resurrection of judgment.

After the verdict is announced, the sentence passed down is the second
death (21:8). A passage from 2nd Thessalonians describes the
consequence of this second death, namely, eternal exclusion from the
presence of the Lord:

> 2 Thessalonians 1:7b when the Lord Jesus will be revealed
> from heaven with His mighty angels
> 1:8 in flaming fire, dealing out retribution to those who do
> not know God, and to those who do not obey the gospel of
> our Lord Jesus.
> 1:9 These people will pay the penalty of eternal destruction,
> away from the presence of the Lord and from the glory of
> His power.

The unrepentant are now cast into the eternal lake of fire (20:15). This
is the everlasting fire of hell, which the angel promised in 14:10-11 K42.
Jesus warned two thousand years ago that it would come:

> Matthew 13:41 The Son of Man will send forth His angels,
> and they will gather out of His kingdom all stumbling blocks,
> and those who commit lawlessness,
> 13:42 and they will throw them into the furnace of fire; in
> that place there will be weeping and gnashing of teeth.

In hell, the non-believers will join the antichrist beast, the false
prophet, and Satan, who acted through them. Many embraced Satan's
lies. But after all the opportunities they had during their lifetimes to
seek the true God, their fate is now sealed. They will see Satan for who
he really is, the ultimate beast. This will fulfill the prophecy made
earlier in Revelation: they will be in the presence of the beast who "was,
and is not, and is about to come up out of the abyss and go to
destruction" (17:8 K02). They will continue in existence forever in this
place of eternal perdition.

Hell is terrible to think about. But for unbelievers, it will be a real place. It makes the love of God even more surprising, for those who embrace it will be brought to heaven.

For believers, death and hades are cast into the lake of fire (20:14). They will never again torment the coming new creation. The days of evil are done, forever.

Comparison. In both the Hadiths and the Bible, the earth is destroyed by fire in the lead up to the final judgment.

In the Hadiths this happens with flames that spread from Yemen, and drive people to the place of assembly. Then occurs the final extinction of all living beings in the *fana'*. The dead are then transmogrified.

In the Bible, the sequence is reversed. All unbelievers are resurrected from the dead, to appear before the great white throne beyond space and time. Afterward, the action of fire occurs. "Earth and heaven [are] fled, and no place was found for them" (20:11). "The heavens will pass away with a roar and the elements will be destroyed with intense heat" (2 Peter 3:10). Thus occurs the dissolution of the entire universe.

A universal destruction is a common factor in both accounts. The Bible explains that this is needed to renew the material creation, and fulfill its hope that the sinful human race be purified:

> Romans 8:19 For the eagerly awaiting creation waits for the revealing of the sons and daughters of God.
> 8:20 For the creation was subjected to futility [decay], not willingly, but because of Him [God] who subjected it, in hope
> 8:21 that the creation itself also will be set free from its slavery to corruption into the freedom of the glory of the children of God.

As we shall see in the next section (K47), the result will be a new creation that is cleansed and released from its subjection to decay.

In Muslim tradition, not only do all earthly creatures die, but so do the angels as well. In contrast, nowhere does the Bible describe the future death of angels, who are spirit creatures. This is because God created spirits to live forever. The souls of both humans (spirit-soul creatures) and animals (soul creatures) became subject to death after the human race fell into sin. Thus, animals suffer death, and all of material creation decays, because of man's sin.

In both accounts, all humanity that has not already been judged comes before the divine throne for the last and final judgment. It will decide the fate of each person: heaven or hell. In the Hadiths, the people are questioned one-by-one. In the Bible, the books that record the lives of every person are opened (20:12). Then they are asked to give an account of their works, or their testimony of faith (Romans 14:12).

Who sits on the throne? In the Hadiths and the Qur'an, it is Allah of course. But the Bible tells us it will be Jesus Christ, the son of God, fully God and fully man, who will sit on the throne and be our judge (Matthew 25:31). This is an abomination to Islam, which teaches that Allah can only be a unitary God, and that to worship Jesus as the son of God is the unforgiveable and highest form of idolatry *(shirk)*.

The criteria for judgment are very different in the two accounts. In the Islamic tradition, Allah will use the great *mizan*, or balance, and will also selectively allow for intercession from a limited set of angels and people. That is what is known of the process of judgment. But the criteria for judgment are uncertain. They were not enumerated in the revelation written into the Qur'an, or in Muhammad's oral sayings. The disagreements of Islamic scholars lead to the conclusion that the criteria are subjective and arbitrary. But all agree that one is saved by a positive measure of his or her works on Allah's balance. Or perhaps by Allah's mysterious and arbitrary will, as expressed in the Arabic word *Inshallah*, "if Allah wills."

Given this uncertainty as to which sins deserve hell, it is surprising that the Hadiths give certainty that only a tiny number of people, one out of a thousand, will be accepted into paradise. The remaining 999 will be rejected, though many of them would profess to be Muslim. "From Yajuj and Majuj nine-hundred ninety-nine will be taken out and one from you. You Muslims (compared to the large number of other people) will be like a black hair on the side of a white ox, or a white hair on the side of a black ox."

The Bible agrees that only a minority of people will be saved, though nowhere does it give numbers or percentages. In the words of Jesus himself:

> Matthew 7:13 "Enter through the narrow gate; for the gate is wide and the way is broad that leads to destruction, and there are many who enter through it.
> 7:14 For the gate is narrow and the way is constricted that leads to life, and there are few who find it."

In Islam, the sins that definitely lead to hell are *shirk* (idolatry), and questioning *tawhid*, the doctrine that Allah is the one and only god who is absolutely and utterly alone. To believe that Jesus is the son of God violates both of these principles, with no room for doubt.

It is interesting that in the Bible almost the exact opposite is taught. Unbelievers who expect their good works to out-balance their bad ones, will not enter heaven. Instead, they will certainly end up in hell. The pure and righteous God will not allow them to bring their sinful nature into heaven. But the repentant man, woman, or child, who puts their trust in Christ, the son of God, to takes their place before God the Father – that person shall be embraced and welcomed into heaven.

The role of intercession is also present in the Bible. But it has a much different perspective.

Some people seek after God, who will be found by them:

> Proverbs 8:17 "I love those who love me; And those who diligently seek me will find me."

But the seeking is also in the opposite direction, and involves the intercession of Jesus. He is the good shepherd who intercedes and seeks after them, even though they might be the only one who is lost, while 99 already follow him:

> Matthew 18:12 "What do you think? If any man has a hundred sheep, and one of them goes astray, will he not leave the ninety-nine on the mountains, and go and search for the one that is lost?
> 18:13 And if it turns out that he finds it, truly I say to you, he rejoices over it more than over the ninety-nine that have not gone astray.

> 18:14 So it is not the will of your Father who is in heaven for
> one of these little ones to perish."

The ratio of one out of 99 in this parable gives great hope for salvation, in contrast with the 999 out of a thousand who are destined for hell in the Hadiths.

The terror of Muslims at the time of the final judgment will be palpable. Will they be in the 999 who will be condemned by Allah to hell? How can they know if their devotion to him is compromised by inconsistency in their life and actions? Only a tiny number will be found acceptable, even out of the Mahdi's warriors. The vast majority will be sent into the hell fire of eternal death. And how does one know if Allah, the unapproachable one, has not changed his will? Perhaps he now demands an even higher level of obedience than what they knew during their lifetime. To the end of their days before they die on earth, they will not find certainty as to whether they will survive the mizan on the day of judgment.

Can you be certain of your salvation, if you trust in Jesus? The testimony of the Bible is that yes, you can be sure, for the following reasons.

You are born again to a new life by the will of God:

> John 1:12 But as many as received Him, to them He gave the
> right to become children of God, to those who believe in His
> name,
> 1:13 who were born, not of blood, nor of the will of the flesh,
> nor of the will of a man, but of God.
>
> 1 John 5:1 Everyone who believes that Jesus is the Christ has
> been born of God, and everyone who loves the Father loves
> the child born of Him.

Salvation is not by your flawed works, but by faith:

> Ephesians 2:8 For by grace you have been saved through
> faith; and this is not of yourselves, it is the gift of God;
> 2:9 not a result of works, so that no one may boast.
>
> 2 Corinthians 5:7 for we walk by faith, not by sight.

> 1 John 5:4 For whoever has been born of God overcomes the
> world; and this is the victory that has overcome the world:
> our faith.

You are adopted into God's family. As a son or daughter, God will
discipline and correct you in a loving way, if you bring your sins to him
in repentance:

> Romans 8:15 For you have not received a spirit of slavery
> leading to fear again, but you have received a spirit of
> adoption as sons and daughters by which we cry out, "Abba!
> Father!"

> 1 John 1:9 If we confess our sins, He is faithful and righteous,
> so that He will forgive us our sins and cleanse us from all
> unrighteousness.

> Hebrews 12:9 Furthermore, we had earthly fathers to
> discipline us, and we respected them; shall we not much
> more be subject to the Father of spirits, and live?

Your sins, past, present, or future, cannot cancel out your salvation,
even at the time of God's fearsome throne of judgment:

> John 10:28 "and I [Jesus] give them eternal life, and they will
> never perish; and no one will snatch them out of My hand.
> 10:29 My Father, who has given them to Me, is greater than
> all; and no one is able to snatch them out of the Father's
> hand.
> 10:30 I and the Father are one."

You have new life in Christ, in which you will grow in your love for him,
and seek his righteousness.

> John 14:15 "If you love Me, you will keep My
> commandments."

To summarize, the Bible says you can be sure that you are going to
heaven, because you are born of God. This is not of your own making,
but by the faith that God has gifted you. He promises to be with you
forever.

Who will be sent to hell? In Islam it is the people of Yajuj and Majuj, the
infidels, the innovators, and the Muslims whose lives were inadequate.
Together they measure to 999 out of 1,000 people, or 99.9% of

humanity. In the Bible it is the unbelievers, who have refused to put their faith in Christ, and have not given their lives to him.

What happens to the Islamic Shaytan at the time of final judgment? The Hadiths do not discuss this topic. This is not surprising, if Satan was instrumental in their production. He would want to draw attention away from Revelation's pointed account of his demise in the eternal lake of fire (20:10 K45). We are left only with the words of Surah 26:94-95, that in addition to those people "thrown headlong into the (Fire),- they and those straying in Evil," with them will also be "the whole hosts of Iblis together."

In the Bible, the tortures of hell are mostly left to one's imagination. The Qur'an almost takes pleasure in enumerating them, which would certainly be true if Satan was involved in inspiring its words.

What will be the fate of death itself? The hadith speaks of a white ram at the end, who symbolizes death. Allah uses it to remind everyone, most of whom are now in hell, that death will not be an option for them to escape the torments that await.[287]

Revelation ends the day of judgment on a far more optimistic note. It says, "death and hades were thrown into the lake of fire" (20:14). This is the greatest encouragement for those who follow Jesus into heaven. They know that never again will they be tormented by sin and death.

---

[287] For an exhaustive treatment of the torments of hell in the Qur'an and the hadiths, see Raj Kripalani, *Judgment and Hell in Islam*, Conservative Theological Journal Volume 8 No. 23, Tyndale Theological Seminary, March 2004, p. 106ff, digested in *Judgment and Hell Behind the Veil of Islam*, https://learntheology.com/islam-judgment-hell.html, accessed March 9, 2024.

K47 :
The new heaven, the new earth, and the new Jerusalem

21:1 Then I saw a new heaven and a new earth; for the first heaven and the first earth passed away, and there is no longer any sea.

21:9 Then one of the seven angels who had the seven bowls, full of the seven last plagues, came and spoke with me, saying, "Come here, I will show you the bride, the wife of the Lamb."

21:10 And he carried me away in the Spirit to a great and high mountain, and showed me the holy city, Jerusalem, coming down out of heaven from God,

21:2 And I saw the holy city, new Jerusalem, coming down out of heaven from God, prepared as a bride adorned for her husband.

21:11 having the glory of God. Her brilliance was like a very valuable stone, like a stone of crystal-clear jasper.

21:12 It had a great and high wall, with twelve gates, and at the gates twelve angels; and names were written on the gates, which are the names of the twelve tribes of the sons of Israel.

21:13 There were three gates on the east, three gates on the north, three gates on the south, and three gates on the west.

21:14 And the wall of the city had twelve foundation stones, and on them were the twelve names of the twelve apostles of the Lamb.

21:15 The one who spoke with me had a gold measuring rod to measure the city, its gates, and its wall.

21:16 The city is laid out as a square, and its length is as great as the width; and he measured the city with the rod, twelve thousand stadia; its length, width, and height are equal.

21:17 And he measured its wall, 144 cubits, by human measurements, which are also angelic measurements.

21:18 The material of the wall was jasper; and the city was pure gold, like clear glass.

21:19 The foundation stones of the city wall were decorated with every kind of precious stone. The first foundation stone was jasper; the second, sapphire; the third, chalcedony; the fourth, emerald;

21:20 the fifth, sardonyx; the sixth, sardius; the seventh, chrysolite; the eighth, beryl; the ninth, topaz; the tenth, chrysoprase; the eleventh, jacinth; the twelfth, amethyst.

> 21:21 And the twelve gates were twelve pearls; each one of
> the gates was a single pearl. And the street of the city was
> pure gold, like transparent glass.
> 21:3 And I heard a loud voice from the throne, saying,
> "Behold, the tabernacle of God is among the people, and He
> will dwell among them, and they shall be His people, and
> God Himself will be among them."
> 3:12 The one who overcomes, I will make him a pillar in the
> temple of My God, and he will not go out from it anymore;
> and I will write on him the name of My God, and the name of
> the city of My God, the new Jerusalem, which comes down
> out of heaven from My God, and My new name.

Revelation. When God created the universe, there was no one on hand
to watch, not even the angels.

But when God re-creates a new heaven and a new earth after the
judgment of the white throne, there will be an entire throng of
onlookers. It will consist of the holy angels, and the resurrected born-
again believers of all ages, now in glorified bodies. These observers are
somehow outside of space and time.

The God who miraculously created the universe in six days is certainly
able to create a new one, in the manner that he chooses. This one
cannot possibly be corrupted.

John's vision of a new heaven and new earth, here near the end of
Revelation, is in fulfillment of prophecies in both the New and Old
Testament:

> 2 Peter 3:13 But according to His promise we are looking for
> new heavens and a new earth, in which righteousness
> dwells.

> Isaiah 65:17 "For behold, I create new heavens and a new
> earth; And the former things will not be remembered or
> come to mind."
> 66:22 "For just as the new heavens and the new earth,
> Which I make, will endure before Me," declares the Lord ,
> "So will your descendants and your name endure."

Revelation adds a great amount of detail to these passages. John sees
that in this future creation, "there is no longer any sea" (21:1). This is
likely not referring to oceans, lakes, or inland seas, because John also

sees that there will be a river of life (22:2 K49). Instead, the word "sea" takes us back to the verses that start the Bible:

> Genesis 1:1 In the beginning God created the heavens and the earth.
> 1:2 And the earth was a formless and desolate emptiness, and darkness was over the surface of the deep, and the Spirit of God was hovering over the surface of the waters.

The idea of "sea" is hidden above in the Hebrew word for "deep," or *tehom*. It means the deep sea, the primeval ocean, the waters below, the abyss or the grave. In the context of God's act of creation, the sea is therefore the uncreated state, which is the chaos, the nothingness that was prior. Verse 21:1 is encouraging us that there will never again be chaos in heaven or on earth.

How can heaven become new? The Bible tells us of three heavens that God created, which are part of our current experience.[288] They help us consider how the new heaven will be better.

The *first heaven* that we know consists of the clouds and the atmosphere. In the six-day creation account, it is called the *expanse*: "Let there be lights in the expanse of the heavens to separate the day from the night" (Genesis 1:14). It is also called the *sky*, as in "the floodgates of the sky were opened. The rain fell upon the earth for forty days and forty nights" (Genesis 7:11-12).

The *second heaven* is beyond our atmosphere. It consists of the sun, moon, solar system, milky way, and all the galaxies and astronomical objects to the edges of space. In the Bible it is called "the heavenly lights" (Jeremiah 8:2), and "the heavens" (Matthew 24:29).

The *third heaven* is mentioned by the apostle Paul, who knew someone (probably himself) who was there briefly, and then came back to earth:

> 2 Corinthians 12:2 I know a man in Christ, who fourteen years ago—whether in the body I do not know, or out of the body I do not know, God knows—such a man was caught up to the third heaven.

---

[288] *How many heavens are there and what is the third heaven Paul speaks of in 2 Corinthians 12*, http://letusreason.org/Biblexp130.htm, accessed July 29,2022, no author.

This third heaven is not within the dimensions that are familiar to us, or even in the extra dimensions that are hypothesized by particle physicists and string theory. It is the home of the holy angels who are loyal to God. There they have access to his presence (Isaiah 6:1-3). The resurrected church believers will join them there after the rapture.

The third heaven is also called the *heaven of heavens* (Deuteronomy 10:14), the *highest heaven* (1 Kings 8:27), and *paradise* (2 Corinthians 12:3).

Here, at the beginning of the new age, God replaces these three heavens with the new heaven (21:1). He breaks down the wall of separation between the second and third heavens, which came about because of mankind's fall into sin. In the new universe, there will be no more sin. Therefore, all who inherit the new heaven will have access to the presence of God, people as well as angels. In the new heaven, we shall see God face-to-face (22:4 K49). The separation between the second and third heavens will be gone.

It is my belief that there will be no limiting speed of light to prevent us from traveling to the furthest reaches of the new heaven. We will be able to follow the pathway that John sees next in the vision – the one blazed by the new Jerusalem which descends from heaven to earth (21:10,2).

The new Jerusalem is more than a fabulous city. It is a bride adorned for her husband, Jesus (21:9,2); the Alpha and the Omega (21:6 K49); the beginning and end of all things (1:8 K00). It will be the dwelling place of God (21:3), his new home. It is the eternal city that Abraham looked forward to:

> Hebrews 11:9 By faith he [Abraham] lived as a stranger in
> the land of promise, as in a foreign land, living in tents with
> Isaac and Jacob, fellow heirs of the same promise;
> 11:10 for he was looking for the city which has foundations,
> whose architect and builder is God.

In the upcoming section, it will welcome another bride: the church saints of the rapture (19:7-9 K48).

The new Jerusalem is the perfected version of the Jerusalem known to us from the Bible.

The Old Testament describes how the Jews went to Jerusalem to offer sacrifices, for the atonement of their sins before God. In the New Testament, it is where Jesus offered himself as the final sacrifice. Before he went to the cross, Jesus told his disciples where he was going afterward:

> John 14:1 "Do not let your heart be troubled; believe in God, believe also in Me.
> 14:2 In My Father's house are many rooms; if that were not so, I would have told you, because I am going there to prepare a place for you.
> 14:3 And if I go and prepare a place for you, I am coming again and will take you to Myself, so that where I am, there you also will be."

After his death, resurrection and ascension into heaven, Jesus is saying that he will go to prepare a place. That place is the new Jerusalem. He has been getting it ready for the past two thousand years, and will certainly attend to it during the time of the tribulation and the millennial kingdom. Since we know that heaven and earth was extinguished at the time of the great white throne (20:11 K46), the new Jerusalem will somehow be preserved apart from them.

When God creates the new heaven, the new Jerusalem will be taken there. We know that must happen, because the city will descend from the new heaven to the new earth. John saw this in his vision (21:10,2). Undoubtedly all of God's people and the angels will see it descend in real time.

Next, God makes a point of giving John a detailed view of the central city of the new universe.

The new Jerusalem will be fully three dimensional. It is pictured to be 12,000 stadia in length and width, but also in height (21:16). That would be a cube the size of Japan on each side. It is left to our imagination how the third dimension of the city is laid out, how it will accommodate millions or billions of people within, and how travel will occur to other locations on the new earth and to the new heaven.

The city will be characterized by the number twelve, which is frequently used to signify completion or perfection in the Bible. It will have a wall that is twelve times twelve cubits high (21:17). The wall will have twelve foundations, with the names of the twelve apostles on them (21:14), garnished with twelve precious stones (21:19-20). It will have twelve gates, made of twelve immense pearls (21:21), with twelve angels posted at them. Each gate will have the name of one of the twelve tribes of Israel written on it (21:12).

The new Jerusalem will glisten with an ongoing bright light, like that of a jasper stone (21:11). The city and its streets will be made, perhaps partially, of clear gold (21:18, 21). Its transparency will magnify the glory of God. It will be a city of unmatched splendor.

The born-again believers have been outside space and time, in their glorified bodies. They have been watching the unveiling of the new heaven and new earth, and the descent of the new Jerusalem from heaven to earth. Now they are transported from their vantage point to the new creation. Never shall they go out of it (3:12). The trials and temptations of this present life will be no more. Instead, they are now welcomed into this city of God. He will dwell among them. They shall be his people, and he shall be their God (21:3).

There was no temple during the New Testament period. The temple of the tribulation period was compromised by the beast and the false prophet (see K23 and K24). And the temple of the millennial kingdom served to memorialize what Jesus did on the cross (see K44).

We shall see that in the new Jerusalem, once again there will be no temple (21:22 K49). Christ himself will be that temple. The followers of Jesus will be its pillars (3:12). He will write upon them the name of the new Jerusalem. And Jesus will also write on them his name: the name of God.

Thus will be fulfilled a passage from the book of Hebrews, addressed to all pilgrims who ever journeyed through this life to someday meet Jesus in the celestial city:

> Hebrews 12:22 But you have come to Mount Zion and to the
> city of the living God, the heavenly Jerusalem, and to
> myriads of angels,

> 12:23 to the general assembly and church of the firstborn
> who are enrolled in heaven, and to God, the Judge of all, and
> to the spirits of the righteous made perfect,
> 12:24a and to Jesus, the mediator of a new covenant.

The inauguration of the new heaven, new earth, and the new Jerusalem is the backdrop for what comes next – the marriage feast celebrating Christ and his bride, the church of God.

Comparison. In the Bible, heaven and earth will be dissolved as a prelude to the great white throne judgment. They will be replaced by a new heaven, a new earth, and a new Jerusalem. The followers of Jesus will live in this new universe. Those who reject him are relegated to live their eternal existence forever apart from God, in hell.

In the Hadiths, the earth is similarly destroyed at the end of time, according to Sunan Ibn Majah 4081 (H46): "then the mountains will turn to dust and the earth will be stretched out like a hide."[289] But no hadith tells that the earth will be reconstituted. This is confirmed by the fact that the earth is missing in the Islamic description of the afterlife. In the Qur'an and the Hadiths, we are only told of the garden of paradise, or *Jannah* (see H49). Though it has some earthly characteristics, it is better thought of as the Islamic version of heaven.

Muslims who survive Allah's judgment inherit paradise. All other people are sent to hell. But a new earth and a new Jerusalem are not found in the Islamic conception of the afterlife.

---

[289] According to Smith and Harrar, p.71, *Kitab ahwal al-qiyama* (*Book of the Phases of Resurrection*), speaks of the dissolution of heaven in addition to earth. However, this work seems to be the speculation of an anonymous Islamic theologian in the centuries after Muhammad, and the mention of heaven being destroyed is not attributable to the prophet. There is no mention in the Qur'an or the hadiths of heaven being reconstituted by Allah in the end time. Therefore it is better to discount the speculation that heaven is destroyed at some point.

K48 :
The marriage supper between Christ and all his church, rejoiced over by believers of other ages

19:5 And a voice came from the throne, saying, "Give praise to our God, all you His bond-servants, you who fear Him, the small and the great."
19:6 Then I heard something like the voice of a great multitude and like the sound of many waters, and like the sound of mighty peals of thunder, saying, "Hallelujah! For the Lord our God, the Almighty, reigns.
19:7 Let's rejoice and be glad and give the glory to Him, because the marriage of the Lamb has come, and His bride has prepared herself."
19:8 It was given to her to clothe herself in fine linen, bright and clean; for the fine linen is the righteous acts of the saints.
19:9 Then he said to me, "Write: 'Blessed are those who are invited to the wedding feast of the Lamb.'" And he said to me, "These are the true words of God."
19:10 Then I fell at his feet to worship him. But he said to me, "Do not do that; I am a fellow servant of yours and your brothers and sisters who hold the testimony of Jesus; worship God! For the testimony of Jesus is the spirit of prophecy."

Comparison. In section H34, we learned that Allah does not relate to faithful Muslims as individuals. Instead, Allah accepts them based on their solidarity with the Muslim community, the *ummah*.

The true God of the Bible is different. He knows each one of his people, and looks after them tenderly. He instructs them to come together for worship and to care for one another, as Christ cares for them. In the age between the cross and the rapture, this assembly is called the church. It is composed of thousands of churches across the world. But they stand together to comprise the holy universal church.

The vision of Revelation has now come to the ultimate destiny of the church – the marriage supper of the lamb. There is no such future gathering between Allah and the ummah that is portrayed in either the Hadiths or the Qur'an.

Revelation. The marriage supper of the Lamb and his bride appears somewhat before the end of John's vision. But it is best placed at this point of the prophetic timeline. The Lamb of God is of course, none other than Jesus Christ:

> John 1:29 The next day he [John the Baptist] saw Jesus coming to him, and said, "Behold, the Lamb of God who takes away the sin of the world!"

A great number of well wishers are at this wedding feast (19:6-7).

Who is the bride, and who are the onlookers? Undoubtedly, the onlookers include the holy angels. The question becomes, are all of God's people the bride of Christ, or is it only a certain number of them?

To answer this, let us consider who were the observers who watched as the new heaven, the new earth, and the new Jerusalem were unveiled in the previous section. An analysis of Bible history would indicate that there will be believers from six different ages present. Each age began with a miracle of global consequences.

The first age was initiated with creation, and extended to the worldwide flood of Noah's day. The first man, Adam, lived for 930 years (Genesis 5:5), which covered most of that period. All his descendants were familiar with his record of God creating heaven, the earth, and paradise, and Adam and Eve's fateful act of disobedience resulting in the human race's fall into sin. Some among them believed in God's promise – that a future seed of the woman would crush Satan (Genesis 3:15). This was the first prophecy of a Messiah. But the vast majority living during that time did not seek to please God. They brought the world to a state of great corruption and immorality, deserving of judgment and the flood.

The believers of the second, post-flood age, were few. Noah lived among them, so they were familiar with what he and his family went through. Yet only some of them also put their trust in the God who preserved Noah's family in the ark, to likewise save them from a future earth-wide catastrophe.

The believers of the third age were mostly from the Jews. God chose them to be his people, and to be the nation out of which the Messiah would eventually come. Every year on the Passover, they celebrated

God's miraculous parting of the Red Sea, and their ancestors' deliverance from Egypt. They knew that he gave them the ten commandments from Mount Sinai, shrouded in fire and smoke. While the other nations were worshipping imaginary gods, God sent a series of prophets to proclaim his word to Israel. The first was Moses starting about 1440 BCE, the last was Malachi around 440 BCE, a period of almost exactly one thousand years. During this time, Israel was God's theocratic kingdom. Numerous prophecies of the coming Messiah were given to the Jews in the Old Testament. He would be God's son.

The faith of the believers of these first three ages was greater in a sense than the faith of those who came afterward. It was based on God's promise of a future deliverer, and not in a Messiah who had already come. Their additional reward will be resurrection and entry into the millennial kingdom, as hinted at in the prophecies of Ezekiel 37:11-12, and Isaiah 11:12 (see K43). The ancient believers who lived before the first coming of Christ, will have the honor of assisting him after his second coming, when he reigns as king. Their subjects will be those who live and die during the millennium in their natural bodies. The thousand years will be a far superior version of God's thousand-year theocratic Old Testament kingdom.

The believers of the fourth age belong to the church of the New Testament era. Some among their first generation walked with Jesus. They watched him give up his sinless life on the cross, and were absolutely amazed when they saw him resurrected from the dead in a glorified body. These eyewitnesses recounted these events in the four gospels of the New Testament. Their testimony rang with truth to those who met them, and to succeeding generations of believers for two thousand years afterward. The church has since spread to almost every people group and language spoken throughout the world. They worship in many individual congregations. Most do so in church buildings. Others meet secretly in house churches, because of persecutions that have occurred in every century. The true believers of the churches have come to faith by the power of Christ, and by the example of others whose lives have been transformed for the better. God's family in the church is far more numerous than the believers from before and after the flood, or from Old Testament Israel. I write this book to you from this church age.

The believers of the fifth age turned away from the antichrist to the true Jesus during the tribulation. Though God had evacuated all church believers from their midst, the violence and persecution unleashed by the godless world government has driven them to find truth in the pages of the forbidden Bible, and in the person of Jesus Christ which the Bible portrays. Many were hunted down and killed as martyrs, but were then resurrected by God. Then they entered into Christ's millennial kingdom. Also entering in are other believers who came to faith during the tribulation, but somehow survived it.

The believers of the sixth age are those born during the millennium. They interacted with Jesus, the king of kings, in person. Their age was unlike all the earlier ones, because also present were resurrected believers who had been martyred during the tribulation, or who had lived before Christ's first coming. The faith of the millennial believers was tested at the end of the thousand years, when Satan was released and made his final bid for supremacy. Sadly, some of the millennials turned rogue, and followed Satan to his doom (K45). Only the true believers are present in the current scene.

The gathering of the saints of all ages must be at this place in the timeline, after the unveiling of the new heaven and earth, because it is the first time when all are together.

The seventh and final age will be eternity, which awaits all these believers in Christ (see K49).

Now that we have reviewed all those present at the marriage supper of the Lamb, who among them will be his wife (19:7)? The rejoicing onlookers, mentioned in 19:6-7, could be limited to the angels. If true, the wife then represents all believers who ever lived.

But a case can be made that the wife is the church of the New Testament age. In the New Testament, an analogy is made between husbands loving their wives, and Christ loving his church:

> Ephesians 5:23 For the husband is the head of the wife, as Christ also is the head of the church, He Himself being the Savior of the body.
> 5:24 But as the church is subject to Christ, so also the wives ought to be to their husbands in everything.

> 5:25 Husbands, love your wives, just as Christ also loved the church and gave Himself up for her,
> 5:26 so that He might sanctify her, having cleansed her by the washing of water with the word,
> 5:27 that He might present to Himself the church in all her glory, having no spot or wrinkle or any such thing; but that she would be holy and blameless.

If the bride is the New Testament church, then the onlookers are the various saints of all other ages, along with the angels.

The new Jerusalem, a shining city like no other, becomes the backdrop to the end-of-time marriage supper of the Lamb and his church.

The bride is seen dressed "in fine linen, bright and clean." The linen represents the righteous deeds of the saints (19:8), which they have done on behalf of their Lord and Savior, in gratitude for their salvation. All who are called to take part in the supper celebration are especially blessed (19:9).

John is so stunned by this vision that he bows down to the one speaking to him, mistaking it as the voice of God. But the speaker comes forth and identifies himself as an angel, and fellow servant of the Lord. He redirects him to worship God instead. The angel adds that "the testimony of Jesus is the spirit of prophecy" (19:10). This encourages believers of all ages to look for Christ expectantly within the prophecies of the Bible.

The millennial kingdom was the almost perfect recapitulation of Old Testament Israel. And so, eternity will be the absolutely perfect recapitulation of the New Testament church. Eternal life in all its glory now opens to all the children of God, including those from the church, and those from all the other ages.

21:22 I saw no temple in it, for the Lord God the Almighty and the Lamb are its temple.
21:23 And the city has no need of the sun or of the moon to shine on it, for the glory of God has illuminated it, and its lamp is the Lamb.
21:24 The nations will walk by its light, and the kings of the earth will bring their glory into it.
21:25 In the daytime (for there will be no night there) its gates will never be closed;
21:26 and they will bring the glory and the honor of the nations into it;
21:27 and nothing unclean, and no one who practices abomination and lying, shall ever come into it, but only those whose names are written in the Lamb's book of life.
22:1 And he showed me a river of the water of life, clear as crystal, coming from the throne of God and of the Lamb,
22:2 in the middle of its street. On either side of the river was the tree of life, bearing twelve kinds of fruit, yielding its fruit every month; and the leaves of the tree were for the healing of the nations.
22:3 There will no longer be any curse; and the throne of God and of the Lamb will be in it, and His bond-servants will serve Him;

(Entering paradise) Nor will they there taste Death, except the first death; and He will preserve them from the Penalty of the Blazing Fire, as a Bounty from thy Lord! That will be the supreme achievement. (Surah 44:56-57)

(The gates of paradise) Paradise has eight gates, and one of them is called Ar-Raiyan through which none will enter but those who observe fasting.[290]

Anybody who spends a pair of something in Allah's Cause will be called from all the gates of Paradise, "O Allah's slave! This is good." He who is amongst those who pray will be called from the gate of the prayer (in Paradise) and he who is from the people of Jihad will be called from the gate of Jihad, and he who is from those who give in charity (i.e. Zakat) will be called from the gate of charity, and he who is amongst those who observe fast will be called from the gate of fasting, the gate of Raiyan.[291]

(The levels of paradise) They are in varying gardens in the sight of Allah, and Allah sees well all that they do. (Surah 3:163)

Not equal are those believers who sit (at home) and receive no hurt,

---

[290] Narrated by Sahl bin Sa`d, *Sahih al-Bukhari 3257*, Vol. 4, Book 54, Hadith 479, https://sunnah.com/bukhari:3257, accessed March 9, 2024.
[291] Narrated by Abu Huraira, *Sahih al-Bukhari 3666*, Vol. 5, Book 57, Hadith 18, https://sunnah.com/bukhari:3666, accessed March 9, 2024.

22:4 they will see His face, and His name will be on their foreheads.

22:5 And there will no longer be any night; and they will not have need of the light of a lamp nor the light of the sun, because the Lord God will illuminate them; and they will reign forever and ever.

21:4 and He will wipe away every tear from their eyes; and there will no longer be any death; there will no longer be any mourning, or crying, or pain; the first things have passed away.

21:5 And He who sits on the throne said, "Behold, I am making all things new." And He said, "Write, for these words are faithful and true."

21:6 Then He said to me, "It is done. I am the Alpha and the Omega, the beginning and the end. I will give water to the one who thirsts from the spring of the water of life, without cost.

21:7 The one who overcomes will inherit these things, and I will be his God and he will be My son."

and those who strive and fight in the cause of Allah with their goods and their persons. Allah hath granted a grade higher to those who strive and fight with their goods and persons than to those who sit (at home). Unto all (in Faith) Hath Allah promised good: But those who strive and fight Hath He distinguished above those who sit (at home) by a special reward. (Surah 4:95)

The seven heavens and the earth, and all beings therein, declare His glory: there is not a thing but celebrates His praise; And yet ye understand not how they declare His glory! Verily He is Oft-Forbear, Most Forgiving. (Surah 17:44)[292]

So He completed them as seven firmaments in two Days, and He assigned to each heaven its duty and command. And We adorned the lower heaven with lights, and (provided it) with guard. Such is the Decree of (Him) the Exalted in Might, Full of Knowledge. (Surah 41:12)

(The landscape of paradise) In it (the Garden) are rivers of water incorruptible; rivers of milk of which the taste never changes; rivers of wine, a joy to those who drink; and rivers of honey pure and clear. In it there are for them all kinds of fruits; and Grace from their Lord. (Surah 47:15b)

There is a tree in Paradise (so huge) that a fast (or a trained) rider may travel: for one hundred years without being able to cross it.[293]

(Life in paradise) For them will be Gardens of Eternity; beneath them rivers will flow; they will be adorned therein with bracelets of gold, and they will wear green garments of fine silk and heavy brocade: They

---

[292] See also mention of seven heavens in Surah 2:29.
[293] Narrated by Abu Sa'id, *Sahih al-Bukhari 6553*, Vol. 8, Book 76, Hadith 559, https://sunnah.com/bukhari:6553, accessed March 9, 2024.

will recline therein on raised thrones. How good the recompense! How beautiful a couch to recline on. (Surah 18:31)

To them will be passed round, dishes and goblets of gold: there will be there all that the souls could desire, all that their eyes could delight in: and ye shall abide therein (for eye). (Surah 43:71)

There no sense of fatigue shall touch them, nor shall they (ever) be asked to leave. (Surah 15:48)

The first group of people who will enter Paradise … will not urinate, relieve nature, spit, or have any nasal secretions. Their combs will be of gold, and their sweat will smell like musk. The aloes-wood will be used in their centers … All of them will look alike and will resemble their father Adam (in stature), sixty cubits tall.[294]

He who would get into Paradise (would be made to enjoy such an everlasting) bliss that he would neither become destitute, nor would his clothes wear out, nor his youth would decline.[295]

(Disputes in paradise) The gates of Paradise are opened on Mondays and Thursdays, and forgiveness is granted to every man who does not associate anything with Allah, except for a man between whom and his brother there is rancor. Command will be given that they should be given respite till they conciliate.[296] *(sahih)*

(Angels in paradise) In the case of those who say, "Our Lord is Allah", and, further, stand straight and steadfast, the angels descend on them (from time to time): "Fear ye not!" (they suggest), "Nor grieve! but receive the Glad Tidings of the Garden (of Bliss), the which ye were promised. "We are your protectors in this life and in the Hereafter: therein shall ye have all that your souls shall desire; therein shall ye have all that ye ask for! "A hospitable gift from one Oft-Forgiving, Most Merciful!" (Surah 41:30-32)

(The Mahdi in paradise) He is the Mahdi on earth and the Mahdi in heaven.[297] *(athar)*

---

[294] Narrated by Abu Huraira, *Sahih al-Bukhari 3327*, Vol. 4, Book 55, Hadith 544, https://sunnah.com/bukhari:3327, accessed March 9, 2024.

[295] Narrated by Abu Huraira, *Sahih Muslim 2836*, Book 40, Hadith 6802, https://sunnah.com/muslim:2836, accessed March 9, 2024.

[296] Narrated by Abu Hurairah, *Sunan Abi Dawud 4916*, Book 42, Hadith 4898, https://sunnah.com/abudawud:4916, accessed March 9, 2024.

[297] `Abdullah ibn `Amr (companion of Muhammad), narrated by Abu Yusuf, in al-Hakim and Nu`aym ibn Hammad, quoted in `Ibn Izzat p.26; also referenced in al-Hafidh Jalal ad-Din as-Suyuti, *al-'Arf al-Wardi fi Akhbar al-Mahdi* (*The Rose Scented Perfume: On the*

(Access to Allah in paradise) Indeed, the righteous will be amid Gardens and rivers, at the Seat of Honour in the presence of the Most Powerful Sovereign. (Surah 54:54-55)

When the people of Paradise enter Paradise, a caller shall call out: Indeed you have a promise with Allah. They will say: Did he not whiten our faces, save us from the Fire, and admit us into Paradise? They will say: Indeed. Then the Veil shall be lifted. He said: So, by Allah, He did not grant them anything more beloved to them than looking at Him.[298] *(sahih)*

When the inhabitants of *Jannah* enter Jannah (paradise), Allah, the Glorious and Exalted, will say to them: Do you wish me to give you anything more? They will reply: Have You not made our faces bright? Have You not brought us into Jannah and delivered us from the Hell' And Allah will remove the Veil. The (dwellers of Jannah) will feel that they have not been awarded anything dearer to them than looking at their *Rabb* (master).[299]

(Spouses and families from previous life) Gardens of perpetual bliss: they shall enter there, as well as the righteous among their fathers, their spouses, and their offspring: and angels shall enter unto them from every gate (with the salutation). "Peace unto you for that ye persevered in patience! Now how excellent is the final home!" (Surah 13:23-24)

(Pure heavenly maiden wives in paradise)
And gladden the minds of those who believe and do good deeds, with prophecy that there would certainly be for them gardens underneath which the rivers flow. Every time they are served there with the food of a fruit, they will say, "This is what we had been served with before," and they will be given things resembling one another. And for them therein will be mates purified. And therein will they have lives eternal. (Surah 2:25, Mohammad Shafi translation)

Indeed, We will have perfectly created their mates, making them virgins, loving and of equal age, for the people of the right. (Surah 56:35-38, Clear Qur'an)

And full-bosomed maidens of equal age. (Surah 78:33)

Reports of the Mahdi), no.168, translated by Bismillahi Rahmani Raheem, Assalamu Alaikum, https://ghayb.com/2019/01/al-arf-al-wardi-fi-akhbar-al-mahdi-by-imam-jalal-ad-din-as-suyuti/, accessed March 11, 2024.
[298] Narrated by Suhai, *Jami` at-Tirmidhi 2552*, Vol. 4, Book 12, Hadith 2552, https://sunnah.com/tirmidhi:2552, accessed March 9, 2024.
[299] Narrated by Suhaib, *Riyad as-Salihin 1896*, https://sunnah.com/riyadussalihin:1896, accessed March 9, 2024.

> And Houris (chaste virgins) with wide lovely eyes, like guarded pearls, as a reward for what they used to do (good deeds). (Surah 56:22-24, Abdul Hye translation)

> In them will be (Maidens), chaste, restraining their glances, whom no man or Jinn before them has touched; Then which of the favours of your Lord will ye deny? Like unto Rubies and coral. (Surah 55:56-58)

> Fair (Companions) … in (goodly) pavilions … reclining on green Cushions and rich Carpets of beauty. (Surah 55:70,72,76)

> They shall recline on couches arranged in rows; and We shall wed them with beautiful Houris (damsels) (Surah 52:20, M. Farook Malik translation)

> So; and We shall join them to fair women with beautiful, big, and lustrous eyes. (Surah 44:54)

> *(Number of wives in paradise)* The first batch to enter Paradise will appear like the moon of a night that is full. The second will appear like the color of the most beautiful star in the sky. Each man among them shall have two wives, each wife wearing seventy bracelets, with the marrow of their shins being visible from behind them.[300] *(sahih)*

> The martyr receives six good things from Allah: he is forgiven at the first shedding of his blood, he is shown his abode in paradise, he is preserved from the punishment in the grave, he is kept safe from the greatest terror, he has placed on his head the crown of honour a ruby of which is better than the world and what it contains, he is married to seventy-two wives of the maidens with large dark eyes, and is made intercessor for seventy of his relatives.[301]

> The believer shall be given in paradise such and such strength in intercourse …. He will be given the strength of a hundred.[302] *(hasan)*

Hadiths. Here we collect verses on the topic of paradise from the Qur'an, and from the words spoken by Muhammad as recorded in the Hadiths. From these original sources, we will find that the information can be grouped into a number of headings. By far the largest disclosure

---

[300] Narrated by Abu Sa'eed Al-Khudri, *Jami` at-Tirmidhi 2522*, Vol. 4, Book 11, Hadith 2522, https://sunnah.com/tirmidhi:2522, accessed April 20, 2024.

[301] Narrated by Al-Miqdam b. Ma'dikarib, *Mishkat al-Masabih 3834*, https://sunnah.com/mishkat:3834, accessed March 9, 2024.

[302] Narrated by Anas, *Jami` at-Tirmidhi 2536*, Vol. 4, Book 12, Hadith 2536, https://sunnah.com/tirmidhi:2536, accessed April 20, 2024.

is on the topic of the *houris*, the heavenly maiden companions that will be given to Muslim men.

Entering paradise. The judgment of all humanity in front of Allah took place in section H46. He used the great *mizan*, or balance, to determine the level of Islamic devotion of each person. The Hadiths tell us that 999 out of each thousand were found inadequate. They were sent to hell. This included many who their whole life regarded themselves as Muslims.

But those who have earned their way to paradise, by total submission to Islam, will not taste a second death in hell. With this great achievement, they will be preserved from the blazing fire. They will be allowed to enter *jannah*, the gardens of paradise.

The gates of paradise. Each true Muslim will be called into paradise from one of its eight gates. Some of them are mentioned in the Hadiths at the top of this section. Here is the full listing of gates according to Islamic scholars:

> - *Baabus Salaah.* Those who were consistent in observing their *Salaah* (worship) will be granted entry through this door.
> - *Baabul Jihad.* Those who participated in Jihad will be granted entry through this door.
> - *Baabus Sadaqah.* Those who frequently gave *Sadaqah* (charity) will be admitted into Jannah through this door.
> - *Baabur Rayyaan.* The people who constantly observed the fast will be granted entry through this door.
> - *Baabul Hajj.* Those who observe the pilgrimage will be admitted through this door.
> - *Baabul Kaazimeenal Ghaiz Wal Aafina Anin Naas.* This door is reserved for those who suppress their anger and pardon others.
> - *Baabul Aiman.* This door is reserved for the entry of such people who are saved from reckoning and chastisement (The *Awliyah* or faithful ones).
> - *Baabuz Zikr.* Those who excessively remembered Allah will be admitted through this door.[303]

The levels of paradise. The Qur'an tells us that "not equal are those believers who sit (at home) and receive no hurt, and those who strive

---

[303] *Day 23 - The 8 gates and 8 levels of Jannah,*
https://30daysoframadan.tumblr.com/post/162020655247/day-23-the-8-gates-and-8-levels-of-jannah, accessed April 14, 2024

and fight in the cause of Allah with their goods and their persons."
Thus, "they are in varying gardens in the sight of Allah." Islamic
theologians understand this to mean that Allah will assign each person
to a different level, a different heaven, based on their attainment.
Though there are Hadiths that speak of a hundred grades,[304] in several
passages of the Qur'an the number of heavens is said to be seven.
Scholars have scoured the Qur'an to determine each heaven. The proof
texts, and the typical Islamic theological interpretations for each
heaven,[305] are as follows:

- *Jannat-al-Adan* (Surah 9:72), the eternal place. Repentant Muslims
  received there will find the greatest acceptance from Allah. Its gardens
  will provide every blessing. Under them flow rivers that fulfill every
  desire.
- *Jannat-al-Firdaws* (Surah 18:107), the exquisite garden. It teems with
  diverse plant life, including grapevines. The Hadiths describe it as the
  most prestigious level.[306]
- *Jannat-an-Naim* (Surah 10:9), the garden of delight, with rivers
  flowing beneath them. It is for those with unwavering faith in Allah,
  committed to a life of good works. *Naim* means a prosperous and
  peaceful life, with wealth, welfare and blessings. This level is built of
  iron.
- *Jannat-ul-Mawa* (Surah 32:19), the refuge of brass, or the garden of
  adobe. It is a resting place for devotees and martyrs. It is anchored by
  a lote-tree at the periphery of heaven.
- *Dar-ul-Khuld* (Surah 25:15), the garden of immortality. It is the place
  where one attains eternal life. (This is of course true of the other
  heavens, but is not the primary emphasis in them). It is great
  consolation for those who faced much evil and suffering during their
  earthly lives.

---

[304] For example, "Paradise has one hundred grades, each of which is as big as the
distance between heaven and earth" in *Sunan Ibn Majah* 4331,
https://sunnah.com/ibnmajah:4331, accessed April 14, 2024.

[305] Babar ali, *7 Level Of Jannah in Islam*, September 21, 2023, https://alquran-
edu.com/7-level-of-jannah-in-islam/; *Day 23 - The 8 gates and 8 levels of Jannah*,
https://30daysoframadan.tumblr.com/post/162020655247/day-23-the-8-gates-and-8-
levels-of-jannah, accessed April 14, 2024; Kashif Ali, *7 Heavens in Islam: Seven levels of
Jannah*, May 21, 2023, https://wordofprophet.com/7-heavens-in-islam.

[306] Narrated by Anas, *Mishkat al-Masabih 3809*, https://sunnah.com/mishkat:3809,
accessed April 13, 2024.

- *Dar-ul-Maqaam* (Surah 35:33), the safe place of eternal essence, where all pain, suffering, and weariness are forever gone. There the soul is untouched by toil or external influences.
- *Dar-us-Salam* (Surah 6:127), the abode of well-being, the place of security and peace. It is for those whom Allah chose to walk the straight path. All speech there is *salaam* (peace), free of any negative and evil connotations. There will be no enmity nor hatred among its inhabitants. There Allah will forever be their protector.
- *Illiyyun* (Surah 83:18-20). Some scholars believe this is an eighth heaven, the highest level of Jannah for the most perfect Muslims. It is said to be a place below the throne in the seventh heaven. The illiyyun is also the book that records all the good deeds of believers who are sincere in their faith.

Scholars are not in agreement which of these levels of heaven are higher than others.

The landscape of paradise. The different heavens will be spectacular. They will have rivers of water, rivers of milk, rivers of delicious fruit, and rivers of honey. They will be covered with luxuriant gardens and trees. One of the trees will be so vast that it would take a hundred years to traverse it.

Life in paradise. Existence will be one of unending ease. The followers of Allah will recline on thrones. Fruit will be brought to them, along with anything else they desire. No one will ever become destitute. Nor would their clothes ever wear out.

All people will have eternal youth, and will never grow tired. Everyone will be similar in appearance. They will find themselves to be over 25 meters tall. They will not experience the bodily fluid functions of our present world. Even their sweat will be pleasant, like musk. They will be adorned with golden combs.

The drink of paradise is not like the wine of the present world. It will not intoxicate, nor bring on poor judgment.

Disputes in paradise. When there is contention between the Muslims of paradise, they will be allowed to approach any gate of paradise on Mondays and Thursdays (note the days of the week, which imply day and night in paradise). At the gates, they will receive forgiveness. But if a dispute rises to a level of hatred, they will be commanded to separate until they are ready to be reconciled. The hadith also implies that individuals may go to one of the gates to receive forgiveness, after they have committed an action which is unbecoming to a devotee of Allah.

Angels in paradise. The Muslims of paradise will have the ever-present hospitality of angels as encouragement, so that they will never fear nor grieve. The angels will minister to them, and grant them whatever their souls desire.

The Mahdi in paradise. The same Mahdi, who guided the world to the Islamic silver age of seven years, will also be present in paradise. He will continue there as Allah's foremost representative.

Access to Allah in paradise. Though Allah is wholly transcendent, in some sense his presence will be felt among the inhabitants of paradise. He will lift the veil that separates their vision of him.

Spouses and families from the previous life on earth. The faithful will be reunited with their parents and descendants who have likewise been true to Islam. Muslim scholars believe that Allah will allow those who have been designated to a lower heaven to visit those at higher levels.[307]

Pure heavenly maiden companions in paradise. Now we come to the most prolific topic in the Qur'an and the Hadiths that pertains to paradise – the *houris.*

Surah Rahman (Surah 55) is known as the bride of the Qur'an, because it talks about them in two groups of verses.

The houris are otherworldly maidens, stunningly beautiful in appearance. They are sinless and pure, created by Allah to live in heaven at the end of time. They serve as consorts for Muslim men in paradise. They are described as wed to their partner, but "this does not literally mean that a marriage ceremony is held ... it simply means that the houris will be given to them as a reward for their good deeds."[308]

---

[307] https://quraanteacher.com/unveiling-the-beauty-of-paradise-quran-verses-hadith-about-jannah/, accessed April 17, 2024.

[308] Abu Mahdi, *Houris In The Quran: The Lovely Big-Eyed Maidens Of Paradise,* November 2, 2023, https://islam4u.pro/blog/houris-in-the-quran/.

They will be virgins, of similar age as their men, with very sympathetic and loving dispositions. They are described as shapely, well endowed, with full figures. Their lips are red, like rubies and corals, with wide, lovely black eyes. Their eyes are so distinctive that they are named after them – the full word for houri is *al-hour al-'in*, which refers to the sharp contrast between the whiteness of their eyes and the blackness of their iris.[309]

A houri will be completely dedicated to her man. She will dwell in his pavilion, and recline on green cushions and lovely carpets. Her gaze will not fall on other men.

The number of wives in paradise. Muhammad left no doubt there would be houris for each man in paradise.

What he left unclear was how many houris each would have. Also uncertain is whether men would also be reunited with the wife or wives they had during their lives on earth, or if some other women who earned entrance into paradise would be matched up with them.

Many scholars would say that two wives each will be from among the women of this world, and seventy more wives from among the houris. Seventy is the minimum, and there is no maximum limit. But "there is no sound hadith which specifies the number of houris that the believer will have in Jannah. The scholars are agreed that he will have a minimum of two wives, but they differ as to whether they will be from among *al-hour al-'in* or from among the women of this world."[310]

The math of two earthly wives per man in heaven has difficulty squaring with the prophecy that the majority of the inhabitants of hell will be women (Sahih al-Bukhari 3241 in H46). This prevalence of women in hell is perhaps mitigated by Allah providing an abundance of the heavenly houris, who would be preferable to wives that followed the men during their lives on earth.

The Hadiths that close this section say that martyrs who died in the cause of jihad will definitely receive seventy-two wives from the houris.

----

[309] Ibid.

[310] *https://islamqa.info/en/answers/257509/number-of-huris-a-muslim-will-get-in-jannah,* accessed April 20, 2024.

And each man, whether they be martyrs or not, will be given the strength of a hundred men, so that they will never be lacking for vigor in sexual intercourse with their various wives.[311]

Earthly women in paradise. The Qur'an and the Hadiths do not spell out the fate of Muslim women who enter into paradise. This leaves modern day commentators to wonder whether they also will be given handsome spouses.

The answers they give are based on reasoning and speculation. One male scholar maintains that "women can choose to be with their own husbands, or they can choose to live with another person who inhabits paradise…. however, it must be noted that Allah has created women in such a way that they only like to live with one husband."[312]

Another says "probably women in general might not enjoy 72 males in paradise. We must realize that the likes of men versus women are quite different. Men generally desire women, while women are far more diverse in their desires. Women's nature is to have only one husband so the women in paradise will not wish for multiple husbands and they will not be jealous to complain about their husbands having more than one wife. Assuming otherwise is belittling Allah's justice."[313]

Comparison.

Entering paradise. In the Qur'an and the Hadiths, the Muslims who survived Allah's *mizan* balance are summoned to paradise without any preliminaries. In Revelation, before entering into eternal life, the true believers who lived by faith in the Messiah were first treated to the unveiling of the new heaven, the new earth, and the new Jerusalem, followed by the marriage supper of the Lamb and his bride the church.

---

[311] Muslims will share in the vigor of the perfect Muslim, Muhammad: "According to Anas ibn Malik, the Prophet Muhammad used to visit all eleven of his wives in one night; but he could manage this, as he had the sexual prowess of thirty men." https://wikiislam.net/wiki/Muhammad%27s_Marriages, accessed August 24, 2024.
[312] Abu Mahdi, *Houris in the Quran: The Lovely Big-Eyed Maidens of Paradise,* https://islam4u.pro/blog/houris-in-the-quran/, November 2, 2023.
[313] About Islam Counselor, *72 Virgins for Men, What Do Women Get in Paradise?* November 26, 2018, https://aboutislam.net/counseling/ask-about-islam/72-virgins-men-women-get-paradise/, accessed March 9, 2024.

The gates of paradise. The Islamic paradise is said to have eight gates. True Muslims will enter in through the gate they are called to, the one appropriate to each person's nature.

In Revelation, heaven and earth do not have gates, but as explained in K47, the new Jerusalem will have twelve of them. They will each have the name of a tribe of Israel inscribed, and twelve different angels associated with them. The city will have twelve foundations, each garnished with one of twelve precious stones.

The levels of paradise. Islamic paradise has seven or eight levels. Higher levels are superior to the lower ones. A true Muslim will be summoned to the level earned by the works that he or she performed for Allah while on earth. Since family members and friends will end up on separated levels in the process, Muslim scholars speculate that Allah will allow them to visit one another from time to time.

On the other hand, the eternal age depicted in the Bible consists of three interconnected places: the new heaven, the new earth, and the new Jerusalem, which was brought down from heaven to earth in front of all the resurrected believers. Believers will never be separated from one another, not even for a time.

The Bible speaks of rewards that will be given to individual believers in heaven, based on the good works they did in gratefulness for their salvation:

> 1 Corinthians 3:11 For no one can lay a foundation other than the one which is laid, which is Jesus Christ.
> 3:14 If anyone's work which he has built on it remains, he will receive a reward.

But the nature of the rewards is not spelled out, and certainly does not result in separation from those with a greater or lesser number of them.

In the Islamic version of paradise, even within a given level, there will be men with a greater or lesser number of wives based on their earthly efforts to further Islam.

The landscape of paradise. Both the Muslim paradise and the new Jerusalem of Revelation feature rivers and trees.

In Jannah there are numerous rivers. Some will be of water, and others of various sweet beverages. In certain levels of heaven, they flow under the gardens. One of the trees will be greater than the earth in size, overwhelmingly awesome.

The new Jerusalem, by contrast, will have the river of water of life, and the tree of life straddling it (22:1-2). We will discuss both below.

Life in paradise. The recurring theme in Islamic paradise is indulgence for Muslim men. For Muslim women, the aim will be to please their husbands and to serve them.

We shall see below that in the Bible, the new heaven and the new earth is characterized by the devotion of the people of God to their Almighty Father, and to Jesus their savior. Each person will have the deepest relationship with both of them.

Disputes in paradise. Muslims will go to any of the gates to seek forgiveness from Allah, if they commit a wayward action, or to resolve disputes with each other. This makes it evident that the resurrected Muslims of paradise will not be perfect. They will still sin occasionally against each other, and against Allah's edicts.

The Christ followers of Revelation's eternal age will be like Jesus and the angels – they will not even be able to sin. We will discuss this below.

Angels in paradise. Both the Islamic prophecies and the Bible speak of angels in the eternal age. They will be pleased to see men and women in their resurrection.

The Mahdi in paradise. Though the Mahdi is the rightly guided one who brought the seven-year silver age of Islam, the Qur'an and the Hadiths do not mention his presence in the gardens of paradise. We only have the words of Muhammad's companions in an athar, that the Mahdi is the rightly guided one in heaven, as he was on earth. This hints at a prominent role for the resurrected Mahdi during the eternal age.

His counterpart in eternity in Revelation is Jesus Christ. We shall see below that he is the all in all of eternity. He will reign forever. All people of all centuries who trusted in him for their eternal life shall have intimate relation with Christ the son of God.

Access to Allah in paradise. In comparison, the Islamic version of eternity does not involve a direct relationship between Allah and those Muslims who are adequate to enter paradise. There is no description of faithful ones serving Allah in his courts. There are some Hadiths that speak of them "looking at him" in paradise. Some Islamic commentators try to magnify this by referring to verses from the Qur'an where believers seek the presence or countenance of Allah in the context of prayer (Surah 13:22), or when asking for guidance (Surah 30:38). But Islam is averse to the kind of relationships that the Bible speaks of, between the children of God and their loving Father, and with Jesus their savior.

Spouses and families from the previous life on earth. Muslims expect to dwell in the same level of paradise as their worthy ancestors and descendants. This suggests that the level of Islamic devotion of a Muslim is determined by bloodline, similar to caste membership among Hindus.

The hadith also says that Muslims will be reunited with their spouse, if they were also allowed into heaven. This is not surprising, given the dominance of men over their wives in Muslim culture, per the example of Muhammad the perfect Muslim.

In the Bible, bloodlines do not determine one's future. Salvation is an individual matter between the believer and God.

Pure heavenly maiden companions in paradise. In both the Qur'an and the Hadiths there is a heavy emphasis on wives as providers of ongoing delight in paradise, almost to the point of obsession. The graphic description of houris leaves no doubt that they will be heavenly objects of sexual arousal for men.

In Islam, women are assigned an inferior status to men. In paradise, they will remain inferior to men. And the women resurrected from earth will not be as desirable as the houris, whose origin is in heaven.

In the Bible, marriage on earth is between one man and one woman, in holy matrimony. In this relationship, sanctioned by God, the two become one flesh (Genesis 2:24). The marriage relationship is meant to be pure, and not to be diverted by external objects of sexual arousal, whether they be multiple wives, illicit affairs with other women and men while married, prostitutes, pornographic media, or fantasizing about mates in heaven.

In the biblical description of heaven, there is definitely no class of specially created female beings, assigned to their men as consorts. Instead, Jesus had this to say about marriage in heaven:

> Matthew 22:30 For in the resurrection they neither marry nor are given in marriage, but are like angels in heaven.

The only marriage mentioned in Revelation is in connection with the marriage supper of the Lamb, between Christ and his church (19:7-9 K48).

The main relation of all believers will be with Christ and God the Father, and then with one another.

The number of wives in paradise. The greatest role model for Muslims, Muhammad, was married to at least fifteen women (see K08). He looked for continual satisfaction by collecting wives during his life, in the confident expectation that in the life to come he would graduate past the limitations of earthly wives to the pleasures of the heavenly houris.

The perfect houris that await Muslim men in the afterlife certainly distracts some of them away from a "one flesh" relationship with a wife in this world. In addition, lust for sexual pleasure in paradise has always been a driver for jihadist martyrs.

Earthly women in paradise. In Jannah, Muslim women will continue their subordinate status to men. They will serve them, while being eclipsed in affection by the perfect and vivacious houris. The best they can hope for is that Allah will also satisfy their pleasures.

In the Bible, though husbands are heads of their earthly marriages, wives have equal status spiritually before God. But in heaven there will not be marriages, only friendships. Both men and women will find ultimate fulfillment in a beautiful relationship with their creator God and savior.

Revelation. Christ came to earth in his second coming to rule over the millennial kingdom. It was a preview of the eternal age. The beneficiaries of his rule included the resurrected tribulation martyrs and believers from the Old Testament age, all in glorified bodies and without sin. But it also included sinners who made the kingdom less than perfect: survivors of the tribulation, and the children born to them during the thousand years.

After that, Christ the King of kings now rules the absolute perfection that is the eternal age, on a new earth, in a new heaven. He rules from the new capital of the cosmos, the new Jerusalem.

Here, near the end of the book of Revelation, we get a glimpse of eternal life in this new universe.

The Jerusalem of the Old Testament, the tribulation, and the millennial kingdom, featured a temple in its central precincts. It served as an intermediate place, where priests acting as representatives made supplication on behalf of people to the invisible God of the universe.

But there will be no temple and no intermediaries in the new Jerusalem. The Lord God Almighty and his son the Lamb will be the temple (21:22). The shadows of things to come (Hebrews 10:1) are replaced with the reality of eternity. All believers will now have direct access to God the Father and Jesus Christ. The faithful will be able to see them with their very own eyes, not the eyes of some substitute artificial intelligence, or some heavenly creature created to resemble them:

> Job 19:26 "Even after my skin is destroyed, Yet from my
> flesh I will see God,
> 19:27a Whom I, on my part, shall behold for myself, And
> whom my eyes will see, and not another."

The new Jerusalem will have no sun or moon for light (21:23, 22:5). Christ will be the light. This will be the ultimate fulfillment of his words to his disciples:

> John 8:12 Then Jesus again spoke to them, saying, "I am the
> Light of the world; the one who follows Me will not walk in
> the darkness, but will have the Light of life."

Before eternity, Jesus was the light of the world in a spiritual sense. Now he will also be the light in a literal sense, in some wonderful way that believers will discover.

There will never again be enemies that would threaten the city of God. The city gates will therefore always be open. Moreover, the city will not have night (21:25). There will be no need for sleep, because people granted glorified bodies will never get tired.

A magnificent throne will be the centerpiece of the city. God and his son the Lamb will frequently make their appearance there in a public manner, with great joy before all (22:3). From it, a unique river with "water of live" will constantly flow through the middle of the city (22:1, 21:6). Even urban planners will be dazzled. We know from the Bible that Jesus is the source of that living water:

> John 4:10 Jesus replied to her [the woman at the well of Samaria], "If you knew the gift of God, and who it is who is saying to you, 'Give Me a drink,' you would have asked Him, and He would have given you living water."
> 4:14 "But whoever drinks of the water that I will give him shall never be thirsty; but the water that I will give him will become in him a fountain of water springing up to eternal life."

This living water will be the fountain of eternal life.

The tree of life of the original garden of Eden (Genesis 2:9) disappeared from history after Adam and Eve were expelled for their sin. But now, in the sinless universe, it makes its reappearance (22:2). The vision that John sees has it straddling the river of water of life. It will produce twelve kinds of fruit every month. Its leaves are for "the healing (Greek: *therapeian*) of the nations." Since there is no sickness or death in eternity, this must mean that the tree of life will be the source of health for the re-created universe.

The garden of Eden was created perfectly, but in it Adam and Eve were able to sin, and able not to sin (Latin: *posse peccare posse non peccare*). They abused this ability, and chose to disobey God. All of us ever since have been not able not to sin (*non posse non peccare*). But the testimony of the Bible is that if you accept Jesus as your Savior and repent of your sins, he sends his Holy Spirit to live in your heart. The Spirit helps you to be able not to sin *(posse non peccare)*.

In the new heaven and new earth, the resurrected Jesus-followers will go beyond that. Like the angels, you will be not able to sin *(non posse pecarre)*. You will know everlasting innocence. There will be never again be temptation – no lie, no corruption, no sin, no curse (22:3); no more death, tears, or sorrow; no more crying or pain (21:4).

Christ makes all things new (21:5). The new heaven and new earth will be created perfect, and it will remain perfect.

Those who, before all time, were written into God's book of life (21:27), will be thrilled to be in his presence. They shall see God and be with him, as his sons (21:7) and his daughters, from many nations (21:24), owning his name (22:4). They will inherit all things (21:7), becoming heirs of God alongside his son the Christ (Hebrews 1:2).

This is the extent to which Revelation describes the new Jerusalem, the new earth, and the new heaven. God does not give us more detail. But in Romans 8:19,21 he does hint that life will flourish so much more than it does now, because the new creation will not be subject to decay (see the discussion in K46). Believers in Jesus will learn the joys of living eternal life.

Jesus Christ, the Alpha and Omega, the beginning and end of all things, declares "it is done" (21:6). The splendors of eternal life will be his reward to all those who belong to him.

K50 :
Concluding revelations and exhortations

22:6 And he said to me, "These words are faithful and true"; and the Lord, the God of the spirits of the prophets, sent His angel to show His bond-servants the things which must soon take place.

22:7 "And behold, I am coming quickly. Blessed is the one who keeps the words of the prophecy of this book."

22:8 I, John, am the one who heard and saw these things. And when I heard and saw them, I fell down to worship at the feet of the angel who showed me these things.

22:9 And he said to me, "Do not do that; I am a fellow servant of yours and of your brothers the prophets, and of those who keep the words of this book. Worship God!"

22:10 And he said to me, "Do not seal up the words of the prophecy of this book, for the time is near.

22:11 Let the one who does wrong still do wrong, and the one who is filthy still be filthy; and let the one who is righteous still practice righteousness, and the one who is holy still keep himself holy."

22:12 "Behold, I am coming quickly, and My reward is with Me, to reward each one as his work deserves.

22:13 I am the Alpha and the Omega, the first and the last, the beginning and the end."

22:14 Blessed are those who wash their robes, so that they will have the right to the tree of life, and may enter the city by the gates.

22:15 Outside are the dogs, the sorcerers, the sexually immoral persons, the murderers, the idolaters, and everyone who loves and practices lying.

22:16 "I, Jesus, have sent My angel to testify to you of these things for the churches. I am the root and the descendant of David, the bright morning star."

22:17 The Spirit and the bride say, "Come." And let the one who hears say, "Come." And let the one who is thirsty come; let the one who desires, take the water of life without cost.

22:18 I testify to everyone who hears the words of the prophecy of this book: if anyone adds to them, God will add to him the plagues that are written in this book;

22:19 and if anyone takes away from the words of the book of this prophecy, God will take away his part from the tree of life and from the holy city, which are written in this book.

22:20 He who testifies to these things says, "Yes, I am coming quickly." Amen. Come, Lord Jesus.

22:21 The grace of the Lord Jesus be with all. Amen.

Revelation. The Hadiths and the Qur'an do not have a divinely inspired afterword at the end of the human history timeline. But Revelation does. At the end of this last book of the Bible, God provides concluding revelations and exhortations.

John, the apostle who received all the visions of Revelation, was so overcome that he "fell down to worship at the feet of the angel who showed me these things." But the angel refuses him, saying "do not do that! ... worship God" (22:8-9). We can similarly become consumed in trying to stitch together the prophecies of the vision. Let us not forget that God's purpose behind them is to draw us into a saving relationship with his son Jesus.

The voice of the angel gives way to the voice of Christ (22:12). Jesus again speaks in the first person, as he did early in the vision when he dictated the letters to the seven churches (chapters 2 and 3, K06 through K12). "I am the Alpha and the Omega, the first and the last, the beginning and the end" (22:13). God is pleased to speak to us through his son, who is one with him in divinity and glory.

By his words to John, Jesus encourages all believers alive during the church age that he will soon return. "Behold, I am coming quickly" (22:7,12,20). "The time is near" (22:10). These words remain true at the time that I write this book, though written almost two thousand years ago. In K13 we learned that this looks forward to the rapture. That will be his first return, when he will spare his church from the terrors of the tribulation.

"I am the root and the descendant of David, the bright morning star" (22:16). Christ will appear like the morning star, to take his followers, both the living and the dead, to a new day in heaven. All of them will be completed with glorified bodies.

"Behold, I am coming quickly, and My reward is with Me, to reward each one as his work deserves" (22:12). For those believers who live by faith and not by works, this reward will be heaven. But for those who refuse the son and stand by their own works, they will experience a first death, and a second in hell.

"Blessed are those who wash their robes, so that they will have the right to the tree of life, and may enter the city by the gates" (22:14). With these words, Jesus calls on all believers to proceed past the step of faith to a life of holiness, to be one of his disciples.

The Bible offers this free gift of Christ at any time, for "now is a day of salvation" (2 Corinthians 6:2). To anyone who wishes it, God will answer their prayers by sending his Holy Spirit to live in their hearts. No matter what future troubles come your away, you will have peace with God and a spring of joy flowing through you. You will ultimately be welcomed into heaven as another of his adopted children.

But Jesus also reminds us that outside heaven there is a burning lake of fire. It will be the ultimate destination of those who spurn him and his commandments. "Outside [heaven] are the dogs, the sorcerers, the sexually immoral persons, the murderers, the idolaters, and everyone who loves and practices lying" (22:15). In eternity, people will never be able to cross the boundary between hell and heaven: "let the one who does wrong still do wrong, and the one who is filthy still be filthy; and let the one who is righteous still practice righteousness, and the one who is holy still keep himself holy" (22:11).

It is notable that in this final part of the book of Revelation, an angel gives express instructions from God regarding its transmission to future generations. "Do not seal up the words of the prophecy of this book" (22:10). This emphasizes how important it is to convey the vision in writing to future generations. Undoubtedly the Holy Spirit led John to perfectly recall all the details of the vision, and commit it to pen and ink. The church fathers in the early centuries followed John's lead. They recognized that Revelation was rightfully part of the New Testament and the Bible, God's inerrant word.

God also warns us to handle the words of the book very carefully. In seeking to understand the vision, we should not add to it (22:18), or take away (22:19). This is clear instruction to take the words of Revelation literally wherever possible. We should not skip over or interpret away portions of the book. We should also be watchful not to embellish the book by forcing preconceived notions or interpretations onto it. The church of my time should take heed. It should be wary of false ideologies that subvert the prophecies of the book to their own ends. We must also question those who teach that the prophecies are purely symbolic, who say their scholarly words are better than God's own word to explain them. "Blessed is the one who keeps the words of the prophecy of this book" (22:7).

We have not encountered the word church since the letters to the seven churches early in the book, in chapters 2 and 3 (K06 through K12). It was not mentioned during the tribulation, or the millennial kingdom. But afterward, the church finally reappeared as the bride of Christ and wife of the Lamb, in the marriage supper of the new Jerusalem (19:7-9 K48).

In this concluding section, we have one last mention of the church. "I, Jesus, have sent my angel to testify to you of these things for the churches" (22:16). Revelation begins and ends with the church, the body of Christ (Ephesians 4:12). It is such a unique gift of blessing to us of the New Testament age.

Whether you read it before the rapture, during the tribulation, or as someone born into the millennial kingdom; whether you are a Muslim, Hindu, Buddhist, spirit worshipper, atheist, progressive, or Marxist – the prophecies of Revelation offer you to trust your eternal life to Jesus Christ. He invites you to do so. He will be your Lord and savior. "Let the one who is thirsty come; let the one who desires, take the water of life without cost" (22:17). If you do, the grace of the Lord will be with you (22:21).

Conclusion

We have reached the end of our journey. We have compared the prophetic timeline of Revelation against the end-time Hadiths. On their own, the Hadiths defy comprehensive attempts to place them into a coherent sequence. My book has shown that it is possible to do so, with the help of a literal reading of Revelation.

This is a very telling point. By itself it indicates that the book of Revelation and the Christian Bible have a position of preeminence. This can be traced to the Bible's richness, structure and coherence. It is in keeping with its claim to be the inerrant word of God.

Before we began our journey, I challenged you to choose one of five alternatives for interpreting the prophecies. Let us conclude by revisiting them.

The Mahdi will rule for seven years: "He will be the glorious one sent by Allah to establish Sharia across the world. The Muslim end-time prophecy is the true one. Allah is supreme, and it is blasphemy to say that he has a Jewish son who is a god. Islam is the true religion, and the falsehoods of Christianity and the Jews will be smashed once and for all." Satan, that great student of the Bible, has been formulating and guiding this scheme ever since he read the book of Revelation.

The question posed by my book is: are there Ancient Prophecies of the Mahdi that were given before Muhammad?

From Satan's point of view, the answer is yes. His plan is to hijack the prophecies of the Bible given by his enemy, Jesus Christ. He will morph the characters within them into others more to his liking. The main one would be the Mahdi, the future savior of Islam. He will be backed by billions of people who have accepted Islam, which Satan inspired in its founding.

Satan has always looked for moments in history to maximize his advantages and find a way to sideline God. Since he cannot see into the future, he must be the opportunist. He and his demonic cohorts therefore work by suggestion and deception. The result is that huge streams of humanity willingly and unknowingly are channeled to their doom.

One alternative where Satan has heavily invested effort is to try to bring forth the Mahdi. As the final caliph, he will bring the glories of an Islamic silver age to the entire world.

The Mahdi is the star of Satan's Islamic antichrist scenario.

After Revelation was written, Satan undoubtedly did much planning. After five centuries of preparation, he found an excellent vehicle to launch his scheme, the young Muhammad, that devotee of the Meccan god Allah and hater of polytheists. Muhammad quickly became a charismatic leader, who could create history that had the potential of ultimately dethroning the God of the Bible. And so, Satan arranged for Muhammad to have many visitations, supposedly by the angel Jibreel, who delivered to him the written words of the Qur'an. In reality they were the words of Satan.

Muhammad was a man specially groomed to launch a contrary religion with its own literal end-time chronology. In it, Satan, taking on the role of Allah, would achieve divine supremacy.

The corpus of the Qur'an and the Hadiths strongly suggest that they are the outcome of long planning by Satan. He saw that Revelation's literal account culminated with him being cast into the lake of fire. He needed to stop that from happening.

Satan knew that he could not compete with Revelation and the Bible head on. Better to have a written book of his own, the Qur'an, with its own end-time events. Then it would be supplemented with a list of future Major Signs, having no set chronology. Next, to add to them the massive oral tradition of the sayings and actions of Muhammad in the Hadiths. As such, they are not directly from the mouth of Satan, but are inspired by him, and are in keeping with the Qur'an.

In the Hadiths, Satan arranged many parallels to Revelation. They would have his own versions of the antichrist beast (the Mahdi), the false prophet ('Isa ibn Maryam), the woman of Babylon (the Romans), the two witnesses and Jesus Christ (the Dajjal) , God (Allah), even of himself (Iblis or Shaytan). And they would also prophesy the mass beheadings of Christians and Jews.

Generations of Muslims are taught that their standing before Allah includes an acceptance of the Major Signs, and a yearning for their fulfillment. With the Qur'an of only partial help to them, and no mention of the Mahdi in it, they therefore look to the Hadiths for guidance.

Unfortunately, the end time scenario painted by Hadiths is disjointed. The Major Signs are sprinkled among the tens of thousands of somewhat contradictory Hadiths. They become a morass that keeps Muslims under suspense and uncertainty. Many therefore accept instruction from hadith teachers about the Mahdi, in order to faithfully believe in the Major Signs.

The Hadiths are so voluminous in their content, that when the end time does finally arrive, the actual events that occur could be substantiated by suitable Hadiths that will be cherry picked for their validity.

With Muhammad's framework of Islam, Sharia, the Qur'an, and the Hadiths in place, Satan has been waiting patiently century after century to take over the narrative of Revelation.

Once again in my day, Satan is using human agents to try to hotwire an end time configuration that he can better control. For example, in 2008-2016, the rise of the Mahdist ISIS caliphate spawned a flood of Muslim refugees into globalist European Union countries. These events were enabled by an American president who was bent on removing Judeo-Christian values, who took all those countries on a road to appeasement, and opened them to more Islamic terrorism. But in 2017 a new and somewhat God-fearing American president reversed the course, and wiped out ISIS. The refugee crisis that was furthering jihadist Islam within the heart of Europe was suspended.

Then Russia launched a debilitating war against Ukraine in 2022. That lessened its superpower status, and ability to project force in conjunction with possible Islamic allies in an end-time scenario. The Russian action also served to divert world history away from the jihadist-globalist alliance that had been forming against Judeo-Christian values and the God of the Bible.

It will take Satan time to queue up another attempt to hot wire an Islamic takeover. Perhaps he will try to coordinate a push from some other completely different direction, to spin world events away from God's control.

But Satan cannot dictate future events, he can only influence them.

In my day, Satan is therefore resetting for another attempt to hijack prophecy, and recruit a man to be the Mahdi. If Satan is successful, that man will proudly be an Islamic antichrist, who will turn the tables on the prophecy of Revelation. Satan will use the Mahdi to finally gain ascendancy over his ancient nemesis, Jesus Christ.

An Islamic antichrist will rule for seven years: "The Christian end-time prophecy is the true one, in all its literal detail, with the Mahdi and an impostor Jesus, 'Isa ibn Maryam, taking on the roles of the beast and the false prophet. They will act in the name of Allah. But they will be the ones defeated by Jesus Christ the son of God at the battle of Armageddon. God the three in one – Father, Son, and Holy Spirit – is the true God over all."

We have devoted hundreds of pages to comparing Revelation with the Hadiths. The similarities are eerie. The evidence that the Mahdi will be the antichrist, and that 'Isa ibn Maryam will be the false prophet, can be piled up.

But the evidence is circumstantial. There is much in the Hadiths that lines up poorly. The timeline after the Mahdi's heroic works and his death completely diverges from Revelation, even if one attempts to see them as anti-parallels.

A non-Islamic antichrist will rule for seven years: "The Christian end-time prophecy is the true one, again in all its literal detail, including an evacuation (rapture) of church believers to heaven before the tribulation period, and a thousand-year kingdom of Christ that follows it. But the beast and the false prophet of the tribulation will not be Muslims."

This is the predominant view of those Christian prophecy scholars who believe in the rapture. They forecast that the antichrist will arise from Europe. The distinction between the beast and the woman of Babylon is explained by a political versus ecclesiastic bifurcation within the governance of the antichrist's world order.

Some go on to say that the ecclesiastic control structures will be an evolution of the Roman Catholic Church. That largest worldwide denomination will wander further and further away from teaching God's word and salvation in Christ, to the point that it will no longer be a true church. Perhaps the end-time religious institution will be an outgrowth of the apostate liberal wing of Roman Catholicism, which has managed to coalesce around itself apostate Protestant churches into an end-time politically correct ecumenical movement. This false church will try to accommodate itself to the antichrist, and the political realities of the end time. In this way it will take on the role of the woman of Babylon. Nonetheless, this false church will be overthrown by the antichrist midway through the tribulation.

The Roman Catholic Church started gaining negative end-time associations during the sixteenth century, in the period of the Reformation, when it persecuted those who were rediscovering the truths of the Bible (see K10). At that time it was accused of already being the end-time whore of Babylon. Later, in the nineteenth century, prophecy commentators started working out a possible confluence with the literal events of Revelation. After World War II, with the formation of the European Community followed by the European Union, a fascination arose that a certain ten of the member countries would assist the antichrist in overthrowing the false church (see 17:12 K21).

These commentators properly see the antichrist's future kingdom as a reestablishment of the ancient Roman empire. The fact that the Pope is also based in Rome makes it logical to include his church as the spiritual lynchpin of this kingdom.

However, by the time of my day, the Roman Catholic Church has become almost irrelevant in the planning of globalists and statists who are putting in place underpinnings of a future world order. That church offers no advantages to them. Nor does a conglomeration of all apostate churches. If the antichrist needs a basis for a new worship system, modern technologies of the Internet will offer many options. That will be more relevant to generations who have been born into a Europe that has dispensed with its Christian heritage.

Though most commentators pull back from offering the Roman Catholic Church as the woman of Babylon, they do insist that the antichrist will be a European.[314] Based on this premise, they object to the idea that the antichrist may be a Muslim.

The world will eventually be ensnared in an antichrist spirit: "The Christian end-times prophecies foresee a spirit of antichrist and lawlessness descending upon the world, perhaps spearheaded by a charismatic leader; to be followed by the second coming of Jesus; a final judgment; and concluding with the eternal state. But the other images of Revelation do not correspond to an intricate series of additional future events."

Revelation is so different from any other written account that it seems to be unacceptable at face value. It is easier to regard it as largely fictional, rather than as a documentary account of future history.

Christians who start from this premise, but who still regard the book as the inerrant word of God, can accept some of Revelation as literal. But they assert the freedom to choose which sections of John's vision are literal, and which are not.

The vision of the thousand-year millennial kingdom thus becomes just a symbol of eternity. The physical cataclysms unleashed upon the earth and the universe are dream sequences that merely exaggerate the difficulties of the tribulation, or anticipate the terrors of hell. It is granted that in the end time there will be an antichrist figure, who leads a world government that persecutes Christians more than ever before. But it is unreasonable duplication to expect more than one additional coming of Christ, more than one resurrection, and more than one judgment before the throne of God. Therefore, the battle of Armageddon must coincide with the second coming of Christ, to be immediately followed by the resurrection of all the dead, and the judgment of both believers and unbelievers at the great white throne.

---

[314] For example, Nathan E Jones, *Will The Antichrist Be A Muslim? No*, June 5, 2009, https://christinprophecyblog.org/2009/06/will-antichrist-be-muslim-no/, says "Twelve different Bible prophecy experts were asked this question. The previous three out of the twelve answered Yes or Maybe. The following nine answered No."

This is the amillennial position. It maintains that there will not be an actual one-thousand-year kingdom. Hence the prefix *a-* in amillennial.

But it does not explain why God provides so much detail on the happenings within a seven-year period where the church is nowhere to be found. And why he shows John the vision of a thousand-year long kingdom with Christ reigning on earth, occurring before the judgment at the great white throne, and before all eternity.

It is interesting that many amillennialists also do not accept that the flood of Noah's day recorded in Genesis 6-9 was an actual worldwide flood, or that the six days of creation described in Genesis 1 were 24-hour days.

Fortunately for them, the Bible is clear that entrance into heaven is based on faith in Jesus Christ alone, and his sacrifice for our sins on the cross of Calvary. Salvation is not also based on one's understanding of creation or the end time.

But the faith of people who accept Christ as their savior can grow all the more, if they accept the awesome works of God in Genesis and Revelation as literal events. Pastors of the churches of my day ought to be bold in proclaiming the power of God from these bookends of the Bible, and not just the grace of God from the middle.

Skepticism: "Neither the Muslim nor the Christian so-called prophecies are prognostications of the future. Both are merely expressions of ingrown belief patterns among hardened segments of humanity."

If you have read my letter starting from this point of view, hopefully you have noticed that skeptics are major players in both ancient prophecies. They are calling you out.

In Revelation, the descendants of the skeptics of my day will fall in behind the woman of Babylon, and the global government that she represents. Skepticism will be ascendant above all ideologies for a time. It will express itself by stamping out all vestiges of God, and establishing mechanisms for conformity. It will be regarded as immoral to question its morality. The skeptics will be stunned when their ally the antichrist suddenly overthrows their system.

In the Hadiths, the sexualized culture that is a product of skepticism is a great offense and obstacle to establishment of worldwide Sharia under the Mahdi.

This trend toward a uniform godless culture was begun in twentieth century Europe. In all the prior centuries, end-time interpreters of prophecy rarely saw skepticism as a player. But in the twenty-first century, the godless ideologies spawned by Europe are now coming into prophetic focus.

At the time that I write this letter, the United States of America, a daughter nation of Europe and world superpower of my day, is succumbing to the godless path blazed by Europe. John Price in his book *The End of America*,[315] makes the case that it will eventually come under divine judgment for this. This will be in fulfillment of the "daughter of Babylon" prophecies in the book of Jeremiah:

> Jeremiah 50:40 "As when God overthrew Sodom And Gomorrah with its neighbors," declares the Lord, "No one will live there, Nor will anyone of mankind reside in it.
> 50:41 "Behold, a people is coming from the north, And a great nation and many kings Will be roused from the remote parts of the earth.
> 50:42 "They seize their bow and javelin; They are cruel and have no mercy. Their voice roars like the sea; And they ride on horses, Drawn up like a man for the battle Against you, daughter of Babylon."
> 51:33 For this is what the Lord of armies, the God of Israel says: "The daughter of Babylon is like a threshing floor At the time that it is tread down; In just a little while the time of harvest will come for her."

God will punish the country that he so richly blessed, the country that originally based its government on biblical principles, for dispensing with those principles in favor of actively promoting sin. I believe this judgment on the United States may occur sometime before the seven-year end-time period.

What is more clearly prophesied in both Revelation and the Hadiths, is the end-time alliance of convenience between the forces promoting

---

[315] John Price, *The End of America*, Christian House Publishers, Indianapolis US, 2009, p.49.

godlessness and the beast/Mahdi. It will result in a changeover, from the soft persecution of Christians by Europe and America, to a hard persecution with widespread deaths of Jesus-followers in the end time. A prelude to this in my time is the suppression by various media platforms of the reporting of soft persecution.

The question then becomes, which prophecy offers proof of its fulfillment?

Islam claims that the Qur'an and the Hadiths are the final revelation of the true god Allah, who was misunderstood until the coming of his foremost prophet Muhammad. It teaches that its holy writings therefore supersede the Old and New Testaments, which had been earlier corrupted by Jews and Christians. Those two groups had been valiant attempts by Allah to establish his theocratic rule. But both deserve his eternal curse because of their innovations. Only a small remnant of his true people, the Muslims, will be worthy of the Mahdi and the seven (or eight) heavens of the afterlife.

Muhammad, after bedding fifteen wives, died. He made sure to communicate the sure hope that seventy-two heavenly houris will be given to each warrior who ever serves in the Islamic jihad, if they also successfully run the gauntlet of Allah's mizan balance judgment.

Jesus Christ, the only sinless one who ever lived, also died. But God raised him from the dead, in fulfillment of dozens of prophecies. His resurrection and those prophecies do not represent corruption in the words of the Bible. Instead, they who reject those words show forth a different corruption, one that is poisoning their hearts and minds.

The amazing fulfillment of those prophecies validates the thorough truthfulness of the Bible. They make it rewarding to look for the fulfillment of the prophecies concerning the future return of Jesus Christ. Those are scattered through many books of the Bible. Many of them are concentrated in that final book of the Bible, Revelation.

Fulfillment of prophecies occurs among real people, in real times. They will happen in the midst of current events. Satan, unlike God and Christ, can only operate within the plane of time. He must use current events to try to nullify the prophecies. He will also come up with his own counter-prophecies. The Islamic narrative of the end times is one main tool for doing both.

After all the analysis, it could be admitted that the prediction of an Islamic antichrist is more cognizant of upcoming current events, than those Christian theologians who insist on a European and non-Islamic antichrist. They continue at guessing which set of ten European Union countries will help him overthrow an apostate church headquartered in Rome. They should take notice that God is permitting Islam to make inroads into Europe, bringing with them the dream of reestablishing the caliphate in Constantinople, the second Rome. The result could be the antichrist who is both Islamic and European.

This is possibly the outcome that God has planned since the beginning of time. Satan realized this shortly after John recorded his vision in the book of Revelation. "The demons also believe, and shudder" (James 2:19). He then prepared his best plan to counter it, and got involved in the formation of the new religion of Islam.

But Satan is working in the domain of the true God of the Bible, who is sovereign to the ends of the universe, and in all the corners of the world. By God's will, the ancient prophecies of Revelation may find fulfillment in coming of the Mahdi, whom God will defeat by sending his son Jesus Christ to be the true savior.

Both the prophecy scholars and Satan may be wrong as to the identities of the future beast and false prophet. The book of Revelation may find unexpected, yet literal fulfillment. If so, my *Letter to the Tribulation* should become an excellent guide.

In the conclusion of that earlier book, I lamented that the church of my time is becoming desensitized to the assault of godlessness in the world around it. The players of the end times are starting to appear on the chessboard of history. Out of them will arise the woman of Babylon, the beast and the false prophet. A man whom many Muslims will anoint may gain the title of Mahdi. Out of many false prophets, one claiming to be Jesus son of Mary, 'Isa ibn Maryam, might arise. This may happen at the two-hundred-year anniversary of the demise of the Ottoman caliphate, or perhaps later, or perhaps even on the two-thousand-year anniversary of Christ's resurrection.

There will be an uncertain and dark time ahead before the rapture happens. No country will be exempt, though some may fare better than others.

The church's role should be to seek the leading of the Holy Spirit of God. He was the one who founded the church on the day of Pentecost, fifty days after Christ's resurrection. When the church forgets to seek the Holy Spirit, it will fall away. That may be the end-time *apostasia* foreseen in 2 Thessalonians 2:3. The Holy Spirit will simultaneously withdraw from the church. He will also withdraw his common grace of daily provision which blesses all unbelievers, though they do not realize it. Finally, he will no longer restrain sin in the world (see 2 Thessalonians 2:6-7 in K13).

The world will then choose tribulation.

It is great comfort to true Christians that Jesus promises to come for them, before the woman of Babylon and the antichrist take full power. They will not experience the terrors of the seven years.

But we don't know how many years of the church sliding into lethargy will occur first. God calls on Christian pastors, priests, and leaders to be bold in efforts to intervene in the world outside, and be God's agents in rescuing people who are lost in their sin. They can bring them to the foot of the cross, where Jesus prayed, "Father, forgive them; for they do know not what they are doing" (Luke 23:34).

Postscript

The year I am finishing this book is 2024, the hundred-year anniversary of the Istanbul caliphate's demise. In this special year, a new caliphate has not been founded, despite the efforts of the current president and strongman of Turkey and many others.

A year ago, on October 7, 2023, the jihad tried to force the issue with Operation Al-Aqsa Flood, a surprise invasion of Israel from Gaza. Hamas fighters breached the Gaza-Israel barrier, attacked military bases and massacred Jewish civilians in 21 communities. But the countries of the world were divided in their response. Of all the major Muslim countries, only Iran launched follow-up attacks on Israel.[316]

This effort to hotwire an Islamic end-time scenario did not succeed in time for 2024. The Mahdi still has not appeared. The next predictable date for his arrival is 2076, which will be year 1500 AH of the Muslim community.

The unity within the community was shaken by the brutality and inhumanity of the Hamas jihadist fighters. Even inside the leadership of Hamas, there are sons and daughters who are ashamed that Islam is a religion of violence, not a religion of peace. At the risk of death, some of them choose Christ and his message of love, forgiveness, and salvation, over the vengeful, brutal, conquering ideology that is Islamic jihad.[317]

Israel defended itself by counterattacking. The two million Muslims of Gaza were trapped. But God, the true God, did not abandon them. According to a report just six weeks into the war, from underground Christian ministries in Gaza:

---

[316] https://en.m.wikipedia.org/wiki/2023_Hamas-led_attack_on_Israel, accessed September 9, 2024.

[317] One of them was Mosab Hassan Yousef, son of a founding leader of Hamas, see https://www.standingforfreedom.com/2023/10/the-son-of-a-founding-leader-of-hamas-is-a-christian-convert-who-denounces-the-savagery-and-violence-of-hamas/, Freedom Center, October 24, 2023.

> "Over the past two days, we have ministered to hundreds of fathers who have lost most, if not all, of their children in the war. As we moved these men to safety, we fed them, washed their clothes, and began to read the Bible to them – sharing the way of peace through Jesus. Then, a big miracle happened. Last night, Jesus appeared to more than 200 of them in their dream! They have come back to us to learn more from God's word and are asking how to follow Jesus."[318]

The Bible has its own example of a jihadist whose heart was changed. That would be Saul of Tarsus. He was a highly educated but violent man, who believed that God could be one and only in nature. To believe otherwise was the height of blasphemy, deserving of death.

Saul was not a Muslim, because he lived almost 600 years before Muhammad. Saul was a Jew.

He studied under the foremost rabbi of the time, Gamaliel. In his late twenties, only a few years after the crucifixion of Jesus, Paul was consumed with anger at all Jews who were believing that Jesus was Messiah and resurrected, and that he was the divine son of God. They had already formed the first church, in Jerusalem. He took action.

With the approval of the rabbis, "Saul began ravaging the church, entering house after house; and he would drag away men and women and put them in prison" (Acts 8:3). He then set his sights beyond Jerusalem, to where Jews lived in the diaspora. Damascus in Syria was the closest such large city. "Saul, still breathing threats and murder against the disciples of the Lord, went to the high priest, and asked for letters from him to the synagogues in Damascus, so that if he found any belonging to the Way, whether men or women, he might bring them in shackles to Jerusalem" (Acts 9:1-2).

---

[318] Michael Licona, https://m.facebook.com/story.php?story_fbid=863924311780322&id=1000448 82823305, November 10, 2023, quoted in Talia Wise, *Supernatural Move of God in Gaza as Hundreds Reportedly Meet Jesus in Dreams*, November 20, 2023, https://www2.cbn.com/news/cwn/supernatural-move-god-gaza-hundreds-reportedly-meet-jesus-dreams.

He was convinced that he was serving God in this. Ironically, he was one of the first to fulfill the words that Jesus had spoken only a few years earlier:

> John 16:2b yet an hour is coming for everyone who kills you to think that he is offering a service to God.

Along the road to Damascus, Saul, the zealot for God, was stopped dead in his tracks by a sudden blazing light from heaven. He recounts what happened next:

> Acts 9:4 and he fell to the ground and heard a voice saying to him, "Saul, Saul, why are you persecuting Me?"
> 9:5 And he said, "Who are You, Lord?" And He said, "I am Jesus whom you are persecuting,
> 9:6 but get up and enter the city, and it will be told to you what you must do."
> 9:7 The men who traveled with him stood speechless, hearing the voice but seeing no one.
> 9:8 Saul got up from the ground, and though his eyes were open, he could see nothing; and leading him by the hand, they brought him into Damascus.
> 9:9 And for three days he was without sight, and neither ate nor drank.
> 9:10 Now there was a disciple in Damascus named Ananias; and the Lord said to him in a vision, "Ananias." And he said, "Here I am, Lord."
> 9:11 And the Lord said to him, "Get up and go to the street called Straight, and inquire at the house of Judas for a man from Tarsus named Saul, for he is praying,
> 9:12 and he has seen in a vision a man named Ananias come in and lay his hands on him, so that he might regain his sight."
> 9:13 But Ananias answered, "Lord, I have heard from many people about this man, how much harm he did to Your saints in Jerusalem;
> 9:14 and here he has authority from the chief priests to arrest all who call on Your name."
> 9:15 But the Lord said to him, "Go, for he is a chosen instrument of Mine, to bear My name before the Gentiles and kings and the sons of Israel;
> 9:16 for I will show him how much he must suffer in behalf of My name."
> 9:17 So Ananias departed and entered the house, and after laying his hands on him said, "Brother Saul, the Lord Jesus, who appeared to you on the road by which you were coming,

> has sent me so that you may regain your sight and be filled with the Holy Spirit."
> 9:18 And immediately something like fish scales fell from his eyes, and he regained his sight, and he got up and was baptized;
> 9:19 and he took food and was strengthened. N ow for several days he was with the disciples who were in Damascus,
> 9:20 and immediately he began to proclaim Jesus in the synagogues, saying, "He is the Son of God."
> 9:21 All those hearing him continued to be amazed, and were saying, "Is this not the one who in Jerusalem destroyed those who called on this name, and had come here for the purpose of bringing them bound before the chief priests?"
> 9:22 But Saul kept increasing in strength and confounding Jews who lived in Damascus by proving that this Jesus is the Christ.

Saul, the man of violence, became Paul, the man of great faith and wisdom. He set across much of the Roman empire preaching the gospel message of repentance and forgiveness, of peace with God. He loved his savior Jesus with all his soul and strength the rest of his days. God spoke through him, to write thirteen books of the New Testament.

Saul had a profound desire to know God and serve him. He was misdirected into violence. He would not listen to the followers of Jesus, like the deacon Steven. Instead, he stood by with satisfaction as he was stoned. But Jesus loved Saul, and reached into his life directly. Saul immediately knew that this resurrected Jesus truly was the son of God.

Many Muslims are like Saul. You may have scoffed at the pleadings of Christian missionaries. But if you open your heart to Jesus, he will come into your life. His appearance in the dreams of the Gazans is one of countless examples.

If you diligently seek Jesus Christ, you will find him. You will then live with him, forever.

Bibliography

Doyle, Tom, with Webster, Greg, *Dreams and Visions, Is Jesus Awakening the Muslim World?*, Thomas Nelson, Nashville US, 2012.

Furnish, Timothy R., *Ten Years' Captivation with the Mahdi's Camps: Essays on Muslim Eschatology, 2005-2015*, self-published, Middletown Delaware USA, 2015.

Ishaq, Ibn, *Sirat Rasul Allah -The Life of Muhammad*, A. Guillaume, translator, Oxford University Press, 1955.

`Izzat, Muhammad Ibn, and `Arif, Muhammad, *Al Mahdi and the End of Time*, Dar al Taqwa press, London, second edition 2007.

McDowell, Bruce, and Zaka, Anees, *Muslims and Christians at The Table*, Phillipsburg NJ USA, P&R Publishing, 1999.

al-Misri, Shihabuddin Abu al-'Abbas Ahmad ibn an-Naqib (1302-1367), *Umdat al-Salik (Reliance of the Traveller)*, translated by Nuh Ha Mim Keller, Amana Publications, 1997.

Muslim Students Association at the University of Southern California (USC-MSA), *The Hadith of the Prophet Muhammad at your fingertips*, https://sunnah.com/.

Qur'an Index, https://www.islamawakened.com/index.php/qur-an.

Rahma, Abu, *Al-Mahdi, The Promised Caliph*, self-published, Middletown Delaware USA, 2018.

Richardson, Joel, *The Islamic AntiChrist*, WND Books, Los Angeles, 2009.

Sa'd, Ibn, *Kitab Al-Tabaqat Al-Kabir*, Vol. I, S. Moinul Haq and H.K.Ghazanfar, translators, Kitab Bhavan, 1967.

Shoebat, Walid, *God's War on Terror: Islam, Prophecy and the Bible*, self-published, United States, 2008.

Smith, Jane I, and Haddad, Yvonne Y, *The Islamic Understanding of Death and Resurrection*, Albany NY US, SUNY Press, 1981.

Spencer, Robert, *The Truth about Muhammad*, Regnery Publishing, Washington, 2006.

Bibliography

al-Tabari, Abu Ja'far Muhammad ibn Jarir, *The History of al-Tabari, Volume VI: Muhammad at Mecca*, W. Montgomery Watt and M.V.McDonald, translators, New York, SUNY Press, 1988.

Bible verse index

Bible topic index

Qur'an and Hadith index

Islamic topic index

About Matthias Key

As a laser physicist working at a world-famous laboratory, Matthias Key was unable to find the secrets of the universe. He then concentrated on his lifelong spiritual quest instead.

Born in the U.S. to persecuted Christians who had escaped Soviet communism, Matthias excelled academically and began his career in advanced physics. He also directed his analytical training toward messages found in different schools of thought: Marxism, New Age, mystical Islam, Judaism, Hinduism, Christianity and mainstream Islam.

At the age of 28, he experienced a profound turning point when he encountered the living Christ, known to others as Yeshua HaMashiakh, ʿIsa al-Maseeh, or Jesus the Messiah. After his awakening, he proceeded to earn a Master of Divinity from a conservative, Bible-affirming seminary.

Professionally, Matthias transitioned to IT, eventually becoming a lead cybersecurity architect with a major U.S. federal contractor. In that role, he developed systems thinking and an eye for complex design — perspectives that now inform his prophetic teaching.

In parallel, Matthias helped start a Russian-speaking Messianic Jewish congregation in a large American city, and later trained for engagement with upper-caste Hindu immigrants. His work reflects both precision and compassion — the heart of a scientist and the soul of a servant.

Matthias Key has moved to devoting himself fully to the study of the Old and New Testaments, the Qurʾan and the Hadiths, and the communication of prophetic truth which they contain. Through his writing, he helps other seekers who are on a spiritual journey to interpret the book of Revelation's "cyber patterns." He shows how they are the key to understanding divine order within end-time prophecies. His aim is to introduce others to the living Christ, who gave his life for them.

> "Revelation isn't chaos—it's code.
> Once you see its divine sequence, everything becomes clear."

You may obtain this and many other fine resources
made available by Proclaim Publishers by contacting us:

Web: proclaimpublishers.com

Email: info@proclaimpublishers.com

Postal Mail:
1317 Edgewater Drive, Suite 4774
Orlando, FL, 32804

SOLI DEO GLORIA

ORLANDO, FLORIDA